Constitutionalizing India

Constitutionalizing India

An Ideational Project

BIDYUT CHAKRABARTY

OXFORD
UNIVERSITY PRESS

OXFORD

UNIVERSITY PRESS

Oxford University Press is a department of the University of Oxford.
It furthers the University's objective of excellence in research, scholarship,
and education by publishing worldwide. Oxford is a registered trademark of
Oxford University Press in the UK and in certain other countries.

Published in India by
Oxford University Press
2/11 Ground Floor, Ansari Road, Daryaganj, New Delhi 110 002, India

ISBN-13: 978-0-19-948762-2
ISBN-10: 0-19-948762-6

Typeset in Adobe Jenson Pro 10.7/13.3
by Tranistics Data Technologies, New Delhi 110 044
Printed in India by Gopsons Papers Ltd., Noida 201301

To the Foot Soldiers of Constitutional Democracy

Contents

Preface

The 1950 Constitution of India is perhaps one of the most fascinating texts that has remained a source of attraction to me since my undergraduate days in Presidency College, Kolkata. I am grateful to my teachers, Sunil Kumar Ray Chaudhuri and Rebati Raman Mukherjee, for having kindled and sustained my interest in the Constitution when it hardly found takers in my class due to being 'terribly dry'. With their persuasive teaching, my teachers had shown me how a particular provision was enacted out of fierce debates and friendly dialogues among the members in the Constituent Assembly. I was drawn to the *Constituent Assembly Debates*, and Bimanda of our departmental library emerged as a messiah by allowing me to consult those volumes in the rare-books collection which was not accessible to a first year student. To be very frank, despite my keenness to go through the engaging debates in the Assembly, I was very selective in my reading then since I was restrained by the prevalent system of learning in which academic results mattered most in one's career regardless of whether they were based on mere mugging of question-answers! I left the *Constituent Assembly Debates* volumes in the library and focused on what I was expected to do to be recognized as 'good student' merely in terms of good grades. Nonetheless, the interest kindled by the volumes persists since those days in my college.

Constitutionalizing India has benefitted a lot from my earlier books. Three books which helped a great deal in defending some of the argument that unfold in the present book are *Social and Political Thought of Mahatma Gandhi* (2006), *Indian Politics and Society since Independence: Events, Processes and Ideology* (2008), and *Localizing Governance in India* (2017). I am thankful to Routledge for having granted me permission to reiterate some of the arguments already made in these books to pursue my academic search for the roots of constitutional liberalism in India.

The present book is just a matter of accident in the sense that when I was working on a project on B.R. Ambedkar's role in constitutionalizing India, I again began consulting the *Constituent Assembly Debates* volumes; this time, I did not consult them in an enclosure in the forbidden area in the library but in my cosy home because now I was the proud owner of the volumes which were affordable because the Lok Sabha Secretariat had reprinted and made them available at a lower price. The initial ideational impulses came from my reading of the *Debates* volumes. An in-depth reading of the arguments that the Assembly members offered led me to the roots of the ideas that informed them. It was a revelation to me because it confirmed my hypothesis that the 1950 Constitution was, not at all, a carbon copy of the 1935 Government of India Act, but an outcome of a historical journey during which the idea of constitutional democracy gained salience. My intellectual journey helped me understand the nature of this historical journey which unfolded in the consolidation of constitutional liberalism in India as colonialism grew strong. It was a satisfying journey because I found out how constitutional liberalism, despite its colonial roots, became an empowering politico-ideological device among the colonized in the nationalist onslaught on colonialism. Notwithstanding the classical liberals' warning, constitutional democracy not only became a source of ideological inspiration to the nationalists during the freedom struggle, it also enabled them to evolve an institutional mechanism to that effect. To capture a complex journey of an idea, such as this, in a single monograph is neither possible nor feasible; hence I dealt with the theme in a way to provide a general understanding of the reality with reference to the identifiable politico-ideological sources out of the dialectical battle between nationalism and its bête noire, colonialism. Needless to say, the task is far from being complete though it can be said that my initiative will provoke further research in this area which will not only be intellectually enriching but will also expose the inherent weaknesses of the theoretical argument defending the conceptualization of the 1950 Constitution of India being a borrowed doctrine.

I am thankful to my email friend Aishwary Kumar of Stanford University, Stanford, California, for being so prompt in procuring articles and other texts for me; without his help, the work would not have been the same. Similarly Bob (Kolondisky), my former colleague at James Madison University, Virginia also supported my work by acquiring those texts quickly so that there was no interruption in my work. My gratitude goes to D.V. Singh, the librarian of our university not only because of his helpful attitude but also because of the human quality (which is rare nowadays) that he evinced whenever I went to his office for a request for books. It was a matter of great joy because he is one of the few who appreciate the scholars simply because they are involved in the creation and also dissemination of knowledge which is also a rare quality especially when the academicians have also become political agents of ideological bosses with or without institutional authority. I would like to thank the team at Oxford University Press without whose support it would not have been possible to undertake this task. Despite not being persuaded by my zeal to work, Barbie and Pablo, my kids, always remain a source of intellectual nourishment by raising questions which allows me to tread an untrodden path to persuasively respond to their queries. By being a fiercely critical wife to me and very caring mother to our kids, Sanchita also helped me understand the intricacies of cooperative existence in an extended family; a significant and also priceless realization which reinforced my belief in being pragmatic but firm, accommodative but principled, and sensitive but critical. My Kolkata-based sisters, Mini and Tinku and their daughters, Debiparna and Sreeja never allowed my emotional quotient to go down by always being a source of joy and self-gratification. Furthermore, my students, both in this campus and other campuses where I had the opportunity to interact with them, sustained my zeal for academic creativity despite odds. I am grateful to them; without them, it would not have been possible for me to remain focused on an activity which does not seem to attract many of my ilk in our society where being in the right network pays more than sustained hard work. If the book adds to their intellectual search, I will consider having achieved my objective as a teacher.

The preface remains incomplete if, in the list of my acknowledgement, I do not mention Professor Granville Austin who inspired a generation of scholars in the study of India's Constitution as 'a cornerstone of a nation'. I had an opportunity to interact with him during his brief visit to our department in February 2000, when he put before me some of the challenging questions on the nature and texture of our Constitution. In fact, my search for answers to those questions landed me in this venture; my regular email interactions with him helped me get a nuanced understanding of the processes leading to the making of the Constitution. Some of the arguments that I offer here to substantiate my claim of the Constitution being an outcome of a long-drawn ideational battle had their roots in those emails. Professor Austin would have been happier had the providence given me a chance to present this book to him. It is a matter of grief and pain that he is not there to cheer me up by saying 'Bidjut [that is how addressed me], keep it up!'

Introduction

Contrary to the widely circulated argument that Indian Constitution is largely a borrowed doctrine, the book underlines that it is also an ideational project in which competing ideas jostled during its preparation. It is an attempt to retrieve the history of constituting the 1950 Constitution of India in the perspective of a politico-ideological design at the behest of the colonizers which the nationalists later endorsed while being opposed to colonial rule. As is commonly known, the Westminster model of democracy that was introduced in India in the wake of colonialism laid the foundation of liberalism as a constitutional practice, which drew its sustenance from the philosophy of British Enlightenment, championing social virtues such as benevolence, compassion, and tolerance. This was complemented by the values of French Enlightenment supporting scepticism and reason and the American Enlightenment exalting liberty and freedom. So, the ideational context in which the Constitution of India evolved was multi-textured and extremely complex that cannot be captured in a monochromatic fashion. The story of the evolution of the constitutional values is further complicated by the unique texture of the Indian polity that was neither completely western nor entirely Indian but a mixed-bag in which multiple ideational influences seem to have converged. India's freedom struggle was a testimony to a creative blending of the so-called 'indigenous' influences with their 'alien' counterparts: the aim of the nationalist struggle was, on the one hand, to create a liberal state while for mobilizing support for the cause, the nationalist leadership drew, on the other, caste–kinship–ethnicity network. This evolved into a pattern as freedom struggle progressed. The battle for freedom was waged at two levels: at the conventional level, it was manifested in open protests against the colonial rule in which, besides the Gandhian satyagraha, several other ideological preferences were also visible. At another level, constitutionalism, conceptualized in liberal terms, was invoked as 'a rallying cry in the struggle against colonialism.'[1] For the nationalists, constitutionalism provided 'contested sites for ideas and practices concerning justice, rights and development and individual associational autonomy.'[2] As will be shown in the book, the efforts that the nationalists made while charting out a constitutional design for India were directed towards creating a set of rule of law which, being free from prejudices (of any kind), would help realize the fundamental principles of the Enlightenment Philosophy, on which the British rule seemingly rested.

The past ideational experiences became critical once the processes towards making the Constitution for the independent India had begun. A perusal of the debates in the Constituent Assembly that came into being in 1946 reveals that the debates hovered around liberalism and the Gandhian idea of Swaraj or self-rule underlining the Kantian emphasis of individual freedom in a collective existence. The fact that the Gandhian insistence on the village-based constitutional democracy did not receive adequate support from the members of Assembly allowed the liberals to shape the Constitution in accordance with their ideological predilections. Nonetheless, by articulating an alternative ideational package, the Gandhians paved the way for differently-textured constitutional principles of governance which gradually became decisive with the increasing importance of democratic decentralization in governance.

In order to conceptualize the complex interplay of processes involving liberalism and the Gandhian approach to self-rule, the book provides a new narrative of constitutionalizing India which is both contextual and ideationally multifaceted. The constitution-making in India is therefore a theatre of contestation in which ideas with completely different socio-economic roots competed with each other for a common ideological aim of making the Constitution for independent India which was acceptable to all.

As is argued, two contrasting perspectives seem to have governed the processes of constitutionalizing India: on the one hand, emphasizing the role of the state as the primary agent of liberal reform, the liberal constitutionalists defended a constitution supportive of the rule of law irrespective of class, caste, and clan; there was, on the other hand, another well-argued perspective in which the idea of village republic prevailed over other considerations while contributing to independent India's Constitution. By seeking to trace the intellectual roots of the processes of constitutionalizing India to an ideational battle spanning over a century, the proposed book deviates from the conventional understanding of the making of India's constitution by arguing that it was merely a legatee of the endeavour of accommodation of differences over contrasting perspectives.

The making of free India's Constitution by the Constituent Assembly over a period of little less than three years is thus reflective of the efforts that the founding fathers undertook to translate the nationalist and democratic aspirations of an independent polity following decolonization. Furthermore, while the Constitution is a continuation at least in structural and procedural terms, it was also a clear break with the past since the 1950 Constitution drew on an ideology that sought to establish a liberal democratic polity following the withdrawal of colonialism. There can be no greater evidence of the commitment to constitutionalism and rule of law on the part of the founding fathers than the Constitution that they framed despite serious difficulties due to partition. The commitment to liberal democratic values, as the Constituent Assembly proceedings suggest, remained paramount in the making of the Constitution.

Set up as a result of negotiations between the nationalist leaders and the members of the Cabinet Mission over the possible constitutional arrangement in the post war-India, the Constituent Assembly began its deliberations on 9 December 1946 and concluded with the acceptance of the draft Constitution on 26 November 1949. This period, little less than three years, was one in which the joy of freedom was severely marred by national trauma, associated with the partition and violence, that resulted in the killing of Mahatma, besides the butchering of innocent people in the wake of the transfer of population in the immediate aftermath of the declaration of freedom. Indian Constitution was born, thus argues Paul

Brass, 'more in fear and trepidation than in hope and inspiration.'[3] There is hardly a strong argument to dispute this proposition presumably because of the context in which the Constituent Assembly began and concluded its proceedings. The Constitution was thus a pragmatic response to the reality that the Assembly confronted while drawing the roadmap for free India. The founding fathers practised, as it has been appropriately suggested, 'the art of the possible and never allowed [their ideological cause] to blind them to reality.'[4] Being most pragmatic, the framers thus prepared a constitution to act as a guardian on the basis of their understanding of the fundamental ethos of liberal constitutionalism. In articulating their choice, they made a simple and yet radical choice. They decided to trust the people. This was a choice which instantly transformed the colonial subjects into free and independent citizens who were given constitutional rights to decide what deemed to have been right for them. In such a scheme of things, they made another radical choice, namely they did not leave any space in which the lawful citizens of the country were to be deprived of their rights, enshrined in the Constitution. The list of rights were thus made constitutionally justiciable, subject only to specified restrictions. Furthermore, in order to evolve a full-proof system, the Constitution also created an independent system of court of law to adjudicate the Executive decisions if they ran contrary to the spirit of the Constitution. Two important ideas seem to be critical here: on the one hand, the purpose was to make the Constitution supreme, following the American traditions in socio-culturally diverse India to cement a politico-ideological bond among the people despite differences on multiple counts. There was also, on the other hand, a concern to evolve an ideological foundation appreciative of values of commonality as perhaps the only option to build 'a nation' on the basis of the 'inherent' civilizational bond that had flourished over millennia notwithstanding regular attacks and challenges. What thus stands out is the founding fathers' steadfast commitment to the Enlightenment principle of 'have courage to use your reason' and their trust on the Indian people to choose their rulers in accordance with their priority. This is not a small achievement when the classical liberals had serious doubts given the absence of the required socio-economic and political context for liberalism to strike roots, let alone, flourish.

—— ·•· ——

The task of constitutionalizing India was not an easy one in view of the contextual difficulties confronting the framers. What was however a source of strength for them was that, despite their political differences, they seem to have been inspired by the Enlightenment principles of constitutional liberalism. There were hardly formidable opponents. The course of history would now be decided and the framers had a great responsibility. It was most eloquently stated by Jawaharlal Nehru when he exhorted:

> India after a long period of being dominated over has emerged as a free sovereign democratic independent country, and that is a fact which changes and is changing history. How far it would change history will depend upon us, this House in the present and other Houses like this coming in future who represent the organized will of the people.[5]

For Nehru, the constitution-making was not merely a technical exercise, but a stepping stone towards evolving complementary norms and values supportive of a liberal constitution. The idea is explicit: the success of the constitution depended on a socio-economic and political milieu in favour of a system of faith for liberal constitutionalism. This was 'a tremendous responsibility', Nehru further argued by saying that 'we have to be conscious of this tremendous responsibility which freedom has brought: the discipline of freedom and the organized way of working freedom'.[6] The effort was directed to work together for the nation on the basis of their unflinching commitment to those values of Enlightenment philosophy that gradually became dominant ideological ethos due to rather symbiotic interactions between the colonizers and the colonized at least in their ideological preferences for constitutional liberalism. It was to be carried forward despite the absence of sizeable sections of the Muslim League in the Constituent Assembly. This was certainly a source of discomfort to the framers because it was a dent to the argument that the Assembly represented the views of the nationalist forces regardless of politico-ideological differences. While underplaying possible adverse impact on the Assembly due to the reluctance of the Muslim League to participate, Nehru, when he moved the Objective Resolution on 13 December 1946, thus emotionally argued:

[W]e are here not to function for one party or one group, but always to think of India as a whole and always think of the four hundred million that comprise India.... The time comes when we have to rise above party and think of the Nation, think sometimes even of the world at large of which our nation is a great part. When I think of the work of this Constituent Assembly, it seems to me, the time has come when we should, so far as we are capable of it, rise above our ordinary selves and party disputes and think of the great problem before us in the widest and most tolerant and most effective manner so that, whatever we may produce, should be worthy of India as a whole and should be such that the world should recognize that we have functioned, as we should have functioned, in this high adventure.[7]

It was an emotional appeal grounded on Nehru's concern for organizing the future Indian polity around constitutional liberalism which was potentially strong enough, he also felt, to wield the nation together. Nonetheless, the criticism that the Constituent Assembly was unrepresentative in character did not seem to be unfounded given the fact that the members were elected on the basis of restricted franchise. Hence, the voice of all did not get represented. The argument was defended by suggesting that (a) it was not representative in character since the Assembly was constituted by restricted franchise and (b) it was convened not by the national or any provincial assemblies, but by the British government who regarded it merely as a conference of the delegates of the major political parties. It was thus not surprising that M.A. Jinnah, the architect of Pakistan, never recognized the Assembly as a sovereign body capable of producing a constitution for the country; the situation was further complicated by the decision of a section of the Muslim League not to participate in the proceedings of the Assembly. According to an estimate, about ten per cent of the Indians voted in the 1946 provincial elections as voting right was based on property and educational qualifications. The chief commissioner' provinces and excluded areas within the Governors' provinces were not allowed to participate in the election; only half of the members who came from the princely states were elected from their legislatures, and the remaining half was nominated by the ruler. In the light of the methods of the composition of the Assembly, the claim that the constitution was drafted in the name of 'We, the people of India', does not seem to be justified.[8]

The issue was raised by the constitutional advisor, B.N. Rau in his intimation to Jawaharlal Nehru where he stated that in the absence of the Muslim League, it would be judicious not to proceed further because that would be a violation of the conditions, stipulated by the Cabinet Mission plan. As the Cabinet Mission insisted, 'the Union Constitution is to be settled only after several Sections have met and settled the Provincial Constitutions and the Group Constitutions, if any', and hence, he deduced, 'if two of the three Sections cannot meet at all, the settling of the Union Constitution will be indefinitely delayed'.[9] Rau thus averred, as Arvind Elangovan informs, that the absence of the members of the League could be an impediment to the constitution-making process and further 'the League would be within its rights to approach the Court in London to invalidate the assembly's proceedings'.[10] A sound legal mind, Rau took a very legalistic stance which was devoid of political substance in a context when the nationalists seem to have reconciled to the partition of India as perhaps the only options available to resolve the communal impasse. It was K.M. Munshi who, while articulating the sentiment of his colleagues in the Assembly, retorted very strongly by saying that Rau's anxiety was totally 'unfounded' because 'the Constituent Assembly ... is clearly a representative of the population of India as a whole, and not of a conference of representative of certain groups'. Representing the nation, the Constituent Assembly, he further emphasized,

> is therefore not a body of delegates representing different communities, but an organ of the sovereign people, which by virtue of its being elected by the sovereign people, inherits a part of that sovereign power so far as constitution making is concerned. The idea that such an Assembly is a meeting ground of delegates representing different groups come to negotiate between themselves, negatives the very concept of Constituent Assembly.[11]

It was not B.N. Rau alone who raised concerns; there were several members who, despite Munshi's strong-worded clarification, corroborated their anxiety by highlighting that the Assembly lacked legitimacy to produce a constitution for independent India since it was not representative of the people for whom the constitution was to be prepared.

One of the first salvos was hurled by Damodar Swarup Seth of United Provinces. He believed

> a constitution-making body of a free country should be able to claim that it represents the will of the entire people of that country. [Since the Assembly] cannot claim to represent the whole country, it has no right whatsoever to embark on this exercise ... at most it can claim to represent fifteen percent of the population of India who had elected the members to the provincial legislatures. The election too, by virtue of which the members of this Assembly are here, was not a direct one; they are here by virtue of indirect election. In these circumstances, when eighty-five percent of the people of the country are not represented in the House and when they have no voice here, it will be in my opinion a very great mistake to say that the House is competent to frame a Constitution for the whole country.[12]

The argument was very clear: the Constituent Assembly lacked the legitimacy to articulate the voice of the country because of the immanent limitations due to the way it was constituted. Since it was not representative of the majority of the people, the entire exercise was dubbed as 'un-democratic and elitist'. Hence, it deserved to be scrapped as Seth further argued, by underlining 'the unrepresentative character of the Assembly'. The contention did not however persuade the majority of the members. Challenging Seth, Balkrishna Sharma of United Provinces questioned the fundamental premise of the statement made by his colleague, Seth. According to him,

> the argument that we are the representative of fifteen percent of the population and that the representatives of eighty-five percent of the population are not with us and therefore we do not have the right to make the Constitution is a fallacious one because (a) nowhere in the world can a model constitution be constituted ... and (b) we are the representatives of the will, emotions and ambitions of the people, and in this capacity representing the whole of India; we are framing the constitution on this basis which is not representation on mere numbers.[13]

The crux of the argument hinges on the fact that the representativeness of the Assembly cannot be conceptualized in absolute terms; it has to be assessed with reference to the context in which the Assembly was constituted. Despite not being representative in contemporary terms, the fact that the Assembly upheld the popular zeal and aspirations had supported its claim of being representative of the people. Furthermore, this was the pattern that was followed in regard to other democratic constitution. By drawing attention to the way the American Constitution was produced in the 1786 Philadelphia Conference, B.R. Ambedkar strongly refuted the charge of his colleagues who strove to undermine the endeavour by saying that since 'the Constitution has been framed by the people who are not the true representative of the general masses ... it will neither be accepted by them nor will work permanently'.[14] For Ambedkar, the argument was without substance, as he defended by comparing the deeds of the US constitution makers with those of India's Constituent Assembly. He mentioned that

> as most members know that the Constitution of the United States of America ... was drafted by a very small body [comprising] representatives from 13 States [who] met in a small conference in Philadelphia. Therefore if these 13 representatives say that what they did was in the name of the people, on their authority, basing on it their sovereignty, ... I personally myself do not understand unless a man was on absolute pedant, that a body of people 292 in number represent this vast continent, in their representative capacity, could not say that they are acting in the name of the people.[15]

Ambedkar defended the point of the Constituent Assembly being representative in character on the basis of his faith in one of the core principles of representation being practised in indirect democracy, namely the representatives represent those who elect them. Conceptually, this is valid since this was perhaps the best possible option available at a particular historical juncture. It is true that the Assembly members were elected by a very limited franchise though they were ideologically tuned to India's independence; hence they appeared to have had the legitimacy to represent the rest of the countrymen. By referring to the Philadelphia Conference which framed the American Constitution, he reinforced his argument to confirm that what the Constituent Assembly did was not an exception, but conformed to the pattern. There was possibly a personal aspect to his argument: he did not want to miss this opportunity to create a liberal framework of constitutional governance which, he strongly felt, was in need in a society heavily prejudiced against the so-called untouchables due to their social origin. With a liberal constitution in place, this could be stopped once for all. Hence, not only did he challenge the efforts towards undermining the entire exercise of the Assembly for allegedly being unrepresentative, he also created a strong group within the House to defend his point of view. As a result, the voice that was raised against him lost its steam in no time.

—— ·•· ——

The processes of constitutionalizing India are both simple and complex at the same time: simple because it was a fait-accompli for colonized India since the British rulers wanted to follow a specific mode of constitutional governance. In other words, there was hardly a choice. A deeper probing of the processes however reveals that the processes do not seem to be as simple as they appear on the surface. The available evidence shows that the efforts towards constitutionalizing India did not immediately succeed; there were hurdles and the British ruling authority was also divided in its appreciation for constitutional rule for India. In opposition to those who justified despotic rule as an appropriate means to accomplish the colonizers' civilizing mission, a prominent group of British liberals strongly argued for constitutional governance in conformity with the principles of Enlightenment. One has to put a caveat here because constitutionalism had a restricted meaning to begin with, though it had created and gradually consolidated a foundation for constitutional values, norms, and principles to flourish. The idea was thus allowed to unfold under the paternalistic care of the rulers and despotic rule was necessary to provide a strong grounding to liberal constitutionalism, a politico-ideological means for the colonized India to realize the exalted values of the philosophy of Enlightenment. It was not surprising that J.S. Mill announced that 'despotism is a legitimate mode of government in dealing with barbarians, provided the end can be their improvement, and means justified by actually effecting that end'.[16] The idea of improvement seems to have been fundamental to Mill's conceptualization of 'imperial despotism'. The liberal model of imperialism or, to borrow Karuna Mantena's expression, 'liberal imperialism' which, she further argued, 'tied together a theory of imperial legitimacy with the project of improvement represented the most fully developed moral justification of the Empire in the nineteenth century Britain'.[17] The idea however did not gain salience immediately since (a) it was not appreciated by those who mattered in the decision making and (b) the British rulers did not realize, as Macaulay emphasized, that they 'were bound to discharge towards [the colonized] the duties of rulers'.[18] It was a rule that was bereft of 'English morality', argued Macaulay which accounted for aberrations in governance. Core to the argument that 'the liberal imperialists' put forward was a concern to couch the British imperial rule in India in a morally-justified liberal constitutional format with adequate checks and balances against the consolidation of 'an arbitrary and despotic' governance.

The British liberals were surely a formidable source of inspiration behind the growth and consolidation of the processes of constitutionalization in India. This was strengthened by the complementary efforts of the Indian liberals who, being politically baptized in British liberal ethos, articulated by those justifying liberal imperialism. As will be shown in Chapter 2, being convinced of the obvious impact of the British rule in India, the Indian liberals supported the endeavours that were undertaken to instil liberalism as an effective means to bring about the radical social and political changes that they aspired. The process appears to have unfolded at two levels: at a rather uncritical level, liberal values gained currency presumably because it was felt that they would not only counter the age-old archaic values which were impediments to 'improvement' or 'progress' but also destroy their foundational roots to usher in an era of liberty, equality, and fraternity. It was justifiably internalized, at another level, by the Indian intellectuals who, by simultaneously supporting the British endeavours towards constitutionalizing India, strove to build 'a new society' in accordance with the techniques of Enlightenment which passed the test of time by being effective in the context of Britain. Here too, the fundamental concern was to allow the processes of change that the British rule set in motion in a backward India. The most categorical confession came from M.G. Ranade, the mentor of Gopal Krishna Gokhale, when, in a speech of 1897 at Amaravati, he argued that with the onset of the British rule in India, 'a new mode of thought ... cast on lines of fraternity, a capacity to expand outwards, and to make more cohesive inwards the bond of fellowship [by recognizing] the essential equality between man and man'.[19] A true liberal, Ranade further appreciated the colonial drive toward female education which, he felt, was 'revolutionary' in spirit and content. Being aware that the experiments remained 'incipient, ... the signs are clearly visible that throughout India, the national awakening to the necessity of developing the moral and intellectual capacities of our sisters has found universal recognition'.[20] What is clear that Ranade, one of most vociferous proponents of British liberalism among the Indian liberals, expressed his choice unambiguously since he felt that liberalism arising out of the philosophy of Enlightenment was not only an empowering politco-ideological design of effective social engineering but also strong enough to replace 'the devilish' social values by 'the modernizing ethos'. Despite being an instrument for colonial exploitation, the prudent Ranade had thus reasons to campaign for the British system of governance in India which was, according to him, 'a stepping stone' towards constitutionalizing India in the long run.

The history of India's constitutionalism is unique in reconceptualizing liberalism by also recognizing group rights. In other words, the trajectory of liberalism in India shows how pluralism evolved integrally with the appreciation of individualism, the staple for liberalism. Rights for 'a plurality of vulnerable groups should not be seen', as the argument goes, 'as illiberal additions but integral to the conception of liberalism'.[21] The idea does not seem to be stunning in the context of India where liberal democracy constitutionalizes individual as an autonomous entity with an identity given by belongingness to one or more groups. In view of India being an extremely diverse society along the lines of religion, language, caste, and tribe, the pluralistic existence of individuals deriving identity from belonging to different groups seems to have become instinctively ordained. Hence, the argument was made by scholars that, 'a regime of group preference, predating the establishment of liberal democracy, [was] thus in place prior to a system of equal individual rights'.[22] This does not seem to be peculiar in the non-Western context. In the multicultural West, the argument is being forcefully made by many analysts. In his endeavour to conceptualize the pluralist existence of individual in the liberal west, Will Kymlicka, for instance, reframed the terms of discourse on group rights within a liberal framework by recognizing that there is hardly a conceptual incongruity between individual being an atomistic unit and individual being part of a collective identity. He thus forcefully made the point that minority rights could cohabit with liberal principles.[23] Indian experience substantiates the claim. Individual also exists as a part of a plurality, and collective identities are legitimate makers of an individual who also articulates his/her self in a collective.

The above preface highlighting the conceptual intricacies of 'liberal-plural normative model of individual existence' situates the Indian experience in a plausible theoretical foundation. History demonstrates that the British rule, once it was constitutionalized by various legislative decrees and political designs, recognizes the importance of group identity by not denying individual of his/her legitimate space within a constitutional-liberal framework of governance. Recognition of groups as important players in the political processes was evidently an integral part of the grand imperial strategy of *divide-et-impera*. Nonetheless, the argument can be said to have been drawn on India's diversity and also obvious socio-economic imbalances within the prevalent social order. What is being emphasized here is that colonial laws, being 'accessories to imperial domination',[24] set in motion processes whereby group identity received adequate importance in the framework of governance. Furthermore, the effort towards constitutionalizing India thus provides new conceptual inputs to reconcile the existence of atomistic individuals in conjunction with pluralistic collective being. This is most eloquently articulated by Baxi when he stated that constitutionalizing endeavours in British India provided 'contested sites for ideas and practices concerning justice, rights and development and also individual associational autonomy'.[25] Two important points are being made here: on the one hand, constitutionalism during the British rule was an empowering device because it created a space where issues were raised, debated, and also clinched; this was also a site, on the other, where individual acted both as an autonomous agent as well as one who also flourished by being part of a collectivity. Specific constitutional designs were adopted by the British rulers to simultaneously ascertain individual rights and also group rights. In other words, the preferential treatment that was meted out to specific socio-cultural and religious groups in the constitutional framework of governance in British India was, in fact, an expansion of the fundamental principles of liberalism to articulate India's peculiar social reality by emphasizing group and individuals as integral to the social compact. One of the first instances of constitutionalizing preferential treatment to a group was the 1927 Communal G(overnment) O(rder) which codified caste quota for the non-brahmins. The most significant step in this regard was the 1932 Communal Award which guaranteed 'separate electorate' for the Muslims. The architect of the award, Ramsay Macdonald, the British premier, justified the preferential constitutional design by declaring that 'separate representation, namely the grouping of a particular category of voters in territorial constituencies by themselves, so as to assure to them an adequate number of members of their faith and race has been favoured'.[26] Undoubtedly a politico-strategic design, drawn largely on imperial priorities, the Communal Award was also a legislative device conceptualizing pluralism in constitutional terms which was perfect in a specific socio-economic milieu. It is also significant in the sense that it also had set a trend that gradually became part of the political vocabulary in the nationalist discourse, especially the one that B.R. Ambedkar had articulated to champion the claim of the untouchables or Dalits in the contemporary lexicon. While attacking the caste system for privileging the upper castes at the cost of those at the lower strata, especially the Dalits, Babasaheb, as Ambedkar was popularly known, by insisting on group rights (of a segment of the population) seem to have added a new leaf in the liberal discourse. Along with his concern for the Dalit collectivity, he thus argued, in a typical liberal language, that constitutional democracy in a liberal mould, represented not merely 'a form of government [but] ... primarily a mode of associated living, conjoint communicated experience [and also] ... an attitude of respect and reverence towards fellowmen'.[27] Ambedkar strove to realize his ideological goal by couching his argument in a liberal framework which was meant 'to justify political rights of Dalits based on democracy, fraternity and liberty'.[28] This, he conceptualized, in a Marathi expression, 'munuski or humanness which ensures self-respect for each other in a community'.[29] So, Ambedkar's concern was to instil a specific behavioural trait of individuals in a collective existence which is derivative of his faith in the Enlightenment paradigm.

This section makes an argument to justify that pluralism is neither illiberal nor an aberration, but is drawn on the peculiarities in Indian socio-economic realities. An expansion of the theory of constitutional liberalism, the efforts towards conceptualizing individuals in a multitude seem to have redesigned the liberal concern for individuals in a creative fashion. What is unique in these endeavours is the conceptualization that it will highly be restrictive if individuals are envisioned as mere entities independent of their cultural identities; instead, the conceptualization that individuals need to be understood both in their individual existence and also being personified in a collectivity vis-à-vis other persons and other collectivity seems to have been an enabling theoretical postulate in reconceptualizing constitutional liberalism in the contemporary era when identities are fuzzy and multidimensional.

—— ·•· ——

The continuity of democracy in India is attributed to the consolidation of constitutional values during colonialism and its aftermath. Contrary to the conventional wisdom on constitutional democracy, as articulated by J.S. Mill in his *Considerations on Representative Government* (1861) constitutional democracy flourished in India. Following Mill's argument linking the success of constitutional democracy with social homogeneity India's well-entrenched social diversity is a serious impediment to the growth of constitutional values of the Western variety. As he argued,

> social homogeneity leads to social ties [and which will] give to each individual a stronger personal interests in practically consulting the welfare of others; it also leads him to identify his feelings more and more with their good, or at least with an ever greater degree of practical considerations for it. He comes, as though instinctively, to be conscious of himself as a being who of course pays regard to others [because] the good of others becomes to him a thing naturally and necessarily to be attended to, like any of the physical conditions of our existence.[30]

While Mill was absolutely sure that social homogeneity was a precondition for the success of constitutional democracy, S.M. Lipset, in his *Political Man: The Social Bases of Politics* (1963) provided a rather nuanced view when he argued that the rise and strengthening of constitutional democracy drew on 'the effectiveness and legitimacy of the political system [which is possible] only with the consolidation of constitutional values'. According to him, 'effectiveness means actual performance, the extent to which the system satisfies the basic functions of the government as most of the population ... see them. Legitimacy involves the capacity of the system to engender and maintain the belief that the existing political institutions are the most appropriate ones for the society.'[31]

Unlike Mill, Lipset felt the need of a system of rule of law to generate confidence among those constituting a political system. In the absence of widely respected rules of governance, the political system, he felt, could neither be effective nor legitimate. Since the rule of law had legitimacy, it would help in large measure, argued Lipset, 'resolve the key issues which have historically divided the society.'[32] In conceptualizing India's constitutional history, the theoretical inputs that Lipset provides seem very useful in two ways: (a) values and principles for constitutionalizing human behaviour do not emerge all of a sudden; instead they are formed historically out of a complex interplay of socio-economic and political processes and (b) they survive only if they provide effective governance which is seen to be legitimate to the most of the population. A cursory look at the evolution of constitutionalism in India confirms that the 1950 Constitution of India was not an outcome of just a little less than three-year endeavour (1946–9) of the founding fathers, but also a culmination of constitutionalizing processes that had its root in the philosophy of Enlightenment which flourished in the heyday of what is commonly known as 'liberal imperialism'. This is not to underestimate the effort that the constitution makers had made to give a specific shape to the 1950 Constitution, but simply to underline how the Enlightenment ideas gradually became an important source of inspiration to the nationalists who, despite being vehemently opposed to British colonialism, derived their ideological sustenance from the philosophy of Enlightenment.

The 1950 Constitution is an articulation of Western liberal values in a non-Western context in a situation when the very existence of newly emerged nation was seriously threatened due to communal bloodbath following India's partition. What was distinctive of the exercise that the members of the Constituent Assembly undertook was their unflinching faith in liberal constitutionalism presumably because they were nurtured in that philosophical tradition. Nonetheless, the 1947 partition set the perspective in which India rose as a free nation. The Constitution that was adopted in 1950 was thus the product of two conflicting cultures: one, representing the national leaders' normative concern for liberal constitutionalism and India's multicultural personality, shaped by her unique history and geography and the other underlining their concern for unity, security, and administrative efficiency. While the former led to the articulation of secularism and federalism in the 1950 Constitution and the latter resulted in the retention of the very state machinery which consolidated the colonial rule in India. The net result was the emergence of a semi-hegemonic state that drew largely upon the 1935 Government of India Act. If the new Indian political elites received a legacy of government from their predecessors, they assuredly carried over also, argued W.H. Morris-Jones, 'a legacy from their own immediate past, from the experience of the nationalist movement'.[33] The independent India's politics drew on, at least in the initial years, these two legacies. The nationalist ideology, that was not exactly derivative, remained the driving force in charting out India's future. Hence, political institutions despite their imperial roots acted in a manner which was reminiscent of an independent state, imbued with enthusiasm for a new beginning. Yet, the importance of the prevalent social order, the divided social structure, and the inevitable social conflicts in shaping the political process cannot be overlooked. There were also rich civilizational traditions that preceded the British rule which remained a binding force despite the triumph of divisive politics with the emergence of Pakistan in 1947 as a precondition for independence from the British rule. There is thus no doubt that constitutionalism in India cannot be grasped without understanding the historical processes that remained most critical even after independence for reasons connected with the peculiar circumstances in which India emerged in the comity of free nations. It would however be wrong to suggest that even after decolonization constitutional practices in India remained as they were in the past simply because the historical context underwent massive changes. It would also not be entirely correct to argue that the articulation of constitutionalism in India was absolutely innovative in its postcolonial phase because of the fact that the colonial past, though much derided, has in fact left behind a substantial political imprint.

In view of the claim that the 1950 Constitution is a culmination of long-drawn processes of socio-economic and political churning over almost two centuries, the book offers a conceptual point by suggesting that three major ideological forces—colonialism, nationalism, and democracy—seem to have been critical in the shaping of constitution-alism in India. The colonial, nationalist, and democratic articulation of constitutionalism therefore remains crucial in comprehending the nature and texture of the 1950 Constitution. Two points need to be kept in mind: first, although colonialism and nationalism are surely antagonistic there is no doubt that the former provoked circumstances in which nationalism emerged as a powerful ideology to articulate the voices of the colonized. Second, colonialism also led to a slow process of democratization by gradually involving people, favourably disposed towards alien administration. The colonial state had permitted some measures of representation to carefully selected Indian interests. But it had also ensured that 'the state had always operated at a level removed from the society which it governed'.[34] Appropriating 'the executive privi-lege' for itself, the colonial state appeared to 'stand outside the realm of and therefore free to arbiter over, social conflict and political competition [and its relationship with the subject] continued to be conducted in the language of supplication and concession, grants and demands, charters and petition, grievances and repression'.[35] The British were admittedly influenced by their own 'theories of liberalism and self-government'. Through a mixture of motives that ranged from 'self interests and ideo-logical commitments', the colonial government introduced principles of representation, appropriate for its rule, into the colonial legislature.[36] The British imperial attitudes in India thus seem to be 'highly ambigu-ous' resulting from their efforts to negotiate their liberal regard for self-rule as the best form of government and their vested interests in being imperial masters.[37] The 1935 Government of India Act was an effort that the colonial rulers seriously undertook to accommodate the nationalist zeal within, of course, the colonial administrative format. This is also illustrative of attempts at legitimizing the growing democratic aspirations of the ruled in India through a constitutional intervention. Interestingly, the 1935 Act remained the strongest influence during the making of the 1950 Constitution for free India. Some 250 clauses of the present Constitution were, in fact, lifted from the Government of India Act. Although the political system of independent India draws its sustenance from universal adult franchise and political sovereignty, the governing rules are undoubtedly derived from its colonial past. The most striking provisions that the Constitution of India derived from its 1935 counterpart are the 'emergency provisions' that enable the President to suspend democratically-elected governments and fundamental rights of the citizens. Furthermore, colonial provisions for 'preventive detention' of the so-called 'politically subversive individuals' remain in force in independent India in different forms. The infamous 1972 Maintenance of Internal Security Act (MISA), Terrorist and Disruptive Activities (Prevention) Act (TADA) of the early 1980s and Prevention of Terrorist Act (POTA) in recent times are some of the examples which are drawn on the colonial and authoritarian legislation of the colonial past. Nonetheless, the 1935 Government of India Act is undoubtedly a very significant concession that the colonial government was forced to concede due to the rising tide of nationalism and democratization.

There is no doubt that post-colonial state in India inherited its habits of governance from colonial practices. Its Weltanschauung (world view) is based on 'the mixed legacies of colonial rule' that also upheld rule of law, bureaucracy, citizenship, parasitic landlords, modern political institutions, and 'two-track tradition' of protest and participation.[38] What accounts for relative stability for colonialism in India was certainly its ability to adapt to the changed socio-political circumstances and also gradual but steady 'internalization' of domination by the subjects of colonial rule which led Ashis Nandy to characterize colonialism as 'an intimate enemy' because the dominated saw 'the virtues of being dominated' for their own betterment.[39] Colonialism was not seen as an absolute evil because for the subjects, as Nandy argues,

> it was a product of one's own emasculation and defeat in legitimate power politics. For the rulers, colonial exploitation was an incidental and regrettable by-product of a philosophy of life that was in harmony with superior forms of political and economic organization. This was the consensus that rulers of India sought, consciously or unconsciously ... [while] the subjects collaborated on a long-term basis [because] they seemed to have accepted the ideology of the system, either as players or as counter-players. This is the only way they could preserve a minimum of self-esteem in a situation of unavoidable injustice.[40]

Colonialism drew on such a cultural consensus that was further strengthened by evolving mechanism to defuse threats and also nationalist ire as and when it required. For instance, when the British model of unitary governance proved relatively ineffective for a diverse country like India, the colonial rulers began introducing, by degrees, since the 1920s doses of 'decentralization' and 'federalism' and the 1935 Government of India Act was most significant institutional step in this regard.[41] Although the colonial state was hardly federal in its classical sense, the federal arrangement that the Act stipulated seemed to have provided critical inputs to the founding fathers while deliberating on federalism in the Constituent Assembly.

These selective examples are illustrative of the argument underlining the critical importance of three ideological forces of colonialism, nationalism, and democratization in charting-out a distinctive constitutional path for India. The argument that the book seeks to make draws on the dialectical interaction between colonialism, nationalism, and democratization over a historical time frame leading to India's independence and its aftermath. Hence, it is neither intended to suggest that political freedom from colonial rule wrought no changes to Indian polity nor to argue that post-colonial India is just a continuity of her colonial past. Major political institutions, despite their clear colonial roots, have undergone dramatic metamorphosis in independent India. A careful look at the evolution of institutions in India clearly shows that they evolved creatively to adjust to the changing circumstances. The Westminster model of parliamentary democracy that India adopted was not a clone, for instance, but was responsive to the situation-specific ethos and the existent socio-cultural milieu.

There is however a note of caution. Colonialism contributed to nationalism, but not to a nation state in India for a variety of reasons connected with India's socio-cultural diversity. The post-colonial India was therefore hardly a nation state, but a state-nation simply because the institutions of governance, very much part of British legacy, were already in place when the 1947 transfer of power took place. The nationalist leaders, except M.A. Jinnah, deliberately avoided the nationalist language that could be devastating in view of the absence of cultural and moral unity in India that characterized the rise of nations in the west. The nation, as a conscious political articulation, hardly figured in the political discourse of the day. Indian nationalism was not based on a shared language, religion, or ethnic identity. Perhaps the presence of a common enemy, namely, British colonialism, 'united men and women from different parts of the subcontinent in a common and shared endeavour'.[42] A nation was consolidated, but followed a completely different trajectory that was not, at all, derivative of the European sources. The nation that India is does not privilege a single language or a religious faith. Although the majority of its citizens are Hindus, India is not 'a Hindu Pakistan'. The 1950 Constitution does not discriminate between people on the basis of faith, nor did the nationalist movement that resulted in decolonization. Although the joy of freedom was marred by partition, the failure to avoid the division made Gandhi's political successors determined to construct independent India as a secular republic and the constitutional provisions were drafted accordingly.

Despite being nurtured in Western constitutional traditions, it was not an easy task for the founding fathers when they began deliberating in the Constituent Assembly for a constitution for independent India. There were two factors which will probably explain the difficulties that they had confronted while being involved in the drafting of the constitution. First, the making of the Indian constitution was a difficult exercise not only because of the historical context but also due to the peculiar social texture of the Indian socio-economic reality that had to be translated in the constitution. The collective mind in the Assembly was also defensive as a consequence of rising tide of violence taking innocent lives immediately after partition. Secondly, the founding fathers seem to have been obsessed with their 'own notion of integrated national life'. The aim of the constitution was to provide 'an appropriate ordering framework' for India. As Rajendra Prasad, the Constituent Assembly's President, equivocally declared on the floor of the Assembly, '[p]ersonally I do not attach any importance to the label which may be attached to it—whether you call it a Federal Constitution or a Unitary Constitution or by any other name. It makes no difference so long as the Constitution serves our purpose'.[43] While Prasad seems to have refrained from making a judgment on whether the constitution was adequately equipped to constitutionalize human behaviour, B.R. Ambedkar, the Drafting Committee Chairman, was uncertain about its future which he articulated by stating that 'on the 26th of January, we are going to enter into a life of contradictions: in politics, we will have equality and in social and economic life we will have inequality'.[44] What is being emphasized here is the constitution makers' concern that despite having adopted a liberal constitution, the future of India's constitutional democracy did not seem to be as bright as they had felt at the beginning primarily due to immanent socio-economic chasm in India. Nonetheless, a sense of optimism writ large. As Prasad noted, 'If the people who are elected are capable and men of integrity, they would be able to make the best ... of the Constitution; if they are lacking in these, the Constitution cannot help the country.'[45] Implicit here is a fundamental assumption that the success of India's liberal constitution was dependent on how, in future, it unfolds at the behest of elected representatives. Two points merit attention here: on the one hand, the framers, being drawn to the Enlightenment values, appear to have endorsed, rather uncritically, a system of rule of law that flourished during colonialism presumably because of the consolidation of a mindset in its support; arguments that they marshalled for liberal constitutionalism are a testimony here. The acceptance of liberal constitutionalism also confirms, on the other, the argument that the values and principles of Enlightenment that gradually blossomed in India remain an important source of politico-ideological inspiration not only for the nationalists but also their successors. What it further reinforces is the claim that liberal constitutionalism is not at all a window dressing, but has evolved organically along with the rise of India as a democratic polity in which constitution reigns supreme.

———— ·•· ————

Constitutionalism is a guarantee whereby a community commits itself to those specific values which it seeks to uphold for common well-being. The very identity of a constitution, based on the textual and historical materials from which fundamental constitutional norms, values, and mores are to be extracted, is always an area of attention for constitutional theorists seeking to explain the phenomenon and also the jurists offering the first resistance when it is sought to be infringed. Hence, in the words of Jacobson, 'constitutional identity, a constitution acquires identity through experience: from a mix of political aspirations and commitments that express a nation's past and the desire to transcend that past. It is changeable but resistant to its destruction, and manifests itself in various ways.'[46] The concern here is to understand constitution as a living organism that survives by being adaptive to the changing social, economic, and political milieu.

Constitutional identity is articulated in a historical perspective. For instance, by according priority to religion and religious freedom, secularism, reservation and gender, the 1950 Constitution thus seeks to build and also consolidate a solid constitutional foundation for liberal democracy (primarily of the Western mould) in India. That specific provisions striving to guarantee religious freedom, secularism, reservation, and gender-parity were incorporated in the Constitution also confirms that the founding fathers were unanimous in appreciating those values of liberal constitutionalism which, they felt, were inseparable to India's governance. In a similar vein, the structure of governance that is integral to liberal constitutionalism needs to be built and nurtured. Hence, federalism was espoused by the framers of the Constitution that has always been upheld in independent India to sustain her multifaceted social, economic, and political texture. Article 370 of the 1950 Constitution ensuring special constitutional status the state of Jammu and Kashmir may however appear to be an aberration if one interprets Constitution's federal provisions mechanically without reference to the historical context in which it was incorporated as perhaps the only option to unite a clearly alienated part of the country with the mainland. The most significant endeavour in articulating India's constitutional identity is evident with the formulation of the doctrine of the basic structure by the Supreme Court of India. Reiterating that those politico-ideological values from which the Constitution draws its sustenance cannot, under any circumstances, be bypassed, India's apex court appears to have discharged its role as a custodian of the Constitution in a creative fashion. This is a design that has, in a very innovative manner, redesigned constitutional identity in circumstances when the threat to the democratic governance does not seem to be imaginary but real! The doctrine remains integral to India's constitutional identity by upholding those constitutional values which are sacrosanct so long as liberal democracy continues. Besides being a critical landmark constitutional outgrowth, the doctrine further institutionalizes the critical role that the Supreme Court of India plays in the maintenance of constitutional democracy in India.

—— .•. ——

The book is about the processes and events leading to constitutionalize India in the wake of the British rule. This is also about a journey of contestations and challenges in which multiple politico-ideological viewpoints were articulated and hotly debated before they gained salience. This is also a story of an idea which unfolded in most complex ways in colonized India and also after the attainment of political freedom in 1947. In a nutshell, the effort here is directed to understand how 'liberal imperialism' led to a specific kind of constitutionalism in India which drew its inspiration from the fundamental ethos of the philosophy of Enlightenment. There is no denying that British liberalism flourished in colonized India presumably because it developed organic roots out of its 'strong', if not 'persuasive' appeal to the ruled. As a result, not only did constitutional liberalism become 'an ideology of the natives', but also evolved as an empowering device that seems to have joined people with diverse socio-economic identities together for a common cause.

Comprising nine chapters, besides an introduction and conclusion, the text begins with the contribution of the British liberals in the consolidation of constitutional liberalism in India which is the core concern of the first chapter, 'British Liberals and the Initial Impetus towards Reorganizing the Indian Socio-political Order'. Given the space-restraint, instead of dealing with the ideas of individual thinkers, the chapter focuses on the trends with reference to those defining moments which the leading British liberals captured in their contemplations and writings. This is followed in Chapter 2, 'Nationalist Liberals and the Advent of Liberal Thought' as well while delving into the contribution of the Indian liberals in seeking to conceptualize Indian politics in liberal terms. In conceptual terms, the Indian liberals acted as a bridge between the British rulers and the colonized Indians, and hence they played a significant role in creating and also sustaining a solid support base for liberal values in India. This conceptual journey shall never be complete unless the contribution of the 'radical' or 'rebel' liberals is adequately articulated. Chapter 3, 'Radical Liberals and the Reimagining of the "Nation" through Politics' thus deals with how the radical liberals, Jyotirao Phule and B.R. Ambedkar, articulated their response while championing constitutional liberalism as perhaps a panacea for the lower strata of society, being pushed to the periphery due to the accident of birth. The dilemma that the constitution makers confronted while bringing the representatives of the Princely State in the Constituent Assembly is the main theme of Chapter 4, 'Princely States and the Nationalists' Constitutionalizing Endeavour'. The Princely States participated in the deliberations in the Assembly to evolve a democratic constitution for united India. As the contemporary evidence shows, some of the Princely States expressed resentment but they were finally persuaded presumably because of the obvious adverse consequences which they had to face if they decided not to join the Union. By drawing on the available inputs, the chapter substantiates the argument that bereft of the British help the Princely States were left with no alternative but to endorse what they were asked to. The decision to remain associated with the drafting of the constitution was perhaps the best option for the erstwhile rulers, the chapter argues.

While the first four chapters deal with constitutional liberalism as an ideational intervention that gradually became the dominant discourse for a variety of complex reasons, Chapter 5 'Major Colonial Designs towards Constitutionalizing India' deals with those landmark legislative decrees and regulations which couched Indian governance in a liberal mould. Here too, instead of focusing on each and every legislative designs, the chapter identifies and analyses those landmark designs of governance which translated constitutional liberalism in practice. What is striking to note is that the constitutional designs that the Indian liberals prepared to seemingly provide 'an alternative' to the British constitutionalizing efforts seem to have been hardly different in conceptual terms. As Chapter 6, 'Major Nationalist Initiatives towards Constitutionalizing India', demonstrates, the nationalist interventions in constitutionalizing India did not seem to be exactly different from the British constitutional designs except that they were ideologically charged with the desire to articulate an Indian voice in the making of the constitution. By focusing on the contribution that Mahatma Gandhi made in sustaining 'the pluralistic individual identity', Chapter 7, 'Mahatma Gandhi's Alternative Conceptualization of Liberal Constitutionalism', provides powerful conceptual inputs in reconceptualizing constitutional liberalism in a theoretical mould which is different from its classical articulation. Chapter 8 is a study of the role of India's Constituent Assembly (1946–9) in designing a constitution for decolonized India on the basis of the derivative ideational inputs which were not exactly imitative but creative as well since they were responses to the context which was unique and hardly static. By expanding the argument that constitutional liberalism continues to remain one of the dominant ideological discourses in India even after independence, Chapter 9 concentrates on the unique constitutional conceptualization of 'basic structure' to show that it was not merely a top-dressing imposition but organic to the prevalent politico-ideological milieu. It is thus argued here that constitutional liberalism, despite being a colonizing device, created an Indian self that acted in its favour presumably because of its persuasive appeal in contrast with other competing ideological discourses.

—— ·•· ——

The book is an analytical narrative to capture the journey of an idea, an idea that sought to consolidate colonialism in India, gradually became a source of nationalist zeal and aspirations. The study is not about what constituted the 1950 Constitution but how it came into being out of a fiercely-fought ideational battle over a period of almost two centuries. While seeking to historicize the journey, the book makes two major arguments with one supplementary argument to support the contention that constitutional liberalism is transcendental in spirit and concern. The first argument is about the critical role of the Indian liberals and British liberals in justifying and also popularizing the idioms and also the conceptual appeals of constitutional liberalism in India. Based on the derivative evidences, the argument highlights how the ideas of Enlightenment paradigm evolved their organic roots in India in the context of a decadent feudalism. The second argument, a rather unique endeavour, relates to how the 'radical' or 'rebel' liberals conceptualized constitutional liberalism by insisting on group rights. Justifying group-differentiated rights within a liberal framework, they appear to have put in centre stage concerns which later received adequate attention in the communitarian discourse on rights. Gandhi's idea of village swaraj also complements the argument that liberalism cannot be conceptualized in a straitjacketed manner given the critical importance of the context in which it is conceptualized. Village swaraj was, for Gandhi, a model of human mobilization that drew on the fundamental liberal values of associational individual existence, toleration, and rationality. On the basis of an analytical study of the unfolding of constitutional liberalism in India, the book also makes a supplementary argument suggesting that the pluralistic individual identity deriving from belonging to groups does not seem to be an aberration in constitutional liberalism, but a powerful theoretical input to comprehend how it evolves in a non-Western context in which individuals' group identity cannot be wished away.

Notes and References

1. Vidhu Verma, *Non-Discrimination and Equality in India: Contesting Boundaries of Social Justice* (New York: Routledge, London, 2012), p. 47.
2. Upendra Baxi, 'Postcolonial Legality', in Henry Schwarz and Sangeeta Ray (eds), *A Companion to Postcolonial Studies* (Oxford: Wiley-Blackwell, 2000), p. 541.
3. Paul Brass, 'The Strong State and the Fear of Disorder', in Francine Frankel, Zoya Hasan, and Balveer Arora (eds), *Transforming India: Social and Political Dynamics of Democracy* (New Delhi: Oxford University Press, 2000), p. 60.
4. Granville Austin, *The Indian Constitution: Cornerstone of a Nation* (New Delhi: Oxford University Press, 1999), p. 21.
5. Jawaharlal Nehru, 8 November 1948, *Constituent Assembly Debates*, Book No. 2, p. 319.
6. Nehru, *Constituent Assembly Debates*, p. 319.
7. Jawaharlal Nehru, 13 December 1946, *Constituent Assembly Debates*, Book No. 1, p. 60.
8. Kalyani Ramnath pursues this argument in her 'We, the People: Seamless Webs and Social Revolution in India's Constituent Assembly debates', *South Asia Research* 32(1), 2012.
9. B.N. Rau's views—cited in B. Shiva Rao (ed.), *The Framing of India's Constitution: Select Documents*, Vol. 1 (New Delhi: Universal Law Publishing C Pvt. Ltd., 2004) (reprint), p. 390.
10. Arvind Elangovan, 'The Making of the Indian Constitution: A Case for a Non-Nationalist Approach', *History Compass* 12(1), 2014.
11. K.M. Munshi's views, cited in Rao, *The Framing of India's Constitution*, p. 391.
12. Damodar Swarup Seth (United Provinces), 5 November 1948, *Constituent Assembly Debates*, Book No. 2, p. 212.
13. Bal Krishna Sharma (United Provinces), 5 November 1948, *Constituent Assembly Debates*, Book No. 2, pp. 214–15.
14. Seth, 19 November 1949, *Constituent Assembly Debates*, Book No. 5, p. 694.
15. B.R. Ambedkar, 17 October 1949, *Constituent Assembly Debates*, Book No. 5, p. 455.

16. John Gray (edited and introduced), *John Stuart Mill on Liberty and Other Essays*, Oxford World's Classics (Oxford: Oxford University Press, 2008), p. 78.

17. Karuna Mantena, *Alibis of Empire: Henry Maine and the Ends of Liberal Imperialism* (New Delhi: Permanent Black, 2010), p. 21.

18. Margaret J. Frick (ed.), *Macaulay's Essay on Warren Hastings* (New York: Macmillan, 1900), p. 13, available at https://archive.org/details/macaulaysessayo00unkngoog, (accessed on 22 February 2017).

19. *The Miscellaneous Writings of the Late Hon'ble Mr. Justice MG Ranade* (New Delhi: Sahitya Akademi, 1992) (reprint), p. 193.

20. *The Miscellaneous Writings of the Late Hon'ble Mr. Justice MG Ranade*, p. 182.

21. Chakravarthi Ram-Prasad, 'Pluralism and Liberalism: Reading the Indian Constitution as a Philosophical Document for Constitutional patriotism', *Critical Review of Internal Social and Political Philosophy* 16(5), 2013, p. 676.

22. Rochana Bajpai, *Debating Difference: Group Rights and Liberal Democracy in India* (New Delhi: Oxford University, 2011), p. 7.

23. Will Kymlicka, *Liberalism, Community and Culture* (Oxford: Clarendon Press, 1989).

24. Baxi, 'Postcolonial Legality', p. 541.

25. Baxi, 'Postcolonial Legality', p. 541.

26. India Office Records, London, L/PO/78(1). The Prime Minister's statement for release on Tuesday, 16 August, afternoon in time for publication in the morning newspaper in India and UK of Wednesday, 17 August 1932.

27. B.R. Ambedkar, *Annihilation of Caste* (New Delhi: Critical Quest, 2007), p. 13.

28. Vidhu Verma, *Non-discrimination and Equality in India: Contesting Boundaries of Social Justice* (Oxford: Routledge, 2012), p. 39.

29. Eleanor Zelliot, *From Untouchable to Dalit: Essays on the Ambedkar Movement* (Delhi: Manohar, 1996), p. 159.

30. John Stuart Mill, *Considerations of Representative Government*, reproduced in John Gray (ed.), *John Stuart Mill: On Liberty and Other Essays* (Oxford: Oxford University Press, 2008), p. 165.

31. S.M. Lipset's *Political Man: The Social Bases of Politics* (New York: Anchor Books, 1963), p. 64.

32. Lipset's *Political Man*, p. 64.

33. W.H. Morris-Jones, *The Government and Politics of India* (New Delhi: BI Publications, 1974), p. 27.

34. Rajnarayan Chandravarkar, 'Customs of Governance: Colonialism and Democracy in the Twentieth Century India', *Modern Asian Studies* 41(3), 2007, p. 446.

35. Chandravarkar, 'Customs of Governance', p. 448.
36. Dipesh Chakrabarty, 'In the Name of Politics: Democracy and the Power of the Multitude in India', in Dipesh Chakrabarty et al. (eds), *From the Colonial to the Post-Colonial: India and Pakistan in Transition* (New Delhi: Oxford University Press, 2007), p. 36.
37. D.A. Low, *Britain and Indian Nationalism: the Imprint of Ambiguity, 1929–1942* (Cambridge: Cambridge University Press, 1997).
38. Subrata Mitra, 'Constitutional Design, Democratic Vote Counting and India's Fortuitous Multiculturalism', Working Paper, November, 2004, Heidelberg, pp. 29–34.
39. Ashis Nandy, *The Intimate Enemy: Loss and Recovery of Self under Colonialism* (New Delhi: Oxford University Press, 1989) (reprint).
40. Nandy, *The Intimate Enemy*, pp. 10–11.
41. Morris-Jones, *The Government and Politics of India*, pp. 15–48.
42. Ramchandra Guha, *India after Gandhi: The History of the World's Largest Democracy* (London: Picador, 2007), p. 757.
43. Rajendra Prasad, 26 November 1949, *Constituent Assembly Debates*, Book No. 5, p. 987.
44. B.R. Ambedkar, 25 November 1949, *Constituent Assembly Debates*, Book No. 5, p. 979.
45. Prasad, *Constituent Assembly Debates*, p. 993.
46. Gary Jeffrey Jacobsohn, *Constitutional Identity* (Cambridge: Harvard University Press, 2010), p. 3.

1 British Liberals and the Initial Impetus towards Reorganizing the Indian Socio-political Order

The Constitution of India was inaugurated in 1950 and in its making the Constituent Assembly played a critical role. There is no disputation to this claim. On the surface, the claim is justified. The doubts however arise as soon as one draws attention to the processes that finally culminated in 1950 when the Constitution made its appearance. A casual look at the provisions and the values on which they rest reveals that the 1950 Constitution does not seem to be a break from the past, instead, it is a continuity both in terms of its nature and also texture—the Constitution carries forward some of the cardinal values of the colonial rule. This is, however, not to argue that the independent India's Constitution replicates the design of governance that evolved during colonialism; what is emphasized here is the argument that by imbibing the spirit of liberal constitutionalism of the

Enlightenment philosophy, the Constitution lays out a foundation for a liberal democratic polity following decolonization. There were challenges, especially by the Gandhians who, for their preference for village Swaraj, questioned liberalism for being incompatible with India's socioeconomic and political circumstances. As we know, the Gandhian challenge fizzled out and constitutional liberalism triumphed.

The aim of this chapter is to present a genealogy of the Constitution of India by drawing on various kinds of inputs which were articulated in the wake of colonial rule. This was not a story of a smooth succession of ideas, instead, there were contrasting ideas and perspectives which appear to have acted critically in shaping democratic governance in India. As Mithi Mukherjee argues,[1] there were two competing but also collaborating political discourses—the discourse of the colonial and the discourse of the imperial. While the former was a discourse of governance driven 'by ideas of territorial conquest, power, violence, domination, and subjugation of the colonialized', the imperial, on the other hand, was based on 'a supranational de-territorialized discourse of justice under natural law, and was critical and censorial towards the arbitrary exercise of power by the colonial government even as it claimed to speak on behalf of the people of India'. The story is one of a rivalry between two different perspectives jostling for a space during the colonial rule which also led to democratization of governance. Hence, it is argued further that 'the British Indian polity unfolded as a complex dialectic of the colonial as a discourse of governance grounded in power and domination and the imperial as a critical-censorial discourse of justice'.[2] The contradictory nature of the British rule in India also reveals that the effort towards constitutionalizing India was not a straightforward act, but one of multiple pulls and pressures drawing on heterogeneous practices and expectations. The idea was well-articulated when the Liberal Secretary of State, Lord Kimberley wrote to Lord Dufferin, the Viceroy, saying that 'I have no faith in a repressive policy [because] … democracy will never allow such a policy to be firmly and continuously pursued'.[3] For DA Low, British colonialism in India thus leaves 'an imprint of ambiguity'[4] resulting from the liberal concern for democratic governance, at one level, and also desire to bulldoze the 'native' urge for democracy, at another. While illustrating the argument, Low further stated that the 1935 Government of India Act was 'ambiguity institutionalised' because of its inherent contradictory nature. As he argued, at the all-India level it

> provided for ministers in an All-India Federation government to be drawn from members of the federal legislature and that extent established 'responsibility at the centre' … while, at the same time, there were innumerable imperial 'safeguards' operating at the centre which gave the Viceroy considerable 'reserve' powers over external affairs, defence, public services, currency, credit, etc., along with [along with the overall political control of governance, which was a] grave menace to the peace or tranquillity of India.[5]

The root of this 'ambiguity' can be traced back to the prevalence of contrasting ideological perspectives that appeared to have influenced how colonialism was conceptualized and conceived in governance. This is important and one has to be sensitive to this aspect while narrating the story of constitutionalizing India. There is also another side of the story which cannot be captured by reference solely to the British initiatives. As will be shown below, the democratic constitution that came out of the deliberations in the Constituent Assembly was not merely an outcome of the British grand design but also a product of struggles, waged at different levels, during the nationalist onslaught on colonialism. There were series of endeavours which were undertaken by the British rulers to gradually instil 'the political skill of self-government [and] … [t]hrough a mixture of motives that ranged from self-interest to ideological commitments, they introduced some very limited principles of representation into the colonial legislatures'.[6] The attempt had magical consequences, as history has shown. It is thus argued that the granting of dominion status was a concession that the British government was forced to concede in view of a series of the Gandhi-led nationalist agitations that created, argued Low, 'a deep crisis for the British over precisely what they should do next'.[7] This is not a stray comment, but supportive of the argument that the endeavour towards constitutionalizing India was primarily a strategic design to defuse political crisis challenging the alien authority.

In order to capture the processes leading to the consolidation of values, norms, and principles supportive of liberal governance, the chapter focuses on those major intellectual inputs in favour of preparing a ground for responsible government in India. Surprisingly, the contradiction between those favouring the imperial concern for self-government and their opponents was hardly threatening to the continuity of the British domination in India which also confirms that, at one level, the difference does not seem to be as deep-rooted as it is construed on a surface reading. Two ideas seem to be important here—first, the British imperial design cannot be conceptualized as entirely benevolent since it was also based on an effort to shape constitutionalism in India in accordance with a derivative conceptual framework that had flourished in Britain. Second, the colonialists had hardly posed a serious challenge to their apparent bête noire when the argument for self-government was forcefully made in the public domain in England and later in India. This further substantiates the claim that they also drew on the imperialists who, by insisting on constitutional governance in India, actually countered the nationalist attack which, they painted, was contrary to what the British rulers were keen to establish.

Conceptual Ideas

The 1950 Constitution of India was drawn on the fundamental liberal values which flourished during the long colonial rule. Liberal ideas were articulated both by the British liberals and their Indian counterparts. While the former was paternalistic in their attitude, the latter held liberalism as perhaps the only empowering ideological design of governance which was appropriate for India. In contemporary scholarship, three important types of liberalism have been identified—colonial liberalism, nationalist liberalism, and radical liberalism.[8] Drawn on their paternalistic concern for the colonized, the colonial liberals contributed to the consolidation of a system of governance which would prepare Indians to appreciate rule-driven administration. Although they differed in their assessment of the situation in India, they agreed that colonialism was beneficial to the rise of India as a well-governed polity in due course. While they strongly felt that representative democracy was certain to flourish in Australia and America, given identical civilizational identity, India was simply incapable of self-government, argued one of most influential liberal thinkers, J.S. Mill, because of the lack of social homogeneity.[9] In order to instil liberal values in India, 'the dominant country' had a responsibility to prepare the ground for them to flourish which means that colonialism was conceptualized as a positive influence in the colonized countries. Hence, he argued that countries which were not privileged enough to have socio-economic conditions for representative government 'must be governed by the dominant country or by persons delegated for that purpose by it. The mode of government is as legitimate as any other'.[10] So, in Mill's perception, political subjugation of a country did not seem to be objectionable since it was a stepping stone towards liberal democracy. In view of a series of efforts that the colonial government undertook to organize governance in India around the basic ethos of liberalism, it is fair to suggest that it did not grow in India and it was fashioned 'from an intellectual tradition and experiences that were substantially European, if not exclusively national'.[11] An alien conceptual paradigm gradually became integral to India's governance both during colonialism and its aftermath. A careful reading of the unfolding of liberalism in India reveals how the ideas of dominant liberal thinkers acted critically in creating conditions for the liberal ideas to strike roots and flourish in circumstances which were not exactly in its favour.

Of all the prominent British liberals, J.S. Mill and Henry Sumner Maine seem to have contributed, to a significant extent, to the evolution of a liberal mindset in the colonized India. Guided by the concern for participatory governance, they upheld the view that independent of participation, democracy remained a cosmetic conceptual category with no substance. It is true that Mill was not inclined to believe that India was not fit for representative government because 'her population is [not] in a sufficiently advanced state to shoulder the responsibility'.[12] What was the way out? For Mill, it was an obligation on the part of the colonial rulers to prepare the natives for representative government. If that was not pursued, Mill warned, 'the rulers are guilty of a dereliction of the highest moral trust which can devolve upon a nation; and if they do even aim at it, they are selfish usurpers, on a par in criminality with any of those whose ambition and rapacity have sported from age to age with the destiny of masses of mankind'.[13]

Being trustee of colonies, the rulers were thus entrusted with the noble task of spreading the complementary values for representative democracy. According to Mill, this was not contrary to what England always stood for. While justifying his contention, he thus stated that, 'England has always felt under a certain degree of obligation to bestow on such of her outlying population as were of her own blood and language, and ... representative institutions formed in imitation of her own'.[14]

The paternalistic attitude notwithstanding, Mill also tempered his views by insisting that in order to inculcate values supportive of representative democracy, the rulers needed to be sensitive to the prevalent 'public mood, habits, and concerns'. As he argued, 'it is always under great difficulties, and very imperfectly, that a country can be governed by foreigners, especially when there is extreme disparity in habits and ideas between the rulers and the ruled'.[15] These difficulties are not insurmountable and can easily be overcome by 'the honest' intentions of the rulers in evolving an atmosphere of trust and commitment on their part which was sadly missing, Mill lamented, among those at the top of the East India Company administrators. Hence, he suggested that one of the most effective ways of realizing representative democracy in its true spirit was to draw on 'the Indian practices, habits, and ideas ... than either English politicians, or those who supply the English public with opinions, have hitherto shown any willingness to undertake'.[16] This was one part of his concern; the other part revolved around the design of liberal imperialism which is a distinctive theory of imperial legitimacy, based on 'a specific link between a project of liberal reform or improvement and the ends of empire'.[17] The concern for improvement (namely, the civilizing mission) seems to have gradually lost its appeal with the steady consolidation of what Mill termed as 'imperial despotism' which he justified as necessary to teach the 'barbarians' the lesson of obedience. As he elaborated, 'the rules of ordinary international morality imply reciprocity. But barbarians will not reciprocate. They cannot be depended on for observing any rules. Their minds are not capable of so great an effort, nor their will sufficiently under the influence of distant motives'.[18]

The primary concern was to instil discipline and also willingness to cooperate for common well-being which, according to him, were 'the central attributes of civilized society'. This was a matter of habit which, he knew, could not be developed so soon because it could be learnt 'incrementally through practice and this training in obedience required a vast length of time, perhaps even centuries, to render discipline an unconscious habit'.[19] So, imperial despotism was directed to civilize the barbarous society which was not trained to be obedient to general rules. This involves two stages, as Stephen Holmes informs—the first step was to teach discipline and its importance for collective well-being; and, the second stage was to bring about change in the style of obedience, from obedience to specific commands, to obedience to general rules.[20] Mill's notion of liberal imperialism was seen as a design to consolidate colonialism around those values that justified stringent politico-ideological action in the name of civilizing the savages or barbarians. This provoked criticism since the degeneration of liberal imperialism also signalled 'the collapse of ethical discourse of empire and the concomitant shift in the language of justification towards more straightforwardly realist and pragmatic claims for legitimacy'.[21] Nonetheless, it was also welcome because it created an ambience in which adherence to general rules for the greatest good of greatest numbers did not seem to be an aberration. This was the most significant achievement of those who, while justifying liberal imperialism, pave the way for the rise and consolidation of rule of law as a stepping stone towards laying-out and also strengthening the foundation of constitutional democracy in the long run.

The other English thinker who also contributed to the articulation of constitutional democracy in India was Henry Sumner Maine who, by highlighting the inherent strength of 'village republics of the East', laid out an alternative form of governance which gained salience, especially in the writings of Gandhi in the early part of the twentieth century. In fact, the idea was so persuasive that it caused a division in the Constituent Assembly between those upholding Western liberalism and those supportive of the Gandhian model of village Swaraj. Apart from championing the village republics, Maine was perhaps one of the leading thinkers in the English Pluralist tradition who critiqued liberalism because it was, according to him, a smokescreen to hide the ulterior motives of those seeking to champion the liberal model of imperialism. Implicit here was the idea that liberalism was an ideologically-empowering device in so far as the colonized were concerned. By drawing on the erstwhile village government, Maine cast 'doubt upon the philosophical assumptions underlying and political consequences entailed by, the liberal-imperial idiom of improvement'.[22] It was Maine who had shown that village communities of the East had evolved as perhaps the most dynamic form of governance which was both self-directed and also self-fulfilling. Not only did they create a stable system of governance drawing on participation, they also remained viable across ages by being adapted to the changed socio-economic environment. Being independent and complete onto itself, the village community of India 'is a living institution ... which is too strong and numerous to be accidental'.[23] It survived, argued Maine, further because it 'contains within itself the means of following its occupation without help from outside'.[24] It was thus 'a functional whole, whose self-sustaining capacity allows it to order various social, political, legal, and economic spheres toward a communal purpose'.[25] By championing Indian village community, Maine had fulfilled two goals at one go—on the one hand, he drew attention to the 'self-acting', 'self-governing', and 'self-organizing' village community which was completely unknown to the British intelligentsia; with his sharp attack on the East India Company rule, he, on the other hand, also sharpened his critique of liberal-imperialism by highlighting the devastating role of British colonialism in destroying these self-independent units of localizing governance. What is distinctive about Maine's contribution is his idea of the community-driven system of governance which was functionally effective by being politically cohesive. This was a powerful conceptualization because (a) it challenged the much claimed intellectual-superiority of the liberal-imperial argument in favour of the so-called improvement thesis, and (b) it reinforced a counter idea which had its structural manifestations in well-established system of governance sustaining over centuries.

The Argument

On a surface reading, the conceptualizations that Mill and Maine had provided appear innocent; at a deeper reading, they are integrally connected with a design justifying colonialism and the British rule in India as beneficial for the Indians since it would enable them to realize the most humanistic principles of governance under its care. Historically, the rise and growth of liberal political philosophy in Europe was preceded by the dismantling of the decaying feudal economic order and its gradual replacement by an incipient capitalism. It was felt at that time that capitalism would not likely be a viable economic replacement for feudalism unless it was backed by something other than intellectual explanations of its numerous operational principles. Thus, it was in this background that liberalism had emerged as a solid philosophy to ideologically explain and justify the fundamental tenets of the capitalist system. It soon became obvious that liberalism was being used by the capitalist class to protect its class interests rather than as a means of bringing about a moral regeneration among the masses. As a result, the basic concepts of liberalism provided a legalistic, contractual, competitive, and bargaining code of serving class interests. Even the sense of accommodation in the doctrine of liberalism was prevalent only to the extent needed to keep the socio-economic and political order intact without putting it at risk of greater and sudden upheavals. A self-driven ideological design, liberalism was thus more than a mere conceptual category, but one that provided the colonialists with a powerful theoretical instrument to justify their rule in India. What remained at the foundation of such an attitude was 'paternalism', based on an apparent superiority of what was construed by the colonizers as British 'civilization'. And colonialism was always benign to the colonized because of the obvious benefits that accompanied 'a munificent rule' drawing on the distinct social virtues of benevolence, compassion, and tolerance. This is how colonialism survived and also thrived because in order to remain the only possible option for the colonized, colonialism undertook simultaneously two complementary sets of activities of 'civilizing others' and also keeping them in perpetual 'otherness'.[26] Reflective of the well-entrenched Victorian cultural prejudices, based on paternalism and also the arrogance of power, which always created 'an inferior other', the British liberals appeared to have articulated a voice that simply endorsed the prevalent socio-cultural values in support of what they termed as 'a civilizing mission' in colonies.

Articulating the Preferences

That the British had a civilizing mission in India was always highlighted. Rooted in the Evangelical concern for individual well-being through a series of directed politico-ideological designs, the Evangelicals were, according to Stokes, governed by '(a) intense individualism and exaltation of individual conscience, (b) the belief that human character could be suddenly and totally transformed by a direct assault on the mind, and (c) the conviction that this required an educative process'.[27] Simultaneously with their commitment to the fundamental Evangelical principles, the Evangelists held their mission as 'most noble' and appropriate to raise 'the Hindus' to a level of being civilized. It was evident when Charles Grant

(1746–1823), the chairman of the British East India Company who also became a Member of Parliament, stated that

> upon the whole then, we cannot avoid recognizing in the people of Hindustan, a race of men lamentably degenerate and base; retaining but a feeble sense of moral obligation; yet obstinate in their disregard of what they know to be right, governed by malevolent and licentious passions, strongly exemplifying the effects produced on society by a great and general corruption of manners, and sunk in misery by their vices, in a country peculiarly calculated by its natural advantages, to promote the prosperity of its inhabitants.[28]

For Grant, the inhabitants of India, particularly the Hindus, needed to be rescued and the East India Company rule was a panacea. The British rule was thus welcomed by a majority since it allowed them to be connected with those values which were humane and enlightening. One of the important means for bringing about noticeable changes was, according to Grant, a well-defined legal system which was simply impossible in the east as it was ridden with rather 'obnoxious attitudes', nurtured by an equally debased society. Believed to have been 'divinely-revealed', the Hindu law argued Grant

> [i]s regarded by them [Hindus] ... with a superstitious veneration, which institutions avowedly of human origin do not produce; so that even under foreign yoke, which in various particulars superseded its injunctions, it still maintained its credit. Hence may be deduced, in part, the predilection of that people, especially of the leading orders, for their ancient state and peculiar customs, which in all the long period of Mohamedan rule, prevented them from being assimilated to the institutions of their conquerors.[29]

The legal system was a subject of rebuke because it was based on the personal preferences of the Hindu rulers who executed 'the laws to pursue their whims'. It was simply contrary to the core values of Enlightenment which created a system of law in which discrimination due to one's socio-economic location was an anathema. There was hardly a mechanism to address the concern of those suffering due to well-entrenched social prejudices. Besides creating social despotism, the absence of 'liberal' laws sustained the system which gradually gained salience in the absence of opposition. Hence, despotism was not only 'the principle of the government of Hindostan, but an original, fundamental, and irreversible principle in the very same society'.[30] The worse sufferers were the lowest ranks in society, exhorted Grant, who were

> [d]oomed to perpetual abasement, and unlimited subjection. It has no relief against the most oppressive and insulting tyranny, no hope of ever escaping from its sufferings. ... if the genius of a Newton should arise in that class, it could have no room to expand ... One of the heaviest grievances attending this state degradation, is, that it discourages all liberal exertions, and consigns those who are destined to it, to ignorance, mean opinions of themselves, and consequent meanness of manners, sentiment, and conduct.[31]

Being a true Evangelical, Grant was hardly belligerent in his opinion presumably because he was confident that the British had no strong opponent in the later eighteenth century when he undertook his Evangelical work in India. For him, the first important task was to purge the Hindu mind of social prejudices which stemmed from the caste system. The soul needed to be purified, for which he emphasized the need of liberal education in the English mould. To free the mind, education needed to be spread, and to prepare it for appreciating what he was preaching, it had 'first to be cleared of error and superstition'.[32] What T.B Macaulay was to suggest in near future was articulated first by Grant who strongly felt that education, especially English education was to be encouraged in India to develop a support base for the Company rule. Justifying an appropriate policy to popularize English education, he thus argued that

> it would be extremely easy for government to establish [its claim by creating], in various parts of the provinces, places of gratuitous institution in reading and writing English: multitudes, especially of the young, would flock to them and the easy books used in teaching, might at the same time convey obvious truth on different subjects. The teachers should be persons of knowledge, morals, and discretion; and men of this character could impart to their pupils, much useful information in discourse; and to facilitate the attainment of that object, they might, at first, make some use of the Bengalee tongue. The Hindoos (sic) would, in time, become teachers of English themselves, and the employment of our language in public business, for which every political reason remains in full force, would, in the course of another generation make it very general throughout the country.[33]

In a very persuasive manner, Grant made a very powerful political point in favour of a system which had helped the rulers to pursue their ideological goal with relative ease. With the spread of education, he further stated, 'the general opinion of the multitude would be rectified, and, above all, they would have access to a better system of principles and morals ... and the mental bondage in which they have long been [subjected to] would gradually dissolve.'[34] By linking language with the fulfilment of the commercial goal of the Company, Grant articulated a view which was to gain support soon. In other words, in a very subtle manner, the Evangelical Grant justified the Company rule as having the benefits which were simply inconceivable in a society, ridden with social prejudices. Hence, he insisted on the English education which would not only defend the British rule but also helped to develop an organic base in the east.

For obvious reasons, these Evangelical ideas did not find favour with the hardcore colonialists who always believed to rule India with an iron fist. Nonetheless, the Evangelicals created a favourable public opinion in England in support of what they stood for. It was William Wilberforce (1780–1825) who is known for his role in abolishing slave trade in Britain. According to him, given the civilizing mission of British colonialism, it was Company's 'moral duty' to transmit the values of Enlightenment while governing the so-called 'backward societies'. The main objective was to build a system of governance that drew on the fundamental ethos of constitutional liberalism. Reverberating some of the ideas that Grant had already articulated, Wilberforce thus stated that 'let us endeavour to strike our roots into the soil by the gradual introduction and establishment of our own principles and opinions; of our laws, institutions, and manners; and, above all, as the source of every other improvement, of our religion, and consequently of our morals.'[35]

In order to inculcate the liberal values, Wilberforce felt that the institutions of governance supportive of these values needed to be implanted in India. Implicit here is also the view that institutions contributing to liberalism in Britain seemed to be appropriate in realizing the Enlightenment principles which evolved out of incessant struggle against the decadent socio-economic and political ideas, patronized by earlier rulers. With an opportunity to civilize the uncivilized, the Company was to undertake steps to build and consolidate a system of governance which was liberal in tenor and also spirit. Framing his argument typically in a paternalistic tone, and also language, Wilberforce thus stated further that, 'the Indian community ... would be bound by the ties of gratitude to those who have been the honoured instruments of communicating them [whereby they] should have exchanged [their] dark and bloody superstitions for the genial influence of Christian light and truth, ... civil order and security, of social pleasures and domestic comforts.'[36]

What is emphasized here is the idea that only by imbibing the British system of constitutional liberalism the 'backward' East could become 'civilized'. And, hence the Company-rule was a blessing in disguise for the Indian community. What is also surprising is the fact that neither Grant nor Wilberforce ever referred to the atrocities that the Company rulers in India were reported to have committed. This was however not the case with T.B. Macaulay, a Whig parliamentarian, who took a leading role in championing liberal values in the British dominions, particularly India. In his speech in the 1813 Charter Debate, not only did he emphasize the critical importance of liberal governance in fulfilling the civilizing mission of the rulers, he also insisted on governmental initiatives in creating a propitious atmosphere where the complementary institutions flourished. He thus never questioned the system of governance since he felt that it was 'human folly' which could have been rectified had the Company been sensitive to 'the moral commitment of civilizing the outlying nations'. In his fiery Charter speech, he accordingly mentioned that

> to have found a great people sunk in the lowest depths of slavery and superstition, to have so ruled them as to have made them desirous and capable of all the privileges, would indeed be a title to glory. [And], the empire, ... a triumph of reason over barbarism, is the imperishable empire of our arts, morals, literature, and laws.[37]

The arguments that Macaulay pursued were a continuity of what Grant and Wilberforce suggested in defence of colonialism. The empire epitomized reason and also progress; colonialism was thus not an impediment but a godsend opportunity for the Indians to shake-off the age-old superstitions and other decadent practices. The instrument which they found appropriate for instilling liberal values in Indian minds was education where the state had a right to intervene.[38] The idea was simple—in order to train the Indian minds in accordance with the core values of liberalism, the prevalent system of education was to be replaced by the English education which would serve two purposes. Not only would it create an English educated elite in India, it would also enable them to understand and appreciate the liberal values following their access to the fundamental literature.

The concern for India was clearly paternalistic. Indians required a benevolent governance of the British variety which was possible only when liberal values were instilled. The idea was justified in two complementary ways—on the one hand, arguments were marshalled to vehemently criticize the prevalent system of governance which was primarily an instrument to keep the Indians in chains. Once that was justified, the liberals suggested specific ways—on the other, to defend their arguments supporting their claim of liberal governance being superior and also appropriate to raise 'an enslaved' nation out of 'priesthood and despotism'. It seems to be thus natural for James Mill to argue that at the root of India's failure to rise as a free society was 'despotism' of caste hierarchy which established 'a pernicious system of subordination, ... built upon the most enormous and tormenting superstition that ever harassed and degraded any portion of mankind, their minds were enchained more intolerably than their bodies, [which made] the Hindus ... most enslaved portion of the human race'.[39] The tyranny was likely to continue unless the system was completely done away with by well-designed secular rules and regulations supportive of liberal values and ethos. The argument had substance and received support from other important liberals, including James Fitzjames Stephen (1829–1894)[40] who defended the contention by saying that

> the establishment of a system of law which regulates the most important parts of the daily life of the people constitutes in itself a moral conquest more striking, more durable, and far more solid than the physical conquest which rendered it possible. It exercises an influence over the minds of the people in many ways comparable to that of a new religion.... Our law is in fact the sum and substance of what we to teach them. It is, so to speak, a compulsory gospel which admits of no dissent and no disobedience.[41]

The objective here was to evolve laws which, being universal in character, were to be applied to all regardless of one's socio-economic locations and political views. This was the idea that gained ground in the context of the impeachment motion that the British liberals had supported against the East India Company ruler, Warren Hastings in the late 1780s. In view of the atrocities committed by the top Company officers in violation of the basic liberal values, there are many who raised voice against this. Insisting that 'all power is limited by law and ought to be guided by discretion and not by arbitrary will [where former] must be referred to the conservation and benefit of those over whom power is exercised and must be guided by rules of sound political morality'.[42] Dismayed by the arbitrary rule of Warren Hastings in India, Edmund Burke (1729–1797) admitted that the rule of law was replaced by the rule of greed— 'The order of Natural Law will be destroyed if the will of the individual becomes supreme', he further stated which he reinforced by adding that 'an arbitrary system indeed must always be a corrupt one [because] ... corruption and arbitrary power are of natural unequivocal generation, necessarily producing one another'.[43] Reiterating Burke's point, Fitzjames Stephen of the Viceroy's Reform Council went a step further by expressing his angst against the Company rule because it was contrary to those values of Enlightenment for which Britain was universally known. In place of rule-driven system of liberal governance, there were Company officers who failed miserably to transmit them to the colonies. In his letter to *The Times* on 1 March 1883, Fitzjames Stephen left no qualms in criticizing the Company rule as being 'barbarian' in some respects when he wrote that

the British Indian government is essentially an absolute government, founded, not on consent, but on conquest. It does not represent the native principles of life or of government, and it can never do so until it represents heathenism and barbarism. It represents a belligerent civilization, and no anomaly can be so striking or so dangerous as its administration by men who, being at the head of a government founded upon conquest, implying at every point the superiority of the conquering race, of their ideas, their institutions, their opinions, and their principles, and having no justification for its existence except that superiority, shrink from the open, uncompromising, straightforward assertion of it, seek to apologize for their own position, and refuse, from whatever cause, to uphold and support it.[44]

Being appreciative of the sentiments in which Fitzjames Stephen couched his argument, while challenging the Company rule since it was contrary to the espoused liberal ideals, Burke pursued the point forcefully by admitting that the people who were considered

> barbarian ... lived under the Law which was formed even whilst we ... were in the forest, before we knew what Jurisprudence was ... it is a refined, enlightened, curious, elaborate, technical Jurisprudence under which they lived, and under which their property was secure and which yields neither to the Jurisprudence of the Roman Law nor to the Jurisprudence of this Kingdom; [i]t was a law, ... which is binding upon all, from the crowned head to the meanest subject—a law interwoven with the wisest, the most learned, and most enlightened jurisprudence that perhaps existed in the world'.[45]

Nonetheless, neither Burke nor Fitzjames Stephen ever questioned the British occupation of India which, they coalesced, was a panacea because it would (a) lead to the consolidation of liberal values in India and (b) usher in an era of Enlightenment there. Their concern was to evolve a society on the basis of their vision based on their unflinching commitment to the philosophy of Enlightenment. However democratic they were in their views and also perception, both Burke and Fitzjames Stephen can also be accused of being 'paternalistic' since they privileged the British form of administration over the prevalent systems in India as perhaps the only option to realize the exalted values of liberal governance.

The Macaulay Minutes

In the transmission of liberal values to India, there were many who had contributed. As argued above, despite differences, even staunch critics like Burke and Fitzjames Stephen did neither challenge the colonial expansion in India nor endorse the system of governance that existed before the advent of the British rule. This was universally accepted that the British rule in India was needed to civilize a barbarian nation and it was an opportunity not to be lost. It was also believed that unless there was a complementary mindset supportive of the British rule, the historical role of the Empire in civilizing the savaged nations would remain unrealized. One of the most significant steps in this regard was what T.B. Macaulay, a member of the Supreme Council of India (1834–1838), undertook to help build a set of native intellectuals, capable of acting as 'interpreters' between the rulers and the ruled. He elaborated,

> I feel ... that it is impossible for us, with our limited means, to attempt to educate the body of the people. We must at present do our best to form a class who may be interpreters between us and the millions whom we govern—a class of persons Indian in blood and colour, but English in tastes, in opinions, in morals and in intellect. To that class we may leave it to refine the vernacular dialects of the country, to enrich those dialectics with terms of science borrowed from the Western nomenclature, and to render them by degrees fit vehicles for conveying knowledge to the great mass of the population.[46]

The argument was unambiguous—in to order govern India efficiently, the rulers needed a group of people who, being equipped with their knowledge of English, could be of great help to them. The concern for creating a class of persons who, despite being Indian in blood and colour, would invariably act on their behalf, was articulated in the 1835 Minutes on Education. As history has shown, the idea that the British needed a group of English-knowing people was also enunciated by the Evangelicals, like Charles Grant and William Wilberforce long before it was articulated by Macaulay. It was also suggested by James Mill when he 'voiced his opinion in the matter of instructing Indian students attending government supported colleges in India' who needed to be given 'some useful knowledge as opposed to Hindu knowledge'.[47] Implicit here is also inbuilt paternalistic bias that the colonizers had always evinced. A careful reading of the Minutes confirms this. While prefacing his arguments, Macaulay left no ambiguity, and it was articulated unambiguously when he stated:

> I certainly never met any orientalist who ventured to maintain that the Arabic and Sanscrit [*sic*] literature could be compared to that of the great European nations [and] ... it is no exaggeration to say that all the historical information which has been collected from all the books written in

Sanscrit language is less valuable than what may be found in the most paltry abridgments used in preparatory schools in England.[48]

In his defence, he put forward another argument, namely, English was spoken by the rulers and also that class of the natives at the seats of government. So, English was likely to evolve as a language of communication between the rulers and the ruled. Now, Macaulay justified his claim of English as the principal mode of communication in the colony by stating that 'whether we look at the intrinsic value of our literature or at the particular situation of this country, we shall see the strongest reason to think that of all foreign tongues, the English language is that which would be the most useful to our native subjects.'[49] Opposition was scuttled and English was championed as an enabler for the natives to gain access to the European literature. The ruling class arrogance seemed to have prevailed when Macaulay further stated that 'we are free to employ our funds as we choose, … we ought to employ them in teaching what is best-worth knowing, … and English is better worth knowing than Sanscrit or Arabic.'[50] A complacent Macaulay thus concluded that given the obvious advantage of knowing English, 'the natives are desirous to be taught English, and are not desirous to be taught Sanscrit and Arabic, [and, hence] these languages do not have any peculiar claim for government funds.'[51] With efforts on the part of the rulers, it was possible 'to make the natives of this country thoroughly good English scholars', he thus insisted that 'to this end our effort ought to be directed'.[52] His effort had paid off; English became a lingua franca in India.

With the official endorsement of the Macaulay Minute, the Orientalists, William Jones, and his colleagues lost a battle that they had been relentlessly fighting since the idea was mooted. Available evidence suggests the inference, as Elmar H. Cutts has shown, that 'evangelical pressure in behalf of the English-language educational programme for India upon the officials of the East India Company, members of Parliament and the British public'[53] finally culminated in the acceptance of the Minute in 1835 in the midst of the opposition, led by the Orientalists, especially, Mountstuart Elphistone, Thomas Munro, and B.H. Hodgson. The role of the Utilitarians, including that of the father-son duo, James and J.S. Mill, was derivative of the Evangelical inputs which Macaulay seemed to have internalized while preparing his defence for English education in India. The young Macaulay had access to the views of the prominent Evangelicals like Charles Grant and William Wilberforce who were his father, Zachary Macaulay's close associates.[54] It was easier for Macaulay and his colleagues to accomplish the goal also because of the support that they received from the indigenous elites, including Ram Mohan Roy and Bankim Chandra Chattopadhyay. Not only did they accept the decision as most appropriate, they also campaigned for English education in Calcutta by urging the city's philanthropists to open schools for training in English; their interest in English language instruction provided Macaulay and his administrative boss in India, Governor-General Bentick, with a source of strength in countering the argument that it was likely to disrupt the political balance in the country.

The Macaulay Minute was not just an administrative design for change of the language for official purposes; it was a new beginning for India in the sense that the it represented the final attack on the Hastings educational policy privileging indigenous languages. As a result of the withdrawal of government patronage of Oriental studies, a large number of academic positions created for teaching Sanskrit and Arabic became redundant. Once the decision was accepted, Governor-General Bentick received petitions supported by the leading Orientalists. In principle, the learning of a language did not seem to be objectionable to Macaulay; he however was not persuaded to endorse the endeavour if the government funds were to be spent. In his Minute, he was categorical in his preference when he said:

> all those petitions ... proceeded on the supposition that some loss had been sustained that some wrong had been inflicted [and, they thus] demand compensation for having been educated gratis, for having been supported by the public for their education, and then sent forth into the world well-furnished with literature and science, [which means that] ... they have wasted the best years of life in learning what procures for them neither bread nor respect.[55]

In two ways, he attacked the critics—on the one hand, he silenced them by highlighting the obvious inadequacies of the Oriental languages which could be a source of knowledge but was not enough to earn a living, let alone respect. Hence, the government decision to support the learning of these languages was a faulty one. Given their inherent limitations to make the learners competitive for the changed social and economic environment, Macaulay, on the other, defended the withdrawal of government patronage. He minced no words to muzzle his critics by saying that 'it would be bad enough to consult their [Indian] intellectual taste at the expense of their intellectual health. But we are consulting neither. We are withholding from them the learning which is palatable to them. We are forcing on them the mock learning which they nauseate'.[56] There is another argument that he offered to dissuade the government from funding the learning of these 'archaic' languages. Why should the government pay people to learn Sanskrit and Arabic, asked Macaulay. Evidently because it was universally felt, he further argued, that 'the Sanscrit and Arabic are languages the knowledge of which does not compensate for the trouble of acquiring them'.[57] Implicit here are two important ideas—on the one hand, since these Oriental languages lost their marketability, they should not receive government support; the other idea reinforces the argument that English learning was justified primarily because it equipped the learners to become marketable in a competitive globe.

For the rulers, the English-learning was meant to create a bridge between them and the ruled; it was an instrument to expand their sphere of influence. For the ruled, it was a device to acquire marketable skills for gainful employment. This is a narrow view of the possible impact of English language instruction for it also allowed the native Indians an easy access to the vast literature championing liberalism as a libertarian ideology. The Macaulay Minute was welcome by the Indian elites because it provided them with an opportunity to engage with the ideas which radically altered the human perception about humanity. In order to qualify the colonized Indians for progress and liberty, it was necessary for them to learn from the Western history and Western literature, and, in that respect, the learning of English was unavoidable. So, being an empowering device, English needed to be learnt as quickly as possible. The concern was to learn from the West, and English was an effective aid. The argument gained momentum and the opponents lost their steam in a context when liberal values seemed to have acquired salience due largely to a propitious environment in which they were dubbed as socio-politically useful for progress and liberty. What is required to be remembered, as Partha Chatterjee warned, is the fact that the process of intermingling with the West cannot be understood independent of the concern of the natives to retain their independent space in the spiritual domain. While, in the material domain, the West maintained their superiority, in the spiritual domain, the European Enlightenment had little to contribute; in this domain, the East was superior, and there it was 'undominated'.[58] So, there is a space in which a battle is waged between the derivative liberal ethos and their indigenous counterpart in the spiritual domain which further confirms that constitutional liberalism that evolved organic roots in India does not seen to be an unalloyed idea; instead, it was a creative blending of what the colonial authority had carried from the West with what had evolved out of a dialectical inter-connection between the derivative inputs and the so-called indigenous concerns.

Concluding Observations

This chapter attempts to identify the possible intellectual sources of liberal political ideas that gradually became critical in governance in India. The basic argument that this chapter defends relates to the contention that liberalism evolved in India at the patronage of the colonial authority. The above analysis of the ideas of a selective group of British thinkers confirms that the civilizing zeal of the rulers appears to have governed their priorities in India as soon as she became a British colony. Notwithstanding the serious differences, among those who shaped the cognitive understanding of colonialism, there was hardly a formidable opposition to the continuity of colonial rule till when the British paramountcy was severely challenged by the nationalists. Besides the obvious economic gain, India as a colony was also a laboratory for testing some of the interesting ideas which were considered to be integrally connected with the fundamental civilizing mission of the colonizers. This was never seriously questioned and the leading thinkers, despite their concern for liberty, fraternity, and compassion, appeared to have endorsed the colonial practices as being needed to elevate the colonies to an improved state of being civilized. As shown earlier, it was James Mill who endorsed colonialism as it was a panacea for the natives to avoid despotic rule justifying priestcraft. Despite being hailed as an important treatise on British India, Mill's views in the History of British India are so simplistic and 'so unremittingly dark, often so pathetically foolish in their lack of nuance'[59] that they are criticized, rightly so, for being rooted in self-obsessed racial prejudices. This was evident when Thomas Munro, one of the most important British administrators and also known for his contribution to some of the major agrarian policies during the Company rule, wrote:

> we should look upon India not [as] a temporary possession, but as one which is to be maintained permanently, until the natives shall in some future age have abandoned most of their superstitions and prejudices, and become sufficiently enlightened to frame a regular government for themselves, and to conduct and preserve it. Whenever, such a time shall arrive, it will probably be best for both countries that the British Control over India shall be gradually withdrawn.[60]

Implicit in the statement is the superiority complex that the colonizers had always evinced; they took onto themselves a divinely-ordained responsibility to civilize a savaged nation by imbibing the spirit of a messiah. It was, as if, a noble duty that the colonizers had to accept for a noble cause. By conceptualizing their role in such a way, the colonial masters had taken onto themselves, it has been rightly argued, 'a pedagogical mission whose ultimate goal was to introduce the discourse and practice of liberty in its most visible form as self-government in India'.[61] This was a self-propelled discourse in which India was shown to be a country of total disorder, chaos, and violence that corresponded with the Hobbesian description of the state of nature as 'nasty, brutish, and short'. So, what naturally followed next was the marshalling of arguments for British rule in India which was based on the idea that it was the British rule which would prepare India for an improved social, economic, and political existence. It was this argument that justified the British rule in India as nothing but a mission for civilizing and also creating an environment in India for self-government in the liberal conceptual mould.

There were, of course, dissenting voices, as shown in the chapter which also confirms the prevalence of contrasting ideas seeking to conceptualize India differently. Edmund Burke or Fitzjames Stephen (who claimed to fame for his contribution to the 1872 Indian Evidence Act), for instance, held views contrary to the dominant discourses. Nonetheless, they were bound together since they always felt that colonialism was beneficial to India for not only would it bring about the required changes for liberalism to strike roots, but it would also lead to the blossoming of liberal ideas contributing to a social order free from superstition and prejudices. Both the critics and the supporters of colonialism appear to have joined hands in their appreciation of British colonialism in India. In other words, there was hardly a substantial difference between the colonizers and those who conceptualized colonialism slightly differently because, as it is argued, 'the judgment of other people's experiences as provisional and interventions in their lives as legitimate is the conceptual and normative core of the liberal justification of the Empire'.[62] The idea is crystal clear. Colonialism was a benevolent influence for India and hence it was to be encouraged as perhaps the only design to redeem India of her social, economic, and political ills and also inadequacies. In other words, the basic idea that gained pre-eminence was 'the paradigm of a backward society's progression towards the pattern of modern European civil and political society under the tutelage of imperial power'.[63] It was thus not surprising when Fitzjames Stephen, who supported Burke when he impeached Warren Hastings for not being 'adequately liberal' in India, insisted that 'if the authority of the government is materially relaxed, if the essential character of the enterprise is misunderstood and the delusion that it can be carried out by the assemblies representing opinions of the natives is admitted, nothing but failure, anarchy and ruin can be the result'.[64]

For Fitzjames, the British rule was a perfect system allowing the natives to be trained in liberal values which ultimately helped them build a representative form of government in the British mould. The representative government was a form, he believed, should emerge from within which means that there was no way it could be transported from Britain; the local natives were required not only to raise this demand but also to fight for it. Representative government could never be a gratis; but would evolve out of an organized campaign involving the majority of the Indians who, by being drawn to liberal values, found the design both self-fulfilling and self-gratifying. With hindsight one can thus argue that the liberal ideas that the British rule had germinated in India prepared the ground for their growth which finally culminated in massive politco-ideological campaigns in the country against colonialism since it was not liberal in its articulation and manifestation in governance.

There is a well-argued opinion suggesting that 'the providential character of British mission in India was upheld on grounds of lofty moral
ideals'[65] which the colonizers always championed to misguide, if not
deceive, the ruled. The liberals gave the British rule 'a wide ideological
umbrella which', the argument further expands, 'sheltered a whole range
of self-righteous exaltations, romantic images, and contorted visions
wrapped up in unrealizable moral goals and objectives'.[66] The argument
does not seem to be vacuous and it has substance especially because
of the well-substantiated claim that the British rule was unblemished
and free from prejudices. Nonetheless, it is also difficult to dismiss the
substantial contribution that the British liberals had made in questioning the age-old primordial social order as being disturbingly archaic and
not, at all, tenable. Necessarily optimistic, they 'never doubted that the
transformation of society was not only possible, but certain'.[67] With
their well-argued and also persuasive opinion, the liberals sought to lib-
erate individuals from their age-old bondage to priestcraft and despotic
and feudal aristocrats which allowed them to become 'autonomous individuals' capable of making an independent choice, if necessary. While
challenging the hierarchy that graded individuals on the basis of their
ascribed identity, the English liberals can thus said to have set a process
in motion which loomed large in course of the nationalist struggle challenging the very liberal political order that also had a significant role in
its articulation.

Notes and References

1. Mithi Mukherjee, *India in the Shadows of Empire: A Legal and Political
   History (1774–1950)* (New Delhi: Oxford University Press, 2010),
   pp. xv–xvi.
2. Mukherjee, *India in the Shadows of Empire*, p. xvi.
3. Lord Kimberley to Lord Dufferin, 22 April 1886—cited in D.A. Low,
   Britain and Indian Nationalism: The Imprint of Ambiguity, 1929–1942
   (Cambridge: Cambridge University Press, 1997), p. 35.
4. Low, *Britain and Indian Nationalism*.
5. Low, *Britain and Indian Nationalism*, p. 269.
6. Dipesh Chakrabarty, 'In the Name of Politics: Democracy and the Power
   of the Multitude in India', in Dipesh Chakrabarty, Rochona Majumdar,
   and Andrew Sartori (eds), *From the Colonial to the Postcolonial: India*

and Pakistan in Transition (New Delhi: Oxford University Press, 2007), pp. 36–7.

7. Low, *Britain and Indian Nationalism*, p. 32.

8. Rochana Bajpai, 'Liberalism in India: A Sketch', in Marc Stears (ed.), *Liberalism and Ideology: Essays in Honour of Michael Freeden* (New York, Oxford University Press, 2012), pp. 53–76.

9. J.S. Mill, 'Considerations on Representative Government', in *On Liberty and Other Essays* (Oxford: Oxford University Press, 1998) (reprint), pp. 257–68.

10. Mill, 'Considerations on Representative Government', p. 453.

11. Uday Singh Mehta, *Liberalism and Empire: India in British Liberal Thought* (Delhi: Oxford University Press, 1999), p. 1.

12. J.S. Mill, 'Considerations on Representative Government', in John Gray (ed.), *John Stuart Mill, On Liberty and Other Essays* (Oxford: Oxford University Press, 2008), p. 453.

13. Mill, 'Considerations on Representative Government', p. 454.

14. Mill, 'Considerations on Representative Government', p. 446.

15. Mill, 'Considerations on Representative Government', p. 455.

16. Mill, 'Considerations on Representative Government', p. 467.

17. Karuna Mantena, 'Mill and the Imperial Predicament', in Nadia Urbinati and Alex Zakaras (eds), *J.S. Mill's Political Thought: A Bicentennial Reassessment* (Cambridge: Cambridge University Press, 2007), p. 299.

18. J.S. Mill, 'A Few Words on Non-Intervention', in J.M. Robson (ed.), *Collected Works of John Stuart Mill*, Vol. XXI (Toronto: University of Toronto Press, 1984), p. 119.

19. Mantena, 'Mill and the Imperial Predicament', p. 305.

20. Stephen Holmes, 'Making Sense of Liberal Imperialism', in Nadia Urbinati and Alex Zakaras (eds), *J.S. Mill's Political Thought: A Bicentennial Reassessment* (Cambridge: Cambridge University Press, 2007), p. 334.

21. Mantena, 'Mill and the Imperial Predicament', p. 316.

22. Karuna Mantena, *Alibis of Empire: Henry Maine and the Ends of Liberal Imperialism* (New Delhi: Permanent Black, 2010), p. 22.

23. Henry Sumner Maine, *Village Communities in the East and West* (six lectures delivered at Oxford) (New York: Henry Bolt and Company, 1889), p. 12, available at https://archive.org/stream/villagecommunities00main#page/n5/mode/2up, (accessed on 25 April 2016).

24. Maine, *Village Communities in the East and West*, pp.175–6.

25. Mantena, *Alibis of Empire*, p. 84.

26. Ania Loomba, *Colonialism/Postcolonialism*, (London: Routledge, 1998), pp. 67–9.

27. Eric Stokes, *The English Utilitarians and India* (Delhi: Oxford University Press, 1989), p. 30.

28. See Charles Grant, *Observations on the State of Society Among the Asiatic Subjects of Great Britain: Particularly with Respect to Morals and on the Means of Improving It*, 1792, p. 71, available at https://ia800206.us.archive.org/12/items/observationsonst00gran/observationsonst00gran_bw.pdf (accessed 29 January 2017).

29. Grant, *Observations on the State of Society among the Asiatic Subjects of Great Britain*, p. 80.

30. Grant, *Observations on the State of Society among the Asiatic Subjects of Great Britain*, p. 81.

31. Grant, *Observations on the State of Society among the Asiatic Subjects of Great Britain*, pp. 81–3.

32. Stokes, *The English Utilitarians and India*, p. 32.

33. Grant, *Observations on the State of Society among the Asiatic Subjects of Great Britain*, p. 151.

34. Grant, *Observations on the State of Society among the Asiatic Subjects of Great Britain*, p. 152.

35. See, Speech of Wilberforce on the Clause in the East India Bill for promoting the religious instruction and moral improvement of the natives in the British dominions in India, 22 June, 1 and 12 July 1813—cited in Eric Stokes, *The English Utilitarians and India*, p. 35.

36. Speech of Wilberforce on the Clause in the East India Bill, p. 35.

37. T.B. Macaulay's Speech in Parliament on 10 July 1833, cited in Stokes, *The English Utilitarians and India*, p. 45

38. Eric Stokes pursued this argument in detail in his *The English Utilitarians and India*, pp. 45–6.

39. James Mill, *History of British India*, Volume II, pp. 166–7, available at https://ia801409.us.archive.org/26/items/historybritishi23wilsgoog/historybritishi23wilsgoog.pdf, (accessed on 12 January 2017).

40. He is also known for his critique of John Stuart Mill's neo-utilitarianism. In his book, *Liberty, Equality, and Fraternity* (1874), he attacked Mill's thesis and held the defence for legal compulsion, coercion, and restraint in the interest of morality and religion.

41. The statement of James Fitzjames Stephen—cited in Jakob Fortunat Stagl, 'The Rule of Law against the Rule of Greed: Edmund Burke against the East India Company', p. 117, available at http://data.rg.mpg.de/rechtsgeschichte/rg20_104stagl.pdf, (accessed on 4 February 2017).

42. *The Works of Right Honourable Edmund Burke, Speeches of the Impeachment of Warren Hastings and Letters*, Vol. VII, pp. 2–3, available

at https://archive.org/details/speechesofrighth02burk, (accessed on 4 February 2017).

43. Speech of Edmund Burke impeaching Warren Hastings, cited in Jakob Fortunat Stagl, 'The Rule of Law against the Rule of Greed: Edmund Burke against the East India Company', p. 113, available at http://data.rg.mpg.de/rechtsgeschichte/rg20_104stagl.pdf, (accessed on 4 February 2017).

44. The letter of James Fitzjames Stephen of 1 March 1833—cited in Jakob Fortunat Stagl, 'The Rule of Law against the Rule of Greed: Edmund Burke against the East India Company', p. 107.

45. Speech of Edmund Burke impeaching Warren Hastings—cited in Peter J. Marshall (ed.), *The Writings and Speeches of Edmund Burke: The Hastings Trial of 1789–1794*, Vol. VII (Oxford, Clarendon Press, 2000), p. 285.

46. T.B. Macaulay, The Minute on Education, 2 February 1835, available at http://www.columbia.edu/itc/mealac/pritchett/00generallinks/macaulay/txt_minute_education_1835.html, (accessed on 4 February 2017).

47. Elmar H. Cutts, 'The background of Macaulay's Minute', *The American Historical Review* 58(4), 1953, p. 825.

48. T.B. Macaulay, The Minute on Education, 2 February 1835, available at http://www.columbia.edu/itc/mealac/pritchett/00generallinks/macaulay/txt_minute_education_1835.html, (accessed on 4 February 2017).

49. Macaulay, The Minute on Education.

50. Macaulay, The Minute on Education.

51. Macaulay, The Minute on Education.

52. Macaulay, The Minute on Education.

53. Elmar H. Cutts, 'The Background of Macaulay's Minute', *The American Historical Review* 58(4) (July), 1953, p. 826.

54. Cutts, 'The Background of Macaulay's Minute', p. 831.

55. Macaulay, The Minute on Education.

56. Macaulay, The Minute on Education.

57. Macaulay, The Minute on Education.

58. Partha Chatterjee, *The Present History of West Bengal: Essay in Political Criticism* (Delhi: Oxford University Press, 1997), p. 16. For a fuller description of this debate, see Partha Chatterjee, *The Nation and Its Fragments: Colonial and Post-Colonial Histories* (Delhi: Oxford University Press, 1994), Chapter 1, pp. 3–13.

59. Uday Singh Mehta, *Liberalism and Empire: India in British Liberal Thought*, (Delhi: Oxford University Press, 1999), p. 90.

60. See Thomas Munro's Speech, 28 July 1824 in S.V. Desika Char, *Readings in the Constitutional History of India, 1957–1947* (Delhi: Oxford University Press, 1983), p. 141.

61. Mukherjee, *India in the Shadows of Empire: A Legal and Political History*, p. 75.

62. Uday Singh Mehta, *Liberalism and Empire: India in British Liberal Thought* (Delhi: Oxford University Press, 1999), p. 191.

63. Sabyasachi Bhattacharya, *The Colonial State: Theory and Practice* (Delhi: Primus Books, 2016), p. 184.

64. James Fitzjames Stephen, 'Foundations of the Government of India', *Nineteenth Century*, No. LXXX, October 1883, p. 566—cited in Eric Stokes, *The English Utilitarians and India*, p. 303.

65. Suhas Chakravarty, *The Raj Syndrome: A Study in Imperial Perceptions*, (New Delhi: Penguin, 1989), p. 44.

66. Chakravarty, *The Raj Syndrome: A Study in Imperial Perceptions*, p. 44.

67. Thomas R. Metcalf, *Ideologies of the Raj*, (Cambridge: Cambridge University Press, 1998), p. 29.

2 Nationalist Liberals and the Advent of Liberal Thought

Liberalism reached the Indian shore through the colonial liberals who, however, had strong reservation about its application in India. Nonetheless, they inspired the early nationalists who were politically baptised through those texts which articulated the liberal approach to politics and governance. Liberalism gained hegemony in part because of the 'Anglicization of public life'.[1] The political ideas of John Stuart Mill, Herbert Spencer, August Comte among others, were spread to the English-educated classes through English and later vernacular newspapers, books, and pamphlets. Reasons are plenty. Chief among them was to strengthen the campaign against the well-entrenched feudal values impeding the rise of a liberal society in India. It was therefore not surprising that the leading intellectuals such as Ram Mohan Roy and Bankim Chandra Chatterjee hailed the British rule as perhaps a stepping stone towards creating an enlightened society. It was also argued that a mere political change was not adequate to bring about a radical social transformation; what was required was to create a system of constitutional governance supportive of the new politico-ideological order drawing on constitutional liberalism. A consensus seems to have emerged among the Indian liberals cutting across ideological divide. Defending their argument by drawing on the fundamental principles of constitutional liberalism, the Indian liberals devoted their energy to build a system of governance, not restrained by primordial loyalties, but based on the values of enlightenment and human progress. This was easier said than done, especially when there was a section among the colonialists which was considered to be favourably disposed towards the prevalent system of values, morals, and norms which, if disturbed, as they felt, was likely to affect the colonial rule adversely. So, the task did not seem to be as easier as it was surmised when it was launched. Here the role of the Indian liberals appeared to have acted favourably since it was they who, through their sustained campaign for a change of guard, created an environment in India in favour of constitutional liberalism which, they believed, was to create a solid socio-economic and political foundation for India to grow as 'a civilized nation'. The chapter thus argues that with complementary support from the British liberals, their Indian counterpart played a critical role in evolving an environment in which the British liberal values in favour of constitutional rule gained salience. What is striking about the efforts of the Indian liberals is also the fact that they couched their argument for constitutional liberalism by linking it with their attempt to weed out a superstitious mindset that appeared to have stunted, if not restricted, the growth of a liberal society. In other words, the effort was a blending of two goals which are dialectically interconnected since the success of the constitutional liberalism was contingent on the appreciation of values of the philosophy of enlightenment. This assumption provides inputs to the argument that the Indian liberals seem to have been intellectually inspired by the colonialists, both the Orientalists and their bête noire, the Occidentalists, when they strongly defended colonial rule in India as a panacea in those circumstances when human values were hardly respected, if not sacrificed, at the altar of the age-old system of social, political, and economic configurations of human society. The Indian society was governed by those given rules and regulations which were not to be questioned as they were divinely-ordained and thus required to be respected and observed. By fiercely critiquing this assumption supportive of anachronistic social practices, the Indian liberals seem to have upheld the spirit of 'Enlightenment humanism' that was 'a boon' to the colonized since it 'provided a strong foundation on which to erect ... critiques of socially unjust practices'.[2] In other words, the ideational inspiration that the nationalist liberals derived from their British counterparts remained a source of strength in their cudgels against various forms of injustice, being justified in the name of scriptures and age-old archaic social morals, values, and practices.

The chapter argues out the point that in the strengthening of liberal constitutionalism in India the role of the Indian liberals was also critical; in fact, it was most laudable since they had to defend their points in a rather hostile socio-political environment when the feudal mind set remained entrenched, to a significant extent. It is difficult to identify individual contribution separately since there are many Indian liberals who played a critical role in espousing the liberal cause. In order to understand the trend championing liberal socio-political values, the chapter delineates the contribution of those major Indian liberals who while being engaged in pursuing specific political goals articulated very categorically their preferences for constitutional governance as perhaps the best options available for the colonized. This needs to be emphasized here that those who stood out for their contribution built their arguments on the basis of what they drew from their predecessors who took up the cudgels long before they appeared on the scene. In concrete terms, the chapter justifies the argument that the effort towards constitutionalizing India cannot be understood, let alone conceptualized, unless the contribution of Ram Mohan Roy and Bankim Chandra Chatterjee is adequately dealt with. The argument supporting the dialectical interconnection between liberal constitutionalism and radical socio-economic changes seem to have had its roots in the conceptualization of Roy and Chatterjee who, while opposing the prevalent socio-economic and political order, sought to create a persuasive alternative by drawing on the seminal writings of the leading British liberals, including John Stuart Mill, James Fitzjames Stephen, Edmund Burke, among others. It was, in other words, a confluence of thought that finally led to the making of a liberal constitution for India in 1950 in which these ideas were articulated in concrete terms.

The Early Inputs

The chapter draws on the argument that liberalism flourished in India due to the support that the Indian liberals had extended. Once they were exposed to the idea, they also seemed to have imbibed its spirit as perhaps a powerful politico-ideological instrument to bring about the required socio-economic and political changes in India. Being integral to an intellectual wave with significant political import, liberalism was upheld by them when the existent feudal values were not as weak as they gradually became. To start with, the three of the Indian liberals—Ram Mohan Roy, Bankim Chandra Chatterjee, and Surendranath Banerjee— appeared to have laid the foundation of liberalism despite the odds. Inspired by the philosophy of Enlightenment, they were persuaded to believe that the British rule was a boon in disguise notwithstanding its adverse political consequences.

Ram Mohan Roy's Initiatives

Ram Mohan Roy (1772–1833) was one of the first Indian liberals who took the initiative in popularizing liberal ideas in India because he strongly felt that only by imbibing its spirit India could become 'a nation with spirit and intent'. While supporting the British rule, he was said to have created a space for 'liberal-imperial' discourse which was an act of considerable originality that could have been attempted by a man, like Roy, 'of multiple hybridities.'[3] As an anglicized Indian, a Hindu-Briton, a modern-traditionalist, a romantic rationalist, a bourgeois intellectual, and a scholar-aristocrat, Roy was endowed with a rare quality of recon-ceptualizing some of the fundamental social and political ethos which he felt, were not contrary to making India modern. While appreciating Roy's seminal contribution in ushering an era of change, Rabindranath Tagore thus mentioned that his cudgels against the archaic Hindu tradi-tions 'promoted him to accept the message of the West without belittling the East [and, in doing so] he braved the wrath of his countrymen in his attempt to impart to them a knowledge of the universal rights of man as man.'[4] Roy's primary concern was to introduce Indians to the empow-ering liberal ideas—an endeavour which, he felt, would help them to shake-off their superstitious selves. It was not a blanket support to the British rule, but was conditional since it was beneficial for the Indians being ruled by the despotic and tyrannical Mughals and Rajputs; in its place, the British rule created a space for civil liberties regardless of class, creed, and clan. Hence, he gave up 'prejudice against [the British rule] and became inclined in their favour, feeling persuaded that their rule, though a foreign yoke, would lead more speedily and surely to the amelioration of the native inhabitants.'[5] In view of his uncritical belief of the British rule being ameliorative for the Indians, he also appreciated the adoption of the 1793 Permanent Settlement, which gave relief to the tillers of the soil from being exploited by the absentee zamindars who hardly had any concern for them. With tough measures by the rulers against tyrant landlords, Roy was also persuaded to accept that the British rule was certainly an improvement over the erstwhile system of governance. He expressed the following view most categorically in his appeal to the King-in-council:

> Divine Providence at last in its abundant mercy, stirred up the English nation to break the yoke of those tyrants, and to receive the oppressed natives of Bengal under its protection. Having made Calcutta the capital of their domination, the English distinguished this city by such peculiar marks of favour, as a free people would be expected to bestow, in establishing an English Court of Judicature, and granting to all within its jurisdiction, the same civil rights as every Briton enjoys in his native country; thus putting the natives in India in possession of such privileges as their forefathers never expected to attain, even under Hindu rulers.[6]

Central to his argument was the concern for liberty to individuals who did not seem to have the right to enjoy liberty because of the archaic social values, justified in the name of tradition. Based on his understanding of 'the harm principle' he also insisted that the rulers needed to adopt rules and regulations even to the extent of harming those who always stood against the obnoxious (which were also atrocious) primordial values which, he believed, sustained the status quo in favour of those being socially dominant. While being critical of the Brahmin idolatry, he was not hesitant in condemning the archaic practices by saying:

> [M]any learned Brahmans are perfectly aware of the absurdity of idolatry and are well-informed of the nature of the purer mode of divine worship. But as in the rites, ceremonies, and festivals of idolatry, they find the

source of their comforts and fortune, they ... advance and encourage it to the utmost of their power by keeping the knowledge of their scriptures concealed from the rest of the people.[7]

It was clear, as Roy felt, that the priestly class 'invented and sustained those dogmas and doctrines'[8] to perpetuate their authority which prompted him to vehemently oppose the government endowment of Sanskrit learning which he seemed to disparage in 'almost Millite tones'.[9] His opposition to Sanskrit learning which would 'keep the country in darkness' was a stepping stone towards welcoming the English education which was a passport to a world free from age-old prejudices and archaic rules. In his letter of 11 December 1823 to Amherst, he thus argued:

[I]f it had been intended to keep the British nation in ignorance of real knowledge, the Baconian philosophy would not have been allowed to displace the system of the school-men which was test calculated to perpetuate ignorance. In the same manner the Sanskrit system of education would be the best calculated to keep this country in darkness if such had been the policy of the British legislature. But as the improvement of the native population is the object of the government, it will consequently promote a more liberal and enlightened system of instruction, embracing Mathematics, Natural Philosophy, Chemistry, Anatomy, with other useful sciences.[10]

Roy's insistence on English education as opposed to Sanskrit learning was based on his firm belief of Western learning being a driving force against superstition and ignorance. It was an opening for the Indians to internalize some of the fundamental ideas of liberalism which would equip them to fight against those socially debilitating systems contributing to the consolidation of an archaic mindset. The goal was to evolve a space where nothing was to be accepted as given and sacrosanct; instead, they needed to be rationally justified and endorsed. Hence, it is argued:

without the example of Rammohun Roy and other members of an emerging new public before them, it is hard to imagine that Trevelyan and Macaulay would have dared to suggest that the Orientalists were elitist pursuing a private agenda at odds with interests of the Indian public or that Macaulay would have closed his minute with the statement that the British must do their best to form a class who may not be interpreters between us and the millions whom we governed, but a class of persons Indian in blood, in colour but English in taste, in opinion, in moral and in intellect.[11]

As a pioneer of social regeneration against heavy odds, Roy is credited with the articulation of those politico-ideological values which supported the campaign for new political order that owed its sustenance from the endeavour that he undertook along with his likeminded colleagues. By conceptualizing Indian socio-economic reality in the classical liberal mould, Roy was insistent on 'modifying the so-called Orientalist attitude ... according to the progressive values in contemporary Western societies'.[12] The idea was clear that India's rise as a liberal society was possible once the values supportive of liberalism in the West were both inculcated and internalized. It was hardly a smooth sailing for Roy and his colleagues holding identical views as the Orientalists were not completely detested, at the outset, by the British rulers which was always a source of anxiety. The arguments opposed to superstition and the rule that drew on the archaic religious dictum gained ground presumably because of the challenges that the Orientalists encountered especially in the context of the impeachment of Warren Hastings in which Edmund Burke sharpened an attack on how British liberal ideas were a casualty in the colonies. The views that Roy had articulated were thus complementary to an intellectual wave that appeared to have influenced, if not swayed, the political elites in Britain who seemed to have found in liberalism an appropriate ideological package for governance.

Bankim Chandra Chatterjee's Responses

Liberalism seemed to have become a dominant mode of thinking especially among the Indian elites. It was Bankim Chandra Chatterjee (1838–1894) who built a strong case for liberalism on the basis of the arguments that Roy had left, but with a difference. While Roy was critical of the prevalent society which was reeling under superstitions and other archaic value systems, Bankim sought to evolve a political mechanism to translate the liberal values in practice. In other words, for Bankim, the task was easier because Roy had already raised certain objections to the continuity of a feudal political order which was

unlikely to disrupt the existent socio-economic relationship supportive of a divided social order. What Bankim realized was the need for
a political system to weed-off the debilitating influences crippling the
Hindu society.

How did he develop his arguments in favour of a political system drawing on the fundamental ethos of liberalism? First of all, as a hard-core
rationalist, Bankim drew on the received wisdom, as Partha Chatterjee
informs us. Conceptualizing his arguments within what he construed as
rational, Bankim admired the British rule since it brought, with itself,
those positive vibes which were critical to evolve a rational mode of
thinking. The British rule was thus a panacea. By comparing the colonial
order in India with a historical reconstruction of the Brahminical order,
he thus strongly argued that the British rule had established 'a fairer and
more impersonal legal and judicial system, greatest access—at least in
principle—for the lower castes to positions of power and status, and had
made available the means for Indians to acquire the benefits of Western
science and literature'.[13]

Critical of an imbalanced Hindu social order for reasons which were
neither rational nor persuasive because of being accepted as 'axiomatic',
Bankim thus had reasons to welcome the British rule. It was a rule which
allowed human beings to be treated as human beings irrespective of
their birth-driven social location. The British rule meant the demotion
of India to the status of a subject nation. In response to a query whether
British rule was thus better than past regimes, Bankim, by emphasizing that, 'we are a subject people and continue to remain so for a long
time to come', underlined that 'the condition of the upper classes such as
Brahmans and Kshatriyas has declined, but that of Sudras or ordinary
people has improved'.[14] In his perception, the loss of independence was
certainly a source of concern, however, it also allowed the Indians to have
access to science and technology which would not have happened had
they not been ruled by a foreign ruler. So, being subjugated had its benefits because it created 'an opportunity also to be acquainted with those
ideas which are meant to contribute to human well-being'.[15]

The second objective that Bankim had was to create conditions in
which the liberal values would develop organic roots. This was not easily
possible since the prevalent social values were strong enough to combat
the ideas which came with the colonial rule. The context did not seem

to be favourable either because there were campaigns against those who were castigated for being 'blind follower' of the British rule. Nonetheless, true to what he sincerely believed, Bankim felt that the prevalent socio-economic milieu needed to be given a jolt by those who privileged the enlightening liberal values as being essential for India's social well-being. In a rather unambiguous manner, he thus retorted that 'just as children learn to speak by imitating the speech of adults, to act by imitating the actions of adults, so do uncivilized and uneducated people learn by imitating the ways of the civilized and the educated. Thus, it is reasonable and rational that Bengalis should imitate the English'.[16] He defended his argument in favour of imitation by saying that even the European civilization flourished by drawing upon what the Romans did to emerge as 'a civilized entity'. There should be a caveat here because Bankim was also aware that mere imitation might not be a device for realizing the fundamental objectives of the philosophy of Enlightenment. Here he identified two problems—on the one hand, he was at pains to suggest that 'since Bengalis are good at imbibing those qualities which are socially harmful, ... it is not desirable for [them] to be as imitative as they are'. Mere imitation, he further noted, also, on the other, stopped 'creativity, and hence it becomes a restraint'.[17] The idea in his argument is very clear. The British rule was preferable since it was meant to purge the people of their superstitious values and beliefs; in other words, despite having subjugated India, colonialism also evolved a milieu in which new libertarian ideas seemed to have a salience in contrast with those which ruled human life so far.

As argued above, Bankim held a nuanced view of civilization. At one level, he appears to have uncritically accepted the foreign yoke because it had obvious benefits. His primary concern was to create a social environment which would allow people to rise above their parochial concerns. By bringing in the values of Enlightenment, the British rule provided the Indians with an opportunity which could not have been possible in their absence. So, despite demoting India to be a subject nation, colonialism was appreciated for being an empowering design in so far as Indians were concerned. At another level, Bankim's contribution was far deeper. As Kaviraj informs, though he did shape ideas but he shaped the medium with which ideas were articulated and presented. In other words, although his ideas may not have been entirely original, he gave to 'the modern Bengali the palette with which it became possible, for the first time, to paint intellectual and imaginative pictures of modernity'.[18] The mode of communication was as important as its content. In other words, by creating a discursive structure of thinking, it was Bankim who set in motion processes whereby new ideas flourished out of dialogue, discussion, and also contestation.

Bankim also put forward the idea of *anushilan dharma* (righteous practice) for bringing about and sustaining cultural nationalism. In 'The Theory of Religion', an essay written in 1888, he defined it as 'a system of culture', more complete and more perfect than the Western concept of culture, articulated by the Western thinkers like Auguste Comte and Mathew Arnold. Critical of the agnostic Western view of practice, anushilan was based on bhakti that entailed a combination of 'knowledge and duty'. In practical terms, anushilan means that it simultaneously imparts knowledge of what is good for the community and what the community is supposed to do under specific circumstances. Anushilan denotes the performance of an action for which one should not expect a reward. From this, he derived the idea of duty towards the nation and its defence. Such a selfless and non-possessive notion of devotion lay at the foundation of Bankim's conception of *dharma*. By underlining the importance of *dharma* in national solidarity, he sought to create a distinct political identity for the Hindu community.

Intellectually Bankim cannot be identified as a blind follower of colonialism. In his perception, the colonial regime was preferable since it represented those values which allowed human beings to evolve as independent selves. Reasons are not difficult to seek— the cultural structure being created by colonialism appeared to have upheld the values, drawn on the philosophy of Enlightenment. They were thus 'not really propositions or at least truths of Indian history', but represented an effort towards constructing 'a historical self of Europe' entailing 'some deep truths about the manner and methods of the European construction of its other'.[19] In a specific historical context, the Indian liberals hardly objected to such a construction since it was conducive to what they were endeavouring to attain. A new cultural ideal was created in which industrialization and scientific knowledge were to be encouraged, of course, not at the cost of denigrating 'the spiritual greatness of the Eastern culture'. This is what Partha Chatterjee characterizes as 'the national cultural project at its moment of departure'.[20]

The point of departure did not seem to be an aberration since it was good for the incipient nation and Bankim's arguments that justified 'tutelage', presumably until the leaders of the country were ready and its material bases prepared, were also persuasive. The consequences were obvious—colonizers being guardians meant 'a continuation of colonial rule, a sharing of power between colonial officials and a modernized elite, and an emphasis on state action to reform traditional institutions and bring into being modern ones'.[21] In concrete terms, the idea of tutelage was articulated in the indiscriminate borrowing of the system of constitutional governance which the Indian liberals appeared to have been instinctively drawn to as colonialism progressed. Bankim was thus an important link in the history of constitutionalizing India in accordance with the derivative liberal discourse which informed the nationalist struggle to a significant extent.

Surendranath Banerjea's Design

Like his predecessor, Bankim, Surendranath Banerjea (1848–1925) also fought for a liberal India. Expelled from the Indian Civil Service in 1874 due to some technical reasons, he was keen to be a lawyer only to discover that his expulsion disqualified him from being registered as a lawyer in courts. This was an incident which left an imprint in the young Banerjea who felt that if he was 'not an Indian [he] would not have been put to all this trouble, and the head and front of my offence was that [he] had entered the sacred preserves of the Indian Civil Service which so far had been zealously guarded against invasion by the children of the soil'.[22] Despite being frustrated, the decision to expel him seemed to have consolidated his determination to battle against injustice. Drawn on the fundamental liberal commitment of T.B. Macaulay, he also realized that without a struggle liberty would remain an elusive goal. As he stated, 'in the Iron grip of ruin, I had already formed some forecast of the work of [Macaulay] that is awaiting me in life. I felt that I had suffered because I was an Indian, a member of the community that lay disorganized, had no public opinion and no voice in the counsels of their Government'.[23]

Unlike Bankim who worked with the administration, Banerjea opted for teaching as a career which he deliberately chose since it would help him to link the youth with the public life. It was evident when he resolved 'to foster a new spirit and to produce a new atmosphere' by saying:

[I]n my mind my educational and political work were indeed inter-linked. I felt that the political advancement of the country must depend upon the creation among our young men of a genuine, sober and rational interest in public affairs. The beginnings of public life must be implanted in them. They must have their period of apprenticeship and qualify themselves for their civic duties. They must, on one hand, be stirred out of their indifference to politics, which was the prevailing attitude of the student mind of Bengal in recent past, and, on the other, protected against extreme fanatical views, which, as all history shows, are fraught with peril in their pursuit.[24]

Accordingly, the Indian Association was formed in July 1876 to represent the views of the educated middle class and 'inspire them with a living interest in public affairs.'[25] By drawing on the themes of Macaulay's English constitutional history, Banerjea and his colleagues were persuaded to believe that without a sustained struggle against the authority it would be impossible for the Indians to transform into 'subjects who could act in history'.[26] Given their experience of England as a liberal society which did not emerge suddenly, but was the outcome of a long-drawn struggle, they appear to have been swayed by Macaulay's insistence on 'representative government, individual rights, the right to bear arms, no taxation without representation, and institutional checks and balances' as critical to constitutional liberalism. It was paradoxical for Banerjea because 'the English-inspired freedom had to be wrested from the tyranny of Britain'.[27] The task was difficult but not insurmountable as history had shown that only through an organized campaign, these rights could be realized and since the Britons had achieved, Banerjea had reasons to believe that it was bound to happen in India; otherwise, he further added that 'we shall borrow that page from England's history, fasten it on our own banner, and unfurl the banner before the gaze of our countrymen.'[28]

There are two interrelated levels in Banerjea's argument for constitutional liberalism in India. At one level, he, like Bankim, felt that the Empire was a good thing to have happened because it was capable of purging India of all her social ills. In the speech which he delivered while inaugurating the Indian Association he was very candid by saying that 'it is England's mission in the East to save, regenerate, emancipate from the chains of ignorance, error, and superstition, 150 millions of human beings, to heal the wounds that have been inflicted on them by the rapacity of their former rulers'.[29] Similar to his colleagues in the Moderate phase of Indian nationalism, his belief was based on his confidence that the colonial government by being inspired by the core ideas of constitutional liberalism was likely to initiate processes of significant social changes which were inconceivable in the past. At one level, his argument, as shown above, was meant to create conditions for a rejuvenating India for which the role of the government was most critical; at another, it was forcefully pursued to evolve representative institutions to realize 'the exalted goal of British liberalism drawn on the philosophy of Enlightenment'. While defending representative institutions as perhaps the only means to internalize the democratic ethos, he thus elaborated in 1889 speech before the Oxford Student Union by underlining:

> representative institutions are a consecrated possession, which in the counsels of Providence have been entrusted to the English people, to guard their possession, to spread it, and not to make it the property of this people or that people, but the heritage of mankind at large. England is the home of representative institutions; from England as the centre, representative institutions have spread far and wide until this country has justly been called the august mother of free nations. The people of India are children of their mother, and they claim their birth right, they claim to be admitted into the rights of British citizens and British fellow subjects.[30]

Being aware that it was not possible to have representative institutions with the rulers being opposed towards this, Banerjea thus couched his appeal in such a way as to provoke their paternalistic sentiments. In contemporary ideological lexicon, the appeal was an epitome of what is known as 'mendicant politics' which the Moderate leaders were charged with while pursuing their 'limited nationalist' goals. By being candid in his appeal which was perhaps strategic as well, Banerjea announced thus:

> [T]he connexion of England with India is a divine dispensation ordained for the holiest and highest ends. Therefore, do I appeal to you, representative of the European community, members of the Empire, friends of human freedom, to stand by us, to cooperate with us in ensuring the success of the great experiment upon which the honour of England is

staked, and the future of India so largely depends. I am sure, I do not appeal in vain. I am strengthened in this hope by the cordiality that the authority has shown and the kind and sympathetic hearing that it has accorded to us.[31]

Banerjea articulated a loyalist discourse couched in liberal terms since he was persuaded to believe that liberal governance in the British mould was perhaps the best instrument to realize the politico-ideological objectives that he held. The Empire was a boon in disguise because it was the outcome of 'those civilizing influences which Macaulay and his associates were instrumental in planting in government of this country';[32] they were critical of the British rule for being terribly 'un-British' which means that in policy-perspectives, it hardly followed the liberal constitutional means for governance in India. For the Indian liberals, the choice was unambiguous, as Banerjea revealed when he said:

> self-government was the end and aim of our political efforts; constitutional methods the means of its attainment. The Indian National Congress was our great outstanding organization, and it recognized no method except by, and through the constitution for the achievement of self-government within the Empire. For more than thirty years it worked upon these constitutional lines with undeviating singleness of purpose; and marvellous has been its achievement.[33]

The idea was clear—constitutional government within the Empire was the nationalist aim. It was justified by reference to the constitutional governance that had flourished in England. According to Banerjea, liberal values gained salience in England because they were constitutionally safeguarded; with the existence of political institutions supportive of these liberal values, he further added, it was possible for liberal constitutionalism to strike organic roots in England which he articulated by saying that 'the English constitution [drawn] on the Enlightenment philosophy survives and continues to do so because of the institutions on which it rests'.[34] The concern was to build institutions for constitutional governance in the liberal spirit and ideology. It came out clearly when Banerjea introduced the Calcutta Municipal Act in 1921 with the statement that the bill was 'the proudest monument of their civic spirit and the strongest justification for that full measure of responsible government to which we all aspire, and which will be the crowning reward of those working for this to happen'.[35] This was a stupendous success for him and his associates who also believed in constitutional governance which, as Banerjea claimed, 'forced the government to adapt itself to the rapidly progressive tendencies of modern India',[36] though he had reasons to feel discontented because the government was not 'moving fast enough to meet the progressive requirements of the country or the growing aspirations of the people'.[37] The faith in the Empire was absolute since it was adequately equipped to take care of the socio-economic and political concerns of the colonized provided liberal constitutionalism was allowed to strike roots in India. Although Banerjea was not happy being a minister of local self-government within a highly restricted system of government known as diarchy, he hardly wavered from his faith in liberal constitutionalism which means that he not only internalized its ideological spirit but also held those values with unflinching commitment to them while being active in governance.

What runs through these early Indian responses—whether of Ram Mohan Roy, Bankim Chandra Chatterjee, Surendranath Banerjea, and others—colonial liberalism was also a concern for massive reform in Hindu society that was seen to have lost its vitality and also meaning. There was a shared assumption that colonial rule in India rested on the divisiveness and other weaknesses of Hindu society. Colonial rule was also appreciated for its role in introducing Indians to the ideas of European Enlightenment to bear on the reform of the prevalent society. There was also a more or less shared awareness that the Hindu religious or cultural traditions provided a valuable source of anti-colonial identity. Roy and Chatterjee privileged Upanishads, the Vedas, and Bhagvad Gita respectively. By drawing on these exclusively Hindu traditional tracts, these social thinkers ignored or seem to have marginalized the traditions of the Muslim and other non-religious communities, although Roy, given his interests in Persian literature, held views which did not correspond with that of Chatterjee. While his predecessors prepared the context for liberal constitutionalism to evolve organically by their campaign against the superstitious Hindu social order, Banerjea constructed its political foundation by popularizing self-governance not only as a staunch campaigner but also as an active participant by being a minister of local self-government. Being complementary to one another, the traditional liberals like Ram Mohan, Bankim, and Surendranath Banerjea, can be said to have played a historical role in creating conditions for liberal constitutionalism to flourish in a context when the opponents did not appear to have lost the ground as they gradually did in the days to come.

The Congress Effort

Liberal constitutionalism seemed to have acted at two levels—at one level, the hard-core liberals, including the Utilitarians, championed liberalism as perhaps the best available ideology to reorient governance in such a way as to make it people-centric in real sense. At another, perhaps most effective, level, liberal constitutionalism received a boost in India once it was zealously endorsed by the Indian liberals as a politco-ideological doctrine to articulate their nationalist aspirations vis-à-vis the British rule. There were, of course, alternative voices which were probably too feeble to have a noticeable impact. The ground was thus ready and liberal constitutionalism rose to have become seemingly unassailable especially in the late nineteenth and early twentieth century. The influence was so well-entrenched that even the Indian National Congress had no qualms to openly appreciate the British rule because it purportedly drew on the fundamental ethos of liberalism. In its eleventh annual session, Indian National Congress declared thus:

> to England, we look for inspiration and guidance [because] English history has taught us those principles of freedom which we cherish ... We have benefitted by the education that we receive and by the material civilization which annihilates time and distance, and brings us together to feel a common interest in our own elevation under a vivifying influence of a literature and a history, the like of which the world has not known in the past for its triumphs in the emancipation of mankind.[38]

However, the delegates were highly disappointed since colonialism in India had already manifested in its most brutal form. Hence, they made an appeal to the rulers 'to gradually change the character of her rule in India, to liberalize it, ... so that in the fullness of time, India may find itself in the great confederacy of free states, English in their origin, English in their character [and] English in their institutions.'[39] So the main concern was to imbibe the spirit of liberalism in governance. Their main ideal was to secure their representation in the legislature. The demand was continuously made by the Congress since it would allow the Indians to voice their concerns in legislative forums. While justifying the demand, Dadabhai Naoroji (1825–1917), a prominent Moderate liberal, strongly argued for expansion of representation to include Indians in the legislature. As he stated:

> what makes us proud to be British subjects, what attaches us to this foreign rule with deeper loyalty than even our own past Native rule, is the fact that Britain is the parent of free and representative government, and, that we, as her subjects and children, are entitled to inherit the great blessing of freedom and representation ... Britain would never be a slave and could not, in her very nature and instinct, make a slave. Her greatest glory is freedom and representation, and as her subjects, we shall have these blessed gifts.[40]

What Naoroji had initiated was reinforced by his successors, such as Pherozeshah Mehta (1845–1915), Surendranath Banerjea (1848–1925), and G.K. Gokhale (1866–1915) who also insisted that institutions of representation were seen as the sine-qua-non of human freedom. They were also persuaded to believe that it was possible for them to express their views freely in public forums since colonial rulers drew on liberalism. 'It is under the civilizing rule of the Queen and the people of England', thus argued Naoroji, 'that we regularly meet, unhindered by none and are freely allowed to speak our minds without the least fear and least hesitation'.[41] In a similar vein, he further admired British rule by saying that:

> We understand the benefits [that] the English rule has conferred upon us; that we thoroughly appreciate the education that has been given to us, the new light which has been poured upon us, turning us from darkness into light and teaching us the new lesson that kings are made for the people and not people for their kings; and this new lesson we have learned amidst the darkness of Asiatic despotism only by the light of free English civilization.[42]

A careful reading of the early nationalists' intervention reveals that they upheld liberalism to the hilt since they were convinced of its utility as an empowering ideology for the colonized. Hence, they insisted on constitutionalism, gradual reforms, and an appeal to the English traditions which helped build the liberal ethos as integral to governance in Britain. G.K. Gokhale was categorical in stating his preferences for constitutional agitation by fiercely critiquing the argument that Bal Gangadhar Tilak made by saying that constitutional agitation had failed in India. 'The people of India', argued Gokhale, 'has not exhausted even a thousandth part of the possibilities of real constitutional agitation'.[43] Critical of Tilak when he openly campaigned against moderate means, the Moderates, including Gokhale, pursued a line of argument as not to annoy the British authority but to gain maximum by way of constitutional means and methods. This was a strategic design which might have been severely limited in a different context, but became most effective in at least sustaining the zeal for change at the beginning of the consolidation of colonial rule in India.

The arguments that the early nationalists made in favour of liberalism had two complementary components—on the one hand, what it entailed was their concern for political transformation following the fundamental principles of liberalism; their critique of the British rule in India was, on the other hand, drawn on the fact that it had failed, to a significant extent, 'to live up to its own mission as the bearer of liberal and modern institutions and values in India'.[44] They were appalled, in other words, because 'Britain was failing to complete the appointed role, as evidenced by its selfish economic and political policies in India, and by its distrust of the very class that it had brought forth'.[45] What was basic to their arguments was the effort to articulate liberalism in spirit and content and they felt discontented since the British rule in India was not adequately liberal.

Notwithstanding the debilitating effect of colonialism in India, the early liberals seem to have found the British rule most conducive for the growth of a liberal society in India, which was drawn on their, as Bhattacharya argues, 'implicit belief in the superiority of the civilization of Europe and the fitness of Britain to rule India'.[46] In their perception, representative institutions and free press were always identified as critical to the material and moral progress of a country which was plagued by archaic customs and primordial social values. As Surendranath Banerjea noted:

the three great boons which we have received from the British Government are High Education, the gift of a free press and local Self-Government. ... But High Education is the most prized, the most deeply cherished of them all. It is High Education which has made local Self-Government the success that it is admitted to be. It is again High Education which has elevated the tone of the Indian press. [47]

In the creation of a liberal India, the institutional changes were as much critical as the change of the prevalent mindset that had undergone a massive transformation with the introduction of English education, the early nationalists claimed. By recognizing the immense utility of English education, the Deccan Sabha thus exhorted that 'the greatest gift [of the British rule] has been to bring within our reach the blessing and benefit of English education which has helped us to avail of and assimilate the civilizing elements which accompany and distinguish [the rule by the British Parliament]'.[48] This was an unqualified appreciation of how the English education contributed to the consolidation of liberal ideas in society. It was strongly felt that efforts towards building a liberal society were likely to fail unless it was complemented by a conducive-mindset which was possible only by accepting English education. Being critical of political liberals and social Tories, M.G. Ranade, another vocal liberal, thus stated that:

> you cannot be liberal by halves. You cannot be liberal in politics and con-servative in religion. The heart and head must go together. You cannot cultivate your intellect, enrich your mind, enlarge the sphere of your polit-ical rights and privileges, and, at the same time, keep your hearts closed and cramped. It is an idle dream to expect men to remain enchained and enshackled [*sic*] in their own superstition and social evils, while they are struggling hard to win rights and privileges from their rulers. Before long these vain dreamers will find a way their dreams lost.[49]

On another occasion, Ranade emphasized the importance of a strong state, guided by the rule of law in combatting the well-entrenched social evils. In other words, he was in favour of a strong state which was necessary to establish a liberal social format as well. The argument was forcefully made when he stated that 'the history of the suppres-sion of infanticide and Sati shows that these institutions which had grown as excrescences upon the healthy system of ancient Hindu society, were checked and can only be checked by the strong arm of Laws, and once they are denounced as crimes they disappeared from the face of the country'.[50] Justifying state intervention as legitimate, he further argued:

> the diseased corruptions of the body cannot and should not be dealt with in the same way as its normal and healthy developments. The sharp surgical operation and not the homoeopathic infinitesimally small pill is the proper remedy of the first class of disorder and the analogy holds good in the diseases of the body politic as well as the material body in dealing with the parasitical growth of social degeneration.[51]

Two important ideas stand out—first, the early liberals were persuaded to believe that unless there were adequate institutional back-ups, the Westminster form of liberal democracy would remain elusive. Their insistence on having those institutions was thus a natural choice. Second, they were also aware of the fact that without supportive value-systems, not only would the liberal institutions fail to strike organic roots in India they would also become merely cosmetic.

The Moderate preferences for constitutional liberalism of the British variety can thus be said to have been an offshoot of their sincere belief in the ideas of Enlightenment that had flourished in Britain as a result of long-drawn politico-ideological battles. Persuaded to accept a liberal mode of governance for India, they thus raised their voice against 'the un-British rule' in India and, at the same, argued for creating socio-economic conditions for the liberal values to strike roots. It was most explicitly stated by M.G. Ranade who, in the manifesto that he wrote for the Deccan Sabha in 1896, exhorted:

> the spirit of liberalism implies freedom from prejudice and steady devotion to all that seeks to do justice between man and man, giving to the rulers the loyalty that is due to the law they are bound to administer, but securing, at the same time, to the ruled the equality which is their right under the law. Moderation implies the condition of never vainly aspiring after impossible or too remote ideas, but striving each day to take the next step in the order of natural growth, by doing the work that lies nearest to the hand, in a spirit of compromise and fairness. After

all, political activities are chiefly of value, not for the particular results achieved, but for the process of political education which is secured by exciting interest in public matters and promoting the self-reliance of citizenship. This is no doubt a slow process, but all growth of new habits must slow to be real.[52]

There are three complementary parts in this argument. First, the Moderate nationalists were drawn to liberalism since it epitomized freedom and those values which upheld justice for all which implies that the discriminatory rule that the British had established in India was contrary to what was appreciated in Britain. The subjects had been denied their rights which was a source of agony for them because this was neither justified nor pertinent in a system of governance that appeared to have drawn its sustenance from constitutional liberalism. Second, they endorsed a discursive strategy of moderation which, they articulated, by suggesting that the spirit in support of liberalism evolved gradually in a mode of 'compromise' and 'fairness'. What seems to have been critical was both the acceptance of liberal ideals as 'legitimate' and also 'result-driven' and the need to nurture them by creating a conducive environment. Finally, for them, political education which entailed primarily liberal values of governance and also responsible citizenry was most critical. The process was both arduous and slow, which, they felt, was obvious since 'good habits' took longer to grow and prosper.

An analytical scan of Moderate nationalism suggests that it is characterized by two complementary efforts. On the one hand it always endeavoured to instil the British constitutional values, presumably because they were emotionally tilted in their favour. It was thus not surprising that while adopting the 1899 (rather short-lived) Constitution of the Congress they declared that 'the object of the Indian National Congress shall be to promote by constitutional means the interests and well-being of the people of the Indian empire [and also to engage in political activity] on the lines of general appreciation of British rule and of constitutional action for the removal of its defects.'[53] By being loyal to the British rule, they, on the other, expressed their appreciation for the rulers presumably because it was, according to them, a stepping stone towards realizing liberal governance in India. Their well-argued critiques were confined to the charge that the British rule was not adequately liberal and hence deserved to be criticized. In his magnum opus, *Poverty and Un-British Rule in India* (1901), Naoroji thus made the point by highlighting that, instead of attacking the British rule, his whole object was

> to impress upon the British people, that instead of a disastrous explosion of the British India Empire, as must be the result of the present dishonourable un-British system of government, there is a great and glorious future for Britain and India to an extent unconceivable at present, if the British people will awaken to their duty, will be true to their British instinct of fair play and justice, and will insist upon the faithful and conscientious fulfilment of all their great and solemn promises and pledges.[54]

The British rule as it unfolded in India was a cause of disillusionment, as the Moderate felt. Britain failed to discharge its 'anointed role' by being selfish and authoritarian which was hardly consistent with the fundamental principles of liberalism for which she was known. The Moderate critique thus represented a concern for the failure of the colonial government 'to fulfil its historic mission as the bearer of liberal and modern institutions and values in India'.[55] Behind being loyal, the Moderate nationalists appeared to have been swayed by liberal values which, they also felt, were to be imbibed to create socio-economic conditions for liberalism to strike roots. Which means that the description of the Moderates being 'just loyalists' does not seem to be apt since it could have been a strategy to mobilize opinion in a rather unfavourable socio-economic circumstances. In other words, their being loyalists was just one of the strategic means to bring about radical socio-economic changes at the behest of colonial rule in India. Whatever may have been their politics, conceptually the Moderates drew their inspiration from the writings of John Locke, Jeremy Bentham, Auguste Comte, J.S. Mill, Herbert Spencer, among others, which brought them together to fight for a cause on the basis of their own understanding of constitutional liberalism. There is another side also which is striking in their ideological predilections in contrast with what their Extremist counterparts held, namely, that they did not pay adequate attention to Indian traditional thought or took a dim view of it, or valued its cultural and moral, but not social and political achievements which led Bhikhu Parekh to characterize their approach to nationalism as being 'clearly derivative' and without originality.[56]

The Contrasting Extremist Stance

While the Moderate liberals pursued a policy of reconciliation within the British rule, their Extremist counterparts championed violence, if necessary, to harm the ruler. Their idea of Swaraj approximated to self-government of the liberal variety, though the Extremists felt that 'as long as the source of power is situated in Whitehall there cannot be even a beginning of the democratic processes'.[57] What was basic in their politico-ideological campaign was the demand for freedom which would facilitate the formation of a political system of their choice. Hence, it was suggested that the new system involved 'the abdication of the right of England to determine the policy of the Indian government, the relinquishment of the right of the present foreign despotism to enact whatever law they please, the abandonment of their right to tax the people according to their own will and to spend the revenues of the country in any way they like'.[58] Their aim was to form a government according to what the people of India thought which was evident in what Lala Lajpat Rai mentioned by saying that 'in order to be free we must form, guide, and control the national will in such a way as to make it irresistible'.[59] What was unique in the Extremist perception was their belief that sovereignty rested with the people. Unlike the Moderates, Aurobindo Ghose, one of the most vocal extremists, made his preference very clear by stating that 'only by becoming responsible to the people and drawn from the people can the government be turned into a protector instead of an oppressor'.[60] Appreciative of liberal democracy since it drew its sustenance from the people, he reinforced his argument by saying,

> the only effective way of putting an end to executive tyranny is to make the people and not irresponsible Government the controller and paymaster of both executive and judiciary. The only possible method of stopping the drain is to establish a popular government which may be relied on to foster and protect Indian commerce and industry conducted by Indian capital and employing Indian labour. This is the object which the new politics, the politics of the twentieth century, places before the people of India in their resistance to the present system of Government, not tinkerings and palliatives, but the substitution for the autocratic bureaucracy, which at present misgoverns us, of a free constitutional and democratic system of government and the entire removal of foreign control in order to make way for perfect national liberty.[61]

There is a caveat here—the Extremist nationalists appear to have endorsed liberal constitutionalism as a politico-ideological framework of governance which, they also believed, was not possible under the British control because 'British Liberalism will never be', as Aurobindo emphasized, 'strong or sincere enough to accept India as a co-sharer in the great British Empire, standing in terms of perfect equality with its other parts'.[62] Instead of holding grudge against his Moderate colleagues, he tempered his criticism of the Moderate means by saying that 'they were deceived by the apparent benevolent intentions under which the sampan self-interest was concealed'.[63] Despite their strong criticisms of the colonial rule which led to devastations in India, the Extremist thinkers expressed their keenness in adopting a liberal democratic system of governance for two reasons—first, liberal democracy was perhaps one of those forms of government which derived its strength from people; the fact that it nurtured popular sovereignty attracted the Extremists regardless of the fact that it had evolved in Britain. Second, the idea appears to have swayed the Extremist thinkers presumably because of their personal experience of the system of governance that existed in England during their stay as students or otherwise; they thus believed that liberal democracy was not only a libertarian ideology, but also appropriate for meaningfully translating into practice popular sovereignty in spirit and content.

Concluding Observations

In the setting of a politico-ideological trend for liberal values to prosper in India, the role of the nationalist liberals remained critical. With their strong arguments in favour of values of individualism, tolerance, rationality which did not seem to have been seriously opposed presumably because they were considered integral to construct a new India following the liberal path they defended their claim. Their uncritical zeal for liberal values had certainly had elements of an imitative ideological design, which was soaked in the nationalist fervour. This was certainly the case at one level; at another level, by using Indian imageries while mobilizing opinion for liberal nationalism, they appear to have developed a unique nationalist vocabulary which was neither exactly imitative, nor purely innovative, but a creative blending of contextual inputs with the derivative liberal ideas. This argument has two inter-related components—on the one hand, by being proactively involved in the transmission of liberal values, the British liberals had built a definite discursive space which allowed their Indian counterparts to flourish. For instance, in order to sustain the momentum for liberalism, there were complementary institutions which were created simultaneously; it is thus not surprising that T.B. Macaulay was insistent on the introduction of English education in India and consequently an English educated elite to carry forward the tradition that he had ushered in by fighting-out his Oriental colleagues both in England and India. Education was a powerful instrument that created a contingent of Indians, thus argues Sanjay Seth, 'capable of operating and making full use of boons of British rule'. This was a common sentiment shared by the Indian liberals who always appreciated the 1835 Macaulay minute for being 'a powerful instrument' of radical socio-economic and political changes in India. English education was thus not merely a mode of learning, but also a medium whereby liberal values were transmitted to the colony. A useful design which helped consolidate a powerful mindset encouraging 'civilizing values' challenging the prevalent archaic social order. This was most explicitly stated by Gokhale who felt that the British system of education enabled people to understand what 'constitutional freedom and national aspirations' meant. Condemning those opposed to English education, he elaborated his point by further saying,

> those who blindly uphold the existing system and resist all attempts ... to broaden its base, prefer practically to sacrifice the future to the present. The goal which the educated classes of India have in view is a position for their country in the Empire worthy of the self-respect of civilized people. They want the country to be a prosperous, self-governing, integral part of the Empire, and not a mere poverty-stricken, bureaucratically-held possession of that Empire.[64]

This is one side of the story. There is another side which reveals that the Indian liberals, despite being appreciative of the British rule, did not seem to be blind in their appreciation. They 'adapted their ideological onslaught', as Bayly shows, 'to empower their argument against colonial despotism'.[65] One of the powerful proponents of this line of thinking was Dadabhai Naoroji who was also credited with perhaps one of most scathing critique of British rule in a typical liberal mould. Attacking the British rule for becoming 'un-British', the grand old man of Indian nationalism, as Naoroji was characterized in the contemporary discourses, argued that being

> subject to an unceasing foreign invasion carrying away our wealth ... the capacity of the people becomes weakened and the taxation becomes oppressive. The Government wants its pound of flesh for the European services—increases the rate of taxation—the whole vicious circle goes on revolving. The Fundamental cause, the cause of the whole mischief is 'Foreign domination' and as long as that continues, there is no hope.[66]

There is also another dimension of the liberal critique which usually escapes notice of the historians, namely the importance of the people, the multitude if they were pushed to the wall they would end up resorting to even 'illiberal means'. According to Naoroji, the drain was the cause of mass misery and 'the cause must be removed, [otherwise] the evil will never be remedied'.[67] Unless this was done well in time, warned Naoroji, and

> if the mass of the people understood the cause and raised the cry—the British rulers will very soon understand the situation and climb down to meet. ... If the people of India once understood their condition and their strength the British will have either to leave precipitately, or be destroyed in India or if they see the danger of the disaster in good time and apply the remedy, to save the Empire by putting an end to the Drain, and finding their true benefit in trade with a prosperous and vast people.[68]

The argument is crystal clear—'to trade with India and not to plunder India'.[69] A careful reading of the argument suggests that Naoroji was ahead of his time in his political thinking. Unlike his Extremist colleagues, he was thinking of an inclusive nationalism of the Gandhian era when it was neither the educated few nor those associated with the British Raj, but the masses that redefined the anti-colonial discourse by being involved in perhaps the most gigantic nationalist struggle in human history. Nonetheless, that he remained committed to the liberal demand of 'self-government under the British rule' was evident when he unconditionally endorsed self-rule under the British paramountcy. This was not thus surprising that the new constitution of 1908 of the Congress began with the Article underlining that, 'the object of the Indian National Congress is the attainment by the people of India of a system of government similar to that enjoyed by the self-governing members of the British empire and a participation by them in the rights and responsibilities of the empire on equal terms with those members'.[70]

This was a trend of thought that the Indian liberals espoused. Even R.C. Dutt who criticized Naoroji for being 'mild' in his condemnation of the British rule, also felt that the liberal demand for 'self-government under British rule ... will, of itself, cure the economic bleeding'.[71] According to him, the drain of wealth and 'excessive and uncertain Land Tax cause extreme miseries to the millions of Indians [which needed to be] stopped'.[72] What brings Dutt and Naoroji in the same league however was their unstinted commitment to the well-defined liberal-constitutional means to address even the devastating socio-economic imbalances in India due to the ruler's selfish design of draining wealth away from India. It was thus not odd to find that despite his strong language against the un-British design, Dutt reconfirmed his commitment to liberalism by reiterating that he 'will never prove untrue to [the] main objective, viz, Self-Government under British rule'.[73] The Moderate critiques can thus be said to have been tempered by their appreciation for the values of Enlightenment which were not adequately respected by the colonial rulers in India. That was a source of disenchantment for them. So, their nationalist agenda was neither complete independence, nor complete withdrawal of the British rule from India, but to do away with the un-British characteristics of the British rule in India. Whatever may have been the techniques, it is not therefore entirely a correct assessment if the Moderate endeavour is dismissed as merely 'loyalist' since none of the ideologues never accepted the British rule as it unfolded in India; instead, they always took up cudgels against its continuity for it was not adequately 'British' in governance which means that by being dismissive of the fundamental liberal ethos, the British rule in India had lost its moral justification and it was the responsibility of the colonized to raise this. In fact, by charging the British colonial rule as 'un-British', the early liberals provided a powerful critique of colonialism in India by internalizing the fundamental values of what is known as 'Enlightenment humanism' which the colonizers 'both preached to the colonized and at the same time denied it in practice'. This was a major contradiction in British colonialism which was thus charged with being 'illiberal' in manifestation and practice.[74] So, the anti-colonial discourse that the Moderates had articulated may not have been adequately radical in hindsight though there are hardly justified arguments to dismiss the Moderate nationalism as merely 'loyalism' to the British Empire. In fact, it will not be an exaggeration to even suggest that some of the core ideas of participatory governance became integral in the nationalist agenda following the efforts by the Moderates to reorient governance accordingly. In other words, the Moderates' contribution to India's rise as a liberal polity is immensely significant since it was they who, in their sustained campaign against the un-British British rule, prepared the politico-ideological context in which the nationalist agenda for the future was articulated and designed. So, what was initiated in the Moderate phase in support of constitutional liberalism in the British mould continued to remain relevant as the nationalist campaign in India expanded its domain to areas which were peripheral in its earlier leg.

There are therefore reasons to believe that the early liberals, be it Moderates or Extremists, helped create some of the conditions for the rise and consolidation of liberal constitutionalism in India. Supportive of political institutions that articulated liberalism in practice, they also contributed to develop a space for debates over the feasibility of a system of governance that owed its sustenance from liberalism. What is however paradoxical was the fact that their concern for class interests, including property rights clouded their vision for social democracy. As a result, they, despite being critical of inequality during colonial rule, failed to provide a conceptually-persuasive analytical framework for combatting well-entrenched poverty which also had social roots. This confirms the argument that liberalism in India was contextually constructed which means that the classical British liberal ideas were not endorsed as they were but were 'deconstructed and reassembled to reflect Indian conditions and structures of thought'.[75]

Notes and References

1. C.A. Bayly, *Recovering Liberties: Indian Thought in the Age of Liberalism and Empire* (Cambridge: Cambridge University Press, 2012), p. 346.
2. Dipesh Chakrabarty, *Provincializing Europe: Postcolonial Thought and Historical Difference* (New Delhi: Oxford University Press, 2001), p. 4.

3. Theodore Kodischek, *Liberalism, Imperialism and the Historical Imagination: Nineteenth Century Visions of Great Britain* (Cambridge: Cambridge University Press, 2011), p. 93.

4. Rabindranath Tagore, *Bharatpathik Rammohun Roy*, as cited in V.S. Naravane, *Modern Indian Thought* (Bombay: Asia Publishing House, 1964), p. 23.

5. See, *Collected Works of Rammohun Roy* (in Bengali), Haraf Prakashani, Calcutta 1973, cited in Tapan Chattapadhyay, 'Rammohun Roy: An Analysis in Historical Perspective', *Calcutta Journal of Political Studies* 2(1), Winter 1981, p. 108.

6. See Rammohun Roy, 'Appeal to the King-in-Council', reproduced in Jogendra Chandra Ghose (ed.), *The English Works of Rammohun Roy*, Vol. II (Calcutta: Published by Srikanta Roy, 1901), p. 446 available at https://ia802606.us.archive.org/22/items/theenglishworks01rammuoft/theenglishworks01rammuoft.pdf, (accessed on 11 February 2017).

7. Roy, 'Appeal to the King-in-Council', p. 44.

8. Thomas Pantham, 'The Socio-Religious Thought of Rammohun Roy', in Thomas Pantham and Kenneth Deutsch (eds), *Political Thought in Modern India* (New Delhi: SAGE, 1986), p. 35.

9. Kodischek, *Liberalism, Imperialism and the Historical Imagination*, p. 95.

10. Lynn Zastoupil and Martin Moir (eds), *The Great Indian Education Debate: Document Relating to the Orientalist-Anglicist Controversy, 1781–1843* (Surrey: Curzon, 1999), p. 118.

11. Zastoupul and Moir, *The Great Indian Education Debate Debate*, pp. 35–6.

12. David Kopf, 'Rammohun Roy and the Bengal Renaissance: A Historiographical Essay', in V.C. Joshi (ed.), *Raja Rammohun Roy and the Processes of Modernization in India* (Delhi: Vikas Publishing, 1975), p. 28.

13. Partha Chatterjee, *Nationalist Thought and the Colonial World: A Derivative Discourse* (New Delhi: Oxford University Press, 1986), p. 64.

14. Jogesh Chandra Bagal (ed.), *Bankim Rachanabali*, Vol. 2, Bharatvarsher Swadhinata Evam Paradhinata (Bengali), p. 245, available at http://dspace.wbpublibnet.gov.in:8080/jspui/handle/10689/20795, (accessed on 12 February, 2017).

15. Bagal, *Bankim Rachanabali*.

16. Bagal, *Bankim Rachanabali*.

17. Bagal, *Bankim Rachanabali*.

18. Sudipta Kaviraj, *The Unhappy Consciousness: Bankim Chandra Chattapadhyay and the Formation of Nationalist Discourse in India* (New Delhi: Oxford University Press, 1995), p. 162.

19. Kaviraj, *The Unhappy Consciousness*, pp. 110–11.

20. Chatterjee, *Nationalist Thought and the Colonial World*, p. 73.
21. Partha Chatterjee, 'Culture and Power in the Thought of Bankimchandra', in Thomas Pantham and Kenneth Deutsch (eds), *Political Thought in Modern India* (New Delhi: SAGE, 1986), p. 91.
22. Sir Surendranath Banerjea, *A Nation in Making: Being the Reminiscences of Fifty Years of Public Life* (London, Humphery Milford: Oxford University Press, 1927), p. 29.
23. Banerjea, *A Nation in Making*, p. 30.
24. Banerjea, *A Nation in Making*, p. 38.
25. Banerjea, *A Nation in Making*, p. 40.
26. Kodischek, *Liberalism, Imperialism and the Historical Imagination*, p. 287.
27. Kodischek, *Liberalism, Imperialism and the Historical Imagination*, p. 290.
28. Surendranath Banerjea, *Speeches*, Vol. 1, Calcutta, Indian Association, 1970, p. 44.
29. Banerjea, *A Nation in Making*, p. 51.
30. Banerjea, *A Nation in Making*, p. 138.
31. Speech by Surendranath Banerjea before the Rotarians in Calcutta (no date)—reproduced in Sir Banerjea, *A Nation in Making*, p. 336.
32. Surendranath Banerjea, 'The 1895 Presidential Address', in A.M. Zaidi (ed.), *Congress Presidential Addresses*, Vol. 1 (New Delhi: Indian Institute of Applied Political Research), p. 223.
33. Surendranath Banerjea before the Rotarians in Calcutta—reproduced in Banerjea, *A Nation in Making*, p. 401.
34. Banerjea, *A Nation in Making*, p. 387.
35. Banerjea, *A Nation in Making*, p. 361.
36. Banerjea, *A Nation in Making*, p. 491.
37. Banerjea, *A Nation in Making*, p. 491.
38. See Report of the Eleventh Indian National Congress, held in Poona in 1895, p. 3, available at file:///C:/Users/Sony/Downloads/GIPE-014672.pdf, (accessed on 19 August 2016).
39. Report of the Eleventh Indian National Congress, p. 13.
40. Chunilal Lallubhai Parekh (ed.), *Essays, Speeches, Addresses and Writings of the Honourable Dadabhai Naoroji* (Bombay, Caxton Printing Works, 1887), p. 321, available at https://ia802608.us.archive.org/30/items/essaysspeechesa00paregoog/essaysspeechesa00paregoog.pdf, (accessed on 19 August 2016).
41. Parekh, *Essays, Speeches, Addresses and Writings of the Honourable Dadabhai Naoroji*, p. 332.
42. Parekh, *Essays, Speeches, Addresses and Writings of the Honourable Dadabhai Naoroji*, p. 333.

43. D.G. Karve and D.V. Ambekar, Gopal Krishna Gokhale, *Speeches and Writings*, Vol. 2 (Political), (Bombay: Asia Publishing House, 1965), p. 218.

44. Sanjay Seth, 'Rewriting Histories of Nationalism: The Politics of "Moderate Nationalism" in India, 1870–1905', *American Historical Review* 104(1), February 1999, p. 104.

45. Seth, 'Rewriting Histories of Nationalism, p. 104.

46. Sabyasachi Bhattacharya, *The Colonial State: Theory and Practice* (New Delhi: Primus Books, 2016), p. 181.

47. Surendranath Banerjea's 'Presidential Address, 1902, Indian National Congress', in A.M. Zaidi (ed.), *Congress Presidential Addresses*, Vol. 2, (New Delhi: Indian Institute of Applied Political Research, 1986), p. 118.

48. 'Address of the Deccan Sabha, 1901', reproduced in A.M. Zaidi and Shaheda Zaidi (eds), *The Encyclopaedia of the Indian National Congress*, Vol. 4 (On Road to Self-Government, 1901–1905) (New Delhi: S. Chand, 1976), p. 139.

49. Address by M.G. Ranade in The Second Social Conference, Allahabad, 1888 in *The Miscellaneous Writings of late Hon'ble Mr. Justice M.G. Ranade* (New Delhi: Sahitya Academy, 1992), p. 88, available at file:///C:/Users/Sony/Downloads/Miscellaneous-Writings-Of-M-G-Ranade.pdf, (accessed on 20 August 2016).

50. Ranade, *The Miscellaneous Writings of late Hon'ble Mr. Justice MG Ranade*, p. 81.

51. Ranade, *The Miscellaneous Writings of late Hon'ble Mr. Justice MG Ranade*, pp. 81–2.

52. Ranade, *The Miscellaneous Writings of late Hon'ble Mr. Justice MG Ranade*, pp. 38–9.

53. A.M. Zaidi and Shaheda Zaidi (eds), *The Encyclopaedia of the Indian National Congress*, Vol. 3, (Gathering Storms, 1896–1900) (New Delhi: S. Chand, 1976), p. 479.

54. Dadabhai Naoroji, *Poverty and Un-British Rule in India* (London, Swan Sonnenschein & Co., 1901), p. v, available at https://books.google.co.in/books?id=ZoGZDQAAQBAJ&pg=PT181&dq=%22poverty+and+un+british+rule+in+india%22&source=gbs_selected_pages&cad=3#v=onepage&q=%22poverty%20and%20un%20british%20rule%20in%20india%22&f=false, (accessed on 16 February 2017).

55. Sanjay Seth, 'Rewriting Histories of Nationalism: The Politics of "Moderate Nationalism" in India, 1870–1905', *American Historical Review* 104(1) (February 1999), p. 104.

56. Bhikhu Parekh, *Debating India: Essays on Indian Political Discourse* (New Delhi: Oxford University Press, 2015), p. 25.

57. Lala Lajpat Rai, *Ideals of Non-Cooperation* (Madras: Ganesh and Company, 1921), p. 50.

58. Bipin Chandra Pal, *Swadeshi and Samaj: The Rise of New Patriotism*, (Calcutta: Yugayatri Prakashak Limited), 1954, p. 55.

59. Lala Lajpat Rai, *Ideals of Non-Cooperation*, p. 98.

60. Aurobindo Ghose, *The Doctrine of Passive Resistance* (Calcutta, Arya Publishing House, 1948), p. 11, available at https://books.google.co.in/books?id=LL9JAAAAMAAJ&printsec=frontcover#v=onepage&q&f=false, (accessed on 20 August 2016).

61. Ghose, *The Doctrine of Passive Resistance*, pp. 15–16.

62. Aurobindo Ghose, '*Bande Mataram*', 21–2 August 1906 in *Sri Aurobindo: Supplement*, Vol. 27, p. 4—cited in Mithi Mukherjee, *India in the Shadows of Empire: A Legal and Political History, 1774–1950* (New Delhi: Oxford University Press, 2010), p. 144.

63. Mukherjee, *India in the Shadows of Empire: A Legal and Political History*, p. 145.

64. Karve, *et al.*, *Speeches and Writings*, p. 354.

65. Bayly, *Recovering Liberties: Indian thought in the Age of Liberalism and Empire*, p. 348.

66. 'Dadabhai Naoroji to R.C. Dutt, 5 July 1903'—reproduced in S.R. Mehrotra and Dinyar Patel (eds), *Dadabhai Naoroji: Selected Private Papers* (New Delhi: Oxford University Press, 2016), p. 167.

67. Mehrotra and Patel, *Dadabhai Naoroji*, p. 168.

68. Mehrotra and Patel, *Dadabhai Naoroji*, p. 168.

69. Mehrotra and Patel, *Dadabhai Naoroji*, p. 169.

70. Cited in Reginald Coupland, *The Indian Problem: Report on the Constitutional Problems in India* (London: Oxford University Press, 1944), p. 37.

71. Mehrotra and Patel, *Dadabhai Naoroji*, p. 170.

72. Mehrotra and Patel, *Dadabhai Naoroji*, p. 170.

73. Mehrotra and Patel, *Dadabhai Naoroji*, p. 170.

74. Dipesh Chakrabarty pursues this argument in his *Provincializing Europe: Postcolonial Thought and Historical Difference* (New Delhi: Oxford University Press, 2001), p. 4.

75. Bayly, *Recovering Liberties*, p. 346.

3 Radical Liberals and the Reimagining of the 'Nation' through Politics

While the early liberals were keen to build the institutional fabric of the nation since it was, in their perception, unavoidable to realize the fundamental liberal ethos, the radical liberals, especially Jyotirao Phule (1827–1890) and B.R. Ambedkar (1891–1956) strongly argued for rearranging of the prevalent social systems to avoid birth-driven discrimination. Influenced by Thomas Paine's *Rights of Man*, Phule was persuaded to believe that since 'the creator has bestowed upon all men and women equal religious and political liberties, ... [they] should therefore have equality before law and equality of opportunity for entry into the civil service or municipal administration'.[1] Anticipating some of the ideas that Ambedkar was to articulate in future, he attributed social discrimination to Brahmin domination in Hindu society. Being critical of M.G. Ranade for his appreciation of 'Hindu tradition', he maintained that this was a ploy to retain a discriminatory social arrangement in which sudras (untouchables) would always remain subservient to the upper caste, particularly Brahmins. His appreciation of the British rule was governed by his firm belief that it was meant by 'the Creator to rescue the sudras from slavery [and hence he urged upon them] to exploit the golden opportunity given by the British rule to get themselves emancipated from Brahman domination'.[2] What Phule suggested was further developed by Ambedkar who, while challenging the existent heritage-dependent hierarchical social order in India, also welcomed the British rule for being liberal in its approach to governance. He was a vocal supporter of positive constitutional and political discrimination in favour of the untouchables. Ambedkar created and also expanded normative spaces involving not just equality, liberty, and rights but also self-respect and dignity for the historically disadvantaged segments of the population. There is a caveat here because Ambedkar's notion of constitutional liberalism can be said to have redefined its basic thrust by insisting on the group autonomy and dignity (and not merely individual autonomy and dignity) against coercion, whatever the source—the state, society, or any other institution. It was an effort that was translated into reality in the 1950 Constitution of independent India which created a template for liberty, equality, and fraternity regardless of class, clan, and ethnicity. By interrogating the foundational values of Hinduism that tended to justify social inequality, also known as Babasaheb, Ambedkar gave a voice to the critique that subjected the sociologically-justified caste divisions to a thorough scrutiny. In his conceptual framework, the human agency remained central which also reflected a Deweyan emphasis on the role of human beings in the making and unmaking of the world that we lived in. It was thus perfectly compatible with his overall ideological position when he declared that 'do not depend ... for the abolition of caste slavery upon God or Superman. Your salvation lies in political power and not in making pilgrimages and the observance of fasts. Devotion to scriptures would not free you from bondage, want, and poverty'.[3] Central to his argument was a belief in human efforts in re-conceptualizing social mores and values which were contrary to liberal interpretations of human civilization. While defending liberalism, Ambedkar also introduced a unique moral and political framework in public reasoning which owed much to the European variety of Enlightenment paradigm combining social virtues (such as benevolence, compassion, and tolerance) with scepticism and reason and the American variety of republican values. The idea of every person having the right to life, liberty, free speech, and pursuit of happiness and the duty of the state to ensure that they were not violated remained critical in Ambedkar's understanding of liberalism which had clear contextual roots. Being 'an eclectic thinker'[4] who was also sensitive to the social brutalities that he suffered due to his birth as a Mahar, he supported 'vigorous state action to empower the untouchables and lower castes',[5] which however ran counter to the fundamental ethos of classical liberalism. Nonetheless, there are imprints of English liberal idealists, like T.H. Green (1836–1882) and L.T. Hobhouse (1864–1929) who insisted on community, individual welfare rights, and an activist state. Although he drew on multiple philosophical traditions within liberalism, he devised his own model of state-driven social transformation in which his own experiences of humiliation because of the accident of birth remained critical.

The aim of the chapter is to understand Ambedkar's distinct contribution to constitutionalizing India since the 1919 Southborough Committee in which he argued strongly for separate electorate and reservation for untouchables and other religious communities. On the basis of an analysis of the arguments that Ambedkar put forward before the 1919 Southborough Committee and 1931 Round Table Conference the chapter makes the argument that Ambedkar, true to his liberal faith, upheld constitutionalism as a shield against caste-driven social discrimination. As an avowed supporter of equality, he rejected the liberal amnesia about the dogma-based-birth-driven social segregation which, in his views, was contrary to the fundamental ethos of liberalism. He strongly felt that the social order of the caste was antithetical to the political institutions of democracy. Hence, so long as the hierarchical social structure existed, equality, in its substantial sense, would remain elusive. This was undoubtedly a powerful theoretical critique of the Gandhi-led dominant nationalist discourse in which, because of the obvious political compulsions of the freedom struggle in diverse society like India, *varnashrama* was defended possibly not to weaken the multicultural anti-British political platform. So Ambedkar fulfilled, as the chapter argues, a historical role in creating a space for liberal constitutional values to strike roots in India long before 1946 when the Constituent Assembly met for the first time to produce the 1950 constitution for independent India.

In order to understand Ambedkar's contextual constitutionalizing role, the chapter draws on his testimony before the 1919 Southborough Committee and his written intervention in the 1931 Round Table Conference besides his innumerable texts that he prepared in his defence. His role in the making of the constitution for independent India has received adequate scholarly attention.[6] The contemporary scholarship seems to be silent in recognizing that most of the liberal constitutional values that became prominent in independent India's constitution were drawn on those arguments which he made before the Southborough Committee and Round Table Conference. By focusing on these relatively less publicized textual defences, the chapter seeks to fill up the gap in our understanding of Ambedkar's critical role in constitutionalizing India following the well-established ethos and also canons of liberalism of the western variety. In specific terms, the chapter draws on Ambedkar's written evidence before the 1919 Southborough Committee and the 1931 Round Table Conference in which he attacked social discrimination despite being vehemently criticized by the prominent nationalist leadership in India.

Intellectual Genealogy

Ambedkar was heavily influenced by his teacher at Columbia University, John Dewey, and believed that change was fundamental to life and there was nothing in life which was sacrosanct. Thus, he challenged the hegemonic ideas, supported by 'omnipresent providence' or 'manifest destiny' and also the deterministic conceptualization of Marxism. At the same time, their idea of democracy coalesced in the sense that both Dewey and Ambedkar agreed that democracy built not only 'a collegial atmosphere for deliberations', but also on 'associated living' which was free from social prejudices. Hence, in their perception, individuals were not 'atomistic or isolated individual of the Enlightenment thought, but always embedded in the social'.[7]

Ambedkar acknowledged his debt to his teacher, John Dewey by quoting extensively from his text, *Democracy and Education*[8] in the final section of the *Annihilation of Caste* which reverberates the fundamental ethos that both of them had shared. Ambedkar imbibed John Dewey's spirit when he advised the caste Hindus to discard much of what they considered as their heritage since it 'dehumanizes a large section of their brethren'. As he stated, 'the Hindus must consider whether they should conserve the whole of their heritage or select what is helpful and transmit to future generations only that much and no more'.[9] He also questioned the tendencies towards worshipping the past as 'inherently retrogressive' since it blocked 'the visions for future' to strike roots. Following Dewey, he thus argued,

> an individual can live only in the present. The present is not just something which comes after the past; much less something produced by it. It is what life is in leaving the past behind it. The study of past products will not help us to understand the past. A knowledge of the past and its heritage is of great significance when it enters into the present, but not otherwise. And the mistake of making the records and remains of the past [a determinant of the present] tends to make the past a rival of the present and the present a more or less futile imitation of the past.[10]

Hence, an uncritical dependence on the past 'makes the present ... look empty and future distantly connected'. Instead of inculcating healthy practices, such an endeavour was 'inimical to progress and [was] a hindrance to a strong and a steady current of life'.[11] So what was the alternative that Ambedkar sought to build on the basis of his understanding of John Dewey's critique of the dependence on the past? Ambedkar's answer was to create space for social endosmosis to strike roots because he believed that without holding 'an attitude of respect and reverence towards fellowmen' substantial equality remained distant.[12] Here too, Ambedkar reverberated Dewey's understanding of democracy which, in Dewey's perception, was 'more than a form of government [because] it is primarily a mode of associated living, of conjoint communicated experience ... denoting a greater diversity of stimuli to which an individual has to respond'.[13] He reproduced the Dewey formulation *verbatim* in his defence by saying that 'democracy is not merely a form of government, [but also] a mode of associated living, of conjoint communicated experience ... [with] an attitude of respect and reverence towards fellowmen'.[14] This was not possible because 'Hindus and the Untouchables are divided by a fence of barbed wire [which] is actually a cordon sanitaire which the Untouchables have never been allowed to cross and can never hope to cross'.[15] So, there is no scope for social endosmosis to evolve simply because the social reality is 'alarmingly fragmented'. In these circumstances, political freedom meant 'liberty to the strong and powerful to suppress the weak and the down-trodden [because] what a caste or a combination of castes regard "as their own interests" as against other castes remains as sacred and inviolate as ever'.[16] How to guarantee political freedom regardless of castes? Here Ambedkar responded in the language of Dewey by saying that 'the paper rights' (codified in the constitution) were futile because '99 per cent of the people in India are not going to allow me to exercise those rights'.[17] Hence he was insistent on constitutional safeguards in the form of stern punishments once his rights were infringed and violated. This was not enough though because of the prejudiced mindset of the caste Hindus. In his presidential speech in the Mahar Satyagraha Conference in 1927, he elaborated his point by saying that 'constitutional provisions are not adequate to remove the sources of prejudices; it will remove Untouchability in the outer world, but not from inside the house; for that, the ban on inter-caste marriage will have to be removed; only then, Untouchability will vanish from inside the house'.[18] In order to bolster his argument, he further mentioned on another occasion that, 'nothing can do this more effectively in my opinion than the admission of the Depressed Classes to the houses of the caste Hindus as guests or servants. The live contact this establishes will familiarize both to a common and associated life and will pave the way for that unity which we are all striving after'.[19]

The primary purpose of Ambedkar was to create conditions for social endosmosis which was a key to the removal of the sources of untouchability. This was a belief that he held so dear even when he presented the 1950 Constitution of India to the nation. Here too it was John Dewey who provided him with an ideological support in favour of his argument for social democracy which was wider in connotation than political democracy. Like his academic mentor, John Dewey, Ambedkar also believed in the supremacy of the constitutional values in democratic political systems. Mere codification of laws was not enough, as Ambedkar argued, unless 'there is public conscience to behave in accordance with Constitutional provisions [which] is more important that the Constitution itself'. In continuation of the argument, he further stated that, 'the principles of democracy are for the people to respect the system of formation of Government, observance of laws, habit of independent thinking and observance of laws of the majority.'[20]

What was critical for the survival of democracy was civility, a Dewey conceptualization that Ambedkar held so dear while discharging his historical role. It called for tolerance, restraint, and mutual accommodation in public life. Civility was thus 'a moderating influence which acts against the extremes of ideological politics.'[21] In his perception, without civility, 'democracy becomes defunct' and he was also aware that the lack of a living democratic tradition in India was a serious deterrent in the context of rigid caste hierarchy. To transform a society of caste and communities into one of citizens was not an easy task. Nonetheless, he fulfilled his role by seeking to create 'a sense of constitutional morality' while defending his liberal agenda.[22] Here too, Ambedkar was indebted to a classicist, George Grote[23] who he quoted extensively in his speech of 4 November 1948 in the Constituent Assembly. Institutions of governance in a democracy, felt Grote, 'lose salience [unless] there is diffusion of constitutional morality, not merely among the majority of any community, but throughout the whole ... since any powerful and obstinate minority may render the working of a free institution impracticable, without being strong enough to conquer ascendancy for themselves.'[24] By constitutional morality, Grote meant

a paramount reverence for the forms of constitution, obedience to authority acting under and within these forms, yet combined with the habit of open speech, of action subject to definite legal control and unrestrained censure of those in public authorities ... with a perfect confidence amidst bitterness of party contest that the forms of constitution will not be less sacred in the eyes of his opponents than his own.[25]

This long quote from Grote's writings was surely an aid to Ambedkar when he defended a liberal democratic framework of constitutional governance in India though he was aware that it was difficult to instil a sense of constitutional morality in India because democracy which 'complements constitutional morality ... is only a top-dressing on an Indian soil which is essentially undemocratic.'[26] In the absence of constitutional morality, the operation of the constitution, no matter how carefully written, 'tends to become arbitrary, erratic, and capricious.'[27] How to make the constitution an effective instrument of governance in such circumstances? asked Ambedkar. He was in favour of detailed provisions in the constitution to scuttle efforts at derailing the constitution and challenging the fundamental constitutional values from which it derived its sustenance. In his defence, he thus argued that 'one can take the risk of omitting from the Constitution details of administration and leaving it for the Legislature to prescribe them ... if the people are saturated with Constitutional morality such as the one described by Grote'.[28] As is evident, Grote provided Ambedkar with an intellectual justification for a liberal constitution in a context in which basic liberal values of human dignity were brutally bypassed in favour of perhaps most ruthless form of social segregation. So, the idea of constitutional morality was a powerful device which allowed Babasaheb to knit together liberal constitutional principles despite strong opposition by the Gandhians in the Constituent Assembly who insisted that 'instead of incorporating Western theories the new Constitution should have been built upon village panchayats and district panchayats.'[29]

For constitutional morality to strike organic roots, Ambedkar insisted that the obedience to 'constitutional methods of achieving our social and economic objectives [which meant that] we must abandon ... the method of civil disobedience, non-cooperation, and satyagraha [because] when constitutional methods are open, there can be no justification of unconstitutional methods ... and sooner these unconstitutional methods are abandoned, the better for us'.[30] The Gandhian Satyagraha was, according to him, a form of coercion. This is an assessment which probably reflects serious political differences that Ambedkar had with Gandhi since the 1932 Poona Pact which deprived the untouchables of separate electorates in the 1935 Government of India Act. The defence for his opposition to Satyagraha was based on his commitment to constitutional morality which was a key to the success of the constitution. As one who was influenced by Edmund Burke too, Ambedkar was also convinced that violence could never be a permanent solution to human problems because 'the forceful subjection of any community always leads to resentment [which was enough] ... to cause severe dent to democratic ethos'.[31]

While discharging his historical role, he thus upheld the values of British Enlightenment privileging social virtues, such as benevolence, compassion, and tolerance. It was an obvious ideological preference for Ambedkar because he was born and raised in a British colony and was also educated partly in England for his second doctorate in Economics from the London School of Economics. Nonetheless, in his political thinking, there is fine blending of the French Enlightenment that emphasizes scepticism and reason with the American Enlightenment that draws on socio-political values like freedom and liberty.[32] It is therefore not merely coincidental that Ambedkar pursued his ideological critique of Gandhi-led nationalism in a language that had clear roots in three different forms of Enlightenment which were visible in his arguments against disprivileging a significant section of the nation on the basis of an archaic and also logically-indefensible system of caste hierarchy.

Sources and Manifestation of Constitutionalism

Ambedkar's approach to constitutionalism is both context-driven and derivative. He was persuaded to accept the significance of a codified rule of law to address social-imbalance presumably because of the torture that he suffered by being born a Mahar in the absence of meaningful legal protection in colonial India for the outcastes. Critical of the 'saints' for their normative and sacred justification of unjust social institutions, he thus questioned the acceptable ethos for social tranquillity. His exposure to Western liberal values during his student-life first in the US and later in England seemed to have strengthened his firm belief in the effectiveness of legally-induced and also constitutionally backed rules and regulations in creating 'a mindset' in support of those socio-economic and political values which he considered as integral to our existence as 'human beings'. In conceptual terms, the process of creating a mindset also involves the installation of equally powerful political institutions championing the exalted 'liberal' values of liberty, equality, and fraternity. For him, the British colonialism in India was a panacea for the untouchables given its liberal roots. It was evident in his statement defending colonial rule since it was 'meant to provide equal opportunities for all, and that in transferring a large share of the power to popular assemblies, arrangement should be made whereby the hardships and disabilities entailed by the social system should be removed and perpetuated in political institutions'.[33]

For Ambedkar, universal adult suffrage consolidated the foundation of democracy because 'this is a mechanism to regularly change the governing elite'.[34] To make democracy a successful experiment in governance, Ambedkar thus insisted on regular changes of political authority through suffrage; otherwise, democracy was likely to lose its vitality, as he argued by saying, 'the principal aim of [democratic] constitution must be to dislodge the governing class from its position and to prevent it from remaining as a governing class for ever'.[35] Besides arguing for regular replacement of the governing elite, he also talked about 'one man one vote' in his 1919 submission to the Southborough Commission because 'a popular government is not only Government for the people, but by the people as well'.[36]

He attributed the rise and consolidation of a healthy democracy to a specific kind of morality that upheld the spirit of democracy in its true and substantial form. So democracy, in Ambedkar's conceptualization, is not merely 'procedural', but 'an ideology-driven political device' challenging the sources of socio-economic discrimination for establishing a polity on the basis of the trio-principles of the Enlightenment of liberty, equality, and fraternity. This would remain a distant goal unless the restricted franchise was withdrawn. The conditional suffrage was an impediment to realize democracy in its true sense while the universal adult suffrage was a guarantee for a people-centric responsible government which required 'an increasing opportunity to the rank and file of the people to influence the government and franchise cannot [thus] be fairly or wisely confined to the specific sections of society on the basis of certain artificial conditions, like education, tax, or land holding'.[37] The other critical factor that helped imbibe the true spirit of democracy was the nature of representation which was a bone of contention in the colonial context especially with the rise of the Muslims and untouchables as powerful communities since the beginning of the twentieth century. For Ambedkar, representation meant an articulation of multiple voices which remained organically-linked with the prevalent social, economic, and political milieu in which communities were located. So, social conditions remained an important determinant in conceptualizing representation in a differently-textured Indian society. Hence, he vehemently opposed territorial and separate electorates; in its place, he suggested 'the system of joint electorates with reserved seats for the community deserving special attention [which] is the golden mean in representation'.[38] Based on his privileging of social conditions for representation, he found the joint electorate with reserved seats as a protective shield for the untouchables for two reasons: first, it would create a milieu in which the caste Hindus and also other religious groups were to be drawn to the specific issues confronting the so-called outcastes even within the fold of Hinduism, and second, with their participation in the political processes through liberal means, the untouchables would get an opportunity to articulate and also present their distinct voice in the public domain without being diffident due to the hegemonic grip of the religion-driven age-old systems of social discrimination.

The Southborough Committee on Franchise

When the Southborough Committee toured India in 1918–19 to determine the nature of the electorate, Ambedkar got an opportunity to advance his arguments for the representation of untouchables in the decision-making processes. Interestingly, besides Ambedkar, there was another Mahar, G.A. Gawai who made a strong plea on behalf of the Depressed India Association for three seats in the Bombay Legislative Council, to be elected by adult suffrage. This also suggests that Mahars were probably the most politically alert section among the untouchables. While challenging the demand for three seats, a former Congress president of Bombay, R.N. Mudholkar defended the denial by stating that since 'not all of the untouchables were so intelligent as the Mahars … not more than one seat for the depressed classes is justified'.[39] Ambedkar, who testified to the Committee without any organizational support, spoke as 'an advisor to British on issues of franchise in India' and also as an exponent of the rights of the untouchables. This was his first well-argued discourse on untouchability as a system of discrimination that could never be wiped out without adequate legal-constitutional protection to those socially-victimized as untouchables.

Ambedkar's testimony before the Committee confirms his unflinching faith in liberal democratic institutions in carving a distinct, and also respectable, position for the untouchables. According to him, the responsibility of the government was to provide each and every individual 'the opportunity of actively participating in the processes of government'. On this fundamental principle rested the Westminster form of democratic government which made it a government by the people. In India, this principle was violated because non-untouchables were authorized to represent the untouchables since the latter were denied representation in the seats of power. So long as this continued, Ambedkar felt, the untouchables would remain politically peripheral, if not insignificant, for all practical purposes. Hence, he collated facts and figures to justify the demand for representation for the untouchables in the legislative council as perhaps the most effective step to give voice to the voiceless in a caste-ridden society based on discriminatory social stratification.

On the basis of his experience in the US where people despite being ethnically diverse came together to form a unified country presumably because of their appreciation of identical ideological values strengthening the bond among them, he was persuaded to believe that social diversity was not an impediment to a constitutional bond. The desire to come together and remain as one among the migrants who were different in terms of every conceivable socio-cultural parameters were reinforced by meaningful and sustained communication, and out of this emerged like-mindedness. He elaborated his point by saying,

> to cultivate an attitude similar to others to be like-minded with others is to be in communication with them or to participate in their activity. Persons do not become like-minded by merely living in physical proximity, any more than they cease to be like-minded by being distant from each other. Participation in a group is the only way of being like-minded with the group.[40]

Conceptually, this is a valid position—the more the communication, the stronger the bond. But in a socially diverse situation like India, each group tended to create its distinctive type of like-mindedness due to well-entrenched caste identities which would invariably lead to 'conflict among the differently placed like-minded groups'. So long as the groups remained isolated and failed to appreciate certain common grounds for togetherness, 'the conflict is bound to continue and prevent the harmony of action'. Since 'isolation of the groups is the chief evil', Ambedkar prescribed strong constitutional arrangements to create and sustain bonding principles which would act towards generating what he defined as 'endosmosis'[41] which meant 'like-mindedness'. In endosmosis, Ambedkar had found a psycho-analytical idea which could be applied to human existence. While pursuing his argument, he thus stated that endosmosis was a perfect tool to redesign human interactions '[f]or endosmosis among groups makes possible resocialization of once socialized attitudes. In place of the old, it creates new like-mindedness which is representative of the interests, aims, and aspirations of all the various groups concerned'.[42] In other words, endosmosis, by setting in motion a process of being appreciative of differences, was thus a perfect shield against the tendencies towards self-centric, if not self-absorbed, human existence.

Despite the conceptual validity of his formula of endosmosis, Ambedkar also knew that the caste-prejudices were not likely to disappear so quickly given their historical roots; they were offshoots of a mindset that evolved over generations almost without resistance. Based on a certain perception about the untouchables, 'the untouchable Hindus', argued Ambedkar, were usually regarded

> as objects of pity, they are always ignored in any political scheme on the score that they have no interest to protect. And, yet their interests are the greatest. Not that they have large property to protect from confiscation. But they have their very *persona* confiscated. The socio-religious disabilities have dehumanized the untouchables and their interests at stake are therefore the interests of humanity.[43]

In view of the visible sources of dehumanization, untouchables ceased to be human beings in Indian society. What was unfortunate was the fact that even under the British rule the same social bondage was being perpetuated to deny the untouchables of their legitimate claim as a British subject because they were not even citizens in the constitutional sense of the term. To develop his point, Babasaheb referred to the denial of the right of representation and the right to hold offices under the State to the untouchables. So his principal aim was to entrust the untouchables with citizenship rights 'to represent their grievances which are their interests' and also to grow with adequate numerical strength 'to constitute a force sufficient to claim redress'.[44]

In spite of Ambedkar's persuasive argument and Gawai's passionate plea for granting of elected representation to the depressed classes in the newly constituted legislatures, the Southborough Committee did not seem persuaded. Two nominated seats for untouchables were allowed in the Madras legislative assembly, one each in the provinces of Bombay, United Provinces, Bihar, and Central Provinces. Nonetheless, what was unique was Ambedkar's ability to couch his cudgels for social justice with demand for constitutional rights when there were colonial endeavours at accommodating different sections in India. Although the guarantee of legal rights to hitherto politically peripheral sections of society was a part of the grand *divide-et-impera* (divide and rule) strategy, it let lose significant socio-political processes whereby the marginalized gained a voice and also a respectable social location in stratified India. Ambedkar's insistence on a legal guarantee of rights to the untouchables was governed by his firm belief that 'suffrage and political rights are a guarantee for active and direct participation in the regulation of the terms for associated human existence in a civilized way'.[45] This was clearly a liberal defence of political rights in which human beings are 'self-defining subjects' who delineate their own purposes, the purposes that had as their objective the development of humanity and civilization in conditions of substantive equality since an unequal social order was theoretically inconceivable in the liberal discourse. Furthermore, equality and freedom went hand-in-hand and without the former, the latter remained entirely cosmetic. So, Ambedkar's persuasive arguments for equality through a constitutional guarantee of political rights for the untouchables was a concrete step towards guaranteeing freedom which so far remained elusive for the untouchables given the absence of definite legal stipulations to that effect. Although he was insistent on constitutional protection for the outcastes, he was also aware that without social democracy, the constitutional guarantee however unambiguous in its articulation would become vacuous in view of the hegemonic mindset, by not being respectful to the sanctity of the constitution and its complementary values and morals. In an atmosphere of the growing importance of liberal values, Ambedkar's single-point demand did set in motion a process whereby the untouchables acquired a salience in the power struggle not only because of their growing political importance in the calculative colonial governance, but also because of the rise of Ambedkar as an exponent of their point of view in clear liberal terms which, due to being non-threatening in nature, seemed to have gradually endeared him to the colonial authority.

The Round Table Conference

What was initiated by Ambedkar in his testimony before the Southborough Committee was forcefully argued further in the 1931

Round Table conference. As an invited member on behalf of the depressed classes, Ambedkar played on his commitment to liberalism to pursue the cause of the untouchables in the face of well-organized opposition. Appreciative of the British government for the support it had extended in fighting caste atrocities, he mentioned that 'the depressed classes welcomed the British as their deliverers from age-long tyranny though the existing administration is not adequate to solve the problems ... [because] the problem of the depressed classes will never be solved unless they get political power in their own hands.'[46] The British authority seemed to have been persuaded, as was evident in the policy announcement by Ramsay McDonald, the British premier. It was agreed upon that there would be a number of special seats for the depressed classes which would be filled by election from special constituencies in which only the members of the depressed classes who were qualified to vote would take part in election; they would also be entitled to vote for general constituencies. The select constituencies were to be formed in areas where the depressed classes formed a majority demographically. The main purpose of this transitional arrangement was, as McDonald highlighted, 'to place them in a position to speak for themselves.'[47] It was a victory for Ambedkar because he finally got what he had been asking for. The untouchables thus became politically equipped to fight their own battle both within the legislature and also outside. Once their rights were recognized, they could now relate to other groups on equal terms leading to, what Ambedkar optimistically noted, 'social endosmosis'. This was thus socially empowering because following this policy declaration untouchables had a chance to be treated at par with the touchables.

Gandhi expressed his resentment as soon as his attention was drawn to the idea of separate electorate for the depressed classes. He argued that 'while the Congress will always accept any solution that may be acceptable to the Hindus, the Muhammedans, and Sikhs, Congress will be no party to provide special reservation or special electorate for any other minorities'. Although, he was perfectly comfortable with the communal award for the Muslims, he never approved of separate electorate for the untouchable because it meant a clear division among the Hindus which he would never tolerate. He passionately defended his position by saying,

[w]e do not want on our register and on our census Untouchables classified as a separate class. ... Will untouchables remain untouchables in
perpetuity? ... I say that it is not a proper claim which is registered by Dr.
Ambedkar when he seeks to speak for the whole of the Untouchables of
India. It will create a division in Hinduism ... I do not mind Untouchables,
if they so desire, being converted to Islam or Christianity ... But I cannot
possibly tolerate what is in store for Hinduism if there are two divisions
set forth in the villages ... if I was the only person to resist this thing, I
would resist it with my life.[48]

In view of Gandhi's intransigent attitude towards the issue of separate electorates for the untouchables, the possibility of a rapprochement
was remote when Ambedkar was found to be equally adamant about
his demand leading to a head-on collision between them. The conflict
between Gandhi and Ambedkar on the issue of the separate electorates for untouchables and the depressed classes was an articulation of
two contrasting perspectives that fundamentally altered the nature of
political participation by the scheduled castes and tribes in the British
India and its aftermath. Once the separate electorate for the Muslims
was conceded by the Congress while accepting the 1935 Government
of India Act, Ambedkar argued, on behalf of the Dalits, that they
must be allowed to constitute a separate electorate and elect their own
representatives to the central and provincial legislatures. He further
defended the claim by saying that since voting was severely restricted
by property and educational qualifications, the geographically highly
disparate depressed classes were unlikely to have any influence in the
decision making process. So, the solution lay in separate electorate
for them. Ambedkar held the view that untouchables were absolutely
separate from Hinduism and hence he tried 'to find a solution to their
problem through political separatism'.[49] In order to substantiate, he
further argued that the Hindus 'had much to lose by the abolition of
untouchability, though they had nothing to fear from political reservation leading to this abolition'.[50] The matter was 'economic' rather than
'religious'. In an unambiguous way, Ambedkar brought out the economic
dimension of untouchability:

[T]he system of untouchability is a gold mine to the Hindus. In it the
240 millions of Hindus have 60 million of Untouchables to serve as their

retinue to enable the Hindus to maintain pomp and ceremony and to cultivate a feeling of pride and dignity befitting a master class, which cannot be fostered and sustained unless there is beneath it a servile class to look down upon. In it the 240 millions of Hindus have 60 millions of Untouchables to be used as forced labourers ... in it the 240 millions of Hindus have 60 millions of Untouchables to do the dirty work of scavengers and sweepers which the Hindu is debarred by his religion to do and which must be done by non-Hindus who could be no other than Untouchables. In it the 240 millions of Hindus have 60 millions of Untouchables who can be kept to lower jobs ... In it the 240 millions of Hindus have the 60 millions of Untouchables who can be used as shock-absorbers in slumps and dead-weights in booms, for in slumps, it is the Untouchable who is fired first and the Hindu is fired last and in booms the Hindu is employed first and the Untouchable is employed last. [So, untouchability is not a religious] but an economic system which is worse than slavery.[51]

Unable to appreciate Ambedkar's demand, Gandhi declined to accept that the untouchables were a community separate from the Hindus and instead was prepared to have reserved seats for them in general constituencies. For him, the matter was highly 'religious', as he stated, 'for me the question of these classes is predominantly moral and religious. The political aspect, important though it is', he further added, 'dwindles into insignificance compared to the moral and religious issue'.[52] He reacted strongly when a charge was labelled that the upper-caste Congress leaders could never properly represent the untouchables. When his attention was drawn to the Congress acceptance of the 1932 Communal Award, Gandhi insisted that unlike the question of religious minorities, the issue of untouchability was a matter internal to Hinduism and had to be resolved within it. Underlining the adverse consequences of such division on the Hindus, the Mahatma thus emphatically argued,

> I cannot possibly tolerate what is in store for Hinduism if there are two division set forth in the villages. Those who speak of the political rights of Untouchables do not know their India, do not know how Indian society is today constructed, and therefore I want to say with all the emphasis that I can command that if I was the only person to resist this thing I would resist it with my life.[53]

Gandhi's protest against the extension of the separate electorate to the Dalits was double-edged—on the one hand, Gandhi sincerely believed that the separate electorate would also split them from the Hindu society and absolve the latter of its moral responsibility to fight against the practice of untouchability. There were clear political calculations that, as Bhikhu Parekh argues, governed Gandhi's mind for 'the separate electorate would have reduced the numerical strength of the Hindu majority, encouraged minority alliance against it, and fragmented the country yet further'.[54] So, the Gandhian intervention was the result of skilful political strategy as well as of his passionate concern for Indian unity. Ambedkar was equally assertive and insisted on separate electorate as the best device to protect the social, economic, and political interests of the outcastes. As he stated, 'I trust [that] the Mahatma would not drive me to the necessity of making a choice between his life and the rights of my people. For I can never consent to deliver my people bound hand and foot to the caste Hindus for generations to come'.[55] No solution was visible. On the one hand, for Gandhi, the separate electorate for the untouchables was to divide the Hindu society further, perpetuating their inferiority. On the other, Ambedkar denounced this as a strategic argument for using the untouchables as 'weightage for the Hindus against the Muslims'.[56] When the British government endorsed the separate electorate for untouchables in the Communal Award of August 1932, Ambedkar had an edge over his rival. Once the Mahatma's persuasions failed, he resorted to moral blackmailing by declaring a fast unto death which was nothing but 'Gandhi's spiritual coercion over Ambedkar'[57] as no other option was left. He went on a fast rather than approve the demand of the separate electorate for the depressed classes. Gandhi who was in Yeravada prison in Poona began the fast on 20 September 1932. Ambedkar knew the significance and magnitude of the crisis arising out of Gandhi's fast unto death. The Mahatma had hurled 'a most dangerous and fatal weapon at him'.[58] Once Gandhi began his fast, a furious campaign was launched against Ambedkar who was identified as 'a monster' capable of killing Gandhi to fulfil his narrow and partisan interests. To Ambedkar, it was a shock because he failed to fathom as to why Gandhi 'single[d]-out special representation for the Depressed Classes in the Communal Award as an excuse for his self-immolation'.[59] It was shocking to him further because 'separate electorates are granted not only to the Depressed Classes, but to the Christians, Anglo-Indians, and Europeans as well as to Mohammedans and the Sikhs'.[60] If separate electorates to the Muslims and Sikhs did not split the nation, Hindus could not be said, Ambedkar argued, 'to be split up if the Depressed Classes were given separate electorates'.[61] Nonetheless, Gandhi continued his fast which he broke on 24 September once Ambedkar agreed to accept the reservation of seats for the untouchables within the caste-Hindu constituencies as he had run out of options in view of the massive nationalist mobilization against him. An agreement between Gandhi and Ambedkar, known as the Poona Pact, was signed in 1933 and the depressed classes were given a substantial number of reserved seats but within the Hindu electorate.[62]

Despite the fact that Ambedkar failed to fulfil his demand for separate electorate for the untouchables, the Pact, for the first time, placed the backward classes, later classified as the Scheduled Castes in the 1935 Government of India Act, on the centre stage of Indian politics with a separate identity. From now on, the scheduled castes invariably figured in any discussion on national identity. As a dissenter bent on dismantling an oppressive caste system, Ambedkar therefore 'fulfilled a historical role ... not only to question the hateful religious dogma but also unbuckle the consolidating ambitions of the secular state to create a unified citizenry'.[63] Nonetheless, mere constitutional guarantee was not adequate unless there were supplementary institutionalized social measures to that effect. What was critical was, as Ambedkar felt, a change of the prevalent mindset supporting religious prejudices for social segregation. He thus suggested that, 'we should go beyond the political arrangement ... and devise ways and means whereby it would be possible for the Depressed Classes not only to be part and parcel of the Hindu community but also to occupy an honourable position, a position of equality of status in the community'.[64]

In the Round Table Conference, Ambedkar lost an ideological battle to Gandhi since his demand for separate electorate for untouchables was not conceded. Nonetheless, his strong arguments for their electoral protection amidst relentless opposition by the Congress-led caste Hindu leadership, including Gandhi, established Ambedkar's image as a vocal participant who fought against social segregation in a typical liberal fashion. Gandhi was pushed to the periphery, and Ambedkar was hailed for his success in articulating the issues concerning Dalits, which, though important, were never adequately addressed either by the nationalist political leadership or by the colonial government. So, justice and freedom acquired new connotations in the changed milieu when Dalits had already emerged as a politically significant constituency under the stewardship of B.R. Ambedkar.

His commitment to liberal principles of constitutionalism loomed large when he was asked to preside over the Drafting Committee for the Constitution that also had legal luminaries of the day as its members. As is shown above, the twin influences of John Dewey and George Grote remained critical with Ambedkar to defend his distinctive liberal approach to democratic experimentalism in India. The 1950 Constitution of India was thus not merely a text but an endeavour to translate the Deweyan robust sense of democracy by creating an inclusive associated public space for effective political participation regardless of caste or any other socio-economic criteria and also to instil Grote's constitutional morality as a guarantee towards fulfilling his liberal dream. According to Babasaheb, what deterred India to achieve democracy in its unalloyed form was 'the absence of equality and fraternity'. Ambedkar was suspicious of caste society held together by the Hindu order which he thought was a clear impediment to a liberal society based on the individual freedom. Unlike Gandhi who argued that the transformation of modern India had to be effected through change in 'society', what was unique in Ambedkar's constitutional project was that it sought to transform 'society' through 'politics', because, according to him, as Uday Mehta emphasizes, 'it was only through politics and the specific kind of power it sanctions that the nation can be imagined, administered, and made just'.[65] It was not therefore surprising that in the first Round Table Conference, Ambedkar insisted that 'we must have a government in which the men in power ... will not be afraid to amend the social and economic code of life which the dictates of justice and expediency so urgently call for [and he further added] that we feel that nobody can remove our grievances ... unless we get political power in our hands'.[66] The implication of such a claim is very significant. For Gandhi, social discrimination was necessarily 'a social evil' which could be easily mitigated through 'moral re-education of the upper castes'; while, for Ambedkar, it was embedded in the structured violence and coercion that could be effectively addressed by stern political action, including legally-endorsed compensatory discrimination.[67] These are two contrasting perspectives based on two entirely different understanding of the situations—Gandhi upheld an abstract notion of citizens bearing universalized values while Ambedkar while critiquing Gandhi sought to capture the diverse and discrepant parts it contained in practice. Ambedkar's perception enables us to conceptualize 'various challenges to homogeneous national identity posed by struggles around various markers of identity (caste, gender, region, and so forth) which have contributed to a differentiated entry into the domain of citizenship.'[68] By strongly arguing for 'differentiated citizenship' as perhaps the most effective means to establish equality and fraternity in the liberal sense, Ambedkar thus not only took the bull by its horns, but also laid the foundation of a system of constitutional governance, despite being discriminatory, for the historically disprivileged minority for reasons which were never seriously interrogated in the past.

Concluding Observations

The chapter reinforces that Ambedkar's views of the nation and nation-state drew on his liberal activist position which clearly corresponds with John Dewey who was also known for his emphasis on education as an empowering device. Nonetheless, Babasaheb absorbed and transformed what he had derived from his teacher at Columbia through his own understanding of the existential experiences of the African-Americans in the US and India's Dalits and Muslims.[69] While defending liberalism, Ambedkar also introduced a unique moral and political framework in public reasoning which owed much to the European variety of Enlightenment paradigm and the American variety of republican values. The idea of every person having the right to life, liberty, free speech, and pursuit of happiness—and the duty of the state to ensure that they were not violated remained critical in Ambedkar's socio-political ideas. There are two important features that stand out: first, in Ambedkar's perception, reasoning and rationality were two major pillars in public discourse; he was not persuaded to accept anything that went as 'heritage' since it was largely constructed to fulfil partisan aims. Hence, the caste hierarchy (varnashrama) was justified, felt Ambedkar, because it provided the majority Hindu community with a support system that would not have been available if it was discarded. His arguments for separate electorate were based on reasons for political representation at a specific historical juncture of India's constitutional development when it was emphasized as a logical step to protect the constitutional rights of the minorities. Once separate electorate was conceded to the Muslims in the 1935 Government of India Act, Ambedkar found it appropriate to argue for the same for the untouchables. But in the end, his urge for distinct constitutional status for the untouchables was perhaps tempered by his nationalist zeal when he gave up the demand for separate electorate as Gandhi opposed through his fast unto death. The second important point relates to the centrality of human agency in Ambedkar's effort at constitutionalizing India. As a rationalist to the core, Ambedkar questioned the relevance of 'god and superman'. By interrogating the foundational values of Hinduism that tended to justify social inequality, Babasaheb gave a voice to the critique that subjected the sociologically-justified caste divisions to a thorough scrutiny. In his conceptual framework, the human agency remained central which also reflected a Deweyan emphasis on the role of human beings in the making and unmaking of the world that we lived in. It was thus perfectly compatible with his overall ideological position when he declared that 'do not depend ... for the abolition of caste slavery upon God or Superman. Your salvation lies in political power and not in making pilgrimages and the observance of fasts. Devotion to scriptures would not free you from bondage, want, and poverty'.[70] Central to his argument was a belief in human efforts in re-conceptualizing social mores and values which were contrary to liberal interpretations of human civilization. He evolved his ideas first out of his engagement with what he saw as given due to his birth as a Mahar and later in course of his training as a doctoral student at Columbia University with John Dewey as his academic mentor. By rejecting 'tradition' and 'holy texts' endorsing blatant discrimination, Ambedkar set in motion a critique that, despite being ridiculed at the outset, had found takers not only among the victims of caste prejudices but also among those who did not appear to be favourably inclined initially towards Babasaheb's cudgels against heritage-dependent social hierarchy. Simultaneously with his fight for social justice, by being appreciative of reasonable contestation and engagement, he, along with his colleagues holding similar kinds of views, had not only initiated, but also consolidated the argumentative tradition within, of course, liberal framework of thinking. This was most explicit in the 1950 Constitution of India which became a cornerstone of a nation that sought to establish equality and fraternity as significant constitutional values in opposition to the well-established birth-driven social discrimination. Ambedkar's effort at constitutionalizing India was thus not merely an account of making the 1950 Constitution as the chairman of its Drafting Committee, but was also reflective of sustained endeavours towards making a caste-ridden society sensitive towards basic human values of care, compassion, and empathy.

Notes and References

1. Rajendra Vora, 'Two Strands of Indian Liberalism: The Ideas of Ranade and Phule', in Thomas Pantham and Kenneth Deutsch (eds), *Political Thought in Modern India* (New Delhi: SAGE, 1986), p. 107.
2. Vora, 'Two strands of Indian Liberalism', p. 108.
3. Address of B.R. Ambedkar to a felicitation function, Bombay, 4 March 1933—reproduced in Narendra Jadhav (ed.), *Ambedkar Speaks*, Vol. 1 (New Delhi: Konark Publisher Pvt. Limited, 2013), p. 422.
4. C.A. Bayly, *Recovering Liberties: Indian Thought in the Age of Liberalism and Empire* (Cambridge: Cambridge University Press, 2012), p. 305.
5. Bayly, *Recovering Liberties*, p. 310.
6. Granville Austin, *The Indian Constitution: Cornerstone of a Nation* (New Delhi: Oxford University Press, 1966); M.V. Pylee, *An Introduction to the Constitution of India* (New Delhi: Vikas, 2007) (reprint). S.K. Chaube, *Constituent Assembly of India: The Springboard of Revolution* (New Delhi: Manohar, 2000).
7. Arun P. Mukherjee, 'B.R. Ambedkar, John Dewey and the Meaning of Democracy', *New Literary History* 40(2), 2009, p. 348.
8. John Dewey, *Democracy and Education: An Introduction to the Philosophy of Education* (New York: Macmillan, 1916).
9. B.R. Ambedkar, *Annihilation of Caste* (New Delhi: Critical Quest, 2007) (reprint), p. 49.
10. Ambedkar, *Annihilation of Caste*, p. 49.
11. Ambedkar, *Annihilation of Caste*, p. 49.
12. Ambedkar, *Annihilation of Caste*, p. 57.
13. John Dewey, *Democracy and Education: An Introduction to the Philosophy of Education* (New York: Macmillan, 1916), p. 101.

14. Ambedkar, *Annihilation of Caste*, p. 57.
15. B.R. Ambedkar, 'What Congress and Gandhi Have Done to the Untouchables', in Vasant Moon (ed.), *Dr. Babasaheb Ambedkar's Writings and Speeches*, Vol. 9, Education Department, Government of Maharashtra, Bombay, 1991, p. 187.
16. Ambedkar, 'What Congress and Gandhi Have Done to the Untouchables', pp. 191–3.
17. B.R. Ambedkar, Speech before the Round Table Conference in Vasant Moon (ed.), *Dr. Babasaheb Ambedkar's Writings and Speeches*, Vol. 2, Education Department, Government of Maharashtra, Bombay, 1982, p. 538.
18. B.R. Ambedkar, Presidential Speech, Mahar Satyagraha Conference, 25–7 December, 1927—reproduced in Narendra Jadhav, *Ambedkar Speaks: Political Speeches*, Vol. III, (New Delhi: Konark Publishers Pvt. Ltd, 2013), p. 97.
19. Ambedkar, 'What Congress and Gandhi Have Done to the Untouchables', p. 138.
20. B.R. Ambedkar, Lecture in the Legislative Assembly, Trivandrum, 10 June 1950—reproduced in Narendra Jadhav, *Ambedkar Speaks: Political Speeches*, Vol. III (New Delhi: Konark Publishers Pvt. Ltd., 2013), p. 537.
21. Andre Beteille, 'Constitutional Morality', *Economic and Political Weekly* 43(40), 4 October 2008, p. 42.
22. Pratap Bhanu Mehta makes this point in his 'What Is Constitutional Morality', *Seminar*, November 2010, pp. 17–24.
23. George Grote (1794–1871), an English radical who wrote the History of Greece (four volumes) during 1846–56 period was influenced by liberals like Ricardo, James Mill, and Jeremy Bentham.
24. B.R. Ambedkar Speech before the Constituent Assembly on 4 November 1948, *Constituent Assembly Debates*, Vol. VII, p. 38.
25. Ambedkar, Speech before the Constituent Assembly, p. 38.
26. Ambedkar, Speech before the Constituent Assembly, p. 38.
27. Beteille, 'Constitutional Morality', p. 36.
28. Ambedkar, Speech before the Constituent Assembly, p. 38.
29. Ambedkar, Speech before the Constituent Assembly, p. 38.
30. Ambedkar, Speech before the Constituent Assembly, p. 978.
31. Ambedkar, Speech at the Round Table Conference, p. 107.
32. These three versions of Enlightenment are well-elaborated by Gertrude Himmelfarb in his *The Roads to Modernity: The British, French, and American Enlightenment* (London: Vintage Books, 2008) (reprint), pp. 3–13.

33. B.R. Ambedkar's evidence on 27 January 1919 before the Southborough Committee, p. 6, available at www.ambedkar.org/ambed/07 (accessed on 24 May 2017).

34. B.R. Ambedkar on Democracy in Valerian Rodrigues (ed.), *The Essential Writings of B.R. Ambedkar* (New Delhi: Oxford University Press, 2004), p. 61.

35. Ambedkar on Democracy, p. 64.

36. Ambedkar's evidence on 27 January 1919 before the Southborough Committee, p.3.

37. Ambedkar on Democracy, p. 74.

38. Ambedkar on Democracy, p. 91.

39. R.N. Mudholkar's statement is quoted in Eleanor Zelliot, *Ambedkar's World: The Making of Babasaheb and the Dalit Movement* (New Delhi: Navayana, 2013) (reprint), p. 113.

40. Ambedkar's evidence on 27 January 1919 before the Southborough Committee, p. 2.

41. A fundamental concept of Biochemistry, endosmosis refers to a process of the influx of substance form an area of lesser concentration to one of greater concentration, endosmosis is usually referred to as a mechanism for stable bonding among the cells.

42. Ambedkar's evidence on 27 January 1919 before the Southborough Committee, p. 2.

43. Ambedkar's evidence on 27 January 1919 before the Southborough Committee, p. 6.

44. Ambedkar's evidence on 27 January 1919 before the Southborough Committee, p. 6.

45. Ambedkar's evidence on 27 January 1919 before the Southborough Committee, p. 11.

46. B.R. Ambedkar's statement before the first Round Table Conference (12 November 1930–19 January 1931)—quoted in Eleanor Zelliot, *Ambedkar's World: The Making of Babasaheb and Dalit Movement* (New Delhi: Navayana, 2013), p. 130.

47. The statement of Ramsay McDonald is quoted in Upendra Baxi, 'Emancipation as Justice: Babasaheb Ambedkar's legacy and vision', in Upendra Baxi and Bhikhu Parekh (eds), *Crisis and Change in Contemporary India* (New Delhi: SAGE, 1995), p. 131.

48. Gandhi's Statement before the Second Round Table Conference (7 September–1 December 1931), Proceedings of Federal Structure Committee and Minorities Committee, p. 544 cited in Zelliot, *Ambedkar's World: The Making of Babasaheb and Dalit Movement* p. 133.

49. Judith Brown, 'The Mahatma and Modern India', *Modern Asian Studies* 3(4), 1969, p. 331.

50. Upendra Baxi, 'Emancipation as Justice: Babasaheb Ambedkar's Legacy and Vision', in Upendra Baxi and Bhikhu Parekh (eds), *Crisis and Change in Contemporary India* (New Delhi: SAGE, 1995), p. 145.

51. B.R. Ambedkar, *Mr. Gandhi and Emancipation of Untouchables* (Jullander: Bheem Patrika Publications, 1943), pp. 196–7.

52. Gandhi's Press Statement. *Harijan*, 10 June 1933.

53. Gandhi to Tagore, 9 May 1933— reproduced in the *Amrita Bazar Patrika*, 10 May 1933.

54. Bhikhu Parekh, *Gandhi* (Oxford: Oxford University Press, 1997), p. 18.

55. C.B. Khairmode, *Dr. Bhimrao Ramji Ambedkar* (in Marathi), Vol. 4 (Pune: Sugava Prakashan, 1989), p. 42—quoted in M.S. Gore, *The Social Context of an Ideology: Ambedkar's Political and Social Thought* (New Delhi: SAGE, 1993), p. 137.

56. Ainslie T. Embree, *Imagining India: Essays on Indian History* (Delhi: Oxford University Press, 1989), p. 171.

57. Upendra Baxi, 'Emancipation as Justice: Babasaheb Ambedkar's Legacy and Vision', in Upendra Baxi and Bhikhu Parekh (eds), *Crisis and Change in Contemporary India* (New Delhi: SAGE, 1995), p. 128.

58. Dhananjay Keer, *Dr. Ambedkar: Life and Mission* (Bombay: Popular Prakashan, 2009) (reprint), p.206.

59. The statement of B.R. Ambedkar is cited in Dhananjay Keer's *Dr. Ambedkar: Life and Mission*, p. 207.

60. Ambedkar's statement cited in Keer's *Dr. Ambedkar: Life and Mission*, p. 207.

61. Ambedkar's statement cited in Keer's *Dr. Ambedkar: Life and Mission*, p. 207.

62. Ravinder Kumar, 'Ambedkar, Gandhi, and the Poona Pact', Occasional Paper on Society and History, No. 20, New Delhi, Nehru Memorial Library and Museum, 1985.

63. Gauri Viswanathan, *Outside the Fold: Conversion, Modernity and Belief* (New Delhi: Oxford University Press, 1998), p. 213.

64. Quoted in Bhagwan Das, 'Ambedkar's Journey to Mass Conversion', in V. Grover (ed.), *B.R. Ambedkar* (New Delhi: Deep & Deep Publications, 1993), p. 595.

65. Uday Mehta, 'Constitutionalism', in Niraja Gopal Jayal and Pratap Bhanu Mehta (eds), *The Oxford Companion to Politics in India* (New Delhi: Oxford University Press, 2010), p. 27.

66. *Proceedings of the Indian Round Table Conference* —12 November 1930–19 January 1931, Central Publication Branch, Government of India, Calcutta, 1931, p. 125.

67. Mark Galanter pursues this argument in greater depth in his *Competing Equalities: Law and the Backward Classes in India* (New Delhi: Oxford University Press, 1984).

68. Anupama Rao, 'Arguing Against Inclusion', *Economic and Political Weekly*, 22 February 1997, p. 428.

69. C.A. Bayly pursues this argument in his *Recovering Liberties: Indian Thought in the Age of Liberalism and Empire* (Cambridge: Cambridge University Press, 2012), pp. 303–9.

70. Ambedkar, Speech at the Felicitation Function at Wadi Bandar, in V Grover (ed.), *BR Ambedkar*, New Delhi: Deep and Deep Publications, 1993: p. 422.

4   Princely States and the Nationalists' Constitutionalizing Endeavour

The story of India's journey as a constitutional democracy can be told in two interrelated ways: on the one hand, it evolved as complementary to British colonialism that also drew its sustenance from the Enlightenment values; hence, constitutional democracy gained salience since it developed organic roots in India. Equally important was, on the other, the Congress-driven political movements in the princely states which, despite having accepted the British suzerainty, maintained political autonomy in so far as domestic governance was concerned. The point that is made here is to emphasize that significant political changes had also occurred in the princely states due to external ideological stimulus and also in view of personal initiatives of some of the rulers in introducing responsible governments in their kingdoms. As a result, the task was made relatively easier for the framers of the constitution since majority of the princely states agreed to join the Constituent Assembly without much hue and cry, presumably because it was the best choice under the changed political circumstances following the transfer of power to the Congress-led government in India. This is one part of the story suggesting that in view of the vulnerable geographical location of their kingdoms in India, the erstwhile rulers seem to have bought peace in exchange of favourable perks and privileges; the other part, as the following discussion will support, is about the circumstances in which the princely states had no option but to join the Constituent Assembly also because of the growing public discontent leading to the consolidation of opposition which the erstwhile rulers were not equipped to handle in the absence of outside support which was available so long as the British paramountcy prevailed. As a result, majority of the princely states, except Junagadh, Hyderabad, and Travancore, voluntarily surrendered their kingdom and also had agreed to become part of the Constituent Assembly.

Designs and Initiatives

It is well-known that there were ninety three representatives from the princely states in the Constituent Assembly as per the Cabinet Mission's recommendations, though the number of representatives were finally fixed out of intense deliberations in the Negotiating Committee involving the Congress and those representing the princely interests in the presence of the British agents. This was however not the first time when the princely states participated in the evolving of constitutional democracy; they enthusiastically took part in the deliberations in the first Round Table Conference that was inaugurated in November 1930. There were 57 political leaders from British India and sixteen delegates from states that included Sangli, Sarila, besides Akbar Hydari (Hyderabad), Mirza Ismail, and Kalias Narain Haksar from Gwalior. On the first day of the conference, T.B. Sapru, the leader of the delegates representing British India, strongly argued for 'a federal, not a unitary, system of government at the centre and invited the rulers to agree forthwith for the creation of an all-India federation'.[1] As soon as the proposal was mooted, the Maharaja of Bikaner, Ganga Singh, not only endorsed but also most zealously supported the idea by declaring that 'India must be united on a federal basis [with the assurance] that the rulers would join the federal India provided their rights were guaranteed'.[2] The suggestion provoked criticism as well. For instance, the ruler of Bhopal felt that in a federal India, the rights of the princely states were likely to be infringed since the central cabinet retained the defacto authority. Hence, instead of a federal India, he preferred a confederal India or 'Indian India', which he characterized, as a stepping stone towards building 'a collectivity involving the British India and the princely states'.[3] The argument did not seem to have persuaded the other members which was evident with the appointment of 'a federal structure sub-committee' to suggest the modalities of what was to be done to translate the idea into practice.

With the boycott of the second session of the Round Table Conference by Congress, the idea of a federal India seems to have lost its steam. Nonetheless, by defending the demand for federation, the prime minister, Ramsay MacDonald, kept the hope alive by exhorting:

> [T]he great idea of an all-India federation still holds the field. The principle of a responsible federal government, subject to certain reservations and safeguards through a transition period, remains unchanged. And, we are all agreed that the Governors' provinces of the future are to be responsibly governed units, enjoying the greatest possible measure of freedom from outside interference and dictation in carrying out their own policies in their own sphere.[4]

The declaration was formalized by way of adopting a resolution to that effect, which created a space, V.P. Menon informs, for discussion primarily in the princely states. Besides the opposition of the Nawab of Bhopal, two issues seem to have caused a serious concern: they insisted on the adequate representation of the princely states in the federal legislature to enable them to meaningfully pursue their causes; and, they also demanded that the financial liabilities of the federating states needed to be fixed in proportionate to the income being generated from within. While agreeing to the first point, the Sub-Committee suggested that the number of representatives were to be determined by taking into account the views of the princely states; as regards the second point, it was also accepted that the federating units were expected to contribute in accordance with what was feasible from the point of view of their financial strength. The Bill prepared by the Sub-Committee was placed before Parliament in December, 1934 and, in August, 1935, it also received royal ascent. This was a remarkable step towards constitutionalizing the princely states; they not only endorsed the scheme but also expressed their willingness to be associated with a federal India.

The design that the Sub-Committee had proposed appeared in the 1935 Government of India Act which provided a constitutional relationship between the Indian states and British India on a federal basis, though the former was given an option of opting out in case they felt otherwise. The Parliamentary Joint Select Committee explained why the princely states needed to be treated differently:

> [T]he main difficulties are two: that the Indian States are wholly different in status and character from the provinces of British India, and that they are not prepared to federate on the same terms as it is prepared to apply to the Provinces. On the first point, the Indian States, unlike the British Indian Provinces, possess sovereignty in various degrees and they are, broadly speaking, under a system of personal government. Their accession to Federation cannot therefore take place otherwise than by the voluntary act of the Ruler of each State, and after accession the representatives of the acceding State in the Federal Legislature will be nominated by the Ruler and its subjects will continue to owe allegiance to him. On the second point, the Rulers have made it clear that while they are willing to consider Federation now with the Provinces of British India on certain terms, they could not, as sovereign States, agree to the exercise by a Federal Government in relation to them of a range of powers identical in all respects with those which that Government will exercise in relation to the Provinces on whom autonomy has yet to be conferred.[5]

On a surface reading of the above statement, it appears to have given enough autonomy to the Indian states. There was however a condition, contrary to the assurance of the Joint Select Committee, which suggested that the rulers were required to sign an instrument of accession enabling the Crown to decide the course of action vis-à-vis Indian subjects which it deemed appropriate. This was a death-blow to the guarantee that the Joint Select Committee proposed. In other words, although the rulers were enthusiastic about the idea of a federal India when it was mooted, they seem to have been disenchanted soon in view of the conditionalities. Furthermore, for the rulers, the Congress was a source of irritation in view of its strong opposition to the presence on the central legislature of State representative nominated by the rulers. The Congress remained steadfast to its stance while the rulers did not relent either. No solution was thus forthcoming because, as Lothian (who acted as chief Commissioner of Princely States, like Jaipur, Bikaner, Hyderabad, among others) persuasively explained by saying that 'the more trouble-some Congress came to be, the more disinclined the States were to have any organic connection with a Central Government in which Congress would necessarily have a big part'.[6] The offer was formally rejected in 1939 and, the idea of a federal India was shelved, at least, for the time being. For Penderel Moon who was involved in negotiation with the princes on behalf of the Government, the outcome was more or less anticipated long before the federal design was made public because 'it was quite beyond the scope of the more pedestrian talents of Lord Linlithgow [the Viceroy] and it never seemed probable that the Princes would yield to his methods of persuasion'.[7] Nonetheless, it had two significant implications for the endeavour towards constitutionalizing India in future. First, the decision to join a federal India was a continuity of the effort that the rulers had made earlier by joining the Chamber of Prince which came into being in the wake of the 1919 Montague-Chelmsford Reform scheme. The concern was to create a forum to forcefully articulate their demands vis-à-vis the British and also to contain the popular movements that the Congress was alleged to have fomented. The second implication was far more critical in developing a supportive mindset by recognizing the importance of a collective will to meaningfully address the prevalent socio-economic and political difficulties. So, a federal India was a design with immense advantages especially during difficult times which was characterized as 'a Vision Splendid [that] many dreamt of [but] none hoped to realize in their own days'.[8] This was not merely a structure creating a forum for all the constituent units; it was also a design which helped develop a base for democratic processes to strike roots by recognizing the need for being accommodative of diverse socio-economic interests and views. It was thus not surprising for Linlithgow, the Viceroy, to appreciate the rulers for having taken 'a giant step towards strengthening India as a democratic polity'.[9] So, the entire exercise, despite being a failure,[10] put in place for reckoning the idea of federating India which was to gain momentum in the days to come.

Between 1939 when federation was rejected and 1946 when the Cabinet Mission was appointed to constitutionalize India, there were serious parleys between the rulers and some of the Indian leaders, including Vallabhbhai Patel and Jawaharlal Nehru. It was a foregone conclusion by then that the transfer of power was imminent which was evident in the Memorandum on States' Treaties and Paramountcy that the Cabinet Mission presented to the Chamber of Princes. By insisting that the princely states should 'make contribution to the framing of the structure and to take their due place in it when it is completed', the Memorandum exhorted:

> in order to facilitate this [the rulers] will doubtless strengthen their position by doing everything possible to ensure that their administrations conform to the highest standard. Where adequate standards cannot be achieved within the existing resources of the State they will no doubt arrange in suitable cases to form or join administrative units large enough to enable them to be fitted into the constitutional structure. It will also strengthen the position of States during this formative period if the various Governments which have not already done so take active steps to place themselves in close and constant touch with the public opinion in their States by means of representative institutions.[11]

For the Mission, the choice was unambiguous: the Indian states needed to be integrated with British India to realize the democratic goals of governance. Furthermore, the insistence on respecting public opinion and representative institutions also clarified that Mission was in favour of putting in place constitutional democracy as perhaps the best option available to them. It was categorically stated in the Memorandum by highlighting,

> when a new fully self-governing or independent Government or Governments come into being in British India ... the rights of the States which flow from their relationship with Crown will no longer exist and ... all the rights surrendered by the States in the paramount power will return to the States. ... The void will have to be filled either by the States entering into a federal relationship with the successor Government or Governments in British India, or, failing this, entering into particular political arrangements with it or them.[12]

The above direction needs to be understood at two levels: at a rather mundane level, the Mission was very emphatic in suggesting that States were required to negotiate with the new political actors in the new dispensation; at another level, the Mission, in a subtle way, also hinted that in the changed scenario, it would be appropriate for the States to be willing 'to cooperate in the new development of India [though] the precise form which their cooperation will take place must be a matter of negotiation, and the outcome of the negotiation may not prove to be identical for all the States'.[13]

Did the princely state have an option to decide a course of action which was contrary to the above direction? Perhaps not. It was a direction which was expected to be carried forward. The Chamber of Princes had a meeting in August, 1946 in which some of the members resented the direction which was construed to be a threat though couched in a very subtle language. Criticising the direction as an attempt of 'political annihilation of the princely states'[14] by the British, the Nawab of Bhopal candidly expressed his disappointment:

> I am unhappy about everything in this country. The British seem to have abdicated power and what is worse they have handed over ... to the enemies of all their friends. The Princes betrayed by the British are already a lost cause and I feel I am wasting my energies ... in trying to protect their case. I am a Moslem in a crowd of Hindu Princes, who suspect me all round, who are bling to their own interests and who are at the moment only guided by one desire, namely, ... to kill, to destroy ... and wipe off the Moslem from the face of the earth. I am a complete misfit in this crowd and I am sure my place lies somewhere else.[15]

By November, 1946, the Nawab of Bhopal was fighting a losing battle because (a) the possibility of British support for his cause was almost nil in view of the Viceroy's uncritical support to a united India, along with the princely states, and (b) the popular movement against the Nawab for being anti-democratic in Bhopal also weakened his claim as an acceptable ruler of his kingdom. By 1946, it was a foregone conclusion that the princely states had no option but to join the new republic of India. Hence it is argued that 'accession was facilitated by pressure—subtle, gentlemanly, but relentless pressure from the Viceroy who conveyed in so many ways to the princes that unless they agreed to the terms and conditions, they would be coerced to do so in the long run'.[16]

An analytical scan of the processes of integration of the princely states with India reveals that it was an outcome of a grand strategy that the Congress leadership had deployed with unflinching support from the last Viceroy, Mountbatten. The integration however did not happen all at once during 1947–8; rather, it was negotiated over several years well into the 1950s. It has been shown that 'the erstwhile princely states were finally woven into the regional and political tapestry of the new nation, a process that reached its culmination in 1956'.[17] As the situation unfolded, the princely states were forced to surrender under circumstances in which they had no option but to accept the terms and conditions that the Congress laid out for them. For the princely states, the situation became worse with the creation of Pakistan which weakened their case further. In the absence of their imperial patron, they had no one to bank upon to defend their claim. Furthermore, the rising public discontent, backed by Congress and also the threat of military forces seem to have completely foreclosed any option for them. The princes were thus victims of what is dubbed as 'opportunistic paramountcy', which deceived them since they were given an assurance by Cabinet Mission to the contrary.[18] And yet, these loyal allies were 'abandoned' perhaps due to the presence of a far more powerful companion despite their unconditional faith in the British Crown.

Representation in the Constituent Assembly

Barring Hyderabad, Junagadh, and Travancore, all the princely states accepted the suzerainty of independent India. While hailing Vallabhbhai Patel for his astute leadership in this regard, Mountbatten expressed his happiness thus:

> [I]t is a great triumph for the realism and sense of responsibility of the rulers and governments of the States as well as for the Government of India that it was possible to produce an instrument of accession which was equally acceptable to both sides; and one, moreover, so simple and so straightforward that within less than three weeks practically all the States concerned had signed the Instrument of Accession and the Standstill Agreement. There is thus established a unified political structure.[19]

With this declaration, the fate of the princely states seems to have been permanently sealed; they had almost no option but to facilitate the processes of integration. It was thus possible for Gopalaswami Ayyangar of the Negotiating Committee to firmly mention that by accepting the terms and conditions of the Cabinet Mission, 'the princes have already acquiesced that they will join the Constituent Assembly and work with others for the purpose of working out a constitutional machinery and having done that, decide for [themselves] whether to federate as units or come to some other political arrangement with the new Government of India'.[20]

Following integration, the rulers also agreed to join the Constituent Assembly which was constituted to frame independent India's constitution. In a meeting of the princes, held in Bombay in April 1947, they reiterated their 'support of the States to the freedom of the country, and their willingness to render the fullest possible cooperation in framing an agreed constitution and to all genuine efforts towards facilitating the transfer of power on an agreed basis'.[21] As per the Cabinet Mission, the princely states had, in the Constituent Assembly, a share of ninety-three out of a total of 385 members by following the formula of one representative per one million people.[22] On the basis of the rec-ommendation of the Negotiating Committee that the Cabinet Mission had devised, it was decided that the representatives from the princely states were to be 'elected on the proportional representation by means of the single transferable vote'.[23] Despite opposition by some of its mem-bers, especially the Dewan of Baroda state who insisted on nominating at least one member out of three representatives for the state,[24] the Chamber of Princes endorsed the suggestion. With the acceptance of this principle, a major hurdle disappeared. While being critical of the stance that the Dewan of Baroda took since it 'put our Committee in a difficult position and the mass opinion which the Constituent Assembly represents', Jawaharlal Nehru insisted that the representatives from the States 'should come in [Constituent Assembly] through some elective processes, through legislature or electoral colleges, as envisaged by the Chambers of Princes'.[25] At the conclusion of the debates, a joint com-muniqué was issued accepting that 'representatives of the States in the Constituent Assembly ... shall be elected by the elected members of the legislatures or, where such legislatures do not exist, of other electoral colleges'.[26] It was 'a good gesture', as Nehru characterized, 'of the Chamber of Princes that resolves a great difficulty in the making of the constitution of India [though he also believed that] by compul-sion of events they may eventually be forced to accept its decisions'.[27]

The objective was to evolve, he further emphasized, a system of constitutional governance to carry forward the task of building a new nation in accordance with the politico-ideological goals that they had assiduously nurtured while challenging the British Empire. As a true democrat, he tried his best to persuade the representatives of the princely states to appreciate the principle of mutual give and take to avoid unnecessary delay in laying out the foundation of constitutional democracy in India and also the bitterness among the colleagues involved in the task. The concern was evident when he exhorted,

> the situation is that before long British power in India will fade away, it is fading away, and the more it fades away, the people of this country, whether in the so-called British India or the States, have to face the situation and face it by cooperating *inter se* by solving problems *inter se*; there will be no third party to intervene between them. So, whatever happens, we shall have to negotiate today, tomorrow or the day after, at every stage sometimes. If we take longer to produce results, we not only postpone decisions, but create difficulties, but anyhow, ultimately we have got to come together. That is an obvious task.[28]

The above narrative of the negotiations between the representatives of British India and their counterpart from the States (that lasted for almost a year since the arrival of the Cabinet Mission in April, 1946) is useful in two complementary ways: on the one hand, it is clear that, for all practical purposes, the princely states seem to have been bulldozed to accept the point of the view that the Congress held, of course, by following, at least, on the surface, intricate processes of negotiation to arrive at a consensus as regards the composition of the Constituent Assembly. There were contrary points of view which hardly received the attention that it deserved presumably because the States' voice was highly fragmented in contrast with those representing British India who always put forward their views in unison. Furthermore, given their strategic advantages of being democratically elected members and also persuasive arguments, it was relatively easier for Jawaharlal Nehru and Vallabhbhai Patel to persuade their counterparts from the States. There was another dimension, on the other, which is usually downplayed. One of the factors that appears to have enforced the views of the British Indian representatives over those from the States was also a subtle threat of the application of force in case the latter decided otherwise. There is substance in the assumption because Vallabhbhai Patel, in his address in the Negotiating Committee made a passing reference to this aspect when he stated that 'if the States decide to do things contrary to people's sentiments and desire, ... we may have to adopt methods against our will'.[29] That this statement had an impact was evident in the response of the Raja of Bilaspur saying that 'the States [that] do not agree ... would have no where to go but to cooperate with whatever union that might be formed at a certain stage'.[30] So it was a foregone conclusion in so far as the princely states were concerned.

Unfolding of the Discussion

As shown above, conditions were created in which the princely states agreed to be associated with the Constituent Assembly on the terms and conditions which, despite being derivative of what the Cabinet Mission had laid out, also received the approval from Congress. Except Jammu and Kashmir, none of the States had succeeded in securing special constitutional packages for themselves. This confirms that (a) the representatives from the princely states acted as a second fiddle since their views in the Assembly largely corresponded with what they conveyed in their intervention in the Negotiating Committee, and (b) since the matter was settled, the Congress-dominated British Indian members had hardly wavered in pushing what they had decided in the meetings of the Congress Legislative Party for liberal democracy of the Western mould for a united India.

A perusal of the deliberations in the Constituent Assembly shows that it was Vallabhbhai Patel who guided the discussion in accordance with what was decided in the Negotiating Committee, constituted to set out the terms and conditions of the negotiations between the British Indian states and princely states. As argued above, the States were left with no alternative but to concede the moment as it was evident that the British paramountcy would be withdrawn soon. That the princely states were to become part of independent India was thus a foregone conclusion. It was thus possible for Patel to confidently announce that 'by integrating 500 and odd States into sizeable units and by complete elimination of centuries-old autocracies, the Indian democracy has won a great victory of which the Princes and the people of India alike should be proud. This is an achievement which should redound to the credit of any nation or people at any phase of history.'[31]

Patel had reasons to feel proud because by the middle of 1949, the process of integration of princely states with independent India (barring Hyderabad, Travancore, and Junagadh) was complete which led him to further declare that 'as a result of the policy of integration and democratization of States pursued by the Government of India since December, 1947, the process of what might be called "unionization" of States is almost over.'[32] Aware that in the absence of a tradition of democracy in the States, it will not be an easy transition, he further emphasized that 'in the interest of the growth of democratic institutions in these States, no less than requirements of administrative efficiency, the Government of India should exercise general supervision over the Governments of the States till such time as it may be necessary.'[33] The members of the Constituent Assembly joined the chorus, defending Patel's position. For instance, R.K. Sidhwa representing Central Provinces and Berar supported unionization as the only option for the people in the States to realize 'democracy in spirit and content'. While elaborating his views, he further mentioned:

> [T]he conditions in Indian States ... are not parallel to what exist in the provinces; ... it is miserable. ... There is no administration there, ... there is no municipality; there is no local body there. These are the States ... where the public do not know what is a local body, what is a municipality and what are the powers of a municipality. [So], you can understand what sort of administration exists there?[34]

Sarangadhar Das of Orissa expressed the same concern which he articulated by saying that in order to perpetuate 'their brutal rule', the local rulers left no opportunity to gag the democratic voices. The rulers were opposed to establish libraries because, as Das argued, 'the Raja and Dewan were afraid that people by reading books would become rebels.'[35] It did not seem odd to Jainaram Vyas of Jodhpur States since 'the restriction to open schools, libraries, boarding houses ... was a deliberate design to keep the people in the dark.'[36] In such a situation, it was difficult for democracy to strike roots. While commending Patel for his success in bringing together 'the princely States under the democratic governance of India', [37] they however also added a note of caution by warning the independent India's leadership not to go overboard because 'our democracy is still in its infancy'.[38] Despite a cautionary note, both Das and Vyas were persuaded to believe, which they also articulated in so many words, that the British Indian take-over of governance of the States was both a useful and propitious step for the people to realize their democratic aspirations. Even the representatives of the princely states were convinced that the integration of the States was 'a boon for them' because it created conditions in which the people would emerge as 'a defecto ruler'. Being apprecia-tive of the endeavour that Patel undertook, P. Govinda Menon of the Mysore State, thus hailed him as 'a modern day Bismarck' who built 'a real India by bringing the erstwhile independent princely States under one roof'.[39] He was persuaded to believe that 'the unionization of India for democracy' would happen with the inauguration of the constitution of India which was applicable to the country as a whole. In his words,

> once this Constitution is passed, the nature of the Government of India changes. The people from the Provinces should not think that it is a government of theirs only, and the people from the Indian States should not think that it is a government of somebody else. Whenever in Constitution, and wherever in the Constitution, the words, 'Parliament', 'President', and 'the Government of India' are used, it must be remem-bered that these institutions demote or represent the sovereignty of the people of India, including the people of the Indian States. In other words, the Indian States and the Provinces are going to pool their sovereignty and to have a single undivided sovereignty in India.[40]

As well as creating a compact administrative unit, the proposed constitution was also a stepping stone towards fulfilling the self-government, an ideal that remained a distant goal so long as monarchical form of government survived. A strong believer of 'hard steps' causing 'heart-burn to the erstwhile rulers', Annie Mascarene of Travancore and Cochin Union admired the Indian leadership when she uncritically endorsed the military option that the Indian state was contemplating to bring the recalcitrant princely States under constitutional governance. In a very candid way, she thus expressed that, 'the States' people are very much obliged to the Indian political leadership for the work they have done during the last few months. They are able to feel now that they are no more going to be tyrannised by autocracies which under the British Administration represented them; ... With their [Indian leaders] efforts, ... we will also be able to mould our destiny along with that of democratic India ... and we shall be one of the foremost democracies that the world had ever seen when four hundred millions of people have launched on the ocean of self-government and that is going to be the best example ever known in the history of the world.[41]

There was an all-round applause for the Indian political leadership for its efforts to create a united India by an adept design of political manoeuvring which seems to have left no option for the princely states but to join. A careful analysis of the political processes leading to the princely states' integration with India suggests that on the one hand the erstwhile rulers lost their control presumably because of the growing popular discontent in their kingdoms and also the withdrawal of British support, on the other, which emboldened the Indian state to tighten their chokehold on the princely states. With the constitution in force, the Indian states were to become just one of the constituent provinces of independent India. Since the objective was to make India a truly democratic state, it was a foregone conclusion, Patel emphasized which he further elaborated by underling that unlike the 1935 scheme,

> our new constitution is not an alliance between democracies and dynasties, but a really union of the Indian people built on the basic concept of the States and the people of Provinces and, achieves for the first time the objective of a strong democratic India built on the true foundation of a cooperative enterprises of the people of the Provinces and States alike.[42]

Deliberations in the Constituent Assembly reveal that the members, whether from the princely states or British Indian provinces, were unanimous in holding the view that the princely states had to be integrated with sovereign India. With an exception of the Nawabs of Hyderabad, Travancore, and Junagadh, the erstwhile rulers signed the accession treaty more or less on the terms and conditions that the representatives from Government of India laid out for them. Even as regards privy purses which were payable as per Covenants and Agreements of Merger, the princes had no choice but to accept the amount that was calculated as appropriate by the India's new rulers. There were murmurs as some of the rulers were unhappy with what was given as privy purse since the amount was inadequate.[43] The Indian rulers remained unfazed. Instead, Patel stressed that privy purse was not, at all, a compensatory financial package which was consummate to the income that the former rulers had had for themselves, but a recognition of their contribution to 'a great historical settlement [for the] ... consummation of the great ideal of geographical, political and economic unification of India, an ideal which for centuries remained a distant dream and which appeared as remote and as difficult of attainment as ever even after the advent of Indian independence.'[44]

While giving a persuasive argument to assuage the feeling of the deposed Princes, Patel was also aware that this had caused heart-burn to those nationalist colleagues who fought against the brutal system that evolved at the formers' behest. In order to carry his comrades, Patel now defended the stance by saying that it was 'a small price we have paid for the bloodless revolution which has affected the destinies of millions of people.'[45]

Except Jammu and Kashmir, which will be discussed below, none of the princely state had succeeded in securing special privileges for themselves. In face of a unified voice of the Indian leadership that Patel had articulated with great determination, the Indian princes seem to have lost a cause presumably because they neither succeeded in mobilizing public opinion in their favour nor had a representative in the Assembly who could successfully pursue their points of views by the strength of the arguments and facts. Nonetheless, the fact that they were not bulldozed but were persuaded to join the independent Union draws our attention to a relatively unknown chapter in the making of the constitution when the concern for a democratic polity appears to have acted decisively in shaping the politico-ideological preferences of the founding fathers. The foregone conclusion was in the face of the rising tide of people's democratic aspirations that the Constituent Assembly epitomized, that the kingdoms of yesterday, to borrow Lothian's phrase, collapsed so soon that it reminds us of 'a sand castle which looked impressive until the oceanic waves swept the shore.'[46] In other words, with unstinted support of the British Crown, these princely states remained invincible; but, in the changed milieu and also with the growing public mobilization against autocratic rules, the Indians states had hardly had alternative but to succumb to the pressure that the Indian leadership had mounted. Nevertheless, for an appropriate understanding of the ideational battle that finally culminated in the 1950 Constitution of India, the part of the debate in the Constituent Assembly that dealt with integration of the princely states and the issue of privy purse shall always provide useful inputs.

Constitutionalizing Special Status for Jammu and Kashmir

Of all the princely states, Jammu and Kashmir was privileged in terms of guaranteeing special status to the State once it agreed to join India by signing the instrument of accession in October, 1947. While the other Indian states unconditionally merged with the independent Union, the integration of State of Jammu and Kashmir was conditional to the extent of even allowing the State to retain its sovereignty within India's suzerainty. It has thus been argued that 'when one considers the integrative agenda of the 1950, the region of Kashmir defies any exercise of neat labelling'.[47] The treaty of accession that the local ruler Hari Singh had endorsed, stipulated, for instance, the terms and condition for merger with India which were heavily tilted in favour of the State. There was no ambiguity when the Instrument of Accession mentioned:

1. Nothing in this instrument affects the continuance of sovereignty [of the ruler] in and over this State, or, save as provided by or under this Instrument, the exercise of any powers, authority and rights now enjoyed by [the ruler] of this State or the validity of any law at present in force in this State.

2. Nothing in this Instrument shall empower the Dominion Legislature to make any law for the State authorizing the compulsory acquisition of land for any purpose, except without a prior approval of the State which deems it necessary to acquire any land exclusively for her benefit.

3. Nothing in this Instrument shall be deemed to commit in any way to acceptance of any future constitution of India or to fetter the discretion [of the State] to enter into agreement with the Government of India under any such future constitution.[48]

In pursuance of this, the local ruler issued a proclamation announcing the formation of a Constituent Assembly made of the elected representatives of the people. Following the election in August-September, 1951, an elected assembly was constituted. For the leader of the house, Sheikh Abdullah of National Conference, it heralded a new era in Kashmir's history which he elaborated by saying,

> people of Jammu and Kashmir, whose duly elected representatives are gathered here, to shape the future of their country after wise deliberation, and mould their future organs of Government. [They] are free, at last to shape [their] aspirations as people and to give substance to the ideas which have brought [them] here. [And] no person and no power stand between them and the fulfilment of their historic objective.[49]

Besides highlighting that the elected assembly was a significant step in realizing people's democratic aspiration, Abdullah also mentioned that the formation of Constituent Assembly marked the recognition of the people of Jammu and Kashmir being sovereign which means that 'what [they] decide has the revocable force of law. The basic democratic principle of sovereignty of the nation, embodied ably in the American and French Constitution, is once again given shape in our midst'.[50] He further reminded the members of the Assembly that once the constitution was put in place, the state would be free to decide on every issue including the decision of accession to the republic. This provoked consternation in the State and also in Delhi. The 1952 Delhi Agreement involving the state of Jammu and Kashmir and Government of India was a step to quell the resentment; it was an agreement that recognized the distinctive Kashmiri identity within, of course, a wider national constitutional framework, created by the 1950 Constitution of India.

The terms and conditions of the instrument of accession and later the formation of a Constituent Assembly show that in case of the integration of Jammu and Kashmir with the republic, they were favourably disposed towards the state. With the acceptance of these terms and conditions as a precondition for the merger of Jammu and Kashmir with India, the Constituent Assembly had little choice in this regard. The price that the State had put was pretty high, and the Indian leaders had agreed presumably because it would help them defend their claim vis-à-vis Pakistan which because of the deployment of her military for taking over the State, had already alienated the local leadership and its supporters. For India, it was a masterstroke which however had negative repercussions in the days to come. As a result, it was easier for the founding fathers to arrive at an amicable political arrangement with Jammu and Kashmir through the terms and conditions that the Indian representatives had accepted while signing the instrument of accession for the State.

The Making of Article 370

Article 370, which provides special constitutional status to Jammu and Kashmir, is a source of contestation for a variety of reasons. Prominent among them is the argument that guarantee of special status to a constituent state in federal India is constitutionally untenable within the framework of a federal nation. The constitutional sanction for autonomy in certain respects is, in other words, contrary to the ideological mission that the founding fathers had pursued while being involved in the battle for freedom. Ideologically invalid, such a concession did not appear to have been drawn on logic especially in view of the fact that other princely states were simply annexed with the Union following independence. That the Jammu and Kashmir issue was however different and needed to be dealt with differently was the argument that was made in the Constituent Assembly to justify its special constitutional status. This was thus a historical necessity which finally persuaded the members to accept a rather discriminatory stance vis-à-vis this state. The aim here is to understand the processes leading to the formulation of Article 370 in a historical perspective. The question seems to have become far more relevant now with the 2015 High Court judgment supportive of Article 370 despite the consolidation of the contrarians who strongly feel that this is ideologically indefensible and constitutionally flawed in the present constitutional dispensation for India.

Historical Antecedents

The Constituent Assembly of India which framed the Constitution of India debated the issue. A perusal of the debate shows that this article was not as intensively debated as other articles in the proposed constitution. It was N. Gopalaswami Ayyangar of Madras who held the fort against an equally feeble opposition, led by Maulana Hasarat Mohani of United Provinces. Nonetheless, it was an interesting chapter in the Constituent Assembly debates because it enables us to understand (a) how a special status to a state was justified by the dominant section in the Assembly and (b) how a discriminatory provision in India's federal constitution helped build a strong political opinion in the state for merger with the Union.

While presenting Article 306A which later became Article 370 in the Constitution of India, Gopalaswami Ayyangar, minister without portfolio in the interim government, attributed the special nature of the Article to 'the special conditions' that existed in the state. Article 306A was, according to him, 'a discriminatory' constitutional design to enable the state to fully integrate with the Union of India in due course. While elaborating his argument for such a discriminatory constitutional provision, he further argued that 'the discrimination is due to the special conditions in Kashmir. This particular state is not yet ripe for this kind of integration. ... There are various reasons why this is not possible now.'[51] One of the important reasons was linked with 'the unusual and abnormal conditions in the state 'due to war' which resulted in 'the capture of part of the state by the rebels and enemies'. The other critical factor supportive of special provision for Jammu and Kashmir was India's commitment to the people of the state for 'an opportunity ... to decide for themselves whether they will remain with the Republic or wish to be out of it. [The Indian State was] also committed to ascertaining this will of the people by means of plebiscite provided that peaceful and normal conditions are restored and the impartiality of the plebiscite could be guaranteed. [It was also] agreed that the will of the people, through the instrument of a constituent assembly will determine the constitution of the state as well as the sphere of the Union jurisdiction over the State.'[52] According to Ayyangar, the discriminatory status given to Jammu and Kashmir was attributed to the difficult circumstances in which the local habitat was placed due to war and rebellion. And also, the state was allowed to go for a plebiscite to decide whether it would integrate with the Union or not; there was also a concession for creating a constituent assembly for the state to frame its own constitution.

Being entirely politically expedient, the terms and conditions were clearly discriminatory. Interestingly, Ayyangar's defence of a tilted Article 306A did not provoke any of the Assembly members to initiate debates except Maulana Hasarat Mohani who raised his concern by questioning the partiality that the Assembly had shown to the Maharaja of Kashmir at the cost of other princely states. 'Why do you make this discrimination about the Ruler [of Jammu and Kashmir]?' asked Maulana Hasarat Mohani and further argued that 'if you grant this concession to the Maharaja of Kashmir you should also withdraw your decision about [the merger of other princely states] with the Union of India.'[53] The special status clause was questioned for being discriminatory; it was unwarranted, as Mohani strongly felt, because it amounted to a serious compromise to India's suzerainty as an independent polity. For him, this concessional provision was thus not justified since no constituent units in federal India had the authority of having either a plebiscite or an independent constituent assembly to frame its own constitution, especially when the Constituent Assembly was already in the process of making one for the Union.

Mohani had hardly had supporters, and Article 306A which later became Article 370 in the 1950 Constitution was approved without a single dissent. Ayyangar thus concluded:

> the effect of this article is that the Jammu and Kashmir State which is now a part of India will continue to be a part of India, will be a unit of the future Federal Republic of India and the Union Legislature will get jurisdiction to enact laws on matters specified either in the Instrument of Accession or by later addition with the concurrence of the Government of the State. And steps have to be taken for the purpose of convening a Constituent Assembly in due course to frame a constitution for the state.[54]

Ayyangar's aim was to justify that concessions were absolutely 'temporary' since the Assembly agreed to have a plebiscite to ascertain 'the will of the people' and also the formation of a constituent assembly to devise a constitution for the state. That Article 306A was approved without much discussion confirms that the proceedings of the Assembly were stage-managed. As the available media sources suggest that when Article 306A was placed for discussion before the Congress Parliamentary Party, it provoked fierce debate and there was hardly a consensus among the members given the discriminatory nature of the

Article. Nobody in the meeting could digest the discriminatory treatment that was meted out to the state. Vallabhbhai Patel was reported to have been in accord with the discordant opinion though he hardly spoke since it meant a betrayal to the Congress pledge.[55]Jawaharlal Nehru and Vallabhbhai Patel persuaded the recalcitrant colleagues by reassuring them that the concessional Article 306A was likely to mobilize global opinion in India's favour in the light Pakistan's counter claim for the entire Kashmir.

Article 370 thus became integral to the Constitution of India. In the light of the assurances given in the Assembly, the Article guaranteed that the power of Parliament to make laws for the state shall be limited to

> (i) those matters in the Union List and the Concurrent List, which, in consultation with the Government of the State, are declared by the President to correspond to matters specified in the Instrument of Accession governing the accession of the State to the Dominion of India as the matters with respect to which the Dominion Legislature may make laws for that State; and (ii) such other matters in the said Lists as, with the concurrence of the State, the President may by order specify.

The second part of the Article is a further endorsement of the distinct constitutional status for the state. As it stipulates,

> notwithstanding anything in the foregoing provisions of this article, the President may, by public notification, declare that this article shall cease to be operative or shall be operative only with such exceptions and modifications and from such date as he may specify ... [and] that the recommendation of the Constituent Assembly ... shall be necessary before the President issues such a notification.

Article 370 though titled as 'Temporary Provisions', and included in Para XXI entitled 'Temporary, Transitional and Special Provisions' is a permanent feature of the Constitution of India which embodies the conceptual framework of relationship between of the Union of India and Jammu and Kashmir, and also lays down broad features of special status granted to the State. This is constitutionally guaranteed. In a 2015 judgment on reservation in government jobs, the Jammu and Kashmir High Court articulated its response in categorical terms. Very explicit in its articulation, the judgment underlines (a) the State of Jammu and Kashmir retained limited sovereignty and did not merge with the Dominion of India, like other princely states, that signed instrument of accession with the Union. The state continues to enjoy special status to the extent of limited sovereignty retained by the state. The limited sovereignty or special status guaranteed under Article 370 of the Constitution—only provision of the Constitution that applied to the State *ex-propriogorige* or on its own. Without Article 1, no other provision of the Constitution would be applicable to the State, except by Presidential order in consultation with the State in case the provision is akin to subjects delineated in instrument of accession and with concurrence of the State and (b) it is beyond amendment, repeal, or abrogation, inasmuch as Constituent Assembly of the State before its dissolution did not recommend its amendment or repeal. As per Article 370, the President is conferred with power to extend any provision of the Constitution to the State with 'such exceptions and modifications' as may be deemed fit subject to consultation or concurrence with the State government.[56]

As the judicial pronouncement confirms, Article 370 cannot be abrogated. The Division Bench of Justices Hasnain Masoodi and Janak Raj Kotwal categorically states that it is 'beyond amendment, repeal or abrogation' as the mechanism provided under clause 3 of the Article is no longer available with the dissolution of the State Constituent Assembly which was the only authority, endowed with powers to recommend abrogation or amendment in the Article. For the court, the Article does not seem to be an exception because Kashmir had 'limited sovereignty' when the Kashmiri ruler agreed to sign the instrument of accession following India's independence from colonialism.

An Article which was accepted because of the exigency of the situation gradually became an integral part of the existence of Jammu and Kashmir as a constituent province of the Union of India with all the special constitutional privileges. With a specific constitutional embargo, the President of India is restrained to act, according to Article 370, without 'consultation' and concurrence of 'the government of the state. Moreover, the authority of Indian parliament is further curtailed by clause 3 of Article 370 which makes the recommendation of the State Constituent Assembly mandatory in case this Article is sought to be changed or repealed which cannot be possible now.

Constitutional implications notwithstanding, the effort towards abrogating Article 370 will have serious internal political repercussions with global ramifications since strife in Jammu and Kashmir will create a constituency for those anti-democratic forces which are reportedly drawing sustenance from operators, located in different countries. Furthermore, it may not be politically useful for the National Democratic Alliance (NDA) government in Delhi to antagonize its alliance partner, People's Democratic Party (PDP) that is ruling the state of Jammu and Kashmir because (a) it will allow the opposition to characterize any move towards that as anti-secular and (b) it is likely to alienate the people in the state, especially in the Kashmir valley who always view any attack on Article 370 as debilitating for their identity. So, any kind of fiddling with the Article may mean playing with fire. Neither the present National Democratic Alliance Government nor the Government led by the PDP can afford to lose out on this count since both these political outfits had to struggle a lot to be in the saddles of power after a long political hibernation. For those living in Jammu and Kashmir that had suffered terribly due to the consolidation of terrorism-engineered anti-democratic forces, Article 370 is no longer as important an issue as in the past simply because it has become part and parcel of their being. There are important socio-economic issues, like poverty, hunger, and unemployment that need immediate attention. An opinion seems to have gained momentum highlighting the fact that involvement in the campaign for abrogation of Article 370 will lead Kashmiris nowhere except fomenting trouble and creating instability in the state. For the rest of India, the campaign for the abrogation of Article 370 will garner support for the NDA's leading partner, Bharatiya Janata Party (BJP), because of its discriminatory nature while in the Kashmir valley, in particular, it will create a fissure between two coalition partners at the cost of those who are fighting for political stability and consolidation of democratic processes at any cost. By highlighting the constitutional validity of Article 370, the Jammu and Kashmir High Court has raised an issue that cannot be addressed as easily as is construed given its obvious implications on what the country stands for.

Fashioning of a Unique Constitutional Design

Article 370 was a price that the founding fathers agreed to pay to retain Jammu and Kashmir as a constituent Indian province; it was also a concession to Sheikh Abdullah, the undisputed local leader who wanted 'people's raj in Kashmir [which means that] it will not be a government of any particular community but of all—Hindus, Muslims and Sikhs'.[57] Given his popularity, a word from him, informs an analyst, 'would have easily taken Kashmir to Pakistan, when Sardar Patel would have gladly allowed Kashmir to go if that would ensure easy assimilation of Hyderabad and Junagadh into India'.[58] True, it was a political concession that privileged the rights of a State over India's overall federal concern. The founding fathers did not face stiff opposition in the Assembly presumably because, as Granville Austin underlines, decisions were arrived at by consensus in the Assembly and the founding fathers were generally accommodative of diverse views and opinions.[59] This was possible since, Austin further emphasizes, 'the ability to think at different levels, without dogmatism, refusing to confine speculation within narrow systems, pervaded Indian society'.[60]

Article 370 is a source of discontent, if not serious resentment, since it constitutionalizes imbalances in India's federal arrangement. It is also a puzzle because Article 370 does not seem to have been grounded on the fundamental principles of federalism; instead, it justifies a constitutional arrangement supportive of a confederal system of government. Whether it is plausible in today's context cannot be decided so easily in view of the specific historical context in which Article 370 was incorporated in the 1950 Constitution of India. There is no doubt that the special treatment that was constitutionally guaranteed to Jammu and Kashmir despite being included in federal India may not appear to be justified in the changed political milieu. An easy option to address this constitutional anomaly is an amendment to the Constitution which, however, does not seem to be plausible given the adverse political implications in the province and elsewhere in the country. A precarious situation has thus emerged in which neither of the options—abrogation of Article 370 or its acceptance—provides an acceptable solution. A careful reading of the debates in the Constituent Assembly also shows that the founding fathers seem to have faced the same dilemma which was evident in their support for making Article 370 a temporary provision; this means that the Article was to be withdrawn if it was needed. As history has shown, it was a hope that dissipated soon due to a peculiar unfolding of socio-economic and political circumstances in the province. In fact, the idea was shelved and Article 370 became an integral part of India's federal arrangement in which the state of Jammu and Kashmir was allowed to retain its semi-independent constitutional identity.

In the constitutional discourse, Article 370 is a new conceptual intervention in the sense that by constitutionalizing the terms and conditions of the accession treaty between India and the erstwhile ruler of this princely state, it contributes to a persuasive argument in favour of autonomy within a federal structure of governance. Here, the argument draws on the principle of accommodation and reconciliation whereby a federal system is both constructed and consolidated. This further confirms that federalism cannot be understood, let alone conceptualized, merely as 'a constitutional design', but also 'a political arrangement' which is hardly static. This is a significant conceptual formulation in two complementary ways: on the one hand, it endows us with persuasive theoretical inputs to enable us to understand the consolidation of federal practices in a socio-culturally diverse polity; it also helps us comprehend, on the other, the importance of the political will in the shaping of constitutional norms, values, and principles in support of an arrangement which is not ordinarily endorsed within the available discursive tools of analysis for federalism. By being deviant from the conventional understanding of federalism as a 'holding together' mechanism, Article 370 is thus a unique constitutional experiment which is academically refreshing, ideologically innovative, and politically decisive.

Concluding Observations

Princely states were autonomous in the sense that they had the authority to govern their subjects in accordance with what they deemed appropriate; but, it was heavily restricted with their acceptance of the British suzerainty which means that they were not sovereign in the real sense of the term. In other words, it was a quid-pro-quo arrangement which was a source of political dividends for the British, while the rulers acquiesced since it helped them maintain their hegemony in the kingdoms that they had ruled. So long as the British authority was stable, the Indian States did not seem to be inclined to consider the option of being a part of a federal India, as Penderel Moon informs.[61] The scene had however undergone a sea-change as the War came to a close, and with the appointment of the Cabinet Mission in April, 1946, it was clear that the transfer of power was imminent. The fact that the princely states that declined to join a federated India in 1939 were willing to be part of the Constituent Assembly is also indicative of a substantial change in their attitudes. In the changed circumstances, when the British decided to withdraw from India, they perhaps had no option to explore, and, hence they agreed to take part in the deliberations in the Constituent Assembly for drafting the constitution. Nonetheless, there was an apprehension on the part of the States whether

> the Congress which is to rule India soon, ... is an adequate successor to the British Government [because] ... its leaders have shown themselves prone to be governed by their emotions rather than their reason, and it is composed of dissonant elements uneasily united only by their former common opposition to British rule. ... Unless the Congress adopts a policy to assuage the bitterness arising from its treatment of the States, there is grave doubt whether it will be able to withstand for the long the menace from the left, coupled with regionalism from the left.[62]

That some of the States did not seem to be as enthusiastic in joining the Assembly as others was evident when the Hyderabad Nizam distanced from the Negotiating Committee with the hope that the British government would stand by him. With the reluctance of the British government to support the Nizam, he was virtually left in the lurch which came out very clearly in his letter of 9 July 1947 to the Crown Representative. While expressing his helplessness, he thus wrote:

> I was hopeful that, in any event, you will not tolerate any pressure being brought to bear upon Hyderabad to drive (when all responsible leaders of opinion in the UK and in India have promised a free choice) to accept one particular alternative if I feel in my conscience and after grave deliberation that I am bound to reject it.[63]

Although the Nizam's demand was dismissed as 'impractical' and drawn on 'his selfish interest',[64] he however had persuaded the Crown Representative, Arthur Lothian to stand by him because the latter felt that 'no person of British origin who knows the fact can read this dignified and loyal statement without a feeling of shame at our tacit abandonment of Hyderabad to pressure of every sort to join it'.[65] Despite being convinced that the abandonment of Hyderabad was 'particularly amoral',[66] Lothian's suggestion hardly received any sympathetic hearing among those who presided over India's destiny just on the eve of independence. There was hardly a reference to this point in the Negotiating Committee's deliberation which also suggests that in the changed political milieu the States just became mere spectators of processes of which the making of a constitution was a significant step towards consolidating a unified India following the withdrawal of British.

There was another aspect which merits attention. A perusal of the discussion the Negotiating Committee to decide on the mode of election of representatives in the Assembly reveals that the tone of the discussion was not always friendly; in fact, it was acrimonious on occasions presumably because the States' representatives endeavoured hard to bargain as much as possible for themselves. Their claim however did not receive adequate attention since they lost the moral authority in view of the growing public resentment against 'monarchical-autocratic rule at their behest' and in favour of democratic governance in which the supremacy of the demos was to be established beyond question. That there were noticeable changes in their attitude to constitutionalize governance for a unified India was evident in the first meeting of the Assembly when Jawaharlal Nehru presented the Report of the States Committee on 28 April, 1947. Aware that serious differences with the States' rulers had cropped up during the course of the meeting of the Negotiating Committee, Nehru while underplaying this aspect, thus prefaced his observation by emphasizing that 'we have come here not to bargain with each other, not to have heated argument with each other, but to achieve results, and to bring those people, even though they might have doubts, into this Assembly ... to accomplish a task not only for the present but also for the future'.[67]

A great responsibility that the founding fathers had shouldered and Nehru, being a principal architect of constitutional governance in India had further reminded his colleagues by stating:

we meet ... under a heavy sense of responsibility [because] we are building for the future and we want to make sure that the building has strong foundations ... and [because] ... above all, we are meeting at a time when a number of disruptive forces are working in India pulling up this way or that way, and because, inevitably and unfortunately, when such forces are at work, there is a great deal of passion and prejudice in the air and our whole minds may be affected by it. We should not be deflected from that vision of the future which we ought to have, in thinking of the present difficulties. That is a dangerous thing which we ought to avoid because we are not building for today or tomorrow, we are making or trying to make a much more enduring structure.[68]

In an unambiguous way, Nehru set the tempo of the discussion by underlining that States were an integral part of the deliberations over the making of the constitution of India. Hinting at the probable adverse consequences of differences of opinion on the endeavour, Nehru further emphasized that it was detrimental to the gigantic task that they undertook to protect India's future as a nation. Interestingly, the States' representatives who held contrary views in the Negotiating Committee seem to have staged a volte-face when they were asked to present their opinion in the Assembly. In other words, by articulating their voice in an identical fashion, the princely states upheld the politico-ideological mission that Nehru had laid out. In his defence for joining hands with the constitution makers, Brojendra Lal Mitter of Baroda State, for instance, thus categorical mentioned:

we are at one with you [Nehru] in that the Indian Union should be strong in the Centre so that India may hold her head high in the comity of nations. We do not believe in isolated independent existence, which can only weaken the Union. We shall join you wholeheartedly in a spirit of cooperation and not in any spirit of securing special privileges at the cost of the Union. We shall endeavour to make the Constitution develop according to the genius and capacity of different units, so that the development may be natural and healthy.[69]

This was the sentiment which appears to have guided K.M. Panikkar of Bikaner State when he spoke in favour of joining hands with British India to draft a durable constitution. As is well-known, Bikaner's ruler was reluctant to be part of the opposition brigade that had opposed the 1935 federal scheme and also in the Negotiating Committee; he while challenging the proposal of electing representatives for the Assembly from the States, dissented when it was accepted. In the Constituent Assembly, the tone was not only reconciliatory, but also one of endorsement for the sake of creating 'a strong India' in future. As Panikkar argued,

> the taking of seats of certain representatives of Indian States today has a symbolic value which far outweighs the actual number of representatives who have joined, or the insignificance of numbers who have themselves joined. This is indeed a symbol of the unity to come and from the work that begins today, in cooperation between the representatives of the state and those of the Indian Provinces, we can really hope to look forward to the emergence of a Union of India.[70]

While Mitter and Panikkar's arguments drew on their concern for being pragmatic at a time when all other options were foreclosed, there were representatives who defended the decision by infusing with a moral tone. Seeking to placate the opposition, Jainarayan Vyas representing Jodhpur State, thus argued:

> it is a pleasure that we are today making history. We are sitting together with the representatives of the British Provinces and the representatives of the Rulers of the Indian States. ... It is a pleasure to find that we are here in sufficient numbers with you; and we assure you that we will cooperate with you in all possible ways in making the future Constitution, not merely in our self-interest but in that of the whole of India. We consider ourselves as parts of India, although some outsiders had raised walls between us. But these unnatural walls are crumbling today, and we hope that within a short time India would be absolutely one single unit.[71]

In a similar vein, T. Vijayaraghavachariar of Udaipur State was also persuaded. The concern for a stable and strong future India seems to have governed his choice, and, in a forceful manner, he thus mentioned:

> [A]ll of us will so put our heads together and so do our work that our children and our grand-children and generations yet unborn, will say, 'Our fathers and our grand-fathers sat in the year 1947 at Delhi and framed a constitution which stood the test of time' and on which history will say, 'Blessed are these men; they did their work and they laid the foundations rightly, and, on those foundations the future history of India will evolve.'[72]

Not only were they enthusiastic in their preference for a democratic constitution for a unified India, they also claimed to have been inspired by the ideals that Mahatma Gandhi represented. In view of their ideological compatibility with Gandhi's nonviolent struggle, the princely states became, it was claimed, a natural ally of India. This was categorically stated by P. Govinda Menon of Cochin State when he exhorted,

> the hundred millions of people of the Indian States never felt nor do they feel now, that they form an entity or group different from their 300 million brothers and sisters living in what is known as British India. ... Not only did the people of the States admire Mahatma Gandhi and other great leaders [who led India's freedom struggle], they neither felt nor did they take up the attitude that their lot lies elsewhere.[73]

There are three points that need attention to conceptualize the changing stances of the States' representative vis-à-vis the constitution of India and its making. First of all, following the British commitment to transfer power to the Indian hands, the princely states seem to have lost a dependable partner willing to stand by them in case of a threat to their existence as a semi-autonomous political unit under the British suzerainty. In the changed environment, with the creation of India being an independent country, and also their geographical location of being encircled by India put them at a disadvantage from which there was hardly an escape route. Second, the voluntary surrender of the majority of the rulers by signing the treaty of accession more or less on those terms and conditions which the Government of India had set out for them create a situation in which those who held contrary views seem to have lost their zeal to fight for their sovereign existence. Being placed in circumstances when they had hardly had the capacity to independently challenge the Indian claim because of peculiar turns and twists of history, the princely states seem to have been drawn to the Negotiating Committee as perhaps the only means to secure whatever benefits they could accrue for them. So, it was the best possible option for them under the prevalent milieu. Finally, the declaration of India's independence also triggered organized campaigns for democratic rule in most of the princely states which the rulers failed to contain primarily because they seem to have alienated the ruled, to a significant extent, by being partisan and feudalistic in their dealings with them. The examples of Junagadh and Travancore are illustrative here. In the face of the mass opposition from within the States and also Patel's willingness to support the agitating groups, the rulers had no option but to leave the kingdoms. The consequences of their non-cooperation would be 'disastrous', as a note from the Government of India suggests, unless the recalcitrant rulers came to terms with the proposed system of governance drawing on democracy. As the note mentioned,

> in the democratic and free India, large scale administrative and territorial integration of Indian States was as inevitable as the liquidation of autocracy. ... [And], the Princes ... must realise that those amongst them who have set their eye on misplaced ambition, not only follow a suicidal path for themselves but also imperil the future of the entire body of Princes.[74]

The princely states were to become a part of history soon, as the above note stipulates. It was easier for the Indian Government to tighten its grip also because the erstwhile rulers had nobody to bank upon in case of need.

What was, then, the role of the princely states in the making of the 1950 Constitution when they actually endorsed the terms and conditions on which they agreed to be integrated with the Union? Their contribution did not therefore seem to be so critical although by being willing (not so, on occasions) to be a part of the democratic experiment of which the constitution-making was a first significant step, they appear to have reinforced the endeavour of the nationalist forces towards constitutionalizing a formerly colonized nation in and around democratic ethos. The fact that the States' representatives zealously participated in the debates in the Assembly also confirms that not only did they accept democracy but also appreciated the system of governance that it contributed. Even with regard to the fixation of the amount, admissible to the rulers as part of the privy purse, the Princes, as shown above, had hardly had a say. Nonetheless, the adoption of a very discriminatory Article 370 for Jammu and Kashmir also demonstrates that, under different set of circumstances, the founding fathers had succumbed to the conditionalities that the incumbent ruler, supported by a very popular local leader, put forward as a precondition for its integration with independent India. Was it merely a strategic response or a *real-politik* design? No answer can be conclusive for obvious reasons. What can thus be argued now that founding fathers upheld their concern for democracy and democratic governance while justifying the liquidation of the kingdoms of yester-years. The debates in the Constituent Assembly are an ample testimony to this claim. Besides the operation Polo, the code name of police action in September, 1948 by the newly independent India against the Nizam-ruled Hyderabad State and the acceptance of Article 370 for Jammu and Kashmir, there was hardly any significant opposition from among those who represented the erstwhile rulers in the Constituent Assembly. Instead, they readily accepted the Enlightenment values which the framers seem to have privileged while being engaged in drafting the constitution for building a democratic India on its foundation; they may not have been innovative in their approaches to the issues of constitution and constitutionalism though their role was no less insignificant in seeking to build a democratic constitutional fabric for independent India by reiterating powerful, but familiar, arguments in its favour.

Notes and References

1. V.P. Menon, *The Story of the Integration of the Indian States* (London: Longman, 1955), p. 20.
2. Menon, *The Story of the Integration of the Indian States*, p. 20.
3. Menon, *The Story of the Integration of the Indian States*, p. 24.
4. Quoted in Menon, *The Story of the Integration of the Indian States*, p. 25.
5. Quoted in Menon, *The Story of the Integration of the Indian States*, p. 28.
6. Arthur Cunningham Lothian, *Kingdoms of Yesterday* (London: John Murray, 1951), p. 147.
7. Penderel Moon, *Divide and Quit: An Eyewitness Account of the Partition of India*, (New Delhi: Oxford University Press, 1998) (reprint with a new introduction), p. 18.
8. Editorial in *The Times of India*, New Delhi, 5 March, 1938.
9. India Office Records, L/P&S/13/551, Linlithgow to Zetland (Secretary of State), 5 April, 1939.
10. Ian Copland pursues the story in his *The Princes of India in the Endgame of Empire, 1917–1947* (Cambridge: Cambridge University Press, 1997), pp. 80–98.
11. Appendix II, reproduced in V.P. Menon, *The Story of the Integration of the Indian States*, p. 339.
12. Appendix II, Menon, *The Story of the Integration of the Indian States*, p. 339.
13. The Statement of the Cabinet Mission, 16 May 1947, *Transfer of Power*, Vol. VII, p. 585.

14. India Office Records, R/3/1/143, Nawab of Bhopal to Wavell, Viceroy, 17 August 1946.

15. Nawab of Bhopal to Conrad Corfield, 23 November 1946, *Transfer of Power*, Vol. IX, pp. 156–7.

16. Ian Copland, *The Princes of India in the Endgame of Empire, 1917–1947* (Cambridge: Cambridge University Press, 1997), p. 257.

17. As Gyanesh Kudaisya has shown that there were two phases in which the process was completed. In the initial 1947–8 period, several princely states had joined the republic by signing the instruments of accession. The second phase, between 1949 and 1956, was marked by interim arrangements—princely states either joined the republic unconditionally or merged in an ad-hoc manner with the existing British Indian provinces. In this period, many of the leading princes served as *Rajpramukh*s (the head of administration or governor) and performed important constitutional functions. However, the curtain was drawn on the princely states in 1956 when Part C states (which were allowed to retain partial administrative autonomy) were abolished in 1956 on the recommendation of the 1956 State Reorganization Commission. Gyanesh Kudaisya, *India in the 1950s: A Republic in the Making* (New Delhi: Oxford University Press, 2017), pp. 38–44.

18. The rulers of Travancore and Maharaja of Kolhapur expressed their resentment in their letters to Mountbatten of 30 July and 11 August 1947 respectively. *Transfer of Power*, Vol. XII, pp. 414 and 654.

19. Mountbatten's address in the Constituent Assembly quoted in Menon's, *The Story of the Integration of the Indian States*, p. 83.

20. N. Gopalaswami Ayyangar's intervention in the meeting of the Negotiating Committee, held on 8 February, 1947—reproduced in B. Shiva Rao (ed.), *The Framing of India's Constitution* (Select Documents), Vol. 1, (Delhi: Universal Publishing House, 2004) (reprint), pp. 652–3.

21. Resolution adopted at the Princes' meeting held in Bombay, 2 April 1947—reproduced in Rao, *The Framing of India's Constitution*, p. 632.

22. It was made clear by Pethick-Lawrence (one of the three members of the Cabinet Mission which also included Stafford Cripps and AV Alexander) who categorically stated that the Cabinet Mission's proposals provide for the representation of the States in the Constituent Assembly on a population basis. This would give the States 93 seats out of a total of 389. The manner in which these seats would be filled was left for negotiation between a committee appointed by the Indian States and a committee appointed by the British India side of the Constituent Assembly. The States have appointed a Committee for this purpose. When a committee has been appointed by the

British India part of the Constituent Assembly, negotiations on this matter can begin'. *Transfer of Power*, Vol. IX, p. 148.

23. Press communiqué regarding the representation of the princely states, issued by the secretary of the Constituent Assembly, 9 Februay 1947— reproduced in Rao's *The Framing of India's Constitution*, p. 618.

24. In a detailed note of 7 February 1947 to the Negotiating Committee, the Baroda Dewan demanded that 'considering the special obligations which Baroda State has on its shoulder arising out of the integration with the Republic of India, it becomes necessary that one at least of the three members to the Constituent Assembly should be His Highness' nominee. The larger interests of the State need to be properly safeguarded. Taking all these factors into account, the demand is justified'. This proposal of B.L. Mitter, the Dewan of Baroda was placed before the States Committee of the Constituent Assembly on 7 February 1947. This is available in Rao's, *The Framing of India's Constitution*, p. 615.

25. Jawaharlal Nehru's address of 1 March 1947, in the Negotiating Committee, reproduced Rao's, *The Framing of India's Constitution*, p. 696.

26. Joint Press Communiqué of 2 March 1947—reproduced in Rao, *The Framing of India's Constitution*, p. 720.

27. Jawaharlal Nehru's address of 8 February 1947 in the Negotiating Committee, reproduced in Rao, *The Framing of India's Constitution*, p. 672.

28. Jawaharlal Nehru's address of 9 February 1947 in the Negotiating Committee, reproduced Rao's, *The Framing of India's Constitution*, p. 674.

29. Vallabhbhai Patel's address in the Negotiating Committee, 8 February 1947, reproduced in Rao's, *The Framing of India's Constitution*, p. 661.

30. The address by the Raja of Bilaspur on 8 February 1947—reproduced in Rao's, *The Framing of India's Constitution*, p. 666.

31. Vallabhbhai Patel, 12 October 1949, *Constituent Assembly Debates*, Book No. 5, p. 161.

32. Patel, *Constituent Assembly Debates*, p. 162.

33. Patel, *Constituent Assembly Debates*, p. 164.

34. R.K. Sidhwa (Central Provinces and Berar), 13 October 1949, *Constituent Assembly Debates*, Book No. 5, pp. 179–80.

35. Sarangadhar Das (Orissa), 13 October 1949, *Constituent Assembly Debates*, Book No. 5, p. 186.

36. Jainarain Vyas (Jodhpur), 13 October 1949, *Constituent Assembly Debates*, Book No. 5, p. 193.

37. Das, *Constituent Assembly Debates*, p. 187.

38. Vyas, *Constituent Assembly Debates*, p. 194.

39. P. Govinda Menon (Mysore State), 13 October 1949, *Constituent Assembly Debates*, Book No. 5, p. 198.

40. Menon, *Constituent Assembly Debates*, pp. 198–9.

41. Annie Mascarene (Travancore and Cochin Union), 12 October 1949, *Constituent Assembly Debates*, Book No. 5, p. 174.

42. Patel, *Constituent Assembly Debates*, p. 164.

43. The rulers of Bikaner, Gwalior, Kohlapur, among others, tried to mobilize opinion against government decision on the Privy Purse by giving press statements in the leading national dailies. Arthur Lothian, *Kingdoms of Yesterday* (London: John Murray, 1951), p. 38.

44. Patel, *Constituent Assembly Debates*, p. 166.

45. Speech of Vallabhbhai Patel in Lucknow, 6 January, 1948, reproduced in *For a United India: Speeches of Sardar Patel, 1947–1950* (Delhi: Publications Division, Government of India, 1967), p. 69.

46. Lothian, *Kingdoms of Yesterday*, p. 201.

47. Gyanesh Kudaisya, *India in the 1950s: A Republic in the Making* (New Delhi: Oxford University Press, 2017), p. 50.

48. http://www.centralexcisehyderabad4.gov.in/documents/history/1947_2.PDF, *Instrument of Accession of Jammu and Kashmir State*, dated, 26 October 1947 (accessed on 20 November, 2017).

49. Sheikh Abdullah's statement—quoted in AG Noorani, *Article 370: A Constitutional History of Jammu and Kashmir* (New Delhi: Oxford University Press, 2011), p. 78.

50. Sheikh Abdullah's statement—quoted in AG Noorani, *Article 370: A Constitutional History of Jammu and Kashmir* (New Delhi: Oxford University Press, 2011), p. 81.

51. N. Gopalaswami Ayyangar (Madras), 17 October 1949, *Constituent Assembly Debates*, Book No. 5, p. 424.

52. Ayyangar, *Constituent Assembly Debates*, p. 424.

53. Maulana Hasarat Mohani (United Provinces), 17 October, 1949, *Constituent Assembly Debates*, Book No. 5, p. 428.

54. Ayyangar (Madras), *Constituent Assembly Debates*, p. 427.

55. L.K. Advani, 'When the Congress Party opposed Article 370', *The Indian Express*, 17 February 1992.

56. http://judis.nic.in/Judis_Jammu/list_new2_Pdf.asp?FileName=1843, Ashok Kumar and Others versus the State of Jammu and Kashmir, 2015, (accessed on 30 November, 2016).

57. Sheikh Abdullah quoted in M.J. Akbar, *India: The Seize Within: Challenges to a Nation's Unity* (London: Penguin, 1985), p. 234.

58. M.J. Akbar, *India: The Seize Within: Challenges to a Nation's Unity* (London: Penguin, 1985), p. 234.

59. Granville Austin, *The Indian Constitution: cornerstone of a nation* (New Delhi: Oxford University Press, 1966), pp. 311–21.

60. Austin, *The Indian Constitution: Cornerstone of a Nation*, p. 321.

61. Penderel Moon, *Divide and Quit: An Eyewitness Account of the Partition of India* (New Delhi: Oxford University Press, 1998) (reprint with a new introduction), p. 18.

62. Lothian, *Kingdoms of Yesterday*, pp. 197–8.

63. Appendix III, letter of 9 July 1947 of Nizam of Hyderabad to the Crown Representative, reproduced in Lothian's, *Kingdoms of Yesterday*, p. 214.

64. Besides accusing the Nizam of being 'selfish', Mountbatten further stated that 'The Indian Dominion, consisting of [three-fourths] of India, and with immense resources and important strategic position in the Indian Ocean, is a Dominion which we cannot afford to estrange for the sake of the so-called independence of the States'. Mountbatten to Listowel, 8 August 1947, *Transfer of Power*, Vol. XII, p. 587.

65. Lothian, *Kingdoms of Yesterday*, pp. 190–1.

66. Lothian, *Kingdoms of Yesterday*, p. 192.

67. Jawaharlal Nehru, 28 April, 1947, *Constituent Assembly Debates*, Book No. 1, p. 375.

68. Nehru, *Constituent Assembly Debates*, pp. 374–5.

69. Brojendra Lal Mitter (Baroda State), 28 April 1947, *Constituent Assembly Debates*, Book No. 1, p. 367.

70. K.M. Panikkar (Bikaner State), 28 April 1947, *Constituent Assembly Debates*, Book No. 1, p. 368.

71. Jainarayan Vyas (Jodhpur State), 28 April 1947, *Constituent Assembly Debates*, Book No. 1, p. 371.

72. T. Vijayaraghavachariar of Udaipur State, 28 April 1947, *Constituent Assembly Debates*, Book No. 1, p. 370.

73. P. Govinda Menon (Cochin State), 28 April 1947, *Constituent Assembly Debates*, Book No. 1, p. 369.

74. A note of 27 December 1950 of V.P. Menon to Baroda ruler, Pratap Singh—reproduced in Menon's *The Story of the Integration of the Indian States*, p. 293.

5   Major Colonial Designs towards Constitutionalizing India

The Constitution of India had both colonial and national-ist imprints. By devising mechanisms of sharing power with their Indian counterparts, the colonial rulers set in motion processes of constitutionalizing India which drew its inspiration from the fundamental ethos of British Enlightenment. There were concerted efforts by the alien state, in other words, to conceptualize constitutional governance within the theoretical framework of liberalism. The inevitable outcome was the growing support for the Westminster model of democracy as perhaps a panacea for all troubles that the colonized had to face. Despite occasional challenges to liberal democracy by those who did not seem persuaded, parliamentary democracy had prevailed over other ideological options since Indian National Congress and its allies were convinced of its effectiveness as a form of governance for India. How was it possible? At one level, the increasing acceptance of liberal democracy was an offshoot of the British initiatives to involve the Indians in administration which was primarily a colonial strategy to weaken the efforts against colonialism. This was further strengthened by those nationalist leaders, from the Moderates to Gandhi and Jawaharlal Nehru who, unlike the former, demanded complete independence, who, by being ideologically baptised in liberalism during their growing-up years, appeared to have found its merit which was strong enough to sway them for what they stood for. The chapter thus makes two arguments: first, the structure of governance that evolved during colonialism and its aftermath was drawn on the fundamental principles of liberal democracy that was rooted in the efforts that the colonial government undertook as a strategy by dispersing power; in other words, the idea had gradually percolated down to the grassroots presumably because it generated a hope among a sizeable section of the colonized who now became part and parcel of colonial governance. Second, the fact that the leading nationalists accepted liberalism as an empowering ideology strengthened its base in India; it was therefore not surprising that the Moderates who never pressed for complete independence and their opponents converged by being appreciative of liberal constitutional values which also confirms that the British-initiated processes of constitutionalism continued to remain critical whenever the nationalists articulated their preferences for a specific kind of constitution.

Keeping these two arguments in view, the chapter thus proposes to pursue the discussion in two complementary parts: on the one hand, there will be an analytical account of all the legislative endeavours that the colonial government adopted to efficiently manage administration in the context of the growing disenchantment of the colonized with colonialism; the discussion shall also be devoted to explore, on the other hand, the nationalist alternative which, despite having been drawn on contrasting political perspectives, was not radically different in tenor presumably because of the nationalist faith in liberalism as a libertarian ideological design.

Major Initiatives by the Colonial Government

Colonialism expanded its control in India in two distinct ways: first, by tactfully following the *divide et imperā* strategy that created and sustained the schism between the two major communities of Hindus and

Muslims. The British strategy worked favourably because of the socio-economic differences that separated these two communities. In course of time, the divide and rule formula not only consolidated the British rule in India, but also created conditions for the politically under-privileged sections to rise as meaningful partners in governance. So, it cut both ways: on the one hand, the chasm between communities, based on genuine socio-economic differences as well, made the task of governance easier for the ruler; this also, on the other hand, led to a process whereby the peripheral communities became a powerful political voice in the nationalist struggle for independence. Second, drawn on the classical liberal-democratic tradition, the British ruler introduced several legal steps to consolidate the empire by gradually opening-up administration to the Indians. Along with the application of force, the British government also adopted various reform schemes to inject constitutional values that shaped the nationalist campaign to a significant extent. It will therefore not be incorrect to suggest that the British rule survived in India with least coercion because of the role of the Indian collaborators in defending the empire. Except in the context of the 1942 open rebellion, the collaborative network of support had never shown signs of collapse. The adoption of various reforms by the British government created conditions in which Indians felt attached with the imperial rule that finally disintegrated due to its internal contradictions and also the growing nationalist consolidation opposed to foreign rule. Focusing on the landmark constitutional designs during the British rule, this chapter is an analytical statement on the British politico-legal strategies to consolidate the Raj. These designs, undoubtedly concessions to the ruled, were also devices to weaken the nationalist agitation as and when it became a serious threat to the government. In other words, while the British liberal tradition may have contributed to the constitutional reforms, one cannot deny the growing strength of the nationalist campaign, Gandhian or otherwise, that forced the British to introduce measures to defuse crisis.

An uncritical look at the selective, but major landmark constitutional initiatives during the colonial rule may lead one to conclude that these were initiated by the British for the Indians. Hence, the spirit of nationalism is underrated. If one goes beyond the surface, what is evident is that the inclusion of Indians in administration was an outcome of the British effort to defuse popular discontent. Therefore, the argument that every constitutional drive was initiated by the Raj is totally unfounded. History reveals that there were situations which forced the British authority to adopt measures to control agitation. For instance, the Congress campaign in the 1880s contributed a lot to the introduction of the 1893 reforms. Behind the 1909 Morley-Minto Reforms lay the Swadeshi Movement and revolutionary nationalism. Similarly, the 1919 Montague-Chelmsford Reforms were attempts at resolving crises that began with the Home Rule League campaign and climaxed with the 1919 Rowlatt Satyagraha and the Non Cooperation Movement of 1910–21. To a large extent, the Gandhian Civil Disobedience Movement (1930–2) accounted for the introduction of constitutional measures seeking to involve Indian politicians in public administration.

Furthermore, the interpretation of these constitutional designs remains partial unless linked with the broader socio-economic and political processes in which they were conceptualized. An attempt to analyse the structure and dynamics of constitutional politics without reference to the broader social matrix and economic nexus is futile because the political-constitutional structure reflects economic and social networks, religio-cultural beliefs and even the nationalist ideology which impinged on the organized world of administrative and constitutional structure. So an urgent and unavoidable task for an analyst is not to completely ignore the broader socio-economic context but to ascertain its relative importance in shaping a particular constitutional initiative. For instance, the 1932 Communal Award was believed to have been initiated by the British to expand political activity among the Muslims in Bengal and Punjab. But, as studies have shown, it was also a concession the British was forced to grant in order make the maintenance of the Empire easier.[1] The sharing of power with the native elites was thus prompted by considerations other than merely British initiatives.

The evolution of colonialism in India will continue to remain an interesting area for research for a variety of reasons. Prominent among them is certainly the process in which colonialism sustained its grip in India by creating a strong collaborative network and also by successfully pursuing a divide-and-rule strategy to scuttle efforts at unifying socio-economically separated communities. The strength of British colonialism lies in the fact that unlike their European counterparts, the British rulers expanded and also maintained their presence not merely by coercion, but also by creating circumstances in which they emerged as the best possible option by the Indians who remained highly divisive due to various socio-economic and political reasons. The constitutional landmarks that we have referred to are a clear testimony to those imperial efforts that defused opposition rather easily on most occasions. What was distinct about British colonialism was its success in welding a significant section of population to the system of governance that the British introduced. It was possible perhaps due to its triumph in ideologically moulding people towards liberal political values and ethos. Barring the militant nationalists, most of the nationalists were content with the method of three Ps (petition, prayer, and protest) until the rise of Gandhi who radically transformed the complexion of anti-British confrontation.

A careful study of the British rule in its initial phase suggests liberalism created a space for the growing involvement of the Indians in administration. Two substantial events changed the course of colonialism: (a) the founding of the universities of Calcutta, Madras, and Bombay helped develop an articulate opinion of the educated Indians on the British rule. It captured the growing discontent among the Indians who always remained, for obvious reasons, peripheral in administration; (b) The inauguration of the Indian National Congress in 1885 created a new platform to ventilate the grievances of the ruled. This also became a forum for the Indians to articulate demands for better rule. The outcome of which was the 1892 Indian Councils Act. As the Act underlines, its aim was:

[T]o widen and expand the functions of the Government of India, and to give further opportunities to the non-official and native elements in Indian society to take part in the work of the Government, and in that way, to lend official recognition to that remarkable development both of political interest and political capacity that had been visible among the higher classes of Indian society since the Government of India was taken over by the Crown in 1858.[2]

The Act provided for the enhanced membership of the Councils. It was mandatory for the government to consult the representative bodies and institutions, approved by the government, before selecting nominees for the Councils. Besides legislative powers, the Councils were also empowered to pull the Executive on financial matters though it had no power to either revise or reject decisions on this matter. However, the growing weightage of the Councils is indicative of a sea change in colonial rule. As Morley, the Secretary of State, articulated, 'there are two rival schools of thought, one of which believes that better government of Indian depends on efficiency, and that efficiency is, in fact, the end of British rule in India. The other school, while not neglecting efficiency, looks also to what is called political concessions.'[3] This declaration laid one of the foundational principles of the British administration in India. As a first step, a Royal Commission was appointed in 1907 to look into the administration that seemed to have lost its viability in the context of growing discontent among the ruled. The aim of the Commission was to provide an administration which was adapted to the changed social, economic, and political realities of India. While recommending the corrective measures, the Commission was guided by the following factors; (a) the difficulties of ruling the vast sub-continent from a single headquarter and the inevitable failure in the statesmanship and efficiency in administration; (b) the difficulties of applying uniform schemes of development for the provinces which are socio-culturally diverse; (c) to instil a sense of responsibility among those engaged in provincial and local administration; and (d) to strengthen the colonial rule by educating people in the values of strong administration. On the basis of the recommendation of the Commission, a bill was introduced in 1908 which became the 1909 Morley-Minto Reforms. As a political scheme seeking to strengthen colonial rule in India, the 1909 Act introduced a profound change with long-term effects in representation of communities in Councils. This is the beginning of a trend that gradually unfolded, as will be shown below by dwelling on the legislative steps that gave impetus to the steady growth and consolidation of representative institutions in India.

These landmark constitutional experiments had a role in permanently dividing major communities in India on the basis of religion and other socio-economic denominations. Both the Hindus and Muslims redefined their identities through a process of contestation of vision, contestation of beliefs, and contestation of history. The period between 1909 and 1947, when major constitutional experiments were undertaken, sharply shows the mutation in the formation of Hindus and Muslims as communities opposed to each other in the political arena. What was distinctive about this period was the growth of the communities as political units always in a permanent adversarial relationship with the members of the 'other' community. This was further consolidated following the introduction of the communal electorate in the 1937 provincial elections. With the acceptance of the principle of majority, Muslims automatically became most powerful community in Bengal and Punjab by their sheer demographic strength. In other words, religious identity as a demographic category became probably the single most crucial criterion in determining the distribution of governmental power in these Muslim-majority provinces. The 1935 Government of India Act reiterated the divide-and-rule strategy by formally recognizing that Muslims needed to be treated separately as a distinct, but neglected minority in India. This was a decisive constitutional intervention because not only did it establish the principle of majority as sacrosanct in democracy, it also made the Muslims self-conscious of their critical importance in governance in India. It is now possible to argue that the 1935 Act definitely shifted the centre of political activity in Bengal to the east of the province. Not by virtue of any inherent superiority of the Muslims but simply because in a democratically elected legislature, as a contemporary report underlines, 'the weight of numbers tells and the teeming millions of East Bengal—sixty percent of their being Muslims outweighed in point of numbers the more educated Hindus of the South, West and extreme north of the province'.[4] The migration of power to the countryside took place in the context of a major realignment in the social bases of political power.

The 1935 Government of India Act was certainly a powerful constitutional intervention that the colonial rulers made to accommodate the nationalist zeal within, of course, the colonial administrative format. This is also illustrative of the efforts at legitimizing the growing democratic aspirations of the ruled in India through a constitutional device. Interestingly, the 1935 Act remained the strongest influence during the making of the 1950 Constitution for free India. Some 250 clauses of the present Constitution were, in fact, lifted from the Government of India Act. Although the political system of independent India draws its sustenance from universal adult franchise and political sovereignty, rules are undoubtedly derived from its colonial past. The most striking provisions that the Constitution of India derived from its 1935 counterpart are 'the Emergency provisions' that enable the President to suspend the democratically elected governments and fundamental rights of the citizens.

There is no doubt that the postcolonial state in India inherited its habits of governance from colonial practices. Furthermore, its *Weltanschauung* (world view) is based on 'the mixed legacies of colonial rule' that upheld rule of law, bureaucracy, citizenship, parasitic landlords, modern political institutions, and 'two-track tradition of protest and participation'.[5] What accounts for relative stability for colonialism in India was certainly its ability to adapt to the changed socio-political circumstances also gradual but steady 'internalization' of domination by the subjects of colonial rule, which provoked an analyst to characterize colonialism as 'an intimate enemy'[6] because the dominated saw the virtues of being dominated for their own betterment. Colonialism was thus not seen as an absolute evil but complementary to India's rise as an independent nation in future. The statement may not be politically correct. Nonetheless, it can safely be argued that colonialism provided critical impetus to various processes that finally resulted in serious political mobilization against imperialism in India. Whether nationalism or democratization—they had their roots in the long history of colonialism and in this sense colonialism remained a significant force behind the rise of India as an independent nation in 1947.

The Unfolding of the Colonial Design of Governance

The nature of the British administration also varied: under the East India Company, the Crown was not directly involved in administration; it was peripherally linked as the supreme authority controlling the Company was the British Queen and the Company functioned under its overall administrative jurisdiction. Empowered by the Crown, two institutions were entrusted with the operation of the Company in India: the Court of Proprietors and the Court of Directors. These two Courts were largely independent and decided the course of action for the Company in India. The Queen's charter authorized the Courts to fulfil its goal in India without almost any restriction. The Company functioned in a ruthless manner, guided solely by its commercial interests. Although there were attempts by the Company rulers to bring about reforms in administration, they remained largely academic in nature. Complaints against the 'misrule' of the Company poured in and as a result, the House of Commons appointed a Committee of Secrecy to look into the authenticity of the complaints. The findings of the Committee went seriously against the Company. The result was the adoption of the Regulating Act of 1773, the first formal articulation of the British supremacy over a part of India that abolished the Dual Government of the Company.

The Regulating Act of 1773

This Act was the first measure of the British Parliament that directly intervened in the affairs of the Company. Although the power of the Company's Directors remained unaltered, the regulation that the Company was required to keep the Treasury Bench informed reduced its independence drastically. The Governor of Bengal, Warren Hastings, was designated as the Governor General of Bengal who would be assisted by a Council of four members, recommended by the Crown. According to the Act, the supreme authority rested not with the Governor General, but with the Council, guided by the principle of majority while taking a decision vis-à-vis India. While in India, the Council remained supreme, but it had to function under the supervision, direction, and control of the Court of Directors in London.

The Act was a major milestone in India's public administration for four specific reasons: firstly, by restraining the Company, the Act simply endorsed the important values of governance in administration. As the Company was involved in public administration in India, it hardly could avoid its obligations to the ruled. The intervention by the Crown clearly suggests that the British government was not at ease with the way, the Company was managing its affairs in India. So, the Act was largely an outcome of an ideological concern of the rulers in England for the governed in India. There is no denying the fact that colonial interests remained paramount though the Act contributed to a social and political ambience that led to the adoption of ameliorating legal enactments in course of time. Secondly, rejecting the individual-based administration, as epitomized by the Governor, the Act also made the Council accountable to the Crown. This was a significant break with the past because public administration was not merely governance, but governance with a purpose. So, apart from laying the structure of administration, the 1773 Act sought to change the ideological basis of Company rule that was now guided by the well-established principles of administration, evolved in the long tradition of Westminster democracy under the Crown. Thirdly, the Act marked the beginning of centralization. The Governor-General-in-Council became the supreme ruler in India and the Governors of three presidencies of Bengal, Madras, and Bombay were reduced to subordinate governments. Within the overall control of the Governor General, the Act however demarcated administrative domains of the Governors of the presidencies that was critical to the evolution of public administration in India. By involving the Council in administration, the Act also inaugurated a new trend in the Company's rule that no longer remained, at least theoretically, as arbitrary as before. The Governor General was required to consult the Council and was also made accountable to the British Parliament. Finally, the most outstanding feature of the Act was the establishment of a Supreme Court in Calcutta. This Court was founded under the Letters of Patent with Elijah Impey as the Chief Justice and three other judges. Primarily a Court of record, it also had civil, criminal, ecclesiastical, admiralty, equity, and supervisory jurisdiction over the whole Presidency and any person in the employment of the Company even outside the Presidency.

As evident, the Act was most critical to public administration in India because (a) it laid down the skeleton of the governmental system of modern India, and (b) all subsequent enactments can be said to have either enlarged or amplified the basic text of the 1773 Act. Despite its limited appeal in today's context, the Act was certainly radical in its approach and content then. By holding the Company responsible to the Parliament, the Act sought to shape Company's administration in accordance with principles of 'formal' democracy. Although the Act recommended unitary command by suggesting the supremacy of the Governor-General-in-Council, it was also a device for 'limited' decentralization because the Governors of the presidencies remained independent, at least administratively, within their respective domains.

The Regulating Act of 1773 was not sufficiently equipped to address the administrative distortions in India under the Company rule. The parliamentary committee under Edmund Burke exposed the arbitrary functioning of the Governor General and Chief Justice and recommended for their recall. But it was not possible because the Board of proprietors refused to respect the recommendation. This led to a constitutional crisis because it also demonstrated the lack, if not absence, of parliamentary control on the Company rule in India. In response, the Pitt's India Act of 1784 was enacted. According to this Act, the Court of Directors were allowed 'free hands' to manage the commercial affairs of the Company in India while in political sphere, the authority was vested in a new body, known as the Board of Control comprising six Commissioners. Appointed by the King, the Board had in it the Chancellor of the Exchequer, a Secretary of State and four Privy Councillors. The Board retained full powers of 'superintendence, direction and control' of all operations of the civil and military governments of the British territorial possessions in the East Indies. The Court of proprietors lost its hegemony in Company's affairs except in the election of Directors who were given the authority to make appointments of all posts in India though the Crown was authorized to recall any person in the employment of the Company.

In the evolution of public administration in India, the Pitt's Act was an important benchmark for two reasons: first, the Act established the supremacy of the British Crown in territories controlled by the Company. Administration was now an elaborate arrangement involving those appointed by the King and accountable to the Parliament. Through various structural mechanisms, the British government sought to create a system of governance in India which was qualitatively different from any of the preceding administrations. Second, this Act introduced a new policy in relation to the Indian princes by laying down that the Company should follow a policy of 'non-interference' in their affairs. In other words, the Company was restricted to those areas which were already under its control. The non-intervention policy was short-lived and by the end of the eighteenth century, especially with the arrival of Wellesley as Governor General, the British Empire in India was transformed into the British empire of India. Wellesley accomplished his task both by military stringency and strategic 'subsidiary alliances' with the Indian princes. What was remarkable about Wellesley, apart from his role as an empire-builder, was his concern for an efficient administration because he believed that without skilled administrators the Empire could not survive. With this intent, he founded a college at Fort William for the training of the Company's civil servants. From here, one can trace the genesis of Indian Civil Service that was to be founded soon.

The Charter Act of 1833

Of all the acts, enacted by the British Parliament to govern the East India Company in India, the Charter Act of 1833 is perhaps the most watershed legislative intervention in India's public administration. Why was such an Act necessary? The administration, both in India and Britain, confronted new circumstances following the rapid expansion of the British Empire in India. The administrative machinery was not adequate in holding the empire together. In Britain, parliamentary reforms led to a new form of governance largely due to the influence of Enlightenment philosophy with its emphasis on enlightened liberalism. There was a clamour for free trade with India, unrestricted immigration of Europeans into India, reform of laws and improvement of education in India. Two ardent liberals who set forth the changes in the British attitude during this period were T.B. Macaulay and James Mill; while the former, also a parliamentarian, was the Secretary to the Board of Control and latter was the Examiner of India correspondence at India House.

As the Company lost its commercial monopoly in India following the acceptance of the Charter Act, all restrictions to European immigration into India were removed. Besides, the Act introduced new devices of administrative control in India which are as follows:

1. The Governor General, now designated as Governor General of India was vested with supreme authority in so far as civil, military and revenue administration were concerned. In the centralized administration, the Governors of other provinces were subordinates to the Governor General who became the pivot of the British administration in India.

2. All decisions of the Governor General and Governors overriding the decisions of their respective Executive Councils were to be supported by recorded statement of reasons. This was a rider in the stipulation to restrain those holding supreme authority.

3. All legislative powers were vested in the Governor-General-in-Council and the provincial governments lost their legislative

powers. Laws approved by the Governor-General-in-Council came to be designated as acts and the endorsement of the Supreme Court for their validity was withdrawn. These acts were applicable to all Courts.

4. A Law Member who was to be an English Barrister was to be appointed to the Governor-General-in-Council in an advisory capacity. This appointment was certainly a significant step in the constitution of the Imperial Legislative Council. Macaulay, the first Law Member, was also entrusted with the task of codifying laws for India in his capacity as the President of the Indian Law Commission that came into being at the behest of the Governor General.

5. The Charter Act was also a powerful statement against discrimination in employment under the Company due to religion, place of birth, descent, colour or any of these. Although this principle was theoretically endorsed it was practised otherwise for reasons connected with colonialism.

Public administration in India gradually became complex with the expansion of the British Empire. While the 1773 Regulation Act ushered in an era of centralized administration of the Company the 1833 Charter Act marked the culmination of that process by establishing the authority of the Crown over the administration in India. The Governor General became supreme along with Council. As evident, the Indian administration was largely Weberian in spirit and content: it was hierarchical and centralized involving various layers of administration within the overall structure of British rule. Its purpose was defined by colonialism that remained a determining influence, for obvious reasons, until India's independence in 1947.

The Act for the Good Government of India, 1858

Perhaps the most distinctive Act that radically altered the nature of public administration in India was the Act of 1858 which brought the East India Company's century-old rule to an end. In order to strengthen the colonial rule in the aftermath of the 1857 abortive revolt of the Indian army, which is also characterized as the first war of independence, this Act stipulated devices to improve the administrative machinery by which the Indian government was to be superintended and controlled by the Crown in England. As per the 1858 Queen's proclamation that led to the adoption of this Act underlines, the Queen appoints Viscount Canning as 'the First Viceroy and Governor-General in and over our said territories, and to administer the government in our name, and generally to act in our name and on our behalf, subject to such orders and regulations as he shall, from time to time, receive through one of our Principal Secretaries of State'. Furthermore,

> [W]hen, by the blessing of Providence, internal tranquillity shall be restored, it is our earnest desire to stimulate the peaceful industry of India, to promote works of public utility and improvement, and to administer the Government for the benefit of all our subjects resident therein. In their prosperity will be our strength, in their contentment our security, and in their gratitude our best reward.

As evident, the proclamation provides significant inputs to the Act of 1858. By abolishing the Court of Directors and the Board of Control, the Act transferred the government territories and revenues from the Company to the Crown. India was to be governed by the English Sovereign that, by implication, suggests the importance of the British Parliament in governance in India. As the pivot of colonial administration, the Secretary of State for India discharged all powers vested earlier in the Board of Control and Court of Directors. As a member of the cabinet, the Secretary of State drew his salary from the revenues, generated from India. He was authorized to place the annual statement of accounts of all government revenue and expenditure in India and to submit a report of all moral and material progress in India. To assist him in the discharge of his constitutional and administrative responsibilities, he was provided with a Parliamentary and a Permanent Under-Secretary. A council, designated as the India Council, was constituted to help him perform his duties most efficiently. The Council was mainly an advisory aid and its role was thus limited, though on various occasions it acted in a decisive manner to influence the decisions of the Governor General through other constitutional bodies.

The Act of 1858 was not qualitatively different from the earlier acts in the sense that it made no spectacular changes in the colonial administration except that it vested the entire revenue of the country in the Governor-General-in-Council. The provincial governments became totally subsidiary to the Council. Another paramount act which introduced non-official members in the administration was the 1861 Indian Councils Act. The function of the Council was limited to legislation and had no authority to control the executive though it empowered the provincial governments to legislate on provincial matters. The Executive Council was expanded to include the Advocate General of the provinces, in addition to four non-official members who were invariably Indians.

The Indian Councils Act is a remarkable piece of legislation for two important reasons: first, it was certainly an important step towards decentralization of power and in that sense it was a break with the past. For the first time, steps were taken to provide an alternative to centralized British administration. Second, it also introduced Indians in the administration by recommending the inclusion of non-official members. It was a deliberate political design to accommodate the elite Indians in public administration that had an enormous impact especially in the aftermath of the 1857 uprising. Although those who were nominated were either Indian princes or big land owners it was undoubtedly a significant beginning towards involving Indians in public administration.

In the early part of the Crown administration, two processes seem to have worked. On the one hand, attempts were made to strengthen the Governor-General-in-Council and on the other, there were steps towards devolution, especially of financial power. In this connection, the 1870 Mayo resolution is most remarkable which stated:

> Local interest, supervision and care are necessary to success in the management of funds devoted to education, sanitation, medical charity and local public works. The operation of the resolution in its full meaning and integrity will afford opportunities for the development of local self-government, for strengthening municipal institutions and for association of the natives and Europeans to a greater extent than before in the administration of affairs.[7]

Several acts were enacted to constitute municipalities in Bombay, Calcutta, and Madras. The most eventful development in this regard was undoubtedly the 1882 Ripon Resolution that defended the introduction of the local self-government by underlining that it was introduced 'not primarily with a view to improvement in administration. It is chiefly desirable as an element of political and popular education.' In pursuance of this goal, the 1885 Bengal Local Self Government Act was adopted that led to the formation of district local boards in Bengal.

The trajectory of the British rule in its initial phase suggests the phased decentralization of administration and also the growing involvement of the Indians in administration. Two substantial events changed the course of colonialism: (a) the founding of the universities of Calcutta, Madras, and Bombay helped develop an articulate opinion of the educated Indians on the British rule. It captured the growing discontent among the Indians who always remained, for obvious reasons, peripheral in administration, and (b) The inauguration of the Indian National Congress in 1885 created a new platform to ventilate the grievances of the ruled. This also became a forum for the Indians to articulate demands for better rule. The outcome of which was the 1892 Indian Councils Act which underlined its aim as:

> [T]o widen and expand the functions of the Government of India, and to give further opportunities to the non-official and native elements in Indian society to take part in the work of the Government, and in that way, to lend official recognition to that remarkable development both of political interest and political capacity that had been visible among the higher classes of Indian society since the Government of India was taken over by the Crown in 1858.[8]

The Act provided for the enhanced membership of the Councils. It was mandatory for the government to consult the representative bodies and institutions, approved by the government, before selecting nominees for the Councils. Besides legislative powers, the Councils were also empowered to pull the Executive on financial matters though it had no power to either revise or reject decisions on this matter. However, the growing weightage of the Councils is indicative of a sea change in colonial rule. As Morley, the Secretary of State, articulated , 'there are two rival schools of thought, one of which believes that better government of Indian depends on efficiency, and that efficiency is, in fact, the end of British rule in India. The other school, while not neglecting efficiency, looks also to what is called political concessions.'[9] This declaration laid the foundational principles of the British administration in India. As a first step, a Royal Commission was appointed in 1907 to look into the administration that seemed to have lost its viability in the context of growing discontent among the ruled. The aim of the Commission was to provide an administration which was adapted to the changed social, economic and political realities of India. While recommending the corrective measures, the Commission was guided by the following factors; (a) the difficulties of ruling the vast sub-continent from a single headquarter and the inevitable failure of in the statesmanship and efficiency in administration (b) the difficulties of applying uniform schemes of development for the provinces which are socio-culturally diverse (c) to instill a sense of responsibility among those engaged in provincial and local administration and (d) to strengthen the colonial rule by educating people in the values of strong administration. On the basis of the recommendation of the Commission, a bill was introduced in 1908 which became the 1909 Morley-Minto Reforms. As a political scheme seeking to strengthen colonial rule in India, the 1909 Act introduced a profound change with long-term effects in representation of communities in Councils. Once the Muslim league was founded in 1906 there were demands for 'separate electorate' for the Muslims. In his plea to the Governor General, the Muslim League chief, Aga Khan defended separate electorate for the Muslims on the basis of their 'numerical strength', 'political importance', and 'contribution' which they made 'to the defence of the Empire'. Endorsing the argument, Minto assured Aga Khan that the Muslims 'may rest assured that their political rights will be safeguarded'. So, the 1909 Act is remarkable in the history of representation in India. Muslims were recognized as a separate community and their electoral rights were also guaranteed accordingly. The British policy of 'divide and rule' was thus formally articulated. Public administration continued to remain partisan, for obvious reasons. Meanwhile, the nationalist movement gained momentum and the political atmosphere in India changed. The 1909 Morley-Minto Reforms failed to address the genuine grievances of the ruled. Various other acts were enacted to reinforce the repressive system of governance that was articulated by the 1909 Reform scheme.

With the outbreak of the First World War (1914–18), a change in the attitude of the British government was visible which was largely 'strategic' to solicit the support of the Indians in its war effort. The result was the adoption of the 1919 Montague-Chelmsford Reform scheme which was guided by the committed goal of the government 'to increase association of the Indians in every branch of the administration and the gradual development of self-governing institutions in India'. On the surface, the Reform scheme, appears to be novel and drew on the commitment to make public administration India-friendly, as the four major principles that formed the core of the scheme suggest:

1. [T]here should be, as far as possible, complete popular control in local bodies and the largest possible independence for them of outside control.

2. The provinces are the domain in which the earlier steps towards the progressive realization of responsible government should be taken. Some measures of responsibility should given at once, and the aim of the British government is to provide complete responsibility to the Indians in their governance to the extent possible under the present circumstances.

3. The Government of India must remain wholly responsible to the Parliament and saving such responsibility, its authority in essential matters must remain indisputable pending experience of the effect of changes now to be introduced in the provinces. Meanwhile, the Indian legislative council should be enlarged and made more representative and its influence in the processes of policy making needs to be enhanced.

There is no denying that the 1919 Act was a politically appropriate strategy at a time when the nationalist movement was growing in importance especially after the arrival of Gandhi on the scene. Although the administration was guided by the colonial spirit, by involving the loyalist Indians in governance the British rulers provided a new design of public administration in India. In the new dispensation, structural changes in administration were made. The most remarkable step was the adoption of dyarchy. The dyarchy was an administrative device that demarcated functions between those who were to be given to popular control and those who must continue to remain with the British rulers: the former were called 'transferred subjects' and the latter 'reserved subjects'. The Governor-General-in-Council was in charge of the reserved subjects while Governors, acting with the ministers in the provinces, remained supreme in so far as the transferred subjects were concerned.

On the surface, the nature of governance appeared to have undergone radical changes since the enlargement of the electorate created Indian majorities in various councils. But the appearance was misleading since critical roles were retained by the British. Since the Viceroy had the veto power, the transfer of authority to the elected representatives was futile. Devolution was thus 'intended to tie in a large element of society to the status quo'.[10] The design was politically-motivated because 'giving power to the local communities meant that energies that could have applied against the imperial power were dissipated into communal harmony'.[11] An outcome of the grand imperial strategy of *dīvide et imperā*, it worked for ruler's benefit though, as the available literature shows, constitutional articulation of British imperial preferences in India always presented a problem for legislators and British colonial officials in India. For drafting and making 'a democratic constitutional design' what was prior, for obvious reasons, was to ensure that 'Britain's imperial position would not be undermined or worse, eliminated'.[12] Nonetheless, the British authority agreed to go ahead with the reforms presumably because of their self-proclaimed civilizing mission in India that also entailed an endeavour towards evolving a socio-political environment for constitutional democracy to strike roots. The constitutional reforms were thus an outcome of concerns for defending Britain as a champion of liberalism and also its tutelary role in developing a conducive milieu.

Despite being unique, the dyarchy was thus doomed to fail simply because of its ideological roots in colonialism. Even the Alexander Muddieman-led committee which was constituted to examine the functioning of dyarchy concluded that it crumbled because of its inherent weaknesses and dissensions due to the following factors: (a) the demarcation of authorities between reserved and transferred was meaningless since the de facto power always rested with the former (b) as a result, there was hardly an effective dialogue between the provincial ministers and the Governors or the Governor General (c) the Indian ministers were further handicapped since Indian civil service officers hardly cooperated with them and (d) the excessive control by the finance department of the Government of India over the transferred subjects.

As evident, administration was constantly being restructured seemingly to placate the Indians' interests in governance. Although the actual power rested with the British authority, dyarchy was a critical step towards administrative devolution that radically altered the complexion of the British power in India that largely revolved around Governor-General-in-Council. Dyarchy empowered the Governors who exercised independence with regard to transferred subjects in the provinces. Furthermore, the involvement of the Indian ministers had introduced changes, though cosmetic in character, in public administration. Apart from gaining experience in administration, the Indian ministers acquired a first-hand knowledge of how the administration functioned in most partisan manner. This helped them articulate a nationalist agenda which was now readily acceptable to the people at large since it was experience-based. So, dyarchy was very critical to conceptualizing the changing nature of public administration in British India at least in the first two decades of the twentieth century.

The 1935 Government of India Act

Colonialism and centralization of power seem to go hand in hand though public administration in British India underwent changes at least in its content. A change is visible if one follows the evolution of public administration since the adoption of the 1772 Regulating Act. Perhaps the most (and last) significant constitutional measure in India during the British rule is the 1935 Government of India Act that drew on the inputs from the Indian Statutory Commission, the All Parties Conference, the Round Table Conferences and the Joint parliamentary Committee of the British Parliament. Seeking to establish a federal form of government in which the constituent provinces had autonomous legislative and executive powers, the Act paved the way for a parliamentary form of government in which the executive was made accountable within certain bounds to the legislature. This had radically altered public administration in India, including the civil services in the country. Although the well-espoused federation never came into being the Act was nonetheless a powerful comment against the integrated administrative system of the colonial variety. A perusal of the Act draws our attention to the following features:

1. Provincial autonomy was recognized by giving the provinces a separate legal identity and liberating them from central control except for certain specific purposes.

2. A federation of India was established demarcating domains between the provincial governments and the federal central government.

3. Dyarchy, discontinued in the provinces, was introduced at the centre. Subjects of foreign affairs and defence were 'reserved' to the control of the Governor-General; the other central subjects were transferred to ministers' subjects in the provinces.

4. The federal principle was recognized in the formation of the lower house of the central legislature though the de facto ruler remained the Governor-General.

5. Separate electorate was retained following the distribution of seats among the minority communities, as devised by the 1932 Communal or MacDonald Award.

The Act redefined 'public' in public administration. Introduction of provincial autonomy enabled the Indian ministers to directly involve in administration though they had to function under the overall restriction of colonialism. Hence it was characterized as 'a gigantic constitutional façade without anything substantial within it'. The Act was also a sign of the determination of the British government to warp the Indian question towards electoral politics. By involving Indians in administration, (a) the Act had brought more players in the arena of public administration. There is therefore no doubt that the Act introduced the Indian politicians to the world of parliamentary politics and (b) as a result of the new arrangement, stipulated by the Act, politics now percolated down to the localities which largely remained peripheral so far. The available evidence also suggests that the Act was the price the British paid for the continuity of the Empire. What thus appears to be a calculated, generous gesture was very much a politically expedient step. In fact, the surrender of power, though at the regional levels, caused consternation among the votaries of the British power in India who saw an eclipse of British authority in this endeavour.

An uncritical look at these selective, but major, landmark constitutional initiatives during the colonial rule may lead one to conclude that these were initiated by the British for the Indians. Hence the spirit of nationalism is underrated. If one goes beyond the surface what is evident is that public administration underwent changes largely because of the British effort to defuse popular discontent. Hence the argument that every constitutional drive was initiated by the Raj is totally unfounded. History reveals that there were situations which forced the British authority to adopt measures to control agitation. For instance, the Congress campaign in the 1880s contributed a lot to the introduction of the 1893 reforms. Behind the 1909 Morley-Minto Reforms lay the Swadeshi Movement and revolutionary terrorism. Similarly, the 1919 Mont-Ford Reforms were attempts at resolving crises that began with the Home Rule League agitation and climaxed with the 1919 Rowlatt Satyagraha and the Non Cooperation Movement of 1910–21. To a large extent, the Gandhian Civil Disobedience Movement (1930–2) accounted for the introduction of constitutional measures seeking to involve Indian politicians in public administration.

Furthermore, the interpretation of these constitutional designs remains partial unless linked with the broader socio-economic and political processes in which they were conceptualized. An attempt to analyse the structure and dynamics of constitutional politics without reference to the broader social matrix and economic nexus is futile because the political-constitutional structure reflects economic and social networks, religio-cultural beliefs and even the nationalist ideology which impinged on the organized world of administrative and constitutional structure. So an urgent and unavoidable task for an analyst is not to completely ignore the broader socio-economic context but to ascertain its relative importance in shaping a particular constitutional initiative. For instance, the 1932 Communal Award was believed to have been initiated by the British to expand political activity among the Muslims in Bengal and Punjab. But, as studies have shown, it was also a concession the British was forced to grant in order to make the maintenance of the Empire easier. The sharing of power with the native elites was thus prompted by considerations other than merely British initiatives.

Devising a Structure: A Steel-Frame of Governance

All India Civil Services in India (ICS)—their structure, role, behaviour, and interrelationships—had evolved over a long period in history since the designing of the system about the middle of the nineteenth century.[13] The Macaulay Committee Report of 1854 is a watershed in the growth of bureaucracy in India. By recommending a civil service based on the merit system, the Committee sought to replace the age-old patronage system of the East India Company.[14] Defending the idea of a generalist administrator—'all rounder'—the Fulton Committee 'portrayed the ideal administrator as a gifted layman who, gains by moving from job to job irrespective of its subject matter, on the basis of his knowledge and experience in the government'.[15] The efficiency of the members of the ICS as administrators may have been exemplary, but there is no doubt that they were motivated primarily by imperial interests and hence 'the interests of the country were too often postponed to the interests of the [Crown]'.[16] Furthermore, there was a Weberian aspect to the ICS. Drawn from the well-off sections of the society, the civil servants were trained in some of the best universities and were chosen on the basis of a competitive examination. Those within the ICS were therefore secluded from the rest given their exclusive class, caste, and educational backgrounds. In other words, they had the special status within the society that Weber felt was essential to a true bureaucracy. Given their peculiar characteristics the British officials in India formed a most unusual kind of society with no organic links with the society they were to serve.[17] The Indian civil service held a pivotal position in the system of administration that flourished during the colonial rule. Recognizing its immense importance in sustaining the empire, Lloyd George thus declared in the House of Commons in 1922:

> They are the steel frame of the whole structure. I do not care what you build it from—if you take the steel frame out, the fabric will collapse. There is one institution we will not interfere with, there is one institution we will not deprive of its functions or of its privileges, and that is that institution which built up the British Raj—the British Civil Service in India.[18]

The Government of India Act, 1919 introduced administrative decentralization by transferring certain powers to the Indian ministers in the provinces. The dyarchy gave further impetus to the demand for Indianization of civil services. In 1921, only about thirteen per cent of the officers were Indians. This challenged the spirit of the Reform scheme. As against the demand for Indianization of the superior services, the serving European officers sought to scuttle the move by submitting a memorandum to the British Prime Minister, Lloyd George. In his response, Lloyd George made his celebrated 'steel frame' speech. As he emphatically argued, he could foresee no period when 'they (those in service) can dispense with the guidance and assistance of a small nucleus of British civil Servants'.[19] The argument had substance but did not seem to be entirely correct, as Philip Mason, who had more than three decades of association with British Indian administration, countered by saying that it was not surprising that 'some three hundred million people were ruled by a body of never more than twelve hundred picked men, with some fifty thousand British troops behind them [because] ... the administration was light'.[20] Furthermore, the system of administration that the colonial government had instituted functioned well because 'it brought a tranquillity and prosperity to a people that they had not known for centuries'.[21] By being critical of the conceptualization of Indian civil service being 'a steel frame', Mason suggested that 'it was more like a weaverbird's nest than a steel frame [since] ... all kinds of odd fragments were woven into the fabric, thongs found on the spot and made use of because they worked'.[22] Whether it was a weaverbird's nest or steel-frame, the fact remains that colonialism devised a powerful structure of governance which ensured its continuity despite the growing consolidation of the nationalist movement till the outbreak of the 1942 Quit India Movement when cracks were visible in the steel frame.[23]

The issue of retention of all India service was always controversial, as the nationalist leaders considered the retention of these services as 'anachronistic' and 'incompatible' with provincial self-government. The nationalist members of the Reforms Inquiry Committee of 1924 and the members of the Indian Central Committee, 1928–9 that was constituted to liaise with the Indian Statutory Commission sharply argued for the abolition of central services and underlined the significance of 'provincialization' of civil service. The Joint Committee on Indian Constitutional Reform did not however endorse this point of view and the all India services remained integral to the Raj.

How was it possible for the steel frame to continue in India during almost the entire period of British colonialism and also its aftermath? It was Philip Mason, a veteran civil servant who, being associated with British administration, came out with very perceptive comments while explaining the viability of the steel frame in colonial governance. According to him, the administration in India,

> had the immense advantage over those in the later African territories that it was possible to set up the framework of government before the invention of the electric telegraph and close control of England. Use was made of Akbar's machinery and whatever local institutions could be adapted. The whole was controlled by a cadre of district officers, rigorously picked, but trained almost wholly by doing what in fact they were learning to do. Because they were so few they had let their subordinates do their own work. Confidence that they would be backed up from above was the hallmark of their profession and they acquired a confidence in themselves and a confidence that they would be obeyed, which meant that they were obeyed. Few administration can have ruled so many with so slight use of force. Everything was done through Indians and by Indians to whom power was delegated.[24]

Mason attributed the continuity of the steel frame to a well-defined set of rules and regulations that were strictly obeyed by those belonging to civil service. It was a solid arrangement that appeared to have struck an organic roots in governance in India. Lord Dufferin, India's Viceroy between 1884 and 1888, was far more explicit in appreciating the role of steel frame in sustaining a system of governance which gained credibility by building 'an image of being an instrument for service to the people'. Hence, he argued that '[t]here is no service like it in the world. If the Indian civil service were not [as they were], how could the government of the country go on so smoothly? We have 250 million subjects in India and less than 1,000 British civilians for the conduct of the entire administration.'[25] The steel frame was thus a useful instrument which allowed colonialism to strike roots in India and made the British system of governance apparently invincible. However, an argument highlighting the excessive importance of the steel frame in sustaining colonialism does not seem to be persuasive unless it is contextualized which means that it acquired salience presumably because of the ideational defence in its favour that drew on the parallel ideological endeavours justifying constitutional liberalism as perhaps the best design for collective existence.

The question of retention of all India services had again figured prominently in the discussion in the Constituent Assembly in independent

India. Although there were some dissenting voices, the nationalist leaders, including Jawaharlal Nehru and Vallabhbhai Patel, were keen to continue with the steel frame. The stock argument ranged around the highest standard of efficiency, progressive and wide outlook, freshness and vigour in administration and efficiency at different levels (centre, province, and district) that could be maintained if the all India service was retained. As Patel argued in defending the continuity of the services, 'as a man of experience, I tell you, do not quarrel with the instruments with which you want to work. It is a bad workman who quarrels with his instruments. Take work from them. Everyman wants some sort of encouragement. Nobody wants to put in work when everyday he is criticized and ridiculed in public.'[26]

In independent India, the Indian Administrative Service (IAS) succeeded the ICS.[27] Despite its imperial roots, the Indian political leaders chose to retain the structure of the ICS presumably because of its efficient role in conducting Indian administration in accordance with prescribed rules and regulations supporting a particular regime. However, during the discussion in the Constituent Assembly, the house was not unanimous as regards the fate of ICS. The argument opposing its continuity was based on its role as an ally of imperialism. 'The Civil Service as the Steel Frame ... enslaved us [and] they have been guilty of stabbing Nation during our freedom struggle. [W]e should not, therefore,' as the argument goes, 'perpetuate what we have criticized so far.'[28] Vallabhbhai Patel was probably most vocal in defending the ICS and its steel frame. Since they were 'patriotic, loyal, sincere [and] able', Patel was not in favour of tampering with bureaucracy especially when the country was reeling under chaos towards the close of the British rule. As early as 1946, he convened the provincial Premier's Conference to evolve a consensus on the future of which was then All India Services (AIS). In view of their long association with public administration, officers belonging to the AIS 'are most well-equipped to deal with new and complex tasks'. Not only 'are they useful instruments, they will also serve as a liaison between the Provinces and the Government of India and introduce certain amount of brashness and vigour in the administration both of the Centre and the Provinces.'[29] Later while speaking in the Constituent Assembly, he categorically stated that, '[y]ou will not have a united India if you do not have a good all India service' which had the independence to speak out its mind and enjoyed a sense of security. He also attributed the success of the Constitution to the existence of an all India service by saying that, 'if you do not adopt this course, then do not follow this Constitution.... This Constitution is meant to be worked by a ring of service which will keep the country intact. If you remove them', Patel thus apprehended, 'I see nothing but a picture of chaos all over the country'.[30] Seeking to persuade his colleagues in the Constituent Assembly, he further argued,

> if these service people are giving you full value of their Services and more, then try to learn to appreciate them. Forget the past. We fought the Britishers for so many years. I was their bitterest enemy and they regarded me as such.... What did Gandhiji teach us? You are talking of Gandhian ideology and Gandhian philosophy and Gandhian way of administration. Very good. But you come out of jail and then say, 'These men put me in jail. Let me take revenge'. That is not Gandhian way. It is going far away from that.[31]

Patel seemed persuaded because he believed that an efficient, disciplined, and contented civil service assured of its prospect as a result of diligent and honest work was the hallmark of a sound administration under a democratic regime even more than under authoritarian rule. Even Jawaharlal Nehru who was very critical of the ICS for its role in sustaining the imperial rule in India as he felt that the Indian civil service was 'neither Indian nor civil nor service [and] it is thus essential that the ICS and similar services disappear completely'.[32] In view of the contingent circumstances that gripped the young nation, he held a pragmatic view and justified its continuity for 'the security and stability of India, including coping with the slaughter and its aftermath in Punjab, crushing opposition in Hyderabad, and containing it in Kashmir'.[33] While defending his argument, he further elaborated by suggesting that it was 'our responsibility' to build a functional and efficient system of administration. As he mentioned, 'before the birth of freedom we have endured all the pains of labour and our hearts are heavy with the memory of this sorrow. Some of those pains continue even now. Nevertheless, the past is over and the future that beckons to us now'.[34]

With support from his colleagues, Patel seemed to have crossed a big hurdle and he also moved a resolution guaranteeing immunity to those in the all India service; his views were translated in Article 311 of the Constitution of India that stated that no civil servant shall be dismissed or removed or reduced in rank except after an enquiry in which he has been informed of the charges and given a reasonable opportunity of being heard in respect of those charges.[35]

So, an instrument that consolidated the imperial rule in India 'with so slight use of force' survived in completely different political circumstances primarily because there was continuing support for it first from the British Government and then the Congress Government Furthermore, its continuity did not pose any threat to the dominant classes that reigned supreme following the 1947 transfer of power in India. The new civil service for all practical purposes was, as a former bureaucrat comments, therefore 'the continuation of the old one with the difference that it was to function in a parliamentary system of government, accepting the undoubted primacy of the political executive which in turn was responsible to the people through their elected representatives in the legislature.'[36] Besides its structure, which is more or less, an expansion of the steel frame, the continuity is at a deeper level. While the colonial civil servants had paternalistic attitude towards the people, and ruled largely by negative discretionary powers, '[t]heir successors, noting the vast unmet development needs of the people, substituted positive discretionary powers of patronage and subsidies, reinforcing the colonial syndrome of dependency on the *mai-baap* state.'[37]

Apart from its functional utility, the steel frame was retained more or less *intact* was due to fact that, as B.P.R. Vithal, himself an IAS officer, argued, 'the Congress leaders who took office . . . shared the social background of the senior civil servants whom they inherited from the colonial state.'[38] Thus, for example, Nehru felt at ease while working with senior civil servants. Similarly, Rajagopalachari felt more at home with the ICS officers who were placed with him when he was the Prime Minister of Madras (1937–9) than with certain elements in the Congress party. The political processes subsequent to Independence gave rise to changes in the class composition of the political executive that was far-reaching and rapid than changes in the social composition of the civil services. While the political executives, trained in vernacular education, came largely from rural and semi-urban areas, those in the steel frame were generally urban-based and English-educated. The growing disparity between the class background of the political executive and the civil servants led to frequent frictions between the administrators and politicians in the Westminster parliamentary system of governance when the latter had assumed a leading role in building a new nation.

The 3 June Plan and Indian Independence Act, 1947

At the end of the Second World War (1939–45), the British politicians realized that the colonial rule in India could no longer be sustained. The Indian nationalists were vehemently against its continuation. International opinion was also in favour of decolonization. The perspective in which the Indian question was so far articulated had thus radically changed. True to its pledge, the newly elected labour government also responded to the situation in a very different way. Illustrative of their commitment is the announcement on 20 February 1947 where Atlee, the British premier, declared that 'His Majesty's Government wish to make it clear that it is their definite intention to take necessary steps to effect the transference of power to responsible Indian hands by a date not later than June, 1948.'[39] Accordingly, Mountbatten, the last viceroy, was vested with all powers to devise an appropriate scheme to settle the Indian question. It was a difficult task. Nonetheless, the viceroy convinced both the Muslim League and the Congress leadership to agree to the partition of Bengal and Punjab and also assured to complete the process by August, 1947 instead of June, 1948, as decided earlier. It was against this background that the 3 June Plan was prepared which involved 'at every stage a process of open diplomacy with leaders.'[40] The Atlee government was determined to transfer power as the 3 June Plan was unambiguous in stating that 'it has been the desire of His Majesty's Government that power should be transferred in accordance with the wishes of the Indian people themselves.'[41] It was also made clear that the responsibility of framing the constitution for independent India and Pakistan should rest with the people of the respective countries. As the government declaration further stated that 'His Majesty's Government wish to make it clear that they have no intention of attempting to frame any ultimate constitution for India [or Pakistan]; this is a matter to be decided by the people themselves. Nor is there anything in this plan to preclude negotiations between communities for a united India.'[42]

The plan made provision for the constitution of two Boundary Commissions one for the Punjab and the other for Bengal and if necessary for Assam. In case, the award not being implemented before the transfer of power to the Government of Pakistan in August, 1947, the plan provided for 'the notional partition' of the provinces of Bengal and the Punjab purely on the basis of demographic composition of the provinces. It further stressed that the Commission 'shall under no circumstances be conditioned by the provisional boundaries and instead look into the matter afresh.'[43]

The 3 June plan appeared to have guided the entire process of what finally culminated in the division of Bengal and Punjab. According to this plan, the provincial Legislative Assemblies of Bengal and Punjab would 'meet in two parts, one representing the Muslim-majority districts and the other the rest of the Province' to decide 'whether or not the Province should be partitioned.'[44] Unlike Punjab where the Legislative Assembly met amidst demonstrations and communal disorders, the voting in Bengal passed-off in a comparatively peaceful atmosphere. First there was a joint meeting of the members from both the Muslim and Hindu majority districts, presided over by the Speaker of the House, Nurul Amin, in which a majority of 126 members endorsed the demand for a new and separate Pakistan constituent assembly while 90 members voted for participating in the existing constituent assembly that was elected in 1946. At the second stage, members representing Hindu and Muslim majority districts, met separately. In a meeting, chaired by the Maharaja of Burdwan, members from the Hindu-majority districts decided in favour of partition by 58 to 21 votes, while Members from the Muslim-majority districts, sitting separately, opposed partition by 106 to 35 votes. However when the results of the members from the Hindu-majority districts were made known to them, they decided by 107 to 34 votes that district with a clear Muslim-majority should join the proposed Pakistan constituent assembly.

The Indian Independence Act of 1947 that formally transferred power to the people of India was introduced in the House of Commons on 4 July and received the Royal assent on 18 July. Drawn on the spirit of the 3 June Plan, the Act also recognized the independent existence of Pakistan along with India. Since partition was accepted by both the Congress and Muslim League, it was rather easier for the British government to set-out the terms and conditions for the transfer of power. Pakistan was created by bifurcating three Muslim-dominated British Indian provinces—two in the east, Bengal and Assam and one in the west, Punjab. Sind, Baluchistan, and North West Frontier Province were also to be included in the new state of Pakistan. As soon as the Independence Act was approved, the British government transferred its responsibility of governing the country to the new dominions. Similarly, the suzerainty of the British Parliament over the princely Indian states lapsed and with it, all the treaties and agreements between the British government and Indian rulers. This provision provoked criticism from the Congress, and Nehru in his note of 3 July 1947 argued that 'the complete wiping out of all treaties and agreements in force at the date of passing of the Act will create administrative chaos of the gravest kind'.[45] Hence he was in favour of endorsing the Cabinet Mission suggestion that 'pending the new agreements, existing arrangements in all matters of common concern should continue'.[46] The Muslim League hailed the Act just like the Hindu Mahasabha: while the League was happy because Pakistan was carved out, Hindu Mahasabha welcomed partition of Bengal, in particular, as it would give the Hindus an opportunity to govern themselves which was not possible given the demographic preponderance of the Muslims in the erstwhile undivided province.

The Act set in motion processes that finally led to the transfer of power on 15 August 1947. The Constituent Assembly had already begun its deliberations. The two Boundary Commissions were appointed under the chairmanship of Cyril Radcliffe who submitted his recommendations within less than a month after his first meeting on the subject on 16 July 1947. Drawing on probably the best available legal minds, the Radcliffe Award turned out to be an excellent technical document which, due to the utter negligence of the reality in Bengal and Punjab, remained a bone of contention to those adversely affected by 'this whimsical design' even in the aftermath of freedom. Nonetheless, the 1947 Act remained an important statement on India's freedom from colonialism for two interrelated reasons: first, India's struggle for freedom led to a paradox of history because freedom was won with a heavy price in the form of partition of the country; second, this was an Act that despite being a formal declaration of the British withdrawal from India seemed to have translated into reality the British apprehension that imperial control of India was no longer tenable.

For the nationalists in India and Pakistan, the 1947 Indian Independence Act was not merely recognition of what they fought for, but also one of the foundational, perhaps most significant, pillars of freedom. The constitutional arrangement that the Act stipulated was respected by all despite being critical of some of the provisions. This itself is indicative of the extent to which the British colonialism succeeded in warping the Indian minds in typical liberal tradition of the Westminster type. There were hardly scathing criticisms of the provisions of the Act; neither the Congress nor the Muslim League challenged the Act except seeking clarifications or offering technical suggestions for implementing some of schemes that Act found appropriate for smooth transfer of power.

Concluding Observations

The British colonial state evolved a strong constitutional machinery on the basis of a mindset that drew on constitutional liberalism. The journey had begun with the onset of the East India Company rule, though it gained momentum with the approval of the famous 1835 Macaulay Minute. From then onwards, the British rule was guided by the ideology of liberalism, with its optimistic assumption that India, as Metcalf argues, 'could be transformed on a European model'.[47] This was a source of tension between two contrasting concerns that shaped the British rule: on the one hand, the inherent colonial desire of being colonialists seemed to have acted decisively in devising a system of governance to control the subjects, brutally, if necessary; by championing its civilizing role, the British rulers charted, on the other, a different course of action to demonstrate that British colonialism had also a different goal to pursue. It was, to use a metaphor, a stick-carrot combination which was deployed to manage opposition and also to create a mindset in support of constitutional liberalism by emphasizing how it could be an empowering politico-ideological mechanism for the Indians. The legislative feats that were adopted during the British rule to translate constitutional liberalism into practice are illustrative here. The efforts of the colonizers were also supplemented by the nationalists who seem to have zealously endorsed the legislative designs for their representation (though selectively) in governance. Perhaps they welcomed these measures because of their ideological compatibility with constitutional liberalism and agreed to become part of the initiative by couching their demand in the language of representation. In other words, representation, despite being heavily restricted, was readily accepted because it was, as they felt, an empowering device. While the nationalist acquiescence of limited representation is explicable, it led to the unfolding of a process of masses being alienated from the Congress which appeared to be losing its claim to represent the nation.

The period between 1909 and 1947, when major constitutional experiments were undertaken under colonialism, sharply shows the mutation in the formation of Hindus and Muslims as communities opposed to each other in the political arena. What was distinctive about this period was the growth of the communities as political units always in a permanent adversarial relationship with the members of the 'other' community. This was further consolidated following the introduction of the communal electorate in the 1937 provincial elections. With the acceptance of the principle of majority, Muslims automatically became most powerful community in Bengal and Punjab by their sheer demographic strength. In other words, religious identity as a demographic category became probably the single most crucial criterion in determining the distribution of governmental power in these Muslim-majority provinces. The 1935 Government of India Act reiterated the divide-and-rule strategy by formally recognizing that Muslims needed to be treated separately as a distinct, but neglected minority in India. This was a decisive constitutional intervention because not only did it establish the principle of majority as sacrosanct in democracy, it also made the Muslims self-conscious of their critical importance in governance in India. It is now possible to argue that the 1935 Act definitely shifted the centre of political activity in Bengal to the east of the province. Not by virtue of any inherent superiority of the Muslims but simply because in a democratically elected legislature, as a contemporary report underlines, 'the weight of numbers tells and the teeming millions of East Bengal— sixty percent of their being Muslims outweighed in point of numbers the more educated Hindus of the South, West and extreme north of the province.'[48] The migration of power to the countryside took place in the context of a major realignment in the social bases of political power.

The 1935 Government of India Act was certainly a powerful constitutional intervention that the colonial rulers seriously made to accommodate the nationalist zeal within, of course, the colonial administrative format. This is also illustrative of efforts at legitimizing the growing democratic aspirations of the ruled in India through a constitutional device. Interestingly, the 1935 Act remained the strongest influence during the making the 1950 Constitution for free India. Some 250 clauses of the present Constitution were, in fact, lifted from the Government of India Act. Although the political system of independent India draws its sustenance from universal adult franchise and political sovereignty, rules are undoubtedly derived from its colonial past. The most striking provisions that the Constitution of India derived from its 1935 counterpart are 'the Emergency provisions' that enable the President to suspend the democratically elected governments and fundamental rights of the citizens. The Act however stands out in another respect. By recognizing provincial autonomy and federation as integral to governance, the Act fundamentally altered the nature of politics in late colonial India, creating a tension between meeting the requirements of maintaining a political order and allowing multiple and competing interests within such an order. The British rule appeared to been torn between two conflicting aims: on the one hand, in their zeal to couch India in liberal constitutional mould, the rulers agreed to adopt a constitution seeking to build accordingly a system of governance; by constitutionally justifying representative government, the British authority had also, on the other, put forward a scheme to consolidate the ideational foundation of constitutional liberalism. In other words, by devising a scheme of representative democracy, the Act substantially changed both the British approach to constitutional governance in India and also the nationalist take on this. It has been succinctly articulated by Arvind Elangovan when he stated that 'by relinquishing a part of its government, the colonial regime, on the one hand, opened itself to increased demands for self-government from the Indian political parties. On the other, the increased political and representative politics between the Congress and the League, amidst other political interests, legitimized this colonial liberal representative order.'[49]

The Act was thus a watershed in India's journey towards constitutional democracy. Besides highlighting a tussle between liberalism-democracy and the partisan imperial design, it can also be said to have firmed the roots constitutional democracy by formally linking the major nationalist players to complementary politico-ideological processes leading to the constitution of a liberal democratic polity in the days to come.

There is no doubt that the postcolonial state in India inherited its habits of governance from colonial practices. And, its Weltanschauung is based on 'the mixed legacies of colonial rule' that upheld rule of law, bureaucracy, citizenship, parasitic landlords, modern political institutions, and 'two-track tradition of protest and participation.'[50] What accounts for relative stability for colonialism in India was certainly its ability to adapt to the changed socio-political circumstances also gradual but steady 'internalization' of domination by the subjects of colonial rule, which provoked an analyst to characterize colonialism as 'an intimate enemy'[51] because the dominated saw the virtues of being dominated for their own betterment. Colonialism was thus not seen as an absolute evil but complementary to India's rise as an independent nation in future. The statement may not be politically correct. Nonetheless, it can safely be argued that colonialism provided critical impetus to various processes that finally resulted in serious political mobilization against imperialism in India. Whether nationalism or democratization—they had their roots in the long history of colonialism and in this sense colonialism remained a significant force behind the rise of India as an independent nation in 1947.

Notes and References

1. I have shown this in my 'The Communal Award of 1932 and its implications in Bengal', *Modern Asian Studies* 23(2), (1989).
2. The text of the Act is available at http://www.sdstate.edu/projectsouthasia/loader.cfm?csModule=security/getfile&PageID=861833, (accessed on 25 May 2016).
3. The statement of John Morley is quoted from D.A. Hamer, *John Morley: Liberal Intellectual in Politics* (Oxford: Oxford University Press, 1968), p. 111.
4. India Office Records, London, Tyson Papers, Eur E 341/41, John Tyson's note, 5 July 1947.
5. Subrata Mitra, 'Constitutional Design, Democratic Vote Counting and India's Fortuitous Multiculturalism', (working Paper, South Asia Institute, Heidelberg University, Germany, November 2004, pp. 29–34).

6. Ashis Nandy, *The Intimate Enemy: Loss and Recovery of Self under Colonialism* (Delhi: Oxford University Press, 1989) (reprint).

7. India Office Records, London, *Report on the Administration of Bengal, 1871–72,* Government Press, Calcutta, 1872, p. 11.

8. The text of the Act is available at http://www.sdstate.edu/projectsoutha-sia/loader.cfm?csModule=security/getfile&PageID=861833, (accessed on 25 May 2016).

9. The statement of John Morley is quoted from Hamer's *John Morley,* p. 111.

10. Walter Reid, *Keeping the Jewel in the Crown: The British Betrayal of India* (New Delhi: Penguin, 2016), p. 31.

11. Reid, *Keeping the Jewel in the Crown*, p. 31.

12. Arvind Elangovan, 'Constitutionalism, Political Exclusion and Implications for Indian Constitutional History: The Case of Montgue Chelmsford Reforms (1919)', *South Asian History and Culture* 7(3) (2016), p. 6.

13. For a detailed account of the civil service in India during the British rule, see Philip Mason, *The Men who Ruled India* (Calcutta: Rupa & Co., 1997) (reprint).

14. As the Report underlined, '[h]enceforth, an appointment to the civil service of the Company will not be matter of favour but matter of right. He who obtains such an appointment will owe it solely to his own abilities and industry'. The Macaulay Committee Report (1854) in *The Fulton Committee Report,* Vol. 1, (Her Majesty's Stationary Office (HMSO), London, 1975), p. 125.

15. Quoted in *The Fulton Committee Report,* p. 125.

16. George Trevelyan, *The Competition Wallah,* (London: Macmillan, 1907) (second edition), pp. 6–7; quoted in Bernard S. Cohn, *An Anthropologist among the Historians and Other Essays,* (New Delhi: Oxford University Press, 1990), p. 545. Given their stake in the British administration, it is but natural that whatever they did, they were simply acting in the imperial interests and in the process preserving or enhancing their superior positions. However there is a school of thought defending that the imperial logic never appeared crucial in administration since 'the ICS [was] Jeremy Bentham's prototype of the benevolent social guardian committed to achieving the common good'. For details, see Eric Stokes, *The English Utilitarians of India* (Oxford: Oxford University Press, 1959), p. 159.

17. While explaining the nature of the British civil servants Bernard S. Cohn developed this argument further by drawing upon their post-recruitment training first at the Haileybury School and later in Oxbridge colleges that

hardly took into account the rapid socio-structural shifts in India during the colonial rule. S. Cohn, *An Anthropologist among the Historians and Other Essays*, pp. 500–53.

18. India Office Records, London, Lloyd George Papers, Mss. Eur. D. 37/A, Lloyd George's famous 'steel-frame speech of 22 August 1922.

19. India Office Records, London, Lloyd George Papers, Mss. Eur. D. 37/A, Lloyd George's famous 'steel-frame speech of 22 August 1922.

20. Philip Mason, *The Men Who Ruled India* (Noida: Rupa & Co., 1997) (Indian reprint), p. 344.

21. Mason, *The Men Who Ruled India*, p. 344.

22. Mason, *The Men Who Ruled India*, p. 344.

23. India Office Records, London, A note, dated 14 July 1942, by R. Tottenham, additional secretary, Home Department, Government of India.

24. Mason, *The Men Who ruled India*, pp. 345–6.

25. Lord Duffrin's statement was quoted by M.L. Jagmohan in his 'Riveting the Steel Frame of the ICS', *Hindustan Times*, 1 November 1998.

26. Vallabhbhai Patel, 10 October 1949, *Constituent Assembly Debates*, Book No. 5, p. 52.

27. For a succinct account of the evolution of the Civil Service in India both during the British rule and its aftermath, see B. Shiva Rao (ed.), *The Framing of India's Constitution (select documents)*, Vol. V, (New Delhi: Indian Institute of Public Administration, 1968), Chapter 23, pp. 708–23.

28. Shibban Lal Saksena, 10 October 1949, *Constituent Assembly Debates*, Book No. 5, p. 46. Prominent among those who criticized the decision to retain the ICS was M. Ananthasaynam Ayyangar who failed to understand the logic of providing 'guarantee to those persons who have played into the hands of others [and] cared only for money and the salaries they got'. Ayyangar's statement in the debate, 10 October 1949, *Constituent Assembly Debates*, Book No. 5, p. 42.

29. Quoted in S.R. Maheshwari, *Indian Administration*, (New Delhi: Orient Longman, 1984) (reprint), p. 211.

30. Vallabhbhai Patel, 10 October 1949, *Constituent Assembly Debates*, Book No. 5, p. 51.

31. Patel, 10 October 1949, *Constituent Assembly Debates*.

32. Jawaharlal Nehru, *An Autobiography: With Musings in Recent Events in India*, (London: John Land the Bodley Head, 1941) (reprint), p. 445.

33. Jawaharlal Nehru, 14 August 1947, *Constituent Assembly Debates*, Book No. 1, p. 4.

34. Nehru, 14 August 1947, *Constituent Assembly Debates*.

35. For a detailed discussion in the Constituent Assembly during the preparation and finally acceptance of Article 311, see Rao, *The Framing of India's Constitution*, pp. 713–23.

36. P.C. Alexander, 'Civil Service: Continuity and Change', in Hiranmoy Karlekar (ed.), *Independent India: The First Fifty Years* (New Delhi: Oxford University Press, 1998), p. 62.

37. R. Sudarshan, 'Governance of Multicultural Polities : Limits of the Rule of Law' in Rajeev Bhargava et al., *Multiculturalism, Liberalism and Democracy* (New Delhi: Oxford University Press, 1999), p. 111.

38. B.P.R. Vithal, 'Evolving Trends in the Bureaucracy', in Partha Chatterjee (ed.), *State and Politics in India* (New Delhi: Oxford University Press, 1997), p. 224.

39. Prime Minister, Atlee's statement in the House of Commons—reproduced in V.P. Menon, *The Transfer of Power in India*, (Madras: Orient Longman, 1993), Appendix IX, p. 507.

40. Mountbatten's statement—quoted in H.V. Hodson, *The Great Divide: Britian-India-Pakistan* (London: Hutchinson, 1969), p. 204.

41. Statement made by the His Majesty's Government on 3 June, 1947—reproduced in Menon's, *The Transfer of Power in India*, p. 510.

42. Statement made by the His Majesty's Government on 3 June, 1947—reproduced in Menon's, *The Transfer of Power in India*, p. 510.

43. *The Statesman*, Calcutta, 8 June 1947.

44. Statement made by the His Majesty's Government on 3 June, 1947—reproduced in Menon's *The Transfer of Power in India*, p. 511.

45. A note 3 July, 1947 by Jawaharlal Nehru—reproduced in Menon's, *The Transfer of Power in India*, Orient Longman, Madras, 1963 (reprint), Appendix XII, p. 4

46. A note 3 July, 1947 by Jawaharlal Nehru—reproduced in VP Menon, *The Transfer of Power in India*, Appendix XII, p. 4.

47. Thomas R. Metcalf, *Ideologies of the Raj* (Cambridge: Cambridge University Press, 1998), p. 199.

48. India Office Records, London, Tyson Papers, Eur E 341/41, John Tyson's note, 5 July 1947.

49. Arvind Elangovan, *A Constitutional Imagination of India: Sir Benegal Narsing Rau Amidst the Retreat of Liberal Idealism (1919–1950)* (unpublished PhD dissertation, University of Chicago, 2012), p. 311.

50. Subrata Mitra, 'Constitutional Design, Democratic Vote Counting and India's Fortuitous Multiculturalism', (working paper, South Asia Institute, Heidelberg University, November 2004), pp. 29–34.

51. Nandy, *The Intimate Enemy*.

6 Major Nationalist Initiatives towards Constitutionalizing India

The idea that India should have a constitutional government was being nurtured seriously by the Congress leadership since the early 1920. In the 1922 Gaya Congress, it was C.R. Das who also argued for the supremacy of the constitution in governance and asked his colleagues to prepare a blueprint for future. Being raised in the British constitutional tradition, it was perhaps logical to argue that the Congress leadership endorsed the arguments for constitutional democracy rather instinctively which was evident in a number of endeavours that it was to take in the aftermath of the Gaya Congress of 1922. In other words, appreciating the role of the constitution in keeping the state power under checks and balances, the Congress leaders seem to have been instinctively drawn to constitutional democracy as perhaps one of the most persuasive modes of governance. There were, of course, opponents though they were not politically strong enough to scuttle the efforts towards constitutionalizing India. The aim of this chapter is to delve on those attempts which both nurtured the desire and also contributed to the making a constitutional design of governance. Interestingly, in these designs, the imprint of the colonial system of constitutional governance that evolved since the onset of colonialism in India was clearly visible, which also confirms the argument that constitutional liberalism appears to have been critical in India's journey as a constitutional democracy. The chapter has two aims: since it was a journey, the chapter delves, on the one hand, on those landmark constitutional designs which the Congress leaders prepared to pursue their politico-ideological goals; it also seeks to understand, on the other, the unfolding of liberal constitutionalism in India as integral to India's struggle for independence in which liberalism remained an important stream of ideological preferences that the Congress upheld.

Empirical Manifestations

Being persuaded by the principles of constitutional liberalism, the nationalists undertook initiatives to articulate their views in the form of specific constitutional designs. Based on their understanding of Westminster form of democracy which they derived by being nurtured and also educated in the liberal tradition, the nationalists provided models of governance which were derivative in substance but had also represented an independent effort on their part to conceptualize a constitutional design in accordance with their politico-ideological priorities. In this section, we will focus on four important initiatives which were undertaken during the period of little less than two decades since 1928. The first serious endeavour was that of the 1928 Motilal Nehru Committee Report, followed by the 1946 Sapru Committee Report; both these reports were outcome of the Congress initiatives. In 1946, B.N. Rau, the constitutional advisor to the Drafting Committee prepared a draft constitution which informed the debates in the Constituent Assembly and also helped shape some of the major constitutional provisions. Finally, we will concentrate on Gandhi's *Last Will and Testament* of 1946 where the Mahatma jotted down his model of a constitution for future India. Despite being conceptualized in different years, there are two features which appear to have linked all these reports: on the one hand, the framers of these texts were guided by the fundamental ethos of constitutional liberalism which they strove to articulate in the constitution that they had proposed; in a similar vein, these constitutional designs defended, on the other, the liberal principle of representation as the only means of constituting political authority. At the outset, the franchise was restricted which, however, gradually expanded due to circumstances in which the British authority deployed this strategy to defuse the nationalist drive against the British power.

The Motilal Nehru Committee Report

Appointed in 1928, the Motilal Nehru Committee[1] had its root in the 1927 Madras Congress that sought to evolve constitutional governance in India. What finally came out of the effort was known as the Swaraj Constitution which was also an outcome of a series of discussion involving several political parties, including the Muslim League. Realizing that without consensus among the major communities, no effort towards making a constitution was likely to succeed, an attempt was made to frame a resolution in such a way as to create confidence among them, especially the Muslims. The resolution that the Congress had adopted was thus explicit in stating that,

> having regard to the general desire of all political parties in the country to unite together in settling a Swaraj Constitution, and having considered the various drafts submitted to it and the various suggestions received in reply to the Working Committee's circular, [the Madras Congress] authorizes the Working Committee ... to draft a Swaraj Constitution for India on the basis of a Declaration of Rights, and to place the same for consideration and approval before a special convention ... consisting of the All India Congress Committee and the leaders and representatives of the other organizations ... and elected members of the central and provincial legislatures.[2]

On paper, it was a grand design, though it did not succeed because the Congress failed to counter the apprehension of the Muslims that they were likely to be marginalized in the proposed constitutional arrangement despite the Committee's assurance that no community would be allowed to dominate over the other. Asserting that the aim was not to 'give domination to one over another but to prevent the harassment and exploitation of any individual or group by another [the Committee insisted] on the fullest guarantee of religious liberty ... [and] cultural autonomy'.[3] In order to establish group rights in its most substantial form and content, the Committee argued for 'joint or mixed electorates' and discarded Separate Electorates completely 'as a condition precedent to any rational system of representation'.[4] Characterizing Separate Electorates as 'bad and harmful for the growth of a national spirit',[5] the Committee also marshalled arguments to suggest that Separate Electorates ended up creating a permanent fissure between the minority and majority community. Hence, it was argued that 'under Separate Electorates, the chances are that the minority will always, have to face a hostile majority, which can always, by sheer force of numbers, override the wishes of the minority'.[6] The aim of the Nehru Committee was to counter the League's insistence on special constitutional protection to the Muslims by guaranteeing Separate Electorates which was never appreciated given its obvious divisive character. Nonetheless, special care was taken to protect cultural autonomy of the minorities which, as the Committee felt, was needed to sustain India's socio-economic diversity. So the conceding of group rights was not a concessional measure but a politically-contrived design for the sake of sustaining the national spirit.

The 1928 constitutional draft, prepared by the Motilal Nehru Committee was finally rejected due to lack of consensus. Nonetheless, it was one of the first serious endeavours that the Indian nationalists had undertaken to constitutionalize India following the fundamental principles of liberalism which unfolded in the wake of the British rule. In order to realize these principles in public life, the Committee admitted that it imitated the British system of governance which was evident in its submission that recommendations were not 'original'. The Committee was said to have been content 'to follow models which have been tried and tested in other parts of the world and which even the framers of the Montague-Chelmsford constitution professed to follow'.[7] The Committee however maintained that the proposed constitution was not exactly derivative of the available constitutions since in drawing up the constitution, it 'deliberately declined to be overcome by one type or the other'. Aware of India's peculiar socio-economic circumstances, the members strove to provide 'for the development of fullest possible provincial life compatibly with national interests'.[8] Another bone of contention was the minority rights which figured prominently in the Report which introduced group rights in the shape of cultural and religious rights of minorities partly to allay the fears of the religious minorities that they would be swamped in a Hindu-dominated India, partly to stave-off the demand for separate electorates, and partly to devise a principle that helped the Congress to regulate inter-group relations.[9] Similarly, the Committee recommended for adult suffrage despite strong criticism even by the Congress. Two points of criticism were made: first, it was argued that without being adequately educated, the voters would fail to exercise franchise 'intelligently'; secondly, in view of the vastness of the country and the lack of transport, it would be difficult, if not impossible, for the voters to go to the booth to exercise their rights, which would make the system redundant. As a counter to these arguments, the Committee retorted that 'the repeated exercise of the right to vote is in itself a powerful educative factor'.[10] And, it was further argued that 'the average Indian voter understands his business and [that he] can form an opinion that affects him directly'.[11] What was unique about the Nehru Report was an attempt to conceptualize group rights in a liberal way since it also endorsed individual rights by insisting on adult suffrage. This was a revolutionary step which also confirms the nationalists' concern for creating a constitutional arrangement on the basis of their understanding of liberal constitutionalism.

Dissensions surfaced as soon as the Nehru recommendations were made public. Even Jinnah who appreciated Motilal's efforts in drafting a constitution for united India rejected the recommendations demanding that the residual powers should rest with the provinces rather than the centre to scuttle the rise of a unitary and authoritarian Hindu-dominated state. Other Muslim groups joined hands and in January 1929, an All Parties Muslim conference met in Delhi and agreed to abandon the Report that hardly addressed the Muslim concern. While Muslims dissociated from the Report as it was far from their expectations, there were dissidents even within the Congress. Led by Jawaharlal Nehru and Subhas Chandra Bose, a powerful faction within the Congress formed 'Independence India League' that demanded complete independence rather than dominion status as suggested by the Nehru Committee. While elucidating the difference between dominion status and independence, Nehru stated that dominion status 'envisages the same old structure, with many bonds visible and invisible tying us to the British economic system: [complete freedom] gives, or ought to give us, freedom to erect a new structure to suit our circumstances.'[12] Critical of those defending dominion status, Nehru further argued 'for them the problem is one of changing colour of administration, or at most having a new administration ... [and] not a new state.... They can only conceive of a future in which, they or people like them will play the principal role and take the place of the English high officials.'[13] The 1928 Calcutta Congress thus saw an open split between those who defended dominion status and those who advocated complete independence. It was more or less a foregone conclusion that in view of the growing importance of the radical section within the Congress, it had no alternative but to insist on complete independence. With the acceptance of the complete independence resolution in the 1929 Lahore Congress, it was decided to boycott the legislature and the Congress members were asked to resign. Furthermore, the All India Congress Committee was authorized to launch civil disobedience, including non-payment of taxes wherever it deemed appropriate. Gandhi rose as the undisputed leader and was made the sole authority to decide the time and manner of the launching of the civil disobedience movement. Nonetheless, the Nehru Report, the first Congress document outlining a constitutional structure appropriate for India, was also an attempt to couch the nationalist desire in a liberal mould. It was also an endeavour to design a constitution in accordance with the liberal principles enshrined in the bourgeois constitutions of the West. This was also an instance when a subject nation aspired to be governed by an indigenous constitution within the empire as a dominion and not an independent republic.

The 1945 Sapru Committee Report

Like the 1928 Motilal Nehru constitutional draft, the 1945 Sapru Committee[14] also prepared a constitutional design following the fundamental ethos of liberalism. Here too, the institutional arrangements that Indians had inherited as colonial subjects were accepted as integral to the making of a liberal constitution for India. Admitting that it was the British initiatives that led to the consolidation of liberal democracy in India, the Committee had begun its recommendations by quoting Montague's famous declaration in the House of Commons on 20 August 1917, which corroborated the idea by declaring that 'the policy of His Majesty's Government, with which the Government of India are in complete accord, is that of the increasing association of Indians in every branch of the administration and the gradual development of self-governing institutions with a view to a progressive realization of responsible government in India as an integral part of the British Empire'.[15]

This was not a favour that the British government extended, but was the outcome of the challenges that the ruling authority was apprehending in view of the growing discontent. It was a powerful strategy to seek to quell the circumstances that were quite volatile as the nationalists were being regrouped under charismatic Gandhi. The idea was also appreciated by a hardcore colonialist, like Curzon who found the suggestion most appropriate since, as he argued, 'with the modern ideal of nationalism and self-determination making in the circumstances of the times so strong an appeal, the peoples of countries such as India attached much more importance to being governed, even though not so well-governed, by themselves, than they did to being even superbly governed by another race'.[16]

By referring to the early British initiatives, the Sapru Committee justified that the idea of self-government was nothing new; instead, it was perhaps a natural outcome of the British endeavour towards constitutionalizing India in a liberal democratic format. On the basis of this understanding, the Committee built its argument for a constitutional structure that drew on the fundamental ethos of liberalism. The Sapru Committee thus prefaced the Report by declaring:

> we are making a deliberate and conscious attempt to emerge from a state of society, in which inequality was the rule, to a state of society in which we hope equality will be normal standard. ... Fundamental Rights, therefore, will not only be a standing warning to the vested interests, ... but also a declaration that the period of privileges and inequality is over and that what the constitution demands and expects is perfect equality between one section of the community and another in the matter of political and civic rights, equality of liberties and security in the enjoyment of the freedom of religion, worship and the pursuit of the ordinary avocations of life.[17]

A liberal manifesto with an unambiguous emphasis on the fundamental values of the Enlightenment paradigm, the text is also an endorsement of an idea that gradually gained salience and was never compromised despite provocation on various occasions. Here too, the members of the Sapru Committee appear to have been persuaded by their erstwhile colleagues who prepared the 1928 Nehru Report which, despite having accepted dominion status within the Empire, also defended self-government. Being favourably disposed towards the Westminster form of liberal democracy, they thus insisted that 'the future of India lies in adopting a democratic constitution and taking all the risks which a change from the present system of government to a state of real democracy must involve'.[18] Similar to its 1928 counterpart, the Committee strongly argued for adult franchise with a proviso that under the existing circumstances 'it may be excusable to give communities divided on religious lines the right to a fair and adequate share of opportunities for service in the legislature and of executive power'.[19] Hence, by following more or less the same logic as the erstwhile 1928 committee, the Sapru Committee opposed separate electorate and argued that 'it should be replaced by joint electorate with reservation of seats'.[20] Opposition to separate electorate had a clear political tone since those in favour of partition spearheaded a vociferous campaign by arguing that the separate electorate was a shield against the infringement of minority rights. In an unequivocal way, the Committee condemned the efforts by saying that 'we are convinced that the campaign for separate electorate was an attempt to cause a schism between the majority and minorities which [was detrimental] to the growth of India as a nation'.[21] For the Committee members, there was a hidden agenda which the campaigners for separate electorate endeavoured to pursue; in what claim as a mere electoral arrangement, it was also a campaign for the partition of the country which they unambiguously articulated by saying that

the partition of India would be an outrage justified neither by history nor by political expediency. It is incompatible with the greatness, safety and economic development of the country and will lead either to constant internecine war or perpetual foreign domination. It multiplies and complicates the problem of minorities without solving it and threatens to plunge India back into the dark and dismal days of the 18th century'. ... The division of India into two or more separate independent sovereign states is unjustified and will endanger the peace and orderly progress of the whole country without compensating advantage to any community.[22]

Their firm opposition to India's partition notwithstanding, in their zeal to evolve a mindset for constitutional democracy, the Sapru Committee left no stone unturned to create circumstances in which liberal democratic values were to prosper. It was very clear when the Committee exhorted:

[I]f we are going to have a democratic constitution, we feel strongly that we should provide certain standards of conduct, citizenship and fairplay to all the members of the community when we know that we are making a deliberate and conscious attempt to emerge from a state of society, in which inequality was the rule, to a state of society in which we hope equality will be normal standard.[23]

Based on their concern for liberal democracy to strike roots in India, the aim of the Committee was to evolve a constitution, free from prejudices and discrimination on the basis of those ideas which its members seem to have internalized by virtue of being nurtured in the liberal tradition of the British Empire. Hence it was not odd when they declared:

[The] fundamental rights will not only be a standing warning to the vested interests or to the privileged classes but also a standing invitation to the governments, administrators and guardians of the law that the period of privileges and inequality is over, that is what the constitution demands and expects is perfect equality between one section of the community and another in the matter of political and civic rights, equality of liberties and security in the enjoyment of the freedom of religion, worship and the pursuit of ordinary vocations of life.[24]

What is basic is the exhortation for obedience to the fundamental principles of liberal democracy which does not allow discrimination on the basis of one's primordial affiliations. Although B.R. Ambedkar refused to join the Scheduled Caste Committee when he was requested, given the alleged political bias of the members for the Congress, the Sapru Committee was sensitive of its obligations to the Scheduled Castes who had been discriminated due to the prevalent archaic social norms. Realizing that 'the religious and social disabilities to which they have been subjected have been innumerable and that the treatment these castes have received in the past cannot be defended according to modern social ideas,'[25] the Committee recommended for Special Fundamental Rights in the Constitution which are:

1. No public authority shall, in carrying out the functions and duties entrusted to it under any law, recognize any custom or usage imposing a disability on any person on the ground that he belongs to a Scheduled Castes or a menial class.
2. No civil, criminal or revenue court shall, in adjudicating any matter or executing any order, recognize any custom or usage imposing any civil disability on any person on the ground of his caste or status.[26]

At one level, these provisions for Special Fundamental Rights were context-driven with the consolidation of Dalits as a politically vibrant group under Ambedkar's dynamic leadership; the nationalist leadership could not afford to ignore their claim especially when it was more or less a foregone conclusion that partition which was justified by Jinnah's two-nation theory was unavoidable; at another level, it is perfectly conceivable that members of the Sapru Committee genuinely felt that only through constitutional guarantee of their rights the prevalent prejudiced mindset could effectively be combatted.

Along with its appreciation for liberal constitutional values which they considered to be appropriate for a healthy India, the Sapru Committee took ample care in devising principles for constituting a constitution-making body. The aim was to create an assembly comprising those who were elected to the provincial legislatures since they were chosen by the voters. It is true that the representatives were elected when franchise was restricted; nonetheless, they were authorized to speak for the people since they held a popular verdict though in a restricted sense. The princely Indian states were also invited to contribute to the constitution and accordingly they were asked to select representatives in the same proportion to their population as in the case of British Indian states and with the same powers as their British Indian counterparts. In so far as the composition of the constitution-making-body was concerned, the Committee followed a fair principle of representation: the representatives from the princely states were also readily accepted just like their colleagues from the British Indian states.

Willing to concede special privileges to religious and social communities, the Committee was not persuaded by the League's criticism that given the Congress hegemony, it was undemocratic by being submissive to the majoritarian Hindu views. Hence, it was emphatic in its declaration that for the constitution to become an instrument of visible socio-economic and political changes, the Committee emphasized at the outset that 'this body is to frame a Constitution for a Single State [and] … by its very nature it cannot debate, and reach a decision on, any preliminary issue as to whether a Single Constitution is to be framed for a united India or whether a number of Constitutions are to be framed for the different Indian States of a divided India'.[27] Upholding the 1942 Cripps proposal for the setting up only of one constitution-making body charged with the function of framing a constitution for the country, the Committee thus overruled the League's demand for a separate constitution for the proposed independent state for the Muslims. Justifying its argument for a single constitution-making body, it further argued for the system of joint electorate for its constitution by sternly critiquing the system of separate electorates which, in their perception, was 'politically-divisive' and 'constitutionally-futile' simply because it drew on separatism or the urge for 'maintaining a separate identity at the cost of national unity'.[28] Critical of separate electorates for being 'divisive', the Committee, in order to make the constitution-making body democratic, also devised the principle of parity of representation between Hindus and Muslims. When the Committee was severely criticised for being soft to the minorities, Sapru, the chairperson, came out in its defence by drawing upon the fundamental principles of liberal democracy in which the majority was responsible to allay the minority fears. Hence, he urged upon the Hindus that,

in dealing with the minorities [their] attitude should be one not merely of justice but of generosity. It is important that every endeavour in reason should be made to give minorities the feeling that they have nothing to fear at the hands of the majority. The concessions to minorities that we have recommended are inspired by the desire to induce such a feeling. When minorities come to feel in this way, they will adopt a thoroughly progressive attitude and the present spirit of distrust and suspicion will yield to a spirit of mutual respect and cooperation.[29]

Critical to the Sapru Committee's constitutional design was the concern for the minorities which was based on its zeal to develop a truly democratic state in the aftermath of decolonization. The idea that the principle of representation should be sociologically-designed was upheld by the Committee which, in fact, set in motion a process which loomed large in the 1946–9 Constituent Assembly debates over minority rights. The argument that G.B. Pant made on the floor of the Assembly exactly within a gap of two years in 1947 in favour of minority rights, was hardly dissimilar as he argued:

[T]he question of minorities everywhere looms large in constitutional discussions. Many a constitution has founded on this rock. A satisfactory solution of questions pertaining to minorities will ensure the health, vitality and strength of the free state of India that will come into existence as a result of our discussions here. The question of minorities cannot possibly be overrated. It has been used so far for creating strife, distrust and cleavage between the different sections of the Indian Nation. Imperialism thrives on such strife. It is interested in fomenting such tendencies. So far, the minorities have been incited and have been influenced in a manner that has hampered the growth of cohesion and unity. But now, it is necessary that a new chapter should start and we should all realize our responsibility. Unless the minorities are fully satisfied, we cannot make any progress: we cannot even maintain peace in an undisturbed manner.[30]

There are two important aspects to which Pant had referred to while defending special protection for the minorities. On the one hand, he justified minorities being treated differently on the basis of fundamental liberal concern for equality; in a liberal democratic society, discrimination is simply illiberal. While Sapru was reticent about the consequences of minority alienation, despite being aware of the growing Muslim consolidation for a separate state, Pant drew our attention, on the other hand, to its adverse consequences on the rise of India as a healthy nation.

A perusal of two constitutional drafts, prepared by the 1928 Motilal Nehru Committee and the Sapru Committee in 1945, reveals that in the making of the 1950 Constitution for independent India, their inputs were as critical as those of the 1946–9 Constituent Assembly. Although the former endorsed dominion status for India, its role in constitutionalizing India in a liberal democratic mould cannot be disputed. With its support for adult suffrage, the Nehru Committee introduced a fundamental liberal principle of individual being a focal point in governance. Similarly, the concern for minorities addressed the importance of groups in a liberal polity which can be ignored only at its peril. Influenced, to a significant extent, by the 1942 Cripps mission, the Sapru Committee also strongly argued for meaningful constitutional steps to allay the fear of the minorities of being subsumed by the majority. Despite having endorsed Special Fundamental Rights for the minorities, the Committee was however critical of Separate Electorates since it was likely to impede the growth of mutually healthy interactions among the communities whereby they seem to have championed the liberal principle of 'living together separately'. This is a unique conceptualization resonating Kant's effort towards theorizing the role of individual in conjunction with the collectivity and vice versa. In a nutshell, what was basic to these two earlier efforts was a clear preference for constitution-driven institutional arrangements for India, based on what the members of these committees had conceptualized as liberal values which were partly derivative and partly an outcome of their urge to negotiate with contextual peculiarities in a liberal fashion. Although these committees operated in contrasting historical contexts, their objective did not appear to be very different since they were in quest of an appropriate constitutional arrangement which was tuned to their loyalty to liberalism and, at the same time, capable of creating a national self out of the kaleidoscopic texture of India as a nation of nations. Their effort was directed to create a shared space in which both majority and minority communities did not exactly coalesce but remained sociologically connected by virtue of occupying a common space. In view of irreconcilable differences, if not incompatibility, constructing a shared space is a difficult task. In the absence of constitutionally-endorsed institutional protections, minorities are likely to be swamped by the majority. These issues were conclusively addressed by India's Constituent Assembly which finally came out with the 1950 Constitution for the country. Although the processes towards making the constitution were complete in 1950, they had their roots in multiple efforts, both by the nationalists and their bête noire, the colonial rulers, in the past. Here is the significance of a thorough analysis of the 1928 Nehru Report and 1945 Sapru Report which not only foresaw some of the difficulties of creating a shared space in excessively diverse India but also endeavoured to address them within a liberal analytical framework.

B.N. Rau's Constitutional Proposals

Along with these two nationalist alternatives which left a blueprint, the Constituent Assembly members had also another proposal, prepared by B.N. Rau, the Constitutional Advisor to the Constituent Assembly. While acknowledging the contribution of Rau, Ambedkar, the chairman of the Drafting Committee, appreciated his role by saying that 'the credit that is given to me does not really belong to me; it belongs ... to B.N. Rau who prepared a rough draft of the constitution for the consideration of the Drafting Committee.'[31] Appointed as the constitutional advisor in 1946, Rau, a former British civil servant of the ICS cadre, was responsible for setting up the administrative structure and also for providing background materials to the members of the Drafting Committee. Besides discharging his role as an advisor, he also prepared a draft constitution based on his heart-felt desire to avoid partition. As for the structure of governance, Rau thus suggested that 'India is to be a Federation which may be called the "United States of India" [which entailed] that the units, as in a confederal system, are in a sense sovereign states.'[32] In Rau's scheme, the proposed federation comprised three groups: Group A included the existing British Indian provinces of Madras, Bombay, the Central Provinces, and Berar, Orissa, the United Provinces, Bihar, Delhi, Coorg, Panth Piploda, and Ajmer-Merwara; Group B consists of the frontier regions comprising the British Indian provinces of the Punjab, the North-West Frontier Province, Sind, and British Baluchistan on the west and Bengal and Assam and Andaman and Nicobar islands on the east; Group C shall contain the existing Indian states which may be expanded in case any of the provinces belonging to Group A and Group B are keen to join Group C.[33]

The scheme that Rau had proposed was also an endeavour to prevent India's partition. Hence, he was in favour roughly of a confederal arrangement in which the constituent units were to remain sovereign which he articulated when he said that 'the particular Federation here outlined concedes the substance of the Pakistan demand.'[34] The idea did not appear to be realistic given the intransigence that the Muslim League had shown for its demand for Pakistan. Nonetheless, the constitutional design that Rau had left was referred to by the framers while being engaged in deliberation in the Assembly for preparing an appropriate constitution for independent India. There is another aspect which needs to be emphasized. In view of his very close involvement in the system of government that the 1935 Government of India Act devised, it does not seem incongruent that Rau drew heavily upon this constitutional design while articulating his views. According to him, borrowing per se was not 'bad' because he felt that 'to profit from the experience of other countries or from the past experience of one's own is the path of wisdom'.[35] So, for him, the received wisdom was to be taken as a source strength for it would enable the future constitution makers to address the weaknesses in a far more effective manner. He reinforced the point by saying further that 'there is another advantage in borrowing not only the substance but even the language of established constitutions; for we obtain in this way the benefit of interpretation put upon the borrowed provisions by the courts of the countries of their origin and we thus avoid ambiguity or doubt'.[36]

What governed Rau's choice was the idea that the constitutional provisions, precedents and practices that had passed the test of time were preferable. Here it was not simply blind borrowing, but borrowing on the basis of a judgment. It was, therefore, not surprising that while preparing his draft constitution he consulted the constitutions of established liberal democracies and also of the former Soviet Union, besides, of course, the 1935 Government of India Act. A careful scan of the Rau's views on constitutionalism, which he published in three volumes entitled *Constitutional Precedents*,[37] reveals that his primary concern was to ascertain 'procedural equality' in governance which was possible when the constitution was meant to achieve a common goal. Unless this was established, no constitution, however brilliant the constitution makers were, was likely to succeed because, as he believed, 'a constitution is a means to an end, when by working together, the various parties realize that the ends are common, there will be little difficulty in agreeing upon the means'.[38] Being opposed to partition, his primary concern was to evolve 'a workable federation' to bring together both the Congress and League for effective governance which was possible if the constituents transcended 'communal or sectional interests'.[39] The essence of the scheme was that, as he elaborated, 'while domination of one community by another is to be prevented, the unity of India is to be preserved for purposes equally beneficial to all'.[40] Despite being convinced that this was the best option available to avoid India's vivisection, Rao did not seem to be very zealous in pushing his ideas presumably because of the prevalent circumstances which were charged with mutual distrust and enmity between Hindus and Muslims. He thus lamented that it was likely to be attacked from all sides: 'Hindus may attack on the ground that it is almost Pakistan, and the Muslims may attack it on the ground that it is not completely Pakistan.'[41] What he apprehended was not unfounded because neither the Congress nor its bête noire, the League accepted the scheme. Nonetheless, it was an important document that seems to have influenced the deliberations in the Assembly especially in regard to Federation, Fundamental Rights and Directive Principles of State Policy. In order to be an effective constitutional system, a federation had to rise above petty politics, and needed to be guided by politico-ideological goals which were beneficial to all regardless of creed, clan, and colour. The primary concern was to bring about inclusive development and no deviation was to be allowed since it would strike at the foundation of the federation. How to ascertain conditions for federation to succeed? His response was that of a seasoned bureaucrat who always privileged procedural fairness as perhaps the only means to avoid being governed by partisan considerations stemming from political priorities. Similarly, the emphasis that he accorded to the Directive Principles of State Policy instead of Fundamental Rights conveyed a powerful ideological message that radically altered India's constitutional practices. In response to the charge that these Principles were in the nature of 'moral precepts and the constitution ... is no place for sermons', Rau argued that not only were they 'directional in character', these stipulations were also needed 'to protect the moral fabric of the constitution' which would otherwise be 'weakened', if not 'destroyed'.[42] Furthermore, his insistence on Directive Principles had another powerful significance. As a recent study shows, the aim was to emphasize 'group rights as opposed to individual rights' which were to be protected by the court of law while the former, by being a part of the moral precepts that the state had to honour, remained a guiding force for legislative practices and acts.[43] In the Indian context, in view of the rising importance of minority rights, the concern for group rights assumed tremendous significance at the time of the framing of the constitution. While he argued strongly for Directive Principles of State Policy he did not seem to be so enthusiastic in favour of enumerating Fundamental Rights. This may seem strange though logically plausible as Rau defended his stance by stating that these enumerated rights were likely to be detrimental to the smooth functioning of constitutional governance in India. In a 1946 detailed note on Fundamental Rights, Rau elaborated his argument by suggesting that since they were enforceable, the court, by being the custodians of law, would play a determining role even at the cost of legislative stipulations which evolved following democratic deliberations. The role of the court was critical in sustaining the democratic polity and thus needed to be protected as perhaps the only effective means to contain 'an oppressive Legislature'. To enunciate the Fundamental Rights in general terms and to leave it to the courts to enforce them had the following consequences, Rau underlined:

(1) The Legislature not being in a position to know what view the courts will take of a particular enactment, the process of legislation will become difficult; (2) there will be a vast mass of litigation about the validity of laws and the same law that was held valid at one time may be held invalid at another and vice and versa; the law will therefore become uncertain; (3) the courts, manned by an irremovable judiciary not so sensitive to public needs in the social and economic sphere, as the representatives of a periodically-elected legislative body, will, in effect, have a veto on legislation exercisable at any time and at the instance of any litigant.[44]

Rau's democratic concern seems to have governed his choice: courts were basic to democratic governance, but by being extremely proactive, as is the case in contemporary India in the context of 'judicial activism', they, instead of being a facilitator of constitutional democracy, could easily become its Frankenstein. On the basis of a thorough study of a series of judicial pronouncements primarily of the US Supreme Court, Rau endorsed his point of view in favour of privileging Directive Principles of State Policy over Fundamental Rights. This was a persuasive conceptualization in India's constitutional democracy as history has shown. Furthermore, Rau's insistence on procedural equality which gave equal voice to the marginalized sections was also directed towards attaining inclusive development in India. His ideas thus 'cohere around the pivotal idea of separating the realm of politics from the architecture of the constitution'.[45] A caveat is necessary here because Rau's notion of politics, being narrowly conceived, was conceptualized merely as a manifestation of the rivalry of conflicting ideological groups for partisan gains. There is however another aspect which he referred to while insisting on the importance of elected legislatures in framing rules and regulations out of dialogues and deliberations which also means that legislative decisions are also an offshoot of negotiations. This is politics in its substantial sense which, instead of being a deterrent, actually facilitates democratic deliberations.

The Gandhian Alternative

In view of political uncertainty, Gandhi had, at the outset, doubts whether it was possible for a constituent assembly to frame a constitution acceptable to the 'warring' communities. However, on a request from Jawaharlal Nehru, he jotted down his comments in an article entitled 'the only way' which appeared in *Harijan* on 19 November, 1939. On the basis of his understanding of the prevalent reality, he changed, as he admitted, his perception on the constituent assembly which was 'a remedy ... for our communal and other distempers, besides being a vehicle for mass political education'.[46] Persuaded by the formula that communities were to be represented in the assembly in proportion to their share in India's demography, Gandhi felt that 'the Constituent Assembly thus provides the easiest method of arriving at a just solution of the communal problem [and] ... except it there is no other way of doing full justice to rival claims'.[47] If the communities came together to evolve an acceptable constitution on the basis of 'principles, values and norms' protecting their rights regardless of social, economic and political differences, it would help them frame 'a grand constitution'. Any other method, Gandhi apprehended, resulted in 'imposed constitution, mostly undemocratic [and] ... it would mean an indefinite prolongation of imperialistic rule sustained by the help of those who will not accept the fully democratic method of a Constituent Assembly'.[48] On the basis of these inputs, one can surmise that the Mahatma was persuaded to accept the proposal of a constituent assembly responsible for making a constitution of India since it was to be representative of the communities in their exact proportion. That also confirms that Gandhi endorsed the endeavour primarily because it was an effective means to address the communal imbroglio which was a deterrent to the efforts seeking to build an acceptable constitutional design for all.

Once he accepted the importance of a constituent assembly, he also devoted a great deal of his time to prepare a blue print of a constitution. Unlike the classical liberal, he did not accept the atomistic individual as the unit of constitutional governance; in its place, he favoured the village as focal unit of administration. By choosing village as the locus of his authority, Gandhi provided a model of liberal democracy which was drawn more on the Kantian conceptualization and less on J.S. Mill's. He was also convinced, like the classical liberals, that only through representation, democracy could be realized in its true form and substance. Here, there was no confusion and Gandhi couched his argument for an alternative form of governance, Village Swaraj in his parlance, in the mode of representation through adult suffrage. Although he was against the Weberian pyramidal form of governance, by arguing for an authority comprising the elected representatives as a governing unit, he did not appear to be radically different from the classical Weberian approach in this regard. Nonetheless, it was a creative conceptualization of collectivization of authority, being constituted by the classical mode of direct election based on universal adult franchise. A liberal mode of conceptualization with indigenous intellectual resources, the alternative Gandhian approach was also explored by the Gandhians in the Constituent Assembly; they were, however outnumbered by their colleagues when they insisted on village swaraj being accepted as the core of constitutional governance in India by recognizing village, and not individual, as central to independent India's initiative at constitutionalizing a decolonized nation. To the British rulers, it was a source of irritation since it came from Gandhi who had the magical power to mobilize Indians for a cause almost instantaneously. The then secretary of state, Lord Pethick-Lawrence, asked for Gandhi's note to understand what he meant and also instructed the Viceroy, Lord Wavell to prepare a note identifying 'the weaknesses' of the Gandhian scheme. In response, Wavell sent, along with his note, a brochure entitled *Gandhian Constitution for Free India* by S.N. Agarwal[49] which also received Gandhi's approval. Besides highlighting the Gandhian insistence on decentralized system of administration for the whole of 'free India' founded on village, the note underlines two important issues which caused consternation to the British authority as it was potentially 'dangerous' for a peaceful transition that it was contemplating. On the one hand, the Gandhian scheme demanded 'a fresh delimitation of Provinces on a linguistic basis and proposes joint electorates, with reservation of seats, and the right to contest additional seats.'[50] Along with suggestion for redistribution of legislative seats, it also argued for 'a fair share for all communities in public services, as a permanent solution of the minority problem.'[51] The scheme also rejected, on the other, the claim for Pakistan 'on the ground that division of India into two or more separate States will virtually mean national suicide.'[52] By questioning the demand for Pakistan when it was tacitly endorsed by the Congress leadership especially when the negotiation failed despite Cabinet Mission's endeavours in 1946, Gandhi seems to have made an attempt to initiate a counter campaign challenging his Congress colleagues. The other significant point that Wavell identified was Gandhi's argument for a defence force, which he justified 'in derogation of his firm belief in non-violence' as 'a necessity' in case the system was disrupted; this was not be 'a brutal police force [but] should be mainly in the nature of a national organization of guardians with empathy for fellow human beings.'[53] Gandhi's constitutional scheme was not exactly different since it followed the ideas that he developed while elaborating constructive programme except the political point that he pursued against those who insisted on India's bifurcation into two independent nations.

Gandhi articulated his thought on constitutional governance in his so-called 'Last will and Testament' which he prepared exactly a day before he fell to assassin's bullet on 30 January 1948. It was released for public attention on 15 February 1948 in *Harijan*. In this text, he provided a rough sketch of his proposed system of governance. Intellectually, the Last Will and Testament is drawn on his ideas of constructive programme that always became an integral part of his political campaign since his assault on the racist South African regime in the late nineteenth century. By making village as the basic organizational unit of the constructive programme, the Mahatma devised what can be defined as 'a loosely federated village republic'. The village, in Gandhi's conceptualization, would be self-sufficient economically, producing almost what it needed, making it autonomous from outside. It would contribute to a harmonious collective life which would morally empower individuals to effectively contain 'the outer evils'. The idea was not unique since, as Gandhi himself admitted, he drew on Henry Maine's classic, *Village Communities in the East and West* while devising his model of village swaraj which, by conceptualizing village being 'the autonomous nucleus', articulated a radical vision suggesting a complete departure from the colonial conceptualization of governance.[54] Critical of the top down model of governance, Gandhi, like Maine, insisted on beginning from the bottom. As he stated,

> independence must begin at the bottom. Thus every village will be a republic or Panchayat having full powers. It follows therefore that every village has to be self-sustained and capable of managing its affairs even to the extent of defending itself against the whole world. It will be trained and prepared to perish in the attempt to defend itself against any onslaught from without.[55]

Reiterating his idea when he articulated his Last Testament, he further argued that the constitutional unit was to be the village which was to become 'a republic, self-sufficient and autonomous'. Each republic would come together in 'ever-widening, never ascending circles'. The whole structure would be 'an oceanic circle whose centre will be the individual always ready to perish for the village, the latter ready to perish for the circle of village, till at last the whole becomes one life composed of individuals, never aggressive in their arrogance, but ever humble, sharing the majesty of the oceanic circle of which they are integral units'.[56]

In sharp contrast with the Weberian formulation of pyramidal structure of governance, Gandhi sought to build a loose and non-hierarchical structure of constitutional authority in which 'the outermost circumference will not wield power to crush the inner circle but give strength to all within and derive its own from the centre'.[57] As is well-known, the Gandhian model was rescinded in the Constituent Assembly by his own colleagues who felt that it was not only inherently debilitating but also 'ineffective' in pursuing a liberal democratic goal for independent India. On the insistence of the Gandhians in the Constituent Assembly, some of the ideas supporting village swaraj were incorporated in Part IV of the Constitution enumerating Directive Principles of State Policy which was not justiciable. It has thus been argued that while his success as 'anti-colonial political leader remains beyond question he failed completely to form through that movement a structural base for the foundation of an independent Indian state'.[58] The idea however gained salience with the approval of the Seventy-Third Amendment Act in 1992, roughly four decades after the acceptance of the 1950 Constitution of India.

Concluding Observations

The nationalist journey for constitutionalizing India was a testimony to a serious endeavour towards organizing India's governance around the fundamental principles of constitutional democracy that evolved in India during the colonial rule. The effort was directed to build a structure of governance on the basis of the derivative knowledge of constitutional liberalism. In a non-substantial way, the Gandhian model was an attempt to create a system of authority on the basis of his unique conceptualization of village swaraj; the foundational unit of governance was different, though the principles governing the structure of governance were drawn on the Westminster model of representation. Despite the difference in the nomenclature that Gandhi highlighted by his expression of village swaraj, the ideological roots and the concern of the 1928 Motilal Nehru Report and 1945 Sapru Report remained identical. In other words, the liberal ideas that flourished in India in the wake of colonialism became 'hegemonic' and the nationalists despite being opposed to the British rule, articulated their aspirations in the same vocabulary and form. Liberalism became 'instinctive' by virtue of being nurtured over a couple of centuries and it was natural that the nationalist voice was to be articulated accordingly. The idea of constitutional democracy that the nationalists sought to articulate was thus, argues Bhikhu Parekh, 'not an add-on, but was inherent in the India of India as a nation-state'. A loosely defined nationalism cemented 'a sense of belonging [which created] a reasonably cohesive political community [on the basis of] shared identity based on a shared conception of what their country stood for'.[59] These efforts had thus an identical conceptual root in the liberal practices that evolved during colonialism; by being critical of their bête noire, the colonial authority, for not being adequately liberal, the nationalists also provided a powerful ideological critique of British rule in India by being drawn to those fundamental liberal values which were conveniently bypassed for the fulfilment of its partisan aims.

A perusal of the Nehru Report and Sapru Report shows that, in their recommendations, both the committees felt the urgent need of addressing the specific communal concerns of the minorities, especially the Muslims. The Assembly members, particularly B.R. Ambedkar, also insisted on giving adequate constitutional protection to the minorities because unless they were integrated with the nation India's political freedom would just become vacuous. What is also striking is the acceptance by the Constituent Assembly of the structure of governance that these two Reports had laid out. It will thus not be an exaggerated claim to say that independent India's Constitution had its roots in these two nationalist efforts at constitutionalizing India.

The Gandhian model, despite not being favoured by the Constituent Assembly members in general, was also an important source of India's constitutional design, especially in regard to Part IV of the Constitution which enumerated the Directive Principles of State Policy. Here B.N. Rau's persuasive arguments in its defence seem to have supported the Gandhians in the Assembly who were keen to have village swaraj as the basic unit of India's constitutional governance. Although these principles are not justiciable they remain critical to the processes of constitutionalizing India in independent India, as Rau had envisioned. In innumerable judicial pronouncements, India's Supreme Court, by being drawn on the Part IV provisions, expanded the sphere of constitutional obligations that the state has to discharge while fulfilling its liberal commitment to the governed. So, Directive Principles are not at all cosmetic, as was argued by some of the Assembly members; they are defining pillars of constitutionalism in India in a context when democracy is both an empowering and self-fulfilling politico-ideological device.

Finally, an aspect that stands out in these nationalist efforts, namely the endeavour was directed to build a complementary mindset in defence of the liberal values which simultaneously grew in conjunction with indigenous onslaught against the illiberal British authority. The concern was to educate people in liberal values which was possible only when they were made aware of their political rights and privileges; only then, they could fight for them; otherwise, constitutional liberalism would remain elusive. A caveat is necessary here: because it would be conceptually wrong to understand the effort towards constitutionalizing in isolation; we need to grasp the processes leading finally to the making of the constitution in tandem with the freedom struggle. Organized around the core liberal principles, India's battle for political freedom led to the rise of those complementary ideological inputs which strengthened the drive towards fulfilling the goals that the Enlightenment Philosophy stood for. The goal was achieved with the adoption of the 1950 Constitution which, the founding fathers felt, not only provided a solid foundation to constitutional liberalism in India but was also to contribute to the creation of a complementary mindset for its sustenance and consolidation in future.

Notes and References

1. With Motilal Nehru as the Chairman, the committee comprised seven other members: Ali Imam, Tej Bahadur Sapru, M.S. Aney, Sardar Mangal Singh, Shuaib Qureshi, Subhas Chandra Bose, and G.R. Pradhan.
2. The resolution is quoted in *The Nehru Report: The Anti-separatist Manifesto, 1928*, Vol. 1 (New Delhi: Machiko & Panjathan, 1928), p. 25.
3. *The Nehru Report*, p. 35.
4. *The Nehru Report*, p. 36.
5. *The Nehru* Report, p. 36.
6. *The Nehru Report*, p. 36.
7. *The Nehru Report*, p. 62.
8. *The Nehru Report*, p. 65.
9. Neera Chandhoke pursues this argument in her 'the political consequences of ethic mapping', Crisis State Development Research Centre (discussion paper no. 14), LSE, December 2005 (mimeograph), pp. 12–14.
10. *The Nehru Report*, p. 67.
11. *The Nehru Report*, p. 67.
12. Jawaharlal Nehru, *An Autobiography: With Musings on Recent Events in India*, (London: John Lane the Bodley Head, 1941), p. 418.
13. Nehru, *An Autobiography*, p. 417.
14. In response to a resolution adopted in the Standing Committee of the Non-Party Conference at its meeting of 18 and 19 November 1944 for examining the communal and minorities question from a constitutional and political point of view, the Sapru Committee (comprising Tej Bahadur Sapru, M.R. Jayakar, S. Gopalaswami Ayyangar and Kunwar Jagdish Prasad) was constituted in December 1944.

15. *Constitutional Proposal of the Sapru Committee, 1945* (Bombay: Padma Publications, 1945), p. 10.

16. Curzon's statement of 20 August 1917 in the House of Commons in response to Montague's declaration is cited in *Constitutional Proposal of the Sapru Committee*, p. 11.

17. *Constitutional Proposal of the Sapru Committee, 1945*, p. 258.

18. *Constitutional Proposal of the Sapru Committee, 1945*, p. 325.

19. *Constitutional Proposal of the Sapru Committee, 1945*, p. 326.

20. *Constitutional Proposal of the Sapru Committee, 1945*, p. 326.

21. *Constitutional Proposal of the Sapru Committee, 1945*, p. 141.

22. *Constitutional Proposal of the Sapru Committee, 1945*, pp. 161–2.

23. *Constitutional Proposal of the Sapru Committee, 1945*, p. 258.

24. *Constitutional Proposal of the Sapru Committee, 1945*, p. 258.

25. *Constitutional Proposal of the Sapru Committee, 1945*, p. 216.

26. *Constitutional Proposal of the Sapru Committee, 1945*, p. 219.

27. *Constitutional Proposal of the Sapru Committee, 1945*, p. 296.

28. *Constitutional Proposal of the Sapru Committee, 1945*, p. 298.

29. *Constitutional Proposal of the Sapru Committee, 1945*, p. 326.

30. G.B. Pant's address in the Constituent Assembly, 24 January 1947, *Constituent Assembly Debates*, Lok Sabha Secretariat, New Delhi, 2003, book No. 1, p. 331.

31. B.R. Ambedkar, 25 November, 1949, *Constituent Assembly Debates*, Book No. 5, p. 974.

32. *The Outlines of a New Constitution* by B.N. Rau—reproduced in B. Shiva Rao (ed.), *The Framing of India's Constitution: Select Documents*, Vol. 1, (New Delhi: Universal Law Publishing House, 1967), p. 159.

33. Drawn on *The Outlines of a New Constitution* by Rau, pp. 159–60.

34. Rau, *The Outlines of a New Constitution*, p. 159.

35. B.N. Rau, *India's Constitution in the Making* (Bombay: Orient Longman, 1960), p. 361.

36. Rau, *India's Constitution in the Making*, p. 361.

37. B.N. Rau, *Constitutional Precedents*, Vols. I, II, and III, Manager, Government of India, New Delhi, 1946–8.

38. B.N. Rau to MA Jinnah, 22 September 1946 in Nicholas Mansergh (ed.), *The Transfer of Power, 1942–7*, Vol. VIII, p. 564.

39. B. Shiva Rao (ed.), *The Framing of India's Constitution: Select documents*, Vol. I, Universal Publishing Co. Pvt. Ltd., New Delhi, 2004 (reprint), p. 165

40. Rao, *The Framing of India's Constitution*, p. 159.

41. Rao, *The Framing of India's Constitution*, p. 158.

42. Rau, *India's Constitution in the Making*, p. 365.

43. Arvind Elangovan, *A Constitutional Imagination of India: Sir Benegal Narsing Rau Amidst the Retreat of Liberal Idealism (1910–1950)*, (Unpublished PhD dissertation, University of Chicago, 2012), pp. 229–44.

44. Rao, *The Framing of India's Constitution*, pp. 30–1.

45. Arvind Elangovan, 'The Road Not Taken: Sir Benegal Narsing Rau and the Indian Constitution', in Sekhar Bandyopadhyay (ed.), *Decolonization and the Politics of Transition in South Asia* (New Delhi: Orient Blackswan, 2016), p. 144.

46. Rao, *The Framing of India's Constitution*, p. 108.

47. Rao, *The Framing of India's Constitution*, pp. 108–9.

48. Rao, *The Framing of India's Constitution*, p. 110.

49. S.N. Agarwal, *Gandhian Constitution for Free India* (Allahabad: Kitabistan, 1946).

50. Lord Wavell's note to Pethick-Lawrence, 27 February 1946, enclosed in circular of 27 February 1946 prepared by Pethick-Lawrence in Nicholas Mansergh (ed.), *The Transfer of Power, 1942–47*, Vol. VI (New Delhi: UBS Publishers' Distributors Ltd., 1976), p. 1074.

51. Wavell's note to Pethick-Lawrence, 27 February 1946, enclosed in circular of 27 February 1946, prepared by Pethick-Lawrence in Mansergh's, *The Transfer of Power*, p. 1074.

52. Wavell's note to Pethick-Lawrence, p. 1074.

53. Wavell's note to Pethick-Lawrence, p. 1074.

54. This argument is developed by Karuna Mantena in her 'On Gandhi's Critique of the State: Sources, Context and Conjunctures', *Modern Intellectual History* 9(3) (2012).

55. M.K. Gandhi, 'Panchayati Raj' in M.K. Gandhi, *Village Swaraj*, (Ahmedabad: Navajivan Publishing House, 1962), p. 69.

56. Gandhi, 'Panchayati Raj', p. 70.

57. Gandhi, 'Panchayati Raj', p. 70.

58. Drawn on the conceptualization of Sudipta Kaviraj ('On the Structure of Nationalism Discourse' in Sudipta Kaviraj, *Imaginary Institutions of India: Politics and Ideas* (New Delhi: Permanent Black, 2010), Sandipta Dasgupta elaborated this argument in his *Localizing the Revolution*, (unpublished PhD dissertation, Columbia University, 2014), pp. 172–82.

59. Bhikhu Parekh, 'The Constitution as a Statement of Indian identity', in Rajeev Bhargava (ed.), *Politics and Ethics of the Indian Constitution* (New Delhi: Oxford University Press, 2008), p. 46.

7 Mahatma Gandhi's Alternative Conceptualization of Liberal Constitutionalism

An activist-theoretician, Mahatma Gandhi evolved a model of governance which was uniquely textured on the basis of understanding of the available modes of thinking. It is also true that he drew upon indigenous sources while conceptualizing his ideas regarding the most appropriate type of political administration that he aspired for. His ideas can be said to have creatively blended what he learnt during the long anti-imperial struggle that he led. There is an implicit assumption here: Gandhi, despite being an activist who remained paramount in the freedom struggle in India, contributed immensely to the nationalist search for an appropriate form of governance out of his internalization of both indigenous traditions and derivative wisdom from western theoretical discourses. What he evolved was, in other words, a unique model with elements from multiple Western and non-Western sources of knowledge. In his conceptualization of village Swaraj, the self-reliant village remained a cornerstone of governance which, according to him, was to be 'a complete republic, independent of its neighbors for its own vital wants, and yet inter-dependent for many others where dependencies are necessary'. Not only did he write extensively on the theme to provide a blue-print for participatory governance, he also projected himself as a crusader who saw participation as 'an antidote to the community-corroding effects of economic growth and modernization'. His republic was an epitome of a 'perfect democracy' ensuring equality across caste and religions and self-sufficiency in needs.

Two important ideas remained preeminent in Gandhi's quest for a form of governance which was, according to him, appropriate for India. First, his search was obviously governed by the prevalent socio-economic and political circumstances. It does not therefore seem odd when one finds that Gandhi was vehemently opposed to a centralized authority presumably because he confronted the British colonial state which hardly provided a space for individuals to flourish in accordance with their priorities. Second, by insisting on village being the epicentre of governance, the Mahatma gave a powerful voice to a context-sensitive sentiment which, for obvious reasons, was never appreciated in the colonial regime. Nonetheless, by his constant engagement with those thinkers who, like him, fought for democratic decentralization of power and authority, Gandhi built a model of localizing governance which was exactly neither Western nor indigenous, but an admixture of both. Hence it has been argued that Gandhi's socio-political ideas were 'the fortuitous product of very personal responses to a range of experiments in India, England, and South Africa—and to a numerous other stimuli, including Tolstoy' and other Western thinkers.[1] Uniquely-textured and conceptually-persuasive, the Gandhian model as well those values that informed his articulation is a useful endeavour in conceptualizing governance in a non-Western context. The aim of this chapter is therefore to grasp the uniqueness of the model that Gandhi had evolved and also the processes in which his approach gained credibility in adverse circumstances. As Gandhi was integrally connected with the freedom struggle, the chapter also makes the argument that the Gandhian model of governance was not based on his exclusive interaction with the leading Western theoreticians of the era, but also drew on India's peculiar socio-economic and cultural texture which perhaps explains why his model cannot be persuasively captured in a derivative theoretical framework.

Gandhi's Aim

There are two basic themes that Gandhi upheld while articulating his distinct ideas of grassroots democracy which remains the fundamental reference point for his conceptualization. In his conceptual universe, the ideas of (a) *sarvodaya* (welfare to all) and (b) panchayati raj form of governance appear to have critically shaped his approach to localizing governance; while the former underlines the philosophical basis of the idea, the latter provides a clearly defined structural arrangement to organize people in a definite ideological perspective. This was made explicit when he exhorted:

> I shall strive for a constitution which will release India from all thralldom and patronage, and give her, if need be, the right to sin. I shall work for an India, in which the poorest shall feel that it is their country in whose making they have an effective voice; an India in which there shall be no high class and low class of people; an India in which all communities shall live in perfect harmony. There can be no room in such an India for the curse of untouchability or the curse of the intoxicating drinks and drugs. Women will enjoy the same rights as men. Since we shall be at peace with all the rest of the world, neither exploiting nor being exploited, we should have the smallest army imaginable.[2]

The Mahatma's aim was to build an ideal India which was free from both caste and class prejudices; by suggesting for gender equality, Gandhi also laid out a foundation for developing an inclusive society. With the nurturing of these values, India was sure to become a centre of nations appreciative of peace and harmony. Hence, the globe would be a different globe with peace being the driving force for amity among the nation-states. How to translate this objective into practice? For Gandhi, it was the system of panchayati raj governance that would radically alter the prevalent structure of governance which was always tuned to partisan interests. This was not his innovation as he himself admitted that panchayati raj governance had an ancient flavour, though it was relevant in contemporary India because it entailed a system of the involvement of people in decision making. Opposed to parliamentary form, Gandhi strongly argued for panchayats as perhaps the only instrument to develop India in accordance with his stipulated goal. Hence, he stated that,

> the government of the village will be conducted by the Panchayat, annu-
> ally elected by the adult villagers, male and female, possessing prescribed
> qualifications. They will have all the authority and jurisdiction required.
> Since there will be no system of punishments in the accepted sense this
> Panchayat will be the legislature, judiciary and executive combined to
> operate for its year of office.[3]

As a true liberal who also drew on Kantian concern for collectivity, Gandhi, along with creating a structure of governance, also underlined the importance of individuals who, in his perception, remained the prin-cipal driving force in the ideal village that he sought to build. He thus argued that 'the individual is the architect of his own government … and he will suffer death in the defence of his and his village's honour.'[4] Implicit here is the idea of responsibility that individuals had to shoul-der for protecting the collectivity, that is the village because individuals in isolation remained a mere description without any social purpose. Conceptually valid in the liberal perspective and politically empowering in the context of the freedom struggle, such a formulation is also powerful exposition of individualism, enabled him to link individuals with the task of nation-building that he undertook simultaneously with his endeavour towards attaining political freedom from colonialism.

There is a third conceptual parameter which also supported the Gandhian approach to localizing governance. According to Gandhi, pan-chayats were also instruments for realizing Swaraj in its real connotation. True to his idea of inclusive development, Gandhi thus elaborated his notion of Swaraj by saying that 'the Swaraj of my dream … recognizes no race or religious distinctions. Nor is it to be the monopoly of the lettered persons not yet of moneyed men. Swaraj is to be for all, including the farmer, but emphatically including the maimed, the blind, the starving toiling millions.'[5] In response to the accusation that he was championing Swaraj for the majority community, that is Hindus, Gandhi vehemently opposed by arguing that 'if it were to be true, I for one would refuse to call it Swaraj and would fight it with all the strength at my command for to me Hind Swaraj is the rule of all people, is the rule of justice.'[6]

In Gandhi's conceptual universe, discrimination in any form was an anathema. For him, unless and until discrimination was completely rooted out, the idea of Poorna Swaraj remained elusive because it was 'as much for the prince as for the peasant, as much for the rich landowners as for the landless tiller of the soil, as much for the Hindus as for the Musalmans, as much for the Parsis and Christians as for the Jains, Jews and Sikhs, irrespective of any distinction of caste, creed or status in life'.[7]

So in Gandhi's perspective, Swaraj was an ideal arrangement which was neither discriminatory nor prejudiced but tuned to the creation of an environment for absolute freedom where individuals contributed to the realization of the goal by dint of hard work. Opposed to the conventional mode of governance where authority was appropriated by a select group of people, Gandhi justified his point of view by emphasizing that 'real Swaraj will come not by the acquisition of authority by a few but by the acquisition of the capacity by all to resist authority when it is abused. In other words, Swaraj is to be obtained by educating the masses to a sense of their capacity to regulate and control authority'.[8]

As is shown above, Gandhi's Swaraj was also a design of governance which drew on his own distinct ideological predisposition. An ideal form notwithstanding, Swaraj was also devised as effective instrument to bring about sarvodaya by challenging the conceptual inadequacies of colonialism which was meant to be a partisan. Like Julius Nyerere of Tanzania who evolved ujamaa as a model of self-government by his insistence on communalization through villagization, Gandhi too strove to build a new system of governance where the role of community remained most critical. This was also tried in China, as discussed in chapter 3 of my *Localizing Governance in India*,[9] where Mao Zedong laid out communes for community involvement in governance besides agricultural production. Similar to Gandhi's notion of self-government, this was an all-purposive system in which members of the communes remained organically connected with their functioning. There is a fundamental point which needs careful attention, namely the ideas of Swaraj, ujamaa, or commune, despite being rooted in different socio-economic circumstances, are powerful theoretical categories seeking to conceptualize the human endeavour towards building an ideal society; what is striking furthermore is also the fact that notwithstanding their different ideological predilections, Gandhi, Nyerere, and Mao seem to have arrived at a consensus by championing an identical socio-political goal of human salvation in circumstances of despair, agony, and disillusionment.

Intellectual Genealogy

Gandhi was uncomfortable with the modern state. With his scathing critique of western colonialism that engendered a powerful state in the wake of its expansive design, the Mahatma justified his argument for localizing the state. As he argued, 'the state represents violence in a concentrated and organized form [and since] it is a soulless machine, it can never be weaned from violence to which it owes its very existence'.[10] Being opposed to a well-entrenched state that was claustrophobic in character, he hardly wavered while arguing for the dismantling of a hegemonic state; in its place, he was always in favour of panchayats which epitomized his ideas for participatory governance. His insistence on village-centric system of grassroots governance disturbed his colleagues in the nationalist movement, especially B.R. Ambedkar who, as will be shown below, never appreciated Gandhi's preference since it reinforced the same system of atrocities against the socially-peripheral dalits. Nonetheless, the model that the Mahatma evolved on the basis of his own understanding of the phenomenon remains very critical in conceptualizing efforts that were undertaken during the nationalist phase of India's growing-up as polity. As a student of India's civilizational trajectory, it was natural for him to draw upon the past masters' contribution in comprehending the idea of localizing governance in the mould of participatory democracy. It was also surprising for him that the idea was not novel because there were thinkers who upheld the idea of self-sufficient villages in order to understand them as parts of a wider collectivity. Whether the description was eulogistic is a different question; but the fact remains that when he began working on his model of local governance, he had adequate inputs to work upon.

As the available literature shows, there are multiple descriptions highlighting, if not glorifying, India's village life as 'an ideal form of collectivity' that needed to be emulated to translate participatory governance into practice. In fact, what was hinted in these tracts was the presence of 'inner vitality' which sustained these 'village republics' over generations. Although Gandhi referred to Henry Sumner Maine's Oxford lectures in the early 1870s—which was later published with the title *Village Communities in the East and West* (1871)—while elaborating his idea of rural governance, there were two interesting tracts which also appeared to have influenced Gandhi to a significant extent given the way the idea was conceptualized and also expanded. Charles Metcalfe's exposition of village communities in India and the description that Karl Marx had left seem to have provided critical inputs that had resonances, if not explicit references, in the way the idea was drawn out by Maine and Gandhi. So, it is perfectly in order to dwell on how Metcalfe and Marx delved into the idea of perennially sustaining village republics with hardly any significant changes in their nature.

Impressed by their continuity over generations despite radical political changes, Indian villages gave enough conceptual inputs to Charles Metcalfe, a British governor who translated them in the form of a model which remains a constant reference point even today for those seeking to explain India's unique village system. By attributing the continuity of the villages to being self-sufficient, he characterized them as 'little republics'. While adumbrating his argument he further stated that,

> the village communities [which are] little republics [because they] have everything that they want within themselves, and almost independent of any foreign relations. They seem to last where nothing else lasts. Dynasty after dynasty tumbles down; revolution succeeds revolution; Hindoo [*sic*], Pathan, Moghul, Mahratta, Sikh, English are all masters in turn, but the village communities remain the same. ... This union of village communities, each forming a separate little state in itself ... is in a high degree conducive to their happiness, and to the enjoyment of a great portion of freedom and independence.[11]

In the same vein, Karl Marx seems to have been swayed by the Indian villages that were, according to him, symbols of republic. Despite significant socio-political changes due to internal dynamics and also external intervention, these villages managed to sustain their character more or less in the same mould. That Marx was equally struck by the distinct nature of Indian villages was evident in his correspondence with Friedrich Engels when he elaborated his views by reference to Fifth Report of the Select Committee on the Affairs of the East India Company (1812) which stated:

[E]very village is, and appears always to have been, in fact, a separate community or republic. ... Under this simple form of municipal government the inhabitants of the country lived from time immemorial. The boundaries of the villages have been but seldom altered; and although the villages themselves have been sometimes injured, and even desolated by war, famine and disease; the same name, the same limits, the same interests, and even the same families, have continued for ages. The inhabitants give themselves no trouble about the breaking up and division of kingdoms, while the village remains indifferent they care not to what power it is transferred, or to what sovereign it devolves. Its internal economy remains unchanged.[12]

Similar to Charles Metcalfe, Marx drew Engel's attention to the collective existence of the villagers by being appreciative of working together for common benefit. As he mentioned by highlighting the fact that 'in these village communities, LANDS OF THE VILLAGE [ARE] CULTIVATED IN COMMON, in most of them, EACH OCCUPANT TILLS HIS OWN FIELD. Home-weaving and spinning by wives and daughters. These idyllic republics, of which only the village boundaries are jealously guarded against neighbouring villages, continue to exist in well-nigh perfect form in [some parts] of India' (emphasis as per original).[13]

Both Marx and Metcalfe seem to have been swayed by the ability of the Indian villages to evolve as a system that appeared to have resisted change. This was a unique social formation which perhaps explains the continuity of the values that informed India as a civilizational entity. Henry Sumner Maine too supported the assumption that Indian villages remained self-sufficient, in his Oxford lecture in the early 1870s. In his words,

[F]or the most part, the Indian village communities have always submitted without resistance to oppression by monarchs surrounded by mercenary armies. ... I have several times spoken of them as organized and self-acting. They, in fact, include a nearly complete establishment of occupations and trades for enabling to continue their collective life without assistance from any person or body external to them.[14]

The assumption that Marx, Metcalfe, and Maine held appears to be little overstretched because no society remained static and change was instinctive to their evolution. Notwithstanding his appreciation of the idea that 'freedom and independence' were important features of Indian villages, Jawaharlal Nehru did not seem to have been persuaded by these descriptions because they were 'ahistorical' and was not conducive to progress in anything and the villages managed to retain their distinctive characteristics not because of anything else but because of 'the lack of means of communication ... that made it rather difficult for them [to get connected] with the outside world and also for the government to intervene too much in village affairs.'[15] In order to further reinforce his critique of this stance, he forcefully argued that 'the old village system ended and the panchayat ceased to exist for obvious historical reasons. We need not express any great regret for this, as the system had outlived its day and did not fit in with modern conditions.'[16] Although the old village system of governance had historically become redundant, it however left enough conceptual inputs to evolve an alternative system of collective being by drawing upon these indigenous sources of wisdom. The village system collapsed without however creating another comparable form to self-governance in accord with changed conditions, Nehru regretted. Instead of uncritically eulogizing the highly-hyped village system, what he insisted on was to make it appropriate for the modern environment when the reach of the state was far more expansive than in the past. The inputs that Metcalfe, Marx, and Maine left needed to be adapted to the circumstances in which villages no longer remained isolated but formed a part of the organic whole involving the towns as well.[17] The idea reverberated in contemporary research also. Critiquing the glorification of the village system, M.N. Srinivas and A.M. Shah also echoed the viewpoints that Nehru upheld by saying that by virtue of being a part of a wider entitle, 'the Indian village was ... always subject to the winds which blew from without.'[18] As is evident now, the notion of idyllic village system may have been useful in conceptualizing an alternative which is tuned to specific socio-economic circumstances. But it cannot be conceived as a universal model of analysis which is, for obvious reasons, ahistorical and romantic since it is contrary to the socio-historical processes that can never be avoided.

Despite powerful critiques, Gandhi did not seem to have wavered in his appreciation of the village republic, especially the account that Maine prepared in its defence. In his conceptual universe, village thus remains a fundamental unit of analysis; he was not in favour of 'resurrecting old village panchayats, but the fresh formation of independent village units of Swaraj in the context of the present day world'.[19] So, on the one hand, village was, for Gandhi, a space for articulating his idea of alternative governance by reference to the erstwhile village republics; it also provided him, on the other hand, with an opportunity to craft a design for Swaraj in consonance with individual freedom and dignity. In his views, the argument emphasizing self-sufficient villages being integral to Indian polity in the past reinforces, rather persuasively, a perception which was conducive to build a progressive future. The idea was unambiguously articulated in 1931 speech on the future state of India at Chatham House in London where he argued the point by stating:

> Princes will come and princes will go, empires will come and empires will go, but this India living in her villages will remain as it is. Sir Henry Maine has left a monograph, The Village Communities of India [*sic*] in which you will find the author saying that all these villages were at one time and are to a certain extent now, self-contained little republics [that] have their own culture, mode of life, and method of protecting themselves, their own village schoolmaster, their own priest, carpenter, barber, in fact, everything that village could want ... these villages are self-contained, and if you went there you would find that there is a kind of agreement under which they are built. From these villages has perhaps arisen what you call the iron rule of caste [that] has been a blight on India, but it has also acted as a sort of protecting shield for these masses.[20]

Gandhi's purpose of defending what Maine said about little village republics was to identify the factors which supported their continuity despite social and political upheavals. Since they were self-contained, they had hardly to depend on others for their sustenance. Being self-contained, these village republics thus became an alternative model of governance which was uniquely textured. Besides highlighting the vitality of these village republics, Gandhi quoted Maine also to combat 'the image of civilizational inferiority'[21] that was constantly being propagated to demoralize Indians. According to him, by referring to the persistence, Maine had shown to India and the world that 'the village life of India today was what it was five thousand years ago, which did not imply that Indians were barbarians. On the contrary, the writer had made it clear that the Indian village life had so much vitality and character that it had persisted all these long years and weathered many a storm.'[22]

As is clear now, Maine's conceptualization and elaboration of little village republic enabled Gandhi to persuasively defend his claim that village could be an autonomous space to wage an ideological battle against 'the imperial discourse on the apolitical and static nature of Indian society'.[23] In order to posit Indian villages as an intuitively constructed counter-point against the obviously prejudiced imperial conceptualization of India being unfit for self-governance Gandhi religiously pursued his point. With its emphasis on the self-constituting village community, Henry Maine gave a powerful voice to this claim. In an imperial context, it is thus 'no accident that Gandhi repeatedly turns to Maine's *Village Communities in the East and West* to support his claim for socio-political vitality of the Indian village'.[24] It has a clear ideological purpose. As an analyst argues, 'the valorization of the village [by] Gandhi ... was neither a simple evaluative reversal of a well-worn orientalist trope not merely a nostalgic plea for a return to a precolonial and therefore authentic India [but to conceptualize] the village as the site of autonomy [representing] a critical reconstruction and radicalization of the [prevalent] imperial discourse undermining India's civilizational vitality'.[25] So, the glorification of village by Gandhi was clearly ideological. Being critical of the hegemonic state, a line of thinking that he had initiated in the *Hind Swaraj* (1909), he found in the Indian villages a space to articulate his model of village-centric governance. Village thus became, in other words, an alternative space also to build a genre of thought which had reverberated in the ideas of Henry Sumner Maine.

What is basic to Gandhi's argument in favour of Indian village system was the idea of community and its articulation in a wider social context. Like Nyerere and Mao, he was persuaded to believe that unless people are communalized by being appreciative of commonality among them, it would be difficult, if not impossible, to evolve a successful community. As an activist-theoretician, Gandhi had found a means in the idea of ashram or communal farm. Similar to what had prevailed in the Victorian England, Gandhi insisted on creating the village as a self-acting and egalitarian form of collective existence, organized on the basis of collective ownership. Drawn on his firm belief that being together was an easy and also most effective way to evolve a community he thus built

Phoenix Farm (1904), followed by Tolstoy Farm (1906) in South Africa and later Sabarmati Ashram (1916–33) in India primarily to experiment with his idea of communal living which would ultimately lead to what he defined as 'cooperative commonwealth'. They had emerged primarily in response to the difficulties that Indians had encountered in South Africa, as Gandhi's own description revealed. While accounting for the miseries that Indians confronted, the Mahatma felt that Indians suffered largely because they lacked unity. In order to instill the feeling of being united, he thus suggested that they should be together physically to combat these challenges. As he further elaborated,

> [T]here was only one solution, namely that all the families should be kept at one place and should become members of a sort of cooperative commonwealth. Thus there would be no scope for fraud, nor would there be injustice to any. Public funds would be largely saved and the families of Satyagrahis would be trained to live a new and simple life in harmony with one another. Indians belonging to various provinces and professing diverse faiths would have an opportunity of living together.[26]

In order to bind the socio-economically disparate people together, the Phoenix and Tolstoy Farms took every steps to create a milieu of communal living as perhaps the only and also effective option to counter state-atrocities; they represented communal living in the real sense of the term. Hence 'accommodation was shared, and instead of each settler cultivating a separate plot of land, it was decided that the entire acreage would be cultivated jointly to ensure more efficient production of larger crops, and to enhance the cooperative spirit of the exercise'.[27] For Gandhi, the experiment was an opportunity to inculcate values conducive to simple and non-materialistic life which was, he felt, necessary to meaningfully articulate the notion of cooperative commonwealth. As Gandhi confirmed, Indians,

> will have on the farm, a noble life in place of the unclean and monotonous ways of town life. Moreover, what they will learn on the farm will prove useful for a lifetime. Indeed we have seen in the past that the Indian community would be well rewarded if it were to take to agriculture and would be saved from the anxieties incidental to business. We have a heavy price for not recognizing this best of occupations.[28]

Out of such cooperation, Gandhi saw, the growth of 'a sort of republic [which was] self-sufficient in the necessities of life and democratically-governed: a nonviolent community founded on harmony and cooperation between its members'.[29] Ashrams were not merely an institutional structure for cooperative life, but also articulated a way of life to inculcate those values which were useful for communal living. Seeking to build and also permanently instill the value of commonality for common well-being, his main concern was to create an environment where men and women, rich and poor and also people belonging to different castes and regions come together to form an organic community. Hence it is argued that Gandhi's ashrams were 'living laboratories wherein he and his colleagues experimented with ways and means of enabling India's villagers to live in dignity and freedom [which also confirms that] the essence of the communal experiment lay not in the institutional infrastructure that developed, but in the activities themselves and their heuristic value'.[30]

Gandhi's fundamental aim was to bring people together and Ashrams were a useful tool. Here Ashram was a microcosm of Indian village life because it was based on the urge to live together in a common space and with common objectives. The idea was not novel as Ashram as an emotion-driven conceptual space is integral to ancient India. While in the ancient era, it was said to have evolved naturally, in the context of South Africa and India where Indians were victims of racial and colonial exploitations respectively, Ashram provided them with a space for creating an alternative voice and also challenging what was considered to be unacceptable. Ashram was therefore a site of organization and also protest in adverse circumstances. The above analytical account highlights two interesting ideas which are useful in conceptualizing Gandhi's fascination for localizing governance. At one level, it was an ideological agenda with significant theoretical implications; at another it was a powerful alternative which immediately struck chord with those fighting against odds. As is argued above, village was, to Gandhi, a site for contestation because it had the potentials to build and develop a space for change and also harmony. Villagers could be a useful force to make an argument in favour of an alternative. Like Maine who argued that the Indian village system represented an epitome of communal living, Gandhi too drew on its inherent qualities to develop his conceptual framework supportive of an alternative model of governance in contrast with an all-pervasive and hegemonic colonial form of administration. On the basis of what Gandhi felt as the inner vitality of communal living, he made another powerful endeavour in crafting a meaningful ideological course of action in a not so favourable situation. Village became a forum of organization to pursue a differently-conceptualized language of commonality and well-being which informed the Gandhian mode of struggle for national salvation in which the role of individuals was as critical as that of the collectivity of which they were constituents. The underlying thread of his argument is clearly Kantian since in Gandhi's conceptual universe the individual and collectivity are dialectically intertwined. By way of popularizing Ashram at the micro and village at the macro level, Gandhi thus evolved a model of governance which was relevant to a context where village was not merely a geographical notion but epitomized a conceptually-innovative and ideologically-appropriate category to meaningfully understand the differently-textured Indian socio-political reality.

Conceptual Ideas

Being critical of positivist rationalism, Gandhi was opposed to the 'one-size-fits-all' syndrome because each society had its exclusively own track record. The purpose of Gandhi was twofold: (a) to mobilize new segments of Indian society and (b) make such participation meaningful as well as to lend a perspective to the movement. He thus developed a large variety of social and economic programmes which were designed for instantaneous appeal to peasants, artisans, craftsmen, and Harijans—in short, every group of society. According to him, 'true democracy cannot be worked by twenty men sitting at the centre; it has to be worked from below, by the people of every village'.[31] What was unique in Gandhi's conceptualization of civic engagement in public affairs was his notion of 'oceanic circle' that he developed while defending village Swaraj by saying that

> Life will not be a pyramid with the apex sustained by the bottom. But it will be an oceanic circle whose centre will be the individuals always ready [to sacrifice] for the village, the latter ready to perish for the circle of villages, till at last the whole becomes one life composed of individuals, never aggressive in their arrogance but even humble, sharing the majesty of the oceanic circle of which they are integral units.[32]

Two ideas are pre-eminent here: *first*, for him, a circle of interdependent villages remained perhaps the most viable unit for sustained and equitable economic growth for any society; *second*, perhaps more importantly, systematic economic well-being would certainly make the individuals within the circle self-reliant and thus confident. Hence he was very critical of the doctrine of 'the greatest good of the greatest number [that] is a heartless doctrine and has done harm to the humanity. [The only] real and dignified human doctrine is', according to Gandhi, 'the greatest good of all, and this can only be achieved by uttermost self-sacrifice'.[33] It is evident that Gandhi was deeply uneasy with the modern state. For him, a society based on Swaraj, 'true democracy' or non-violence was the only morally acceptable alternative to the modern state. According to him, the swaraj-based polity would be composed of small, cultured, well-organized, thoroughly regenerated and self-governing village communities; elected by these communities, a small body of people would administer justice, maintain order, and take important economic decisions out of interactive dialogues with the community as a whole. These units would thus be not merely administrative but also powerful economic and political units fulfilling their role by seeking to articulate swaraj in its true form. As such they would thus have a strong sense of solidarity, provide a genuine sense of community and act as nurseries of civic virtues. In conceptualizing the village swaraj which would finally lead to Sarvadayo (welfare for all), Gandhi was drawn to *dharma* which, in his views, consisted of sensitivity and responsiveness. After having theoretically justified *Swaraj* as an efficient form of civic engagement emphasizing the importance of both individuals and communities, the Mahatma evolved his model of village swaraj which, according to him, was an authentic form of participatory democracy.

The conceptualization of the oceanic circle is an innovative design to view governance in a participatory mould. This was to be a system of governance in which, as Gandhi argued, 'the last is equal to the first, or in other words, none is to be the first and none the last'.[34] Opposed to hierarchy in any form, Gandhi laid out his model by suggesting an alternative structure of governance which was neither discriminatory nor appreciative of division in terms of class, creed, and power. An egalitarian mode of organizing governance, Gandhi's oceanic circle represents a system where, 'the outermost circumference will not wield power to crush the inner circle but give strength to all within and derive its own from the centre.[35] So, at one level, the Mahatma prepared a mental map to appreciate the values of equality as an antidote to exploitation of human beings by human beings; at another, he laid out the broad outlines of a structure of governance which is constituted by interdependent units pursuing common aims. This may appear to be utopian, as Gandhi himself admitted, which he countered by saying that 'if Euclid's point, though incapable of being drawn by human agency, has an imperishable value, my picture has its own for mankind to live.'[36] The idea has certain obvious limitation unless it is complemented by a comparable mindset which may not be feasible in a real world where human greed for more at others' cost cannot be completely ruled out. Nonetheless, the Gandhian oceanic circle is a powerful conceptual innovation for two complementary reasons: on the one hand, being integrally connected with a well-entrenched global intellectual tradition in favour of creating an egalitarian socio-economic order, the Gandhian intervention articulates its manifestation in the non-Western context where colonialism created a divisive society for consolidating processes in its favour. Not only is the idea—oceanic circle—inventive, it is also a useful intellectual tool to conceptualize, on the other hand, the notion of peaceful coexistence by addressing the sources of irritation and discomfort in the spirit of togetherness and commonality for an identical purpose of common well-being, as it happens, to use Gandhi's metaphor, in the marine life where creatures of different size and strength survive presumably because of certain natural laws governing their behaviour.

The Village Swaraj

Being raised in colonial India, Gandhi naturally imbibed certain specific ideas which were not exactly anti-British but against the prevalent British government that he fought tooth and nail. His critique of racism in South Africa and British colonialism in India was based on his appreciation of Enlightenment philosophy. He was simply not agreeable to a regime that, despite being based on liberalism, had an explicit discriminatory character. This was a contradiction that, Gandhi felt, needed to be meaningfully addressed to avoid further distortions in governance in South Africa and India. At another level of his critique, Gandhi sharpened his counterattack on the regime for its failure to uphold the basic values of liberalism while governing the citizens of the empire. His insistence on Indians being treated equally as citizens of the empire followed from the liberal tenets that he held so dearly. What was unique in Gandhi's approach to racism and colonialism was his emphatic faith in liberalism which was, he strongly felt, an empowering ideology because of its egalitarian nature and its desire to create sameness in humanity. Nonetheless, despite being appreciative of Western liberalism, he also held views which ran counter to the 'liberal-democratic reification, objectification and technocratization of the political and the alienation of the people's political rights'[37] because he firmly believed that 'swaraj will be an absurdity if individuals have to surrender their judgment to a majority[38] ... [and] true democracy cannot be worked by twenty men sitting at the Centre; it has to be worked from below by the village.'[39] Unlike its conventional mould, liberalism was conceptualized differently by Gandhi by drawing on the distinctly-textured village republic which allowed localizing of governance in its true connotation. What is striking is the implicit idea that despite being committed to liberalism, Gandhi, instead of blindly conforming to its fundamental ethos and principles which were not politically relevant, devised village swaraj in which power was dispersed and authority decentralized. His aim was to make governance genuinely participatory by insisting on exercising power by the villagers themselves rather than by their representatives.

Gandhi's entire project was to build a system of governance on the basis of his understanding of liberalism as a guiding principle. As is argued above, being vehemently opposed to state-hegemony, the Mahatma preferred a village-based national polity which drew upon his fascination for village swaraj. So emphatic was his belief about the village being the focal point of India's socio-economic rejuvenation that he exhorted, 'if village perishes, India will perish too.'[40] True to his own conceptualization of the British state, he evolved the idea of village swaraj as the only means to combat the omnipresent colonial state which also prevented individuals from realizing their full potentials. While elaborating his notion of village swaraj, he thus stated,

> my idea of village swaraj is that it is a complete republic, independent of its neighbours for its own vital wants, and interdependent for many others

in which dependence is a necessity. Thus every village's first concern will be to grow its own food crops and cotton for its cloth. It should have a reserve for its cattle, recreation and playground for adults and children.[41]

Two important features of being republic and independent of its neighbours for basic needs are critical to village swaraj. While the former refers to the way the authority is to be constituted, the latter delves into its self-sufficient character. In order to ascertain the republican character of village swaraj, Gandhi prescribed his familiar system of panchayat governance, to be elected by the adult villagers regardless of caste, class, gender or ethnicity. These little village republics needed to be self-sufficient as well, as Gandhi insisted. Such an argument is likely to be misleading if Gandhi's notion of self-sufficiency is narrowly conceptualized. Being aware of such a possibility, Gandhi thus explained that 'to be self-sufficient is not be altogether self-contained [because] in no circumstances would we be able to produce all the things that we need [and hence] ... we shall have to get from outside the village what we cannot produce in the village'.[42] There is a further point that he also offered while making a case for getting stuff from outside in case that was not available in the village. In his scheme of things, villages were also interdependent on one another for their survival. In order to address this aspect of village swaraj, Gandhi thus suggested that 'we shall have to produce more of what we can in order thereby to obtain in exchange what we are unable to produce'.[43] The fundamental point here is how to make village swaraj a workable scheme. The formula is easy to understand: along with his insistence on self-sufficiency in regard to food, cloth and other basic necessities, he also suggested a scheme for mutual exchange of goods which villagers could part with after having satisfied their requirements. Unless this was done, Gandhi warned, village swaraj would cease be a reality, but a utopian construct which could be conceptually thought-provoking without hardly being realistic.

One of the fundamental pillars of village swaraj happened to be individuals who, unless adequately empowered, were just numbers with no consequence whatsoever. Based on his concern for individual freedom, he thus argued that 'individual, [being] guided by nonviolence ... is the architect of his own government ... and will suffer death in the defence of his and his village's honour'.[44] Here Gandhi was talking in a typical liberal language. That he was a true liberal was further evident in his conceptualization of 'an ideal state' where the importance of individuals is established beyond doubt. With the setting of individual as indispensable in village swaraj, Gandhi now talked about its actual functioning. In order to make villages an ideal livable place, he thus suggested,

> there will be no castes such as we have today with their graded untouchability. Nonviolence with its technique of Satyagraha and non-cooperation will be the sanction of the village community. As far as possible, every activity will be conducted on the cooperative basis. [Furthermore,] the village will maintain a village theatre, school and public hall. It will have its own waterworks ensuring clean water supply. This can be done through controlled wells or tanks. Education will be compulsory up to the final basic course.[45]

This is a well-defined structure which is both indicative and elaborate. As a step towards creating 'a communal self' being appreciative of one another, the village swaraj drew its sustenance from stable social relations which were possible by creating a caste-free society. Here, in tune with his basic social view, Gandhi laid out a structure of governance that had no place for caste discrimination, especially untouchability which was, he always felt, a sin in humanity. By creating village theatre and public hall, he put forward a structure for regular social interactions among the members of village swaraj which would act in creating and also cementing a bond among the villagers and also helping to remove the source of irritation by addressing them collectively. As one who always endorsed that human efforts could do miracle, Gandhi laid out a structure of human collectivity based on his belief that 'human beings are capable of building a community [drawing] on cooperation and sharing, on altruism, and on the denial of greed. It is the world of *sarvodaya*.'[46] A unique conceptualization, the village swaraj was thus meant to articulate an aspired world which was free from want, greed, and prejudices. As a pragmatist, Gandhi was also aware that the idea of village swaraj was utopian though he firmly believed that with sincere human endeavours it could easily be translated into reality. According to him, village swaraj,

> will contain intelligent human beings; they will not live in dirt and darkness as animals. Men and women will be free and able to hold their own

against anyone in the world. There will be neither plague, nor cholera nor smallpox; no one will be idle, no one will wallow in luxury. Everyone will have to contribute his quota of manual labour.[47]

Village swaraj provides a model of localizing governance with reference to Gandhi's own understanding of multiple intellectual resources, drawn from both Western and indigenous inputs. A surface reading of the construct reveals that it has utopian characteristics because, as Gandhi himself admitted, it hardly corresponded with what existed as village life in the then India.[48] An idealistic formation undoubtedly, it was also an intellectual device to generate support for village-centric governance in a context when there were opponents, as we will see later. Nonetheless, the idea of village swaraj was a refreshing idea of self-belief in a structure of governance that also had conceptual roots in the Western thinking besides visible indigenous sources of inspiration. What was unique in Gandhi was his ability to put forward a persuasive scheme of things which was also realistic enough to gain acceptance. It was not surprising that his idea of Ashram led to several experiments all over India. What he devised in the context first of Phoenix and Tolstoy Farms in South Africa, and later Sabarmati Ashram in India created a realistic alternative which was not only feasible but also conceptually thought-provoking. A Gandhian alternative, village swaraj thus represented a powerful design of localizing governance during the British rule when a hegemonic state reigned supreme, for all practical purposes.

Basic Principles of Village Swaraj

Since village swaraj was a format of participatory governance, it can be said to have emerged from Gandhi's critique of limited democracy that colonial government in India had adopted. For him, it was not at all democracy in its actual connotation because majority of the population remained peripheral. What was therefore required was to instill the democratic spirit by inculcating the complementary values. This was easier said than done because the prevalent socio-economic processes did not seem to have been favourable in a colonial context. It was a daunting task though the Mahatma, in his familiar style, elaborated some basic principles which were easy to internalize not because they were articulated in a lucid language but because they emerged out of the prevalent socio-economic circumstances. For the majority of Indians, these principles were, in other words, persuasive since they were organically connected with their aspired universe which was free from exploitation due to socio-economic and political reasons.

In all, there were twelve principles[49] that Gandhi had elaborated as integral to village swaraj. Suggestive of Gandhi's concern for inclusive development, these principles are also useful to decode his model of participatory governance.

1. *Supremacy of man-full employment*: In village swaraj, everybody was entitled to get sufficient work to enable him to make two ends meet. This was possible, as Gandhi believed, only when the means of production remained in the control of the masses, and not appropriated by a group.

2. *Body labour*: For inclusive development, everybody was expected to contribute in creating and sustaining resources; otherwise, no society would progress. The idea of body labour is also conceptualized as 'bread labour' which means the physical labour that one needs to put to earn one's bread or livelihood.

3. *Equality*: As per Gandhi, unless there was equality, the talk of village swaraj was absolutely futile. One comes across three complementary levels in Gandhi's argument: at one level, he was insistent that 'an economics that ... enables the strong to amass wealth at the expense of the weak is a false and dismal science'.[50] At the second level, he linked equality with nonviolent revolution because 'working for economic equality means abolishing the eternal conflict between capital and labour [which actually is all about] levelling down of the few rich in whose hands is concentrated the bulk of the nation's wealth on the one hand, and a levelling up of the semi-starved naked millions on the other.' At the third level, he was strongly arguing for equal distribution of wealth which means that 'each man shall have the wherewithal to supply all his natural wants and no more'.

4. *Trusteeship*: The idea of trusteeship seemed to have emerged out of Gandhi's concern for economic equality. He felt rather strongly that political freedom to be meaningful needed to be

complemented by economic equality. The Gandhian political economy consists in the careful possession and just division of human possession. According to Gandhi, 'at the root of this doctrine ... must lie that of the trusteeship of the wealthy for the superfluous wealth possessed by them [and the rich men] may possess nothing beyond what is required for personal needs.'[51] Gandhi was aware that his doctrine of Trusteeship was 'ridiculed' by his colleagues since it derived its sustenance from high moral values which were hardly realizable in reality.

5. *Decentralization*: According to Gandhi, centralization as a tendency was always harmful for democracy because it stifled the natural human growth. The major driving force for the healthy human development was decentralization of authority and power. Like Henry Sumner Maine, the Mahatma was also persuaded to believe that decentralization heralded a new era in democratic governance which lost its momentum in colonialism. The aim was not merely to involve people in governance, but also to empower them socially and ideologically to defend what they endorse as appropriate for the common well-being.

6. *Swadeshi*: In the conventional sense, swadeshi is an economic doctrine referring to being self-dependent in terms of economic needs. Unable to appreciate the restricted connotation of swadeshi as merely an economic design, Gandhi upheld its wider meaning by arguing that swadeshi was also a mindset which instilled the urge for being self-independent. 'Every village in India will almost be a self-supporting and self-contained unit, exchanging' felt Gandhi, 'necessary commodities with other villages as are not locally producible.'[52] So, this is an economic arrangement to make villages stand on their own.

7. The final two components of village swaraj are panchayat governance and *Nai Talim* or new education. While the former refers to a specific administrative structure the latter is about the form of education that Gandhi felt was necessary to build village swaraj. It was Mahatma's masterstroke to convincingly argue for a form of grassroots democracy in the context of colonialism where centralized authority was a norm rather than an exception. Since it was a space for participation, it would create a zeal

among the villagers to get drawn to it without reservation. For the villagers, the panchayats were not merely a forum of governance, but also a way of self-gratification in a situation where they hardly had a respectable place in the colonial dispensation of administrative roles. An empowering device, panchayats therefore became a rallying point in the Gandhi-led political struggle leading to decolonization in 1947.

In order to strengthen village swaraj's spiritual-cultural foundation, Gandhi considered Nai Talim to be an effective means. Nai Talim was not a conventional system of education but a means of 'drawing out of the best in child and man—body, mind and spirit' which was possible only by involving oneself in physical labour'.[53] Appreciative of John D. Ruskin's endorsement of dignity of labour, the Mahatma preferred physical labour as against intellectual labour because the former allowed individuals to really understand that the distinction between them was futile. Instead, Gandhi preferred a creative blending of 'craft, art, health and education as perhaps the only time-tested device to realize the goal of village swaraj. This was, in Gandhi's conceptualization, Nai Talim which was meant to guide individual 'from the time of conception to the moment of death.'[54]

Village swaraj is the Mahatma's mental construct depicting an ideal socio-political order based on his distinct ideological preferences. Despite being drawn on Western sources, village swaraj became readily acceptable presumably because of the obvious indigenous roots. At one level, it was a model of localizing governance; at another, it was a powerful statement suggestive of an alternative in the face of a centralized colonial state which lost its credibility, as Gandhi pointed out, by violating even the basic principles of the Enlightenment philosophy. According to him, village swaraj was a liberal state in its undiluted form which he upheld in his defence by saying that,

here no one would harbor any distinction between community and community, caste and outcaste. Everybody would regard all as equal with oneself and hold them together in the silken net of love. No one would regard another as untouchable. We would hold as equal the toiling labourer and the rich capitalist. Everybody would know how to earn an honest living by the sweat of one's brow and make no distinction between intellectual and physical labour.[55]

The ideas are explicit: the aim of village swaraj was to create conditions for sarvodaya or welfare of all. This was possible with serious human endeavours which also reconfirms that, in conceptual terms, village swaraj is more realistic and less idealistic since it draws on those human qualities which can easily be inculcated. There is a pattern in his thought-process if one places the idea of village swaraj in the scheme of things that Gandhi had put forward to defend the arguments questioning the illiberal British rule in India which were articulated first in the *Hind Swaraj* (1909) and later in other texts. Central to his sustained political effort was his concern for freedom not only from colonialism but also from those structural social impediments which hardly allowed the human beings to realize their full potentials. Village swaraj was thus a twin-edged formula which firmly established, on the one hand, an alternative design of participatory governance, and also an ideology, on the other hand, of self-confidence among those who were usually denigrated as incapable by virtue of being colonized.

Based on his emphatic belief that cooperative efforts would do miracle, he thus built an alternative structure by drawing on the traditional panchayat system of governance. Contrary to the conventional notion of governance linked just with political administration, Gandhi conceptualized the idea in its wider sense; it is also a socio-ideological mode of preparing human being to lead a collective life. In Gandhi's perception, panchayats are that form of collective-disciplining to make people sensitive to common concerns and welfare. This is a self-generating idea which derives its sustenance from those socio-ideological processes which have, at their core, the urge for common good. So, panchayats are not mere structures of governance, but nurseries of civic virtues which are useful to radically alter the existent socio-political prejudices of one against another. Appreciative of the bottom-up mode of governance, Gandhi's core unit was thus village and he believed that once the village was transformed, it would have automatic spiral effect on the entire society. In other words, since he held that 'independence must begin at the bottom',[56] he thus took ample care while laying-out his views on panchayats. Characterizing panchayats as 'a republic having full powers', he further noted that 'every village has to be self-sustained and capable in managing its affairs even to the extent of defending itself against the whole world.

It will be trained and prepared to perish in its attempt to defend itself against any onslaught from without'.[57]

So, the panchayats needed to be self-sufficient in terms of what they required for survival and further growth. This was possible, as Gandhi underlined, when 'every man and woman knows what he or she wants and, what is more, knows that none should want anything that others cannot have with equal labour'.[58] The aim was to create a mutual benefit society in which its members learnt to appreciate the values of being together for the sake of the collectivity of which they were constituents. Here too, Gandhi was banking on 'voluntary play of mutual forces' which, unless they were nurtured, were unlikely to contribute to panchayats. This has two implications: on the one hand, it ensures mutual give-and-take among the members who always feel being connected with each other by being integral to the oceanic circle. Once they are part of the wider circle, they, on the other hand, do not feel isolated but independent at the same time since their primary aim is also to be self-dependent. In the maze of collectivity, Gandhi, a true liberal thinker, was also keen not to submerge the individuals as critical units in his entire philosophical discourse. This he emphatically argued when he stated that 'it is the individual who is the unit' of any collective formation.[59] Hence, in his perception, individuals remained the only critical factor in social transformation which was explicit when he gave the responsibility of building a true nonviolent society to them. He thus exhorted that 'any lover of democracy and village life can take up a village, treat it as his world and sole work by being [a multitasker] who is comfortable in working as a scavenger, spinner, watchman, medicineman and school teacher all at once'.[60]

Very much comparable to what Karl Marx postulated while conceptualizing a communist society, the Gandhian approach is however distinctly textured because of its rejection of the idea of class war. The little village republics are formed on the basis of mutual respect, empathy, and care for one another for a better cause. This is a highly moralist position which may appear to be utopian since the mindset does not seem to be supportive of such processes. Gandhi had a solution which he found out in a situation where everybody got drawn to activities, meant to realize a common goal. Hence, to draw the villagers to work for common well-being, he favoured certain methods, despite being primitive, for engaging them in fruitful employment. As he argued, 'I have no partiality for return to the primitive method of grinding and husking for the sake of them; I suggest the return because there is no other way of giving employment to the millions of villagers who are living in idleness, ... [and] to induce the villagers to utilize their idle hours is in itself solid uplift work.'[61]

In the light of what Gandhi suggested, it is evident that for inclusive development to strike roots, panchayats were a useful stepping stone towards the goal. What was unique in his endeavour was to evolve not only an institutional mechanism of governance but also favourable socio-economic circumstances supportive of a specific mindset endorsing the urge for common good. The scheme that he devised was thus ideologically-inspired in contrast with colonialism which was both restrictive and also restraining in so far as the colonized subjects were concerned. In this sense, panchayats were not merely an innovative alternative, but also another site of contestation and challenge against the dominant ideological discourse in support of the state-centric top-down theoretical paradigm. By critiquing the colonial state, Gandhi created, in other words, a powerful and also persuasive set of arguments which allowed parallel efforts, elsewhere in more or less similar socio-economic milieu, to articulate distinct responses supportive of participatory governance in opposition to the centralization of authority at the behest of a hegemonic state.

Concluding Observations

In his defence for the self-governing village swaraj, Gandhi endorsed the Pluralist approach to state sovereignty, of which Henry S. Maine was one of the exponents.[62] According to Maine, state sovereignty stood in the way of realizing the idea of popular government in its substantial form since the latter could be a threat to the former. What is basic to the Pluralist approach is the notion that a host of voluntary associations—from church to trade unions—holds sovereignty which cannot be abdicated under any circumstances in democracy. The state cannot therefore be allowed to appropriate the space these self-administered organizations independently retain. In opposition to the contractualists—Hobbes, Locke, and Rousseau—they further argued in favour of the pluralization of state or a process of decentralization of authority to legitimately accommodate these self-governed structure of authorities. For Maine, village community was a mode of governance challenging and also supplementing state sovereignty by way of endorsing decentralization as an empowering device. In tune with this argument, Gandhi insisted on village swaraj as the only device to inculcate the spirit of self-governance. He was anti-statist in his theoretical inkling which was manifest in his arguments for village swaraj. As little republics, villages were vested with political authority which they acquired by being directly elected by the people. These republics were 'oceanic circle' comprising village panchayats which held, for all practical purposes, substantial authority to pursue common objectives. Critical of the pyramidal structure of the state because it represented institutionalized hierarchy, Gandhi evolved village swaraj as a decentralized structure of governance which, by creating 'the forms of self-rule, would work to eventually displace the state, [which is] understood to be inherently violent'.[63] He thus looked upon 'an increase in the power of the state with the greatest fear because although while apparently doing good by minimizing exploitation, it does the greatest harm to mankind by destroying individuality which lies at the root of all progress'.[64] Gandhi's choice was very clear: a nonviolent village republic in which individual would be 'the architect of his own government' by transforming the village into 'a perfect democracy based upon individual freedom'.[65]

The story will however be incomplete unless one refers to the tension in Gandhi's idea of village swaraj: despite being critical of the modern industrial state, he did not completely reject the notion of an organized authority which an anarchist would have done. Instead, Gandhi gave an alternative form of authority by drawing on his philosophical preferences for pluralization of state. It was a state of a completely different kind because it was neither exploitative nor insensitive to the importance of individuals. Village swaraj was thus a creative blending of what he derived from Henry Sumner Maine and those from the classical liberal thinkers. At one level, it was thus a derived but uniquely-textured concept, at another, village swaraj also represented a typical Gandhian model of organization of authority that was conceptually compatible with what the Pluralists stood for. The Gandhian arguments in favour of village swaraj are, in other words, both derivative and novel at the same time: derivative because the imprint of the ideas of the Pluralists, including Maine, is visible; creative since the Mahatma left his own stamp while elaborating village swaraj by emphasizing its distinct character of being nonviolent and individualistic. There was also a political purpose: village republic was, as argued above, a site of contestation of two contrasting models of governance: one that came in the wake of the British rule and the other which Gandhi had articulated as little village republics. They are conceptually at variance with each other since the former drew on centralization of power and authority while the latter represented just the opposite; for Gandhi, the success of village republic as a mode of self-generating governance was contingent on meaningful decentralization of authority and power. The urge for localization of power remained, in other words, vacuous unless authority was decentralized in the real sense of the term. What is fundamental in regard to Gandhi's village republic is the fact that it is linked with his overall concern for involving individuals in an effort which allows them to realize their full potentials through their participation.

Notes and References

1. Satish Saberwal, 'Introduction: Civilization, Constitution, Democracy', in Zoya Hasan, E. Sridharan, and R. Sudarshan (eds), *India's Living Constitution: Ideas, Practices and Controversies* (New Delhi: Permanent Black, 2006) (reprint), p. 12

2. M.K. Gandhi, 'India of my dreams', *Young India*, 10 September 1931—reproduced in M.K. Gandhi, *India of My Dreams* (Ahmedabad: Navajivan Publishing House, 2006) (reprint), p. 6.

3. M.K. Gandhi, 'My Idea of Village', *Harijan*, 26 July 1942—reproduced in Gandhi, *India of My Dreams*, p. 11.

4. Gandhi, 'My Idea of Village', p. 12.

5. M.K. Gandhi, 'Defining Swaraj', *Young India*, 26 March 1931—reproduced in Gandhi, *India of My Dreams*, p. 8.

6. Gandhi, 'Defining Swaraj', pp. 8–9.

7. Gandhi, 'Defining Swaraj', p. 9.

8. Gandhi, 'Defining Swaraj', p. 7.

9. Bidyut Chakrabarty, *Localizing Governance in India* (London and New York: Routledge, 2017), pp. 105–28.

10. Gandhi, 'The Sarvodaya State', *The Modern Review*, 1935, p. 412—reproduced in Gandhi, *India of my Dreams*, p. 80.

11. Charles Metcalfe's text on the Indian village system was cited by Jawaharlal Nehru in his *Glimpses of World History* (Gurgaon: Penguin, 2004) (reprint), p. 489.

12. Karl Marx quoted the original English from the *Fifth Report of the Select Committee on the Affairs of the East India Company* (London, 1812, p. 82) in his letter to Friedrich Engels on 14 June 1853—reproduced in Iqbal Husain (ed.), *Karl Marx on India*, (New Delhi: Tulika Books, 2006), pp. 266–7.

13. Karl Marx to Engels, 14 June 1853—reproduced in in Iqbal Husain (ed.), *Karl Marx on India*, p. 267.

14. Henry Sumner Maine, *Village Communities in the East and West* (six lectures delivered at Oxford), Henry Bolt and Company, New York 1889, pp. 124–5, available in https://archive.org/stream/villagecommunities00main#page/n5/mode/2up, (accessed on 25 April 2016).

15. Nehru, *Glimpses of World History*, p. 489.

16. Nehru, *Glimpses of World History*, p. 491.

17. Drawn on the argument that Jawaharlal Nehru advanced in his *Glimpses of World History*, p. 491.

18. M.N. Srinivas and A.M. Shah, 'The Myth of Self-Sufficiency of the Indian Village', *The Economic Weekly*, 10 September, 1960. p. 1377.

19. H.M. Vyas's introduction to M.K. Gandhi, *Village Swaraj* (Ahmedabad: Navajivan Publishing House, 1962), p. xiv.

20. M.K. Gandhi's speech at Chatham House meeting, 20 October 1931, *The Collected Works of Mahatma Gandhi*, Vol. 54, pp. 56–7—cited in Karuna Mantena, 'On Gandhi's Critique of the State: Sources, Contexts, Conjunctures', *Modern Intellectual History* 9(3), 2012, p. 540.

21. Mantena, 'On Gandhi's Critique of the State', p. 542.

22. M.K. Gandhi's speech at YMCA, Calcutta, 25 August 1925, *The Collected Works of Mahatma Gandhi*, Vol. 32, p. 332—cited in Mantena, 'On Gandhi's Critique of the State', p. 542.

23. Mantena, 'On Gandhi's Critique of the State', p. 537.

24. Mantena, 'On Gandhi's Critique of the State', p. 537.

25. Mantena, 'On Gandhi's Critique of the State', p. 537.

26. M.K. Gandhi, *Satyagraha in South Africa* (Ahmedabad: Navajivan Publishing House, 2006) (reprint), pp. 213–14.

27. Mark Thomson, *Gandhi and his Ashram*, (Mumbai: Popular Prakashan, 1993), p. 76.

28. M.K. Gandhi, 'Kallenbach's Gift', *Young India*, 11 June 1910, *The Collected Works of Gandhi*, Vol. 11, p. 66, available in http://www.gandhiserve.org/cwmg/VOL011.PDF, (accessed on 26 April 2016).

29. Mark Thomson, *Gandhi and His Ashram* (Mumbai: Popular Prakashan, 1993), p. 234.

30. Thomson, *Gandhi and his Ashram*, p. 302.

31. Gandhi, *Village Swaraj*, p. 41.

32. M.K. Gandhi, 'Panchayat Raj', *Harijan*, 28 July 1946—reproduced in Gandhi, *India of my Dreams*, (reprint), p. 100.

33. *The Diary of Mahadev Desai* (Ahmedabad: Navajivan Publishing House, 1953), p. 149.

34. Gandhi, 'Panchayati Raj', p. 100.

35. Gandhi, 'Panchayati Raj', p. 100.

36. Gandhi, 'Panchayati Raj', p. 100.

37. Thomas Pantham, 'Thinking with Mahatma Gandhi: Beyond Liberal Democracy', *Political Theory* 11(2), May 1983, p. 173.

38. M.K. Gandhi, *Democracy: Real and Deceptive* (Ahmedabad: Navajivan Publishing House, 1961), p. 45.

39. Gandhi, *Democracy: Real and Deceptive*, p. 7.

40. M.K. Gandhi, 'The Place of Village', *Harijan*, 29 August 1936—reproduced in Gandhi, *Village Swaraj*, p. 30.

41. Gandhi, *Village Swaraj*, p. 31.

42. M.K. Gandhi, 'Self-sufficiency and Cooperation', *Harijan*, 30 November 1935—reproduced Gandhi, *Village Swaraj*, p. 63.

43. Gandhi, *Village Swaraj*, p. 63.

44. Gandhi, 'The Village Swaraj', *Harijan*, 26 July 1942—reproduced in Gandhi, *Village Swaraj*, p. 32.

45. Gandhi, 'The Village Swaraj', *Harijan*, 26 July 1942—reproduced in Gandhi, *Village Swaraj*, p. 31.

46. Peter Ronald deSouza, 'Institutional Vision and Sociological Imaginations: The Debate on Panchayati Raj', in Rajeev Bhargava (ed.), *Politics and Ethics of the Indian constitution* (New Delhi: Oxford University Press, 2008), p. 85.

47. Gandhi to Jawaharlal Nehru, 5 October 1945—reproduced in Anthony J. Parel (ed.), *Hind Swaraj and Other Writings* (Cambridge: Cambridge University Press, 1997), pp. 150–1.

48. In his letter to Jawaharlal Nehru, he thus made it very clear by saying that 'you must not imagine that I am envisaging our village life as it is today'. Gandhi to Jawaharlal Nehru, 5 October 1945—reproduced in Parel, *Hind Swaraj and Other Writings*, p. 150.

49. M.K. Gandhi, 'Basic Principles of Village Swaraj'—reproduced in Gandhi, *Village Swaraj*, pp. 34–43.

50. M.K. Gandhi, 'Equality', *Harijan*, 9 October 1937—reproduced in Gandhi, *Village Swaraj*, p. 37.

51. M.K. Gandhi, *Trusteeship* (Ahmedabad: Navajivan Trust, 1960), p. 19.

52. M.K. Gandhi, 'Swadeshi'—in Gandhi, *Village Swaraj*, p. 38.

53. M.K. Gandhi, 'Nai Talim', *Harijan*, 31 July 1937—reproduced in *The Selected Works of Mahatma Gandhi*, Vol. IV (Ahmedabad: Navajivan Publishing House), p. 507.

54. Gandhi, 'Nail Talim', p. 504.

55. M.K. Gandhi, 'Sarvodaya in Outline', *Harijan*, 18 January 1948—Gandhi, *Sarvodaya* (Ahmedabad: Navajivan Publishing House, 2002) (reprint), p. 5.

56. Gandhi, 'Panchayat Raj', p. 99.

57. Gandhi, 'Panchayat Raj', p. 99.

58. Gandhi, 'Panchayat Raj', p. 99.

59. Gandhi, 'Panchayat Raj', p. 99.

60. M.K. Gandhi, 'Every Village a Republic', *Harijan*, 26 July 1942—reproduced in Gandhi, *India of my Dreams*, p. 97.

61. M.K. Gandhi, 'Dangers of Mechanization', *Harijan*, 30 November 1934—reproduced in M.K. Gandhi, *Village Industries* (Ahmedabad: Navajivan Publishing House, 2004) (reprint), p. 14.

62. I have drawn this argument on Karuna Mantena, 'On Gandhi's Critique of the State: Sources, Contexts, Conjunctures', *Modern Intellectual History*, 9(3), 2012, pp. 535–63.

63. Mantena, 'On Gandhi's Critique of the State', pp. 558–9.

64. M.K. Gandhi, 'The Sarvodaya State', *The Modern Review*, 1935, p. 412—Gandhi, *India of my dreams*, pp. 79–80.

65. Gandhi's statement, no date—quoted in Mantena, 'On Gandhi's Critique of the State', p. 563.

8 The Constituent Assembly and Its Role in Articulating a Distinct Response

Seeking to lay out the background for the Constituent Assembly (1946–9) that drafted free India's constitution, it is conceptually pertinent to focus on two specific constitutional steps that the British government undertook just on the eve of the 1947 transfer of power. While the 3 June Plan set out the agenda for the transfer of power, the 1947 Indian Independence Act translated that into reality. Framing a constitution for independent India was not an easy task. The idea was formally broached in 1937 by Jawaharlal Nehru in his address to the Convention of Congress Legislators when he stated that

> the Constituent Assembly that we demand will come into being only as the expression of the will and strength of the Indian people; it will function when it has sanctions behind it to give effect to its decisions without reference to outside authority. It will represent the sovereignty of the Indian people and will meet as the arbiter of our destiny. ... And

till then, there is no room in India for any other constitution imposed upon us; there is room only, unhappily, for conflict and struggle between an imperialism that dominates and a nationalism that seek deliverance.[1]

The irony of history is that the Constituent Assembly which was to be constituted in 1946 did not represent popular sovereignty because (a) it was formed by restricted franchise and (b) it was also an outcome of an imperial design since it came into being under the authority of a law passed by the British Parliament.[2] Nonetheless, the idea was pursued zealously by the Indian National Congress, and in two years after the provincial election of 1937, it resolved that 'a Constituent Assembly is the only democratic method of determining the constitution of a free country, and no one who believes in democracy and freedom can possibly take exception to it'.[3] Gandhi too supported the endeavour because by being representative of the communities, the Constituent Assembly 'provides the easiest method of arriving at a just solution to the communal problem'.[4] Hailing the exercise as it would bring the communities with contradictory political aims together for an effective dialogue, he further defended his argument by saying that, 'the Constituent Assembly alone can produce a constitution indigenous to the country and truly and fully representing the will of the people. Undoubtedly such a constitution will not be ideal, but it will be real however imperfect it may be in the estimation of the theorists or legal luminaries'.[5]

A scan of the earlier nationalist efforts establishes the point that the idea of having a constituent assembly to frame India's constitution seemed to have been received enthusiastically by the Indian National Congress and also Gandhi who also argued in its favour. That the nationalists were keen to have a constituent assembly was a testimony to their tilt towards a codified constitution as perhaps a definite means to establish a constitutional democracy in the liberal mould. The nationalist endorsed the idea because the constituent assembly would provide them with an opportunity to thrash out the differences since it would give them a chance to sit together for a dialogue.

With the 1942 Cripps Mission's categorical statement for constituting a constituent assembly for India, the process of forming a constituent assembly for preparing a constitution of India started. In the Cripps Mission, it was proposed that 'a Constitution-making body should be set up through which Indians should frame a constitution for India within the Commonwealth subject to the right of any province of British India not to adhere to the constitution so framed'.[6] The idea was carried forward and the 1946 Cabinet Mission enthusiastically supported the formation of a constituent assembly to prepare the constitution for free India although its members were convinced that 'a solution involving the partition of the Punjab and Bengal would be contrary to the wishes and interests of a very large proportion of the inhabitants of these Provinces'.[7] Nonetheless, the subcontinent was partitioned and two independent nations—India and Pakistan—were born in 1947. The Constituent Assembly for India met, for the first time, on 9 December 1946 and in less than three years, the Constitution of India was produced and was adopted by the nation on 26 November 1949.

Besides elaborating the processes that led to the making of the Constitution, the chapter draws on the socio-economic and political circumstances of the era and also the philosophical predilections of the founding fathers to delve into the riddle as to why India's Constitution incorporated some of the draconian provisions of the 1935 Government of India Act despite being opposed to it when it was introduced.

Historical Antecedents

The outcome of the 3 June Act of 1947 was the inauguration of two new nations. India became free on 15 August 1947. A new era dawned and Jawaharlal Nehru captured that moment in his famous 'tryst with destiny' speech:

> At the stroke of the midnight hour, when the world sleeps, India will awake to life and freedom. A moment comes, which comes but rarely in history, when we step out from the old to the new, when an age ends, and when the soul of a nation, long suspended, finds utterance. It is fitting that at this solemn moment we take the pledge of dedication to the service of India and her people and to the still larger cause of humanity.[8]

While Nehru was optimistic, his colleagues were not, given the multiple sources of discontent that the newly-emerged nation was likely to confront. Apprehending that political freedom, by itself, made no sense unless it was articulated to bring about radical changes in governance which was possible once the sources of social, economic, and political discontent were completely eradicated. Hence, Rajendra Prasad, the President of the Constituent Assembly, exhorted:

> India needs today nothing more than a set of honest men who will have the interest of the country before them. There is a fissiparous tendency arising out of various elements in our life. We have communal differences, caste differences, language differences, provincial differences and so forth. It requires men of vision, men who will not sacrifice the interests of the country at large for the sake of smaller groups and areas and who will rise over the prejudices which are born of these differences.[9]

The scene does not appear to be as gloomy as it was made out to be, as he immediately pointed out that 'successful working of democratic constitution requires in those who have to work them willingness to respect the view point of others, capacity for compromise and accommodation.'[10] He was also persuaded to believe that it was not difficult to achieve since 'we have been able to draw this Constitution without taking recourse to voting and division in Lobbies.'[11] Nonetheless, social diversity of India was 'a real, if awkward, fact [which] simultaneously provoked pride in India's civilizational fecundity and plurality, and a fear in its centrifugal potential'.[12] India's partition in 1947 was a testimony to a situation when communal schism was resolved only with the vivisection of the country. One cannot therefore ignore the context in which specific efforts towards constitutionalizing India were made. In other words, what was initiated by the colonial rule in the name of constitutional governance and also those parallel attempts that the nationalists made towards that goal need to be understood with reference to the contemporary democratic politics. Constitutionalism is conceptualized as organically linked with the prevalent socio-economic context. There is a point of view however suggesting that it was a design for 'political exclusion of the masses'[13] which both the colonial rulers and their opponents endorsed while articulating their responses for constitutionalizing India. Despite having contrasting political objectives, the colonizers and the colonized were hardly different in their approach to the masses given their 'shared political language of exclusion [which] was intrinsic to constitutional reforms'[14] that were undertaken so zealously during colonialism and its immediate aftermath. As their ideological goal was identical, the nationalists, like the British, were persuaded to accept that 'in order to achieve any measure of self-government, they had to adopt a language of representation, one that fundamentally agreed with the colonial government that large masses had yet to be tutored in the art of self-government.[15] It is true and the argument draws heavily on this, that there existed two worlds: organized and unorganized; in the former, the appeal of constitutionalism was significant while the latter remained peripheral due to complex socio-economic reasons explaining their exclusion. However, the situation had undergone a sea-change with the arrival of Gandhi who tried to bridge the gulf between the organized and the unorganized words for a nationalist goal. There were other ideological forces representing the interests of the peasants, workers and other marginalized sections of society which also became prominent in struggles which were also directed against socially-entrenched vested interests. The point here relates to the argument emphasizing the dialectical interconnection between democratic politics and constitutionalism. Hence, India's constitutional history is not one of absolute consensus but one that represented a series of conflicts around myriad social, economic, and political issues.

The Constituent Assembly and the Making of the Constitution

The making of free India's constitution by the Constituent Assembly over a period of little less than three years is reflective of the efforts that the founding fathers undertook to translate into reality the nationalist and democratic aspirations of an independent polity following decolonization.[16] Furthermore, while the Constitution is a continuity at least in structural and procedural terms, it was also a clear break with the past since the 1950 Constitution drew on an ideology that sought to establish a liberal democratic polity following the withdrawal of colonialism. There can be no greater evidence of the commitment to constitutionalism and rule of law on the part of the founding fathers than the Constitution that they framed despite serious difficulties due to partition. The commitment to liberal democratic values, as the Constituent Assembly proceedings suggest, remained paramount in the making of the Constitution.

Set up as a result of negotiations between the nationalist leaders and the members of the Cabinet Mission over the possible constitutional arrangement in the post war-India, the Constituent Assembly was not, it is argued, convened 'by any national provisional government but by the British government [to bring together] the delegates of the major political parties'.[17] The task of the Constituent Assembly was to draft a constitution for India. The objective resolution that Jawaharlal Nehru moved was, according to B.R. Ambedkar, 'an expression of the pent-up emotions of the millions of this country'.[18] While defending the objective resolution, Nehru argued strongly for democracy and socialism: he strongly defended 'democracy' as the most appropriate system of government that 'fit in with the temper of our people and be accountable to them'.[19] Similarly, socialism, he firmly believed, would bring about economic democracy to India. For him, political independence was futile unless it was supported by democratic governance and socialistic vision. Hence, he was critical of the princely states that were reluctant to relinquish monarchy for democracy. As a true democrat who had no doubt that socialism was the ultimate solution for India's stark poverty, Nehru set the tenor of the discussion in the Assembly by providing a philosophical lay-out for free India's constitution. Nonetheless, the political context in which the Constitution was being deliberated was full of uncertainty because of (a) Hindu-Muslim rivalry and (b) reluctance of most of the princely states to join independent India. While the former led to the dismemberment of India following the British withdrawal in 1947, the latter necessitated threat or application of coercion, on occasions, to geographically unify India by bypassing the claim of the existing rulers of the princely states. By staying away from the Assembly, the Muslim members clearly stated their preference for Pakistan that gained momentum especially after the adoption of the 1940 Lahore resolution. The 1946 Calcutta and later Noakhali riots confirmed the Congress apprehension that it was possibly strategically correct to accept partition to avoid further bloodbath. What was clear when the Constituent Assembly met for drafting the constitution was that Pakistan was inevitable and a strong state was required to fulfil its socio-economic goals.

The Nature of the Constituent Assembly

The Constituent Assembly convened on 9 December 1946. It was handicapped from the very beginning since the Muslim League decided to boycott the Assembly as it was contrary to its political objective of creating an independent state for the Muslims. For some Assembly members, the League's decision to stay away could hardly question the authority of the Assembly because, as K.M. Munshi argued, 'it is not a body of delegates representing different communities, but an organ of the sovereign people, which, by virtue of being elected by the sovereign people, inherits a part of that sovereign power so far as constitution-making is concerned'.[20] Hence, the claim that the Assembly lost the sanctity of being an acceptable forum was 'unfounded'. The withdrawal of the League was a source of sadness and perhaps discomfort, but did not seem to affect the strength of mind that the framers had evinced. For them, it was a great responsibility that they were about to shoulder. Jawaharlal Nehru articulated the feeling by saying that,

> we who meet here under a heavy sense of responsibility—responsibility not only because the task which we have undertaken is a difficult one or because we presume to represent vast numbers of people, but because we are building for the future and we want to make sure that that building has strong foundations, and because, above all, we are meeting at a time when a number of disruptive forces are working in India pulling us this way or that way, and because, inevitably and unfortunately, when such forces are at work, there is a great deal of passion and prejudices in the air and out whole minds may be affected by it. We should not be deflected from that vision of the future which we ought to have, in thinking of the present difficulties.[21]

Here too, Nehru set the tempo of the effort that was required to be undertaken in such a gigantic task. This was a task for the future of the nation and needed to be accomplished with great care. It was a persuasive speech that not only inspired the members, but also clarified to them the nature of the responsibility that they were asked to shoulder.

A cursory look at the composition of the Constituent Assembly reveals that it had had a very narrow base of representation. The Congress swept the polls for the Constituent Assembly winning 203 of the 212 general seats and in the final tally it had 208 out of a total of 292 seats of the Provincial Assemblies. Of these, 93 members were nominated by the princely states. Election to these seats was based on a restricted franchise following the Sixth Schedule of the 1935 Government of

India Act which conditioned voting on criteria like paid tax, educational qualifications, and property. As evidence shows, less than 30 per cent of the adult population participated in the election. Furthermore, the departure of the Muslim League caused a severe dent in the claim that the Assembly represented the Muslims as well. In fact, the absence of the League made the Assembly, as it was alleged in contemporary media, 'a Hindu body'.[22] The charge was however countered by referring to the fact that out of seventy Muslim League members, twenty-three of them stayed back and took part in the deliberations in the Constituent Assembly.[23] Nonetheless, the fact remains that the Assembly remained a Hindu-dominated body. A scan of the members who attended the proceedings show that 210 of a total of 296 members regularly participated; of these 210 members, Hindus constituted an overwhelming majority with a total of 160 members. The League members did not seem to have shown much interest as there were only four who were regular in their attendance while the Scheduled Caste representatives seemed very enthusiastic as majority of their representatives (30 out of 33) hardly missed a session of the Assembly.[24]

The first major step that the Assembly undertook was the adoption of the Objective Resolution which 'seeks to show how [the founding fathers] shall lead India to gain the objectives laid down in it [and] ... also to give a live message to India and to the world at large to show [what they] have resolved to accomplish by framing a Constitution of their choice'.[25] The Resolution has eight interrelated parts, each focusing on critical aspects of collective existence which the constitution was meant to protect. Primarily, the Objective Resolution contains a list of exalted socio-economic goals that the framers so assiduously aspired to fulfil during the battle against colonialism and its aftermath. Tuned to 'the nation's dream and aspiration', the Resolution[26] runs as follows:

1. This Constituent Assembly declares its firm and solemn resolve to proclaim India as an independent Sovereign Republic and to draw up her future Constitution;

2. wherein the territories that now comprise British India, the territories that now form the Indian States, and such other parts of India as are outside British India and the States as well as

such other territories as are willing to be constituted into the Independent Sovereign India, shall be a Union of them all; and

3. wherein the said territories, whether with their present boundaries or with such others as may be determined by the Constituent Assembly and thereafter according to the Law of the Constitution, shall possess and retain the status of autonomous Units, together with residuary powers, and exercise all powers and functions as we vested in or assigned to the Union, or as are inherent or implied in the Union or resulting therefrom; and

4. wherein all power and authority of the Sovereign Independent India, its constituent parts and organs of government, are derived from the people; and

5. wherein shall be guaranteed and secured to all the people of India justice, social, economic and political; equality of status, of opportunity, and before the law; freedom to thought, expression, belief, faith, worship, vocation, association and action, subject to law and public morality; and

6. wherein adequate safeguards shall be provided to the minorities, backward and tribal areas, and depressed and other backward classes; and

7. wherein shall be maintained the integrity of the territory of the Republic and is sovereign rights on land, sea and air according to justice and the law of civilized nations; and

8. this ancient land attains its rightful and honoured place in the world and make its full and willing contribution to the promotion of world peace and the welfare of mankind.

Being the foundation of the discussion leading to the making of the constitution, the Objective Resolution has four major components: The first part of the Resolution relates to the aim of the exercise that the founding fathers were to undertake soon to draft a constitution for independent India. It is clearly articulated in the first point of the Resolution. The goal of the exercise was to, in other words, develop a solid foundation for India to grow as a Sovereign Republic. It is also interesting to note here that despite having agreed to be in the Commonwealth, the framers were influenced by the idea of republicanism which means that the head of the State was to elected. With their endorsement of republicanism, the founding fathers left no doubt that, unlike Australia or Canada, India would become a republic. Second, there is a categorical statement in item number 4 that people hold sovereign power and all the institutions of governance derive their existence as part of India's constitutional democracy from the *demos*. Perfectly in tune with their commitment to democracy, the planners of the constitution affirmed their faith in people being the sole repository of substantial authority. Only then, a true democracy was likely to emerge which was not a mere copy of the available forms of democratic forms of government, but an improvement, claimed Nehru who further argued that 'in any event whatever system of Government we may establish here must fit in with the temper of our people and be acceptable to them'.[27] It was further endorsed by Alladi Krishnaswami Ayyar who reaffirmed the sentiment by saying that 'the constitution of sovereign independent India is the concrete expression of the will of the people of India as a whole conceived of as an organic entity ... and the authority of the rulers can rest ultimately on will of the people concerned'.[28] Fundamental here is the idea that in a true democracy, the source of authority remains the *demos* and that can never be wished away. The third aspect of the resolution is about certain critical attributes of the democratic polity which are distinctive and place a democratic form of governance in a different class altogether. The constitution was to secure justice to all regardless of one's social and economic location and political predilections. In order to realize democracy in its undiluted form, the constitutional recognition of these values is of utmost importance. It was also hinted that mere codification of rules directed to fulfil the constitutional aims might not be an effective means unless they were endorsed by a supportive mindset. The apprehension was justified and G.B. Pant replied by saying that the elaborate constitutional provisions would, in the long run, create an environment for a conducive mindset to grow. The final component deals with the mechanism for protecting the minority rights for the strength of a constitution is contingent on this aspect; if the constitution fails to safeguard the interests of the minorities, goes the argument, the claim that India is a democratic country will become a false one. As G.B. Pant of United Provinces expressed,

> the question of minorities everywhere looms large in constitutional discussions. Many a constitution has foundered on this rock. A satisfactory

solution of questions pertaining to minorities will ensure the health, vitality and strength of the free State of India that will come into existence as a result of our discussion here. ... So far, the minorities have been incited and have been influenced in a manner which has hampered the growth of cohesion and unity. But now it is necessary that new chapter should start and we should all realize our responsibility. Unless the minorities are fully satisfied, we cannot make any progress; we cannot even maintain peace in an undisturbed manner.[29]

The concern for the minorities seems to have assumed tremendous significance following (a) the endorsement of the Pakistan plan on the basis of the two-nation theory whereby Hindus and Muslims were projected as separate nations and (b) the withdrawal of the Muslims League from the Constituent Assembly since the Muslims felt that it was meant to frame a constitution for 'Hindu India'.

On the whole, the Objective Resolution is about an ideational concern which the founding fathers had shared with one another before they embarked on the gigantic task of preparing an acceptable constitution for India. There were serious difficulties: on the one hand, the unity of India as an independent polity was at stake given the existence of so many princely states which needed to be integrated with the mainland to make it a one unit; the feeling of the minorities were also to be assuaged, on the other, to make them feel being part of the country, not under compulsion, but by being drawn to the ethos of Indian fraternity. The main concern of the founding fathers was to guarantee 'full freedom to its various sections to have themselves whatever administration they liked and we need to give them full freedom in their social and religious affairs'.[30] What is distinctive here is the fact that despite the agony of partition, the planners for India's constitution did not seem to nurture any ill-feelings towards the minorities; instead, they took it to themselves the responsibility of making them feel comfortable in independent India since they, according to them, were as much a part of India as anybody else. The most revealing statement was made by S. Radhakrishnan of United Provinces on 20 January 1947, who seems to have laid out a solid conceptual foundation in this regard by proclaiming that

we are not here asking anything for a particular community or a privileged class, We are here working for the establishment of Swaraj for all the Indian people. It will be our endeavour to abolish every vestige of despotism, every heir loom of inorganic tradition. We are here to bring about real satisfaction of the fundamental needs of the common man of this country, irrespective of race, religion and community. It is therefore essential that our bugle call, our trumpet-sound, must be clear, must give the people a sense of exhilaration, must give the suspicious and abstaining a sense of reassurance that we are here pledged to achieve full independence of India where no individual will suffer from undeserved want, where no group will be thwarted in the development of its cultural life.[31]

The constitution was not just about the rule of law, it was also a tool for building an inclusive society in the real sense of the term. Keeping in view the obvious constraints due to India's socio-economic and political uncertainties following the 1947 Great Divide on the basis of unbridgeable communal schism, Radhakrishnan devoted his attention to both address the individual wants as well as cultural alienation of a collectivity which, he felt, would provoke further cracks in India's socio-economic fabric.

In a nutshell, the Objective Resolution seems to have charted a specific course of action drawn on certain ideological preferences that the founding fathers articulated during their campaign against colonialism. For them, it was a great challenge since the constitution was to serve a future nation. Furthermore, that their goal was clearly futuristic also gave them an advantage of being not being governed by immediate compulsions; it means that since the Assembly members were placed in circumstances where they had no axe to grind, they had an obvious advantage which allowed them to be absolutely insulated from the petty or partisan aims. B.R. Ambedkar thus emphasized that 'the Constituent Assembly in making a constitution has no partisan motive. Beyond securing a good and workable constitution it has no axe to grind. In considering the articles of the constitution, it has no eye on getting through a particular measure'.[32] The impartiality that the Constituent Assembly had shown was simply impossible for the future Parliaments since they had to address the partisan interests of those who chose them as their representative. As Ambedkar clarified,

the future parliament, if it met as a Constituent Assembly, its members will be acting as partisans seeking to carry amendments to the Constitution to facilitate the passing of party measures which they have failed to get through parliament by reason of some article of the Constitution which has acted as an obstacle in their way. ... That is the difference between the Constituent Assembly and the future parliament. That is the reason why the Constituent Assembly though elected on limited franchise can be trusted to pass the Constitution by simple majority and why the parliament though elected on adult suffrage cannot be trusted with same power to amend it.[33]

The argument has substance. The founding fathers were entrusted with the task of evolving a constitutional design for future India. Given their obvious suffering during colonialism, it was quite natural for them to create a system which was to work for the country as a whole. In other words, in their efforts to build a system of governance for independent India, they acted like statesmen who were charged with a historical responsibility of modelling India as a democratic polity. The Objective Resolution and Nehru's elaborate exposition of what India, as an independent nation, should aspire for left enough ideological inputs for the members in the Assembly to build their arguments in their favour. Since the Assembly had 'no axe to grind', as Ambedkar mentioned, it was possible for the members to rise above partisan interests while being engaged in evolving appropriate constitutional provisions for a stable political order in future India.

The Outcome

While Nehru laid down the ideological foundation of the constitution, B.R. Ambedkar created a blueprint with support from his colleagues in the Drafting Committee of seven members,[34] by identifying the areas of concerns that needed attention. In a detailed speech on 4 November 1948, he elaborated both the form of government and the form of the constitution that India was going to have after the conclusion of the deliberations in the Constituent Assembly. At the outset, he explained that the constitution was framed by taking into account the inputs from various committees that were appointed to look into the specific areas of socio-economic concerns. The Draft Constitution consisted of 315 Articles and three Schedules which made Ambedkar to comment that 'the Constitution of no country could be found to be so bulky as the

Draft Constitution.[35] It is true that the 1950 Constitution of India is perhaps the most exhaustive constitution which was framed by taking into consideration the best constitutional practices that were followed in other constitutional democracies in the globe.

Despite being appreciative of India's pluralistic social texture, there was a near unanimity among the Assembly members for a strong state.[36] Even those who were critical of the Emergency provisions also defended a centralized state to contain tendencies threatening the integrity of the country. Emergency provisions in the Constitution were justified because 'disorder' or 'misgovernance' endangers India's existence as 'a territorial state'. Such concerns could only have reflected, argues Paul Brass, 'another kind of continuity' between the new governing elite and the former British rulers, namely 'an attitude of distrust' of the ordinary politicians of the country and 'a lack of faith' in the ability of the newly-franchised population to check 'the misdeeds' of their elected rulers.[37] Nonetheless, the fear of 'disorder' was probably the most critical factor in favour of the arguments for a centralized state despite its clear incompatibility with the cherished-ideal of the nationalist leaders for a federal state. B.R. Ambedkar's contradictory stances on federalism, for instance, thus may appear whimsical independent of the circumstances. In 1939, Ambedkar was clearly in favour of a federal form of government for its political viability in socio-culturally diverse India.[38] By 1946, he provided a radically different view by saying that 'I like a strong united Centre, much stronger than the Centre we had created under the Government of India Act of 1935'.[39] While presenting the final report of the Union Powers Committee, Jawaharlal Nehru also argued in favour of a strong state by stating that '[w]e are unanimously of the view that it would be injurious to the interest of the country to provide for a weak central authority which would be incapable of ensuring peace, of coordinating vital matters of common concern and of speaking effectively for the whole country in the international sphere'.[40]

As evident, federalism did not appear to be an appropriate structural form of governance in the light of the perceived threats to the existence of the young Indian nation. Hence, the constitution-makers recommended for a strong centre because the constitutional design of a country is meant to serve 'the normative-functional requirements of governance'. The constitution was to reflect 'an ideology of governance' regardless of whether they articulate the highly-cherished ideals of the freedoms struggle that a majority of the Assembly members nurtured while participating in the freedom struggle. As G.L. Mehta believed that 'we have to build up the system on the conditions of our country [and] not on any abstract theories'.[41] In the same tune, Alladi Krishnaswami Ayyar argued that 'our constitutional design is relative to the peculiar conditions obtaining here, according to the peculiar exigencies of our country [and] not according to a prior or theoretical considerations'.[42] In the making of the constitution for governance, they were guided more by their views on state craft which would surely have been different without the traumatic experience of partition and communal bloodbath preceding the inauguration of the Constitution in 1950. Hence, one can safely suggest that 'hard-headed pragmatism and not abstract governmental theories' was what guided 'the architects of our Constitution'.[43]

Yet, it was not the entire Assembly that wrote the document. It was clearly the hard work 'of the government wing of the Congress, and not the mass party' and the brunt of the task fell upon 'the Canning Lane Group [because] they lived while attending Assembly sessions on Canning Lane'.[44] There is another dimension of the functioning of the Assembly which is also instructive. According to Granville Austin, Indian's constitutional structure is perhaps 'a good example' of decision-making by consensus and accommodation, which he defends by examining the debates on various provisions of the Constitution.[45] Scholars however differ because given the Congress hegemony in the Assembly, views, held by the non-Congress members were usually bulldozed. As S.K. Chaube argued that at least on two major issues—political minorities and language—both these principles were conveniently sacrificed. As regards political minority, there was no consensus and the solution to the language issue was, as Austin himself admits 'a half-hearted compromise'.[46] By dubbing the Assembly as 'a packed house', the shrunk Muslim League expressed the feeling of being alienated from the house. Even Ambedkar underlined the reduced importance of the Assembly since on a number of occasions, as he admitted, 'they had to go to another place to obtain a decision and come to the Assembly'.[47]

Decision by consensus may not be an apt description of the processes of deliberation. But, as the proceedings show, there was near unanimity on most occasions and divisions of opinion among the Congress Party members who constituted a majority, were sorted-out politically. As Ambedkar admits, '[t]he possibility of chaos was reduced to nil by the existence of the Congress Party inside the Assembly which brought into its proceedings a sense of order and discipline.... The Party is therefore entitled to all the credit for the smooth sailing of the Draft Constitution in the Assembly'.[48] As Shiva Rao informs, on a number of controversial issues, efforts were made to eliminate or at least to minimize differences through informal meetings of the Congress Party's representatives in the Constituent Assembly,[49] which Ambedkar also endorsed when he emphasized the role of the Congress Assembly Party comprising three-fourth of the Assembly members in sorting differences in their regular informal meetings. If the informal discussion failed to resolve the differences, 'the Assembly leadership ... exercised its authority formally by the Party Whip'.[50] As evident, in the Constituent Assembly, no attempt was made to force decision, the accent being on unanimity presumably because 'the leaders were alive to the fact that the constitution adopted on the principle of majority vote would not last long'.[51] It was not therefore surprising that Rajendra Prasad, the president of the Constituent Assembly preferred to postpone debate and allow them to work out agreed solutions rather than take a vote that might, as he apprehended result 'in something not wanted by anybody'.[52] Nonetheless, debates were allowed and consensus were sought to be built though there were occasions when the framers had to concede the point of view which they opposed as perhaps the only way out to break the logjam in the deliberations. Nehru's arguments during the amendment clause debate and Patel's during the expropriation debates confirm this. This was not due simply to 'their magnanimity as leaders', an analyst rightly points out, 'but the real constraints of negotiating the complex and competing interests as a part of the constitution making process'.[53] Fundamental here is the point that the founding fathers, instead of being ideologically inflexible, had shown a remarkable sense of resilience in arriving at a point of agreement provided that was not contrary to the basic ethos of constitutional liberalism.

Two important points emerge out of the preceding discussions: first, the making of the Indian constitution was a difficult exercise not only because of the historical context but also due to the peculiar social texture of the Indian reality that had to be translated in the constitution,

The collective mind in the Assembly was defensive as a consequence of rising tide of violence taking innocent lives immediately after partition. Second, the founding fathers seem to have been obsessed with their 'own notion of integrated national life'. The aim of the constitution was to provide 'an appropriate ordering framework' for India. As Rajendra Prasad equivocally declared on the floor of the Assembly, '[p]ersonally I do not attach any importance to the label which may be attached to it—whether you call it a Federal Constitution or a Unitary Constitution or by any other name. It makes no difference so long as the Constitution serves our purpose'.[54] On the whole, a unitary mind produced 'an essentially unitary constitution doused with a sprinkling of permissive power for a highly supervised level of constituent units'.[55] This was not the goal of the nationalists and, of course, their leader, Mahatma Gandhi, who always stood for decentralized village republic. Besides confirming that constitutionalism in India was not entirely derivative, this assumption directs our attention to the argument that the Indian Constitution was 'cosmopolitan' in character not only 'in its fidelity to the universal principles of liberty, equality and fraternity' but also due to fact that its text and principles, its values and its jurisprudence were drawn from 'the major cross-currents of global constitutional law'.[56]

Cracks in the Mirror: The Contextual Restraints

With their efforts that spanned nearly three years, the Constituent Assembly members had reasons to be proud of since they produced a constitution which translated their commitment to constitutional liberalism into practice. As is evident, the 1950 Constitution of India is a template for liberal values that the founding fathers espoused both during its making and also during the period when they fought British hegemony. Despite having succeeded in their mission, the Assembly members did not appear to be absolutely confident whether the constitutional fabric that they had created was strong enough to sustain constitutional democracy in India. The Assembly was divided since the outcome did not seem to have incorporated the suggestions of some of the members who disagreed with the dominant views, espoused by Ambedkar and his colleagues. Besides the Gandhians who resented because Gandhi's notion village swaraj did not receive adequate attention in the constitution, there was another group who also felt dissociated since the constitution, instead of being 'a political document' was 'a lawyer's constitution' in which 'there is no idealism and [it] is a Constitution foreign to culture and genius of this land [and] ... is meant to protect the interests of the rich'.[57] Powerful critiques notwithstanding from his colleagues, B.R. Ambedkar too was not very confident that the proposed constitution was likely to attain the socio-economic and political objectives that he held so dear. In his valedictory address to the Assembly, he expressed his concern by raising two points to articulate why he felt 'anxious for India's future'.[58] The first source of concern was the apprehension whether independent India was capable of retaining its independence in future. The apprehension did not seem to be unfounded presumably because of the prevalent circumstances of uncertainty due to the partition riots resulting in terrible human loss. For Babasaheb, what was most debilitating than the physical division of the country was the hatred for one another due to well-entrenched caste division. It was unfortunate that Indians became a prey to the design that flourished primarily due to 'our mutual distrust with one another'.[59] The second source of anxiety revolved around the apprehension whether India continued to remain democratic. Democracy needed to be nurtured which was likely to be compromised, Ambedkar apprehended, in an atmosphere of mutual distrust. With partition, Hindu–Muslim–division seemed to have lost its steam. The caste division, being far dangerous than communal chasm, was an impediment to India's rise as a nation, and hence to conceptualize India as a nation was, according to Ambedkar, 'a delusion [because] people divided into several thousand castes can never be a nation'. While supporting his contention, he further argued that 'the castes are antinational: in the first place because they bring about separation in social life. They are anti-national also because they generate jealousy and antipathy between caste and caste'.[60]

The outcome was disastrous. By creating and sustaining an artificial division, India hardly became a collective entity, but one that was divided along castes. The prevalent social imbalances were protected because 'political power ... has too long been the monopoly of a few and the many are not only beasts of burden, but also beasts of prey. The monopoly has not merely deprived them of their chance of betterment, it has sapped them of what may be called the significance of life'.[61]

In view of the political power being appropriated by the upper caste at the cost of the majority, constitutional democracy that Ambedkar held so dear could become a mere structure without substance. As he mentioned, 'without fraternity, equality and liberty, the fulcrum of democracy, will be no deeper than coats of paint'.[62] What was then to be done? According to him, 'the down-trodden classes are impatient to govern themselves, [and] this urge for self-realization ... must not allowed to devolve into a class struggle or class was [which] would lead to a division of the House'. Hence, he suggested that 'the sooner room is made for the realization of their aspiration, the better for the few, the better for the country, the better for the maintenance for independence and the better for the continuance of its democratic structure'.[63] In this note of caution, Babasaheb, by highlighting the pernicious effects of caste system, reiterated the arguments that he always deployed while pursuing his distinctive design of social justice in opposition to his upper caste colleagues.

How did the priest of constitutional democracy seek to safeguard the constitution which was a beacon of light not merely for the founding fathers who worked hard to evolve a constitutional design for democracy in India but also for those who saw in it a means for betterment? In a detailed response, Ambedkar identified the source of the problem and also offered a solution which, he felt, was also linked with creation of a complementary mindset. It was a herculean task indeed because 'democracy in India is only a top-dressing on an Indian soil which is essentially undemocratic'.[64] So a guarantee of political democracy did not seem to be adequate to realize democracy in its actual sense. This was a serious limitation of the democratic discourse that hardly recognized, emphasized Ambedkar, that 'the soul of democracy is the idea of one man, one value. Unfortunately', he further added,

democracy has attempted to give effect to this doctrine only so far as political structure is concerned by adopting the rule of one man one vote which is supposed to translate into fact the doctrine of one man one value. It has left the economic structure to take shape given to it by those in position to mould it. This has happened because constitutional lawyers have been dominated by the antiquated conception that all that is necessary for a perfect constitution for democracy was to frame a constitutional law which would make Government responsible to its people and it prevent tyranny of the people by the Government. They have advanced to the conception that constitutional law of democracy must go beyond adult suffrage and fundamental rights. In other words, old time constitutional lawyers believed that the scope and function of constitutional law was to prescribe the shape and form of the political structure of society. They never realized that it was equally essential to prescribe the shape and form of the economic structure of society, if democracy is to live up to its principle of one man one value.[65]

Implicit here is a powerful critique of democracy as a practice which unfolded in Ambedkar's last speech in the Assembly where he clarified and defended his points one by one. First, in order to maintain democracy 'not merely in form, but also in fact',[66] he insisted on 'the constitutional methods of achieving our social and economic objectives'.[67] In his opinion, both 'the bloody methods of revolution and methods of civil disobedience, noncooperation and satyagraha',[68] were impediments towards realizing constitutional democracy in its true spirit and substance because 'these methods are nothing but the Grammar of Anarchy and the sooner they are abandoned, the better for us'.[69] By characterizing these methods as 'unconstitutional' because there was hardly a scope of dialogue which was a staple for liberal discourse, Ambedkar never found them congruent in his own understanding of constitutional democracy. The second source of concern was the growing ascendancy of a mindset privileging political leaders as 'heroes' which ran counter to the foundational ethos of democracy. Drawn on J.S. Mill's cautionary argument that unconditional support to the leaders enabled them to 'subvert the democratic institutions', Ambedkar strongly felt that,

> this caution is far more necessary in India than in the case of any other country [for] in India, Bhakti or what may be called the path of devotion or hero-worship, plays a part in its politics unequal in magnitude by the part it plays in the politics of any other country in the world. Bhakti in religion may be a road to the salvation of the soul; but, in politics, Bhakti or hero-worship is a sure road to degradation and to eventual dictatorship.[70]

Here too, Babasaheb while critiquing a mindset supportive of hero-worship sought to develop a counter mindset striving to create conditions for value-driven politics in which the importance of the individuals did not seem to be critical at all. The third source of worry stemmed from the concern whether the constitution which consolidated the foundation of political democracy in India was adequate to establish social democracy, without which, democracy ceased to become an empowering device. According to him, 'political democracy cannot last unless there lies at the base of it social democracy [which means] a way of life [recognizing] liberty, equality and fraternity as the principles of life'.[71] A meaningful democratic existence was impossible without 'a union of this trinity in the sense to divorce one from the other is to defeat the very purpose of democracy'.[72] Equality which was primary to constitutional democracy was 'a casualty' in India, due to the prevalence of 'the principle of graded inequality which means elevation for some and degradation for others'; similarly, on the economic plane, India was 'a society in which there are some who have immense wealth as against many who live in abject poverty'.[73] This was a most tragic aspect of India's independence struggle which, despite challenging the prevalent social and economic order, did not seem to have been effective enough to meaningfully address the sources of socio-economic imbalances. Hence, Ambedkar warned:

> on the 26th of January, 1950, we are going to enter into a life of contradictions: in politics we still have equality and social and economic life we will have inequality. In politics, we will be recognizing the principle of one man one vote and one vote one value. In our social and economic life, we shall, by reason of our social and economic structure, continue to deny the principle of one man one value.[74]

Unless these contradictions were resolved soon, those who suffered from inequality, he further underlined, 'will blow up the structure of political democracy which [the Constituent Assembly] has so labouriously built-up'.[75] Finally, the absence of fraternity was what bothered the Chairman of the Drafting Committee. By fraternity he meant 'a sense of common brotherhood of all Indians [which] gives unity and solidarity to social life'.[76] In view of the well-entrenched social schism, nurtured by an age-old traditions receiving nourishment by those who held social and political power in India, it was a difficult thing to achieve, argued Ambedkar. There are two complementary arguments that Ambedkar offered to substantiate his stance: on the one hand, given the hegemonic caste-hierarchy, it was impossible to build a social compact on the basis of democratic ethos; or, in other words, in the absence of social endosmosis, to borrow Ambedkar's expression, the idea of fraternity became an abstract conceptualization with no meaningful substance. By subjecting the sociologically justified caste division to a thorough scrutiny, he, on the other, evolved a set of powerful critiques challenging what had so far been considered axiomatic in Hindu society. By rejecting those foundational values endorsing hierarchical caste division, he articulated a voice which, despite being ridiculed at the beginning, gained momentum as history progressed.

Concluding Observations

On a surface reading of the making of the 1950 Constitution of India, it can be persuasively argued that it was made by the Constituent Assembly which completed the task in little less than three years between 1946 and 1949. Despite having accomplished the assigned responsibility, the Assembly was criticized for not being representative since it was constituted by restricted franchise, and also there were significant absences, namely the Muslim League, the limited representatives of the princely states and the Father of the Nation, Gandhi. The explanation is usually couched in contextual terms: the Muslim League did not attend because it was a foregone conclusion by 1946 that India was to be bifurcated; the majority of the princely states did not seem prepared to decide the best course of action for them due to the sudden political changes, and the Mahatma was busy elsewhere to assuage the feelings of the victims of communal flagrance. The decision of the League and the princely states did not appear to have affected the proceedings though the absence of the Mahatma caused a sense of vacuum, as many of the Gandhians in the Assembly raised their feeling of helplessness while defending the draft constitution. Despite not being present, Gandhi accepted the decision of his Congress colleagues to participate in the Assembly proceedings. The decision could have been tactical in the sense that instead of openly chiding them who agreed to work for the Assembly, he quietly withdrew to avoid open confrontation with those who appeared to have uncritically accepted the so-called British design. Even in the absence of a strong evidence, one can advance an argument to this effect by referring to a letter that

Gandhi wrote to Patel 1 August 1946 in connection with a request that the latter made to interact with Ambedkar on certain issues of national importance. The response that Gandhi gave was unambiguous. As Mahatma stated,

> I see a risk in coming to any sort of understanding with him, for he has told me in so many words that for him there is no distinction between truth and untruth or between violence and non-violence. He follows one single principle, viz., to adopt any means which will serve his purpose. One has to be very careful indeed when dealing with a man who can become Christian, Muslim or Sikh and then be reconverted according to his convenience. There is much more that I could write in the same strain. To my mind, it is all a snare.[77]

This is a significant comment suggesting that Gandhi had reasons not to identify with an activity in which one of the leading priests happened to be Ambedkar who always raised a counter, and also a powerful voice against the Mahatma. It was evident in one of the earlier meetings of the Assembly when Babasaheb rejected the Gandhian model of village swaraj by castigating the so-called village republics as being responsible for 'the ruination of India [by championing] localism, ignorance, narrow-mindedness and communalism'.[78] This was clearly an ideational battle in which Ambedkar had won in the sense that he succeeded in persuading the Assembly members to accept individual as the basic unit of constitutional governance in India.

Nonetheless, the Constituent Assembly came out with a persuasive text of the constitution which was finally approved in 1949 before it was given to the nation in 1950. A careful scanning of the proceedings of the Assembly reveals that the debates in which the founding fathers took part were the culmination of an ideational battle that the nationalist had waged in the past. Processes of constitutionalizing India in a constitutional-liberal mould had begun long before the Assembly had embarked on this exercise. As the argument goes, and the book elaborates in so many chapters, there were complementary politico-ideological forces which had its imprint in the 1950 Constitution of India. On the one hand, there were British liberals who seemed to have laid the foundation for liberal constitutionalism in the wake of colonialism in India which the Indian liberals endorsed, on the other, most zealously.

This was a confluence of thought leading to the articulation and also consolidation of the paradigmatic values of Enlightenment which also helped the nationalists to devise a specific response while challenging the British rule in India. These ideational inputs influenced the constitutional designs, beginning with the 1909 Morley-Minto Reforms till the 3 June plan of 1947 that the colonial state had evolved ostensibly to contain the nationalist onslaught by being gradually accommodative of dissenting forces. So, before the Assembly, there were inputs, both ideational and constitutional, which seemed to have made the framers' task easier. This was both advantageous and restraining: advantageous because the founding fathers had a blue print on which they worked to evolve and also fine-tune the constitutional principles on the basis of their ideological preferences; restraining because by accepting the available inputs as ideologically rejuvenating, they had hardly an urge to explore alternative thought processes which did not allow them to tread beyond the known territory.

In view of the fact that the ideas that the founding fathers had upheld while being engaged with his colleagues were not exactly a break with the past but a continuity, it can now be argued that the Constituent Assembly was a significant point in India's evolution as a constitutional polity in which primarily Western liberalism prevailed over other competing ideological discourses, including the Gandhian model of village swaraj. Nonetheless, in the end, as a result of sustained dialogues and also fierce debates in the Assembly, the founding fathers had succeeded in codifying their views in the Constitution which is not just a juridical text of rules and regulations, but a guide for a specific type of constitutional democracy that arose in the aftermath of the British withdrawal in 1947. Strangely enough, the Constitution drew its sustenance from the politico-ideological ideas of liberalism that also defended colonialism. In view of stronger liberal roots of the Constitution, it is not conceptually improper to argue that it was rooted in those ideas of liberalism which also inspired the nationalists to launch a fierce campaign against the alien state. And, the Constituent Assembly provided a forum in which competing ideas jostled for a space in circumstances where the fundamental socio-economic and political values of the Enlightenment paradigm were privileged for specific historical reasons by those who presided over India's destiny at a critical juncture of her history.

Notes and References

1. B. Shiva Rao (ed.), *The Framing of India's Constitution: Select Documents*, Vol. 1 (New Delhi: Universal Publishing House, 2004) (reprint), p. 90.

2. Sandipta Dasgupta pursed this point in detail in his *Localizing the Revolution* (unpublished PhD dissertation, Columbia University, 2014), pp. 193–7.

3. A.M. Zaidi and Shaheda Zaidi (ed.), *The Encyclopaedia of the Indian National Congress*, Vol. XII (New Delhi: S. Chand, 1987), p. 2017.

4. Rao, *The Framing of India's Constitution*, p. 108.

5. Gandhi on the Constituent Assembly, November, 1939—reproduced in Rao, *The Framing of India's Constitution*, p. 109.

6. Prime Minister, Atlee's telegram to the British Ambassadors in Canada, Australia, New Zealand, and South Africa—reproduced in the Nicholas Mansergh (ed.), *The Transfer of Power, 1942–7*, Vol. VI (New Delhi: UBS Publishers' Distributor Ltd, 1976), p. 1201.

7. M.V. Pylee, *Constitutional Government in India* (London: Asia Publishing House, 1963) (reprint), p. 127.

8. Jawaharlal Nehru's 'Tryst with destiny' speech, delivered at the dawn of independence in India on 15 August 1947—quoted from Rao, *The Framing of India's Constitution*, pp. 558–9.

9. Rajendra Prasad's address in the Constituent Assembly on 26 November, 1949, *Constituent Assembly Debates*, Vol. XI, Lok Sabha Secretariat, New Delhi, 2003, p. 993.

10. Rajendra Prasad's address in the Constituent Assembly, p. 993.

11. Rajendra Prasad's address in the Constituent Assembly, p. 993.

12. Uday S. Mehta, 'Indian Constitutionalism: Crisis, Unity and History', in Sujit Choudhury, Madhav Khosla, and Pratap Bhanu Mehta (eds), *The Oxford Handbook of the Indian Constitution* (New Year: Oxford University Press, 2016), p. 53.

13. Arvind Elangovan, 'Constitutionalism, Political Exclusion and Implications or Indian Constitutional History: The Case of Montague-Chelmsford reforms (1919), *South Asian History and Culture* 7(3), 2016, p. 14.

14. Elangovan, 'Constitutionalism, Political Exclusion and Implications or Indian Constitutional History, p. 14.

15. Elangovan, 'Constitutionalism, Political Exclusion and Implications or Indian Constitutional History, p. 14.

16. The Constituent Assembly comprised (a) 292 members who were elected through the Provincial Legislative Assemblies, (b) 93 members

represented the Indian Princely states, and (c) 4 members came from Chief Commissioners' Provinces.

17. Shibanikinkar Chaube, *Constituent Assembly of India: Springboard of Revolution* (New Delhi: Manohar, 2000), p. 49.

18. B.R. Ambedkar, 17 December 1946, *Constitutional Assembly Debates*, Book No. 1, p. 102.

19. Jawaharlal Nehru, 13 December 1946, *Constitutional Assembly Debates*, Book No. 1, p. 62.

20. K.M. Munshi's views reproduced in Rao, *The Framing of India's Constitution*, p. 391.

21. Jawaharlal Nehru, 28 April 1947, *Constituent Assembly Debates*, Book No. 1, pp. 374–5.

22. Mohammad Akram Khan, the editor of *Dainik Azad* (Bengali), condemned the Constituent Assembly as a Hindu Body in the absence of the Muslims who were represented by the Muslim League. *Dainik Azad* (Bengali), Calcutta, 18 August 1947.

23. *Ananda Bazar Patrika*, Calcutta, 21 August, 1947.

24. *National Herald*, New Delhi, 26 November, 1950.

25. Jawaharlal Nehru, 13 December 1946, *Constituent Assembly Debates*, Book No. 1, pp. 58–9.

26. Nehru, *Constituent Assembly Debates*, p. 59.

27. Nehru, *Constituent Assembly Debates*, p. 62.

28. Alladi Krishnaswami Ayyar (Madras), 19 December 1946, *Constituent Assembly Debates*, Book No. 1, p. 142.

29. G.B. Pant (United Provinces), 24 January 1947, *Constituent Assembly Debates*, Book No. 1, p. 331.

30. P.D. Tandon (United Provinces), 13 December, 1946, *Constituent Assembly Debates*, Book No. 1, pp. 66–7.

31. S. Radhakrishnan (United Provinces), 20 January, 1947, *Constituent Assembly Debates*, Book No. 1, pp. 269–70.

32. B.R. Ambedkar, 4 November 1948, *Constituent Assembly Debates*, Book No. 2, p. 43.

33. B.R. Ambedkar, 4 November 1948, *Constituent Assembly Debates*, Book No. 2, pp. 43–4.

34. Besides B.R. Ambedkar who was its chairman, the Drafting Committee comprised eminent political leaders and constitutional experts like N. Gopalaswami Ayyangar (1882–1953) Alladi Krishnaswami Ayyar (1883–1953), K.M. Munshi (1887–1971), Saiyid Mohammed Sadulla (1885–1955), Madhava Rau (1887–1972) and D.P. Khaitan. Of these members, Khaitan died in 1948 and T.T. Krishnamachari (1899–1974)

was co-opted. B.N. Rau (1887–1953) was the advisor to the Drafting Committee and was not its member.

35. B.R. Ambedkar, 4 November 1948, *Constituent Assembly Debates*, Book No. 2, p. 31.

36. Mohit Bhattacharya, 'The Mind of the Founding Fathers', in Nirmal Mukarji and Balveer Arora (eds), *Federalism in India: Origins and Development*, Vikas Publishing House, New Delhi, 1992.

37. Paul Brass, 'India, Myron Weiner and the Political Science of Development', *Economic and Political Weekly*, 20 July 2002, p. 2132.

38. B.R. Ambedkar, *Federation versus Freedom*, Gokhale Institute of Politics and Economics, Poona, 1939.

39. *Constitutional Assembly Debates*, Vol. 1, 1946, p. 102.

40. Jawaharlal Nehru, Report (of 5 July, 1947) of the Union Powers Committee, 20 August 1947, *Constituent Assembly Debates*, Book No. 1, p. 58.

41. G.L. Mehta (Western India States Group), *Constituent Assembly Debates*, Book No. 1, p. 78.

42. Alladi Krishnaswami Ayyar (Madras), 23 November 1949, *Constituent Assembly Debates*, Book No. 5, p. 839.

43. Bhattacharya, 'The Mind of the Founding Fathers', p. 89.

44. Granville Austin, *The Indian Constitution: Cornerstone of a Nation* (New Delhi: Oxford University Press, 1999), pp. 17, 317.

45. Austin, *The Indian Constitution*, pp. 311–21.

46. Austin, *The Indian Constitution*, pp. 264–307.

47. *Hindustan Times*, 27 November, 1949.

48. B.R. Ambedkar, 25 November 1949, *Constituent Assembly Debates*, Book No. 5, p. 974.

49. Rao, *The Framing of India's Constitution*, p. 835.

50. Austin, *The Indian Constitution*, p. 315.

51. Rajni Kothari, *Politics in India* (New Delhi: Orient Longman, 2005) (reprint), p. 107.

52. Rajendra Prasad's press statement, *Hindustan Times*, 29 December 1949.

53. Sandipta Dasgupta, *Localizing the Revolution* (unpublished PhD dissertation, Columbia University, 2014), p. 211.

54. Rajendra Prasad, 26 November 1949, *Constituent Assembly Debates*, Book No. 5, p. 987.

55. Bhattacharya, 'The Mind of the Founding Fathers', p. 103.

56. Sujit Choudhury, Madhav Khosla and Pratap Bhanu Mehta, 'Locating Indian Constitutionalism' in Sujit Choudhury, Madhav Khosla, and Pratap Bhanu Mehta (eds), *The Oxford Handbook of the Indian Constitution* (New Delhi: Oxford University Press, 2016), pp. 4–5.

57. Brajeshwar Prasad (Bihar), 24 Novemberm 1949, *Constituent Assembly Debates*, Book No. 5, p. 875.

58. B.R. Ambedkar, 25 November, 1949, *Constituent Assembly Debates*, Book No. 5, p. 977.

59. Ambedkar, *Constituent Assembly Debates*, p. 980.

60. Ambedkar, *Constituent Assembly Debates*, p. 980.

61. Ambedkar, *Constituent Assembly Debates*, p. 980.

62. Ambedkar, *Constituent Assembly Debates*, p. 980.

63. Ambedkar, *Constituent Assembly Debates*, p. 980.

64. B.R. Ambedkar, 4 November 1948, *Constituent Assembly Debates*, Book No. 2, p. 38.

65. B.R. Ambedkar's *Memorandum and Draft Articles on the Rights of States and Minorities, 24 March, 1947, Article II, Section II, Clause 4*, in Rao, *The Framing of India's Constitution*, p. 102.

66. Ambedkar, 25 November 1949, *Constituent Assembly Debates*, p. 978.

67. Ambedkar, 25 November 1949, *Constituent Assembly Debates*, p. 978.

68. Ambedkar, 25 November 1949, *Constituent Assembly Debates*, p. 978.

69. Ambedkar, 25 November 1949, *Constituent Assembly Debates*, p. 978.

70. Ambedkar, 25 November 1949, *Constituent Assembly Debates*, p. 979.

71. Ambedkar, 25 November 1949, *Constituent Assembly Debates*, p. 979.

72. Ambedkar, 25 November 1949, *Constituent Assembly Debates*, p. 979.

73. Ambedkar, 25 November 1949, *Constituent Assembly Debates*, p. 979.

74. Ambedkar, 25 November 1949, *Constituent Assembly Debates*, p. 979.

75. Ambedkar, 25 November 1949, *Constituent Assembly Debates*, p. 979.

76. Ambedkar, 25 November 1949, *Constituent Assembly Debates*, p. 979.

77. Gandhi to Vallabhbhai Patel, 1 August 1946, reproduced in *Collected Works of Mahatma Gandhi*, Vol. 85, July 16, 1946—20 October 1946, Publication Division, Ministry of Broadcasting and Information, Government of India, 1982, p. 102.

78. Ambedkar, 4 November 1948, *Constituent Assembly Debates*, p. 39.

9 The Doctrine of Basic Structure and the Reinforcement of Constitutional Liberalism in Post-Independent India

In the constitutional parlance, the basic structure of the constitution entails those distinctive features which form the core of the constitution. Once they are compromised, it would be detrimental to the fundamental character of the constitution. In view of their critical importance in conceptualizing the foundational values on which the constitution rests, these features remain inseparable and can never be belittled for the sake sustaining its basic ideological thrust. This is usually understood in two complementary ways: on the one hand, the constitution evolves out of certain fundamental values and principles which are articulated in the provisions or conventions that also flourish along with specific constitutional practices; there are also, on the other, significant socio-political and economic inputs arising out of the prevalent context with which the constitution is organically linked. Fundamental here is the idea that the doctrine of basic structure of the constitution can never be conclusively defined independent of the context since it is an offshoot of its dialectical interconnection with the context; as a consequence, it cannot thus be articulated as something which is sacrosanct which further means that the features of the basic structure need to be constantly reinvented in response to the demands of the time and space. One has to factor in, in other words, the rapidly transforming socio-economic context to pinpoint what constitutes the basic structure at a particular juncture of India's existence as a democratic polity.

The doctrine of basic structure is conceptually empowering since it also enables us to grasp the foundational basis of democracy. Broadly speaking, in the liberal conceptual mould, there are two major forms of democracy which draws its sustenance from the demos. On the one hand, there is the Westminster form of parliamentary democracy in which it is Parliament which reigns supreme and everything else is subservient; the parliamentary authority is, in principle, unrestrictive and shackle-free, of course, within the ideological boundaries that have been set by the constitutional practices and conventions. The American system of governance provides, on the other, another form of democracy where it is neither the Congress nor the President who holds sovereign authority, but the constitution which remains supreme in so far as the polity is concerned. The idea is very simple: the only source of authority is the constitution and all other institutions of governance derive their constitutional right in governance from the constitution. The Indian Constitution does not follow either of these formats of governance in its undiluted form. Instead, by creatively blending these two unique constitutional experiences, it articulated a third alternative, namely, a parliamentary democracy in which constitution is made the supreme authority though it took a while to establish that the Constitution cannot be bypassed by any of the institutions of political authority. In such a context, basic structure doctrine assumes tremendous constitutional significance.

In the articulation of the doctrine of basic structure, the Indian judiciary has played a very critical role. Not only has the Indian judiciary acted as a guardian of constitutional democracy in India, it has, by creatively interpreting the constitutional provisions in the context of the changing socio-economic circumstances, evolved a new area of jurisprudence drawing on the 'due process of law' doctrine. The interpretation is not exactly drawn on 'the procedure established by law' which the Constitution of India upholds in Article 21, but on the basis of those values emanating from the social compact epitomizing new politico-ideological concerns. Being a proactive player in India's constitutional democracy, the Supreme Court of India has not only created a new domain of its functioning, it has also initiated significant processes of change by privileging the constitution over the executive and legislature. A new era in India's constitutional democracy has ushered in whereby judiciary does not seem to a mere an interpreter of the legislative acts and executive feats, it also provides powerful inputs to the policy makers. The doctrine of basic structure is therefore a watershed in India's constitutional democracy. With the recognition of the doctrine, it is now established beyond doubt that constitutional supremacy can be relegated to futility under no circumstances. Parliament, despite being the voice of the people, is subservient to the constitution which sets out the parameters for its functioning. In other words, the Parliament has to function within the boundary demarcated by the constitution. This has not been readily accepted by the Parliament, and judiciary, as history has shown, had to confront the legislature, on a number of occasions, for being respectful to the basic structure of the Constitution.

The aim of this segment is to acquaint the readers with the basic structure doctrine with reference to how it emerged in India's constitutional discourses by dwelling on the major judicial pronouncements since the inauguration of the 1950 Constitution. This is a narrative of judicial ascendancy in India. An offshoot of creative jurisprudence, the doctrine delineates a critical role for the judiciary which is also constitutionally authorized to ascertain whether Parliament is within its limits while discharging its obligation to the governed. Given the massive significance of basic structure in constitutional governance in India, by drawing on some of the major judicial verdicts which are pertinent here, this section thus concentrates on how it evolved in India's democratic practices by paying adequate attention to its integral features.

Historical Antecedents

The root of the basic structure debate can be traced back to the debates in the Constituent Assembly when it pondered over the choice between 'the procedure established by law' and 'due process of law' which the US

Constitution upholds. The founding fathers favoured the former on the basis of the advice given by Justice Felix Frankfurter of the US Supreme Court to B.N. Rau; they were persuaded to believe that 'the due process law' was likely to be a deterrent to the independent functioning of the Parliament which was, in their views, not justified in democratic governance where Parliament represented the voice of the people; the judiciary being authorized to ascertain the constitutionality of parliamentary acts in accordance with the due process of law would then overpower the Parliament weakening thereby the foundation of constitutional democracy in India. The decision provoked a fierce debates. Kazi Syed Karimuddin of Central Provinces and Berar, for instance did not seem persuaded since he felt that if the constitution incorporated,

> the procedure established by law, instead of due process of law, there will be very great injustice to the law courts in the country because as soon as a procedure according to law is complied with by a court, there will be an end to the duties of the court and if the court is satisfied that the procedure has been complied with, the judges cannot interfere with any law which might have been capricious, unjust or iniquitous. ... As soon as the procedures is complied with, there will, [in other words] be an end to everything and the judges will be only spectators. The clause, as it stands, can [thus] do a great mischief in a country which is a storm centre of political parties and where discipline is unknown. Let us guarantee to individuals' inalienable rights in such a way that the political parties that come into power cannot extend their jurisdiction in curtailing and invading the Fundamental Rights laid down in the Constitution.[1]

An apprehension loomed large because it was felt that that Parliament was to gag individual freedom since political parties might not be sensitive enough of their obligation to the values of constitutional democracy. Sharing the concern, Krishna Chandra Sharma (United Provinces) also argued that

> the term 'without due process of law' has a necessary limitation on the powers of the State, both executive and legislative.... What this phrase means is to guarantee a fair trial both in procedure as well as in substance. The procedure should be in accordance with law and should be appealable to the civilized conscience of the community. It also ensures a fair

trial in substance, that is to say, that substantive law itself should be just and appealable to the civilized conscience of the community.[2]

Here, the argument for parliamentary supremacy was being questioned by reference to the apprehension that it was likely to be misused in future which was not entirely unfounded as the 1975–7 Emergency experiences demonstrates. Despite forceful arguments, the clause, due process of law, was not finally accepted since it was believed that 'the clause may serve as a great handicap for all social legislation [and] would allow the judiciary a free hand in devising major policies'.[3] Such an understanding also reveals that 'the Drafting Committee, ... in suggesting "procedure" for "due process of law" was possibly guilty of being apprehensive of judicial vagaries in the moulding of law'.[4] B.N. Rau's warning that due process was an impediment for Parliament to act, without shackles, for fulfilling mass democratic aspirations seemed to have conclusively settled the issue; and the Constitution incorporated 'the procedure established by law' in Article 21.

It is true that Indian judiciary is constrained to go beyond the constitutional mandate of following the procedure established by law while looking into the justiciability of the policy preferences of the executive and legislative feats. Nonetheless, with the growing acceptance of the idea of basic structure of the constitution which can never be violated, the apex court seems to have carved an independent space in constitutional governance in India. The doctrine of basic structure does not provide the judiciary with the authority that the US Supreme Court possesses because of the constitutional guarantee of due process; it however creates a definite space for the judiciary to act in case the Parliament undermines the fundamental constitutional values and principles for the fulfilment of partisan goals and desires. In the changed socio-economic environment leading to the consolidation of democratic ethos and values, the basic structure doctrine further constitutionalizes judicial intervention in areas which are considered to be critical for sustaining constitutional democracy in India.

The Basic Structure Doctrine

As is mentioned earlier in the chapter, the basic structure doctrine is rooted in the processes leading to democratization of governance in

India. With the growing public disenchantment with the executive and legislature, the judiciary seems to have emerged as a messiah for constitutional democracy. The beginning of the doctrine is usually traced back to the judicial concern for misuse of power by the Parliament as per Article 368 of the Constitution. With the constitutional guarantee, can Parliament amend any part of the constitution for the socio-economic causes—was the question that the judiciary was asked to respond. According to Article 368, Parliament 'may, in exercise of its constituent power, amend by way of addition, variation or repeal any provision of this constitution in accordance with the procedure laid down in this article'. The founding fathers did not seem to have put restrictions on Parliament's authority in amending the constitution. For instance, Jawaharlal Nehru argued:

> while we want this Constitution to be as solid and as permanent a structure as we can make it, nevertheless, there is no permanence in constitutions. There should be certain flexibility. If you make anything rigid and permanent, you stop a nation's growth. So, when you pass this Constitution, ... you will ... lay down a period of years ... during which changes to that constitution can easily made without any difficult process. ... We should not make a Constitution such as some other great countries have, which are so rigid that they do and cannot be adapted easily to the changing conditions. ... Therefore, while we make a constitution which is sound and as basic as we can, it should also be flexible and for a period we should be in a position to change with relative flexibility.[5]

Nehru was keen to make the constitution flexible to keep pace with the changing world while insisting on making it as 'basic' as was possible under the circumstances. This means that the constitution is to have a basic character in politco-ideological terms which can never be compromised. The basic character needs to be sustained. The idea that Nehru offered was made clearer by B.R. Ambedkar who, while elaborating the procedure for amendment to the constitution, clarified that by eliminating the proviso that the constitution could only be amended by 'a decision, adopted in a convention or referendum', the constitution was made flexible which means that legislature, central and provincial, is empowered to revise the constitution by following simple procedures. This is one aspect of the amendment procedure. The other aspect relates to 'the amendment of specific matters' for which 'the ratification of the State Legislatures is required' along with the condition that 'such an amendment shall be done by majority of not less than two-thirds of the members of each House present and voting, and a majority of the total membership of each House'. He also apprehended that future Parliament, being elected on adult suffrage, could be tempted 'to alter the fundamental character of the Constitution ... by acting as partisans seeking to carry amendments to facilitate the passing of party measures'.[6] The idea is crystal clear, namely, there are some values which hold the substance of the constitution and they need to be protected and cannot be allowed to be bypassed under any circumstances. Nehru too endorsed the point by suggesting that there were 'specific areas' in the constitution that could be amended by following a rigid procedure.

Two basic points that had emerged in the Assembly seem to have contributed to the formulation of the basic structure doctrine: first, Indian constitution has certain distinctive features which allow it to be distinguished as a democratic constitution; these features are integral and cannot be fiddled with; second, since these are core to the constitution, they cannot be allowed to be sacrificed by the parliamentarians for the sake of fulfilling their partisan aims.

Conceptual Roots

In conceptual terms, basic structure entails those values and principles which form the core of a constitution. The doctrine is about certain characteristics which are essential since they define the nature of the constitution and once they are separated, the constitution, by implication, loses its identity. The crux of the argument is that given their critical importance in shaping the politico-ideological characteristics of a constitution, they can never be divorced from the constitution. Although the idea has philosophical roots in some of the classical texts on democracy, federalism and republicanism, it was very clearly articulated in a commentary on the Weimer Constitution in the context of the early phases of Nazism in Germany in the early 1930s. Ernest Rudolf Huber, who is infamous for his support to the Nazi regime since it came to power through election, underlined the importance of constitutional norms in governance which, if bypassed, would lead to the collapse of the constitutional structure in no time. In a very categorical way, he thus argued:

> every constitution consists of such principles, which determine the totality of the constitutional order and make up 'the spirit of the constitution'. There is no equality of rank among the numerous provisions of a written constitutional document. The main principles of the common order have clear priority; the remaining legal precepts are derived from them. ... One can say of a constitution that it is valid only so long as this core of the constitution maintains its existence. If the core of the constitution is destroyed, then the entire constitution is wiped out, even if individual constitutional precepts of inferior rank continue to be legally valid.[7]

The argument provides us with three important conceptual inputs to articulate the basic structure doctrine: (a) no amendment is permissible if it effectively alters the basic essential principles of the constitution since it means a stark departure from the purpose for which it was framed, and (b) if the amendment destroys the foundational values of the constitution, it is unconstitutional and thus uncalled for; and finally if the amendment undermines the basic values of the constitution, it has no intention of revising the constitution but desire to eliminate the constitution. Hence, it is argued that 'if certain fundamental principles, values and norms ... are seriously altered, the life of the constitution actually comes to an end; from its ashes, a new political regime emerges'.[8] What is explicitly stated here is that once the core values of a constitution are altered, it results in a complete breakdown of the edifice on which the constitution rests which means that the constitution is no longer the same as it was in the past in its original form.

In India, the idea of basic structure is a judicial invention and is attributed to M.K. Nambyar, a lawyer who pleaded before the Supreme Court in the *I.C. Golaknath v. State of Punjab* in 1967. Nambyar owed this idea to Dietrich Conrad, an academic from Germany who delivered a speech in Banaras Hindu University, entitled 'implied limitation of the amending power' in February, 1965. According to Conrad, 'any amending body organized within the statutory scheme, howsoever verbally unlimited its power, cannot by its very structure change the fundamental pillars supporting its constitutional authority'.[9] The idea was further expanded when he argued:

Could a constitutional amendment abolish Article 21, to the effect that forthwith a person could be deprived of his life or personal liberty without authorisation by law? Could the ruling party, if it sees its majority shrinking, amend Article 368 to the effect that the amending power rests with the President acting on the advice of the Prime Minister? Could the amending power be used to abolish the Constitution and reintroduce, let us say, the rule of a moghul [*sic*] emperor or of the Crown of England? I do not want, by posing such questions, to provoke easy answers. But I should like to acquaint you with the discussion which took place on such questions among constitutional lawyers in Germany in the Weimar period—discussion, seeming academic at first, but suddenly illustrated by history in a drastic and terrible manner.[10]

What Huber had apprehended in the 1930s had resonated in Conrad's assessment of the situation. He also felt that there were certain features in the constitution that could never be abrogated; Conrad also warned that if Parliament was allowed to undertake such an exercise, it would finally contribute to the growth of an authoritarian state, as it happened in Germany following the disintegration of the Weimer republic.

Judicial Pronouncements

As argued above, the basic structure doctrine evolves in India in the course of a series of judicial verdicts, especially since the 1967 Golaknath case. In the history of constitutional laws in India, the idea of basic structure was mooted in the 1964 *Sajjan Singh v. State of Rajasthan*. While endorsing the right to property, Justice P. Gajendragadkar raised a question by saying 'whether the basic features of the Constitution under which we live and to which we owe allegiance are to endure for all time—or at least for the foreseeable future—or whether the yard no more enduring than the implemental and subordinate provisions of the Constitution.'[11] In his note of dissent, J.R. Mudholkar, another member of the bench, also referred to the concept by stating that 'it is a matter of consideration whether making a change in a basic structure of the Constitution can be regarded as an amendment or would it be, in effect, rewriting a part of the Constitution; and, if the latter, would it be within the purview of Article 368?'[12] This is the beginning of the unfolding of the conceptual-legal journey of the basic structure doctrine which passes through a series of judicial pronouncements. The purpose here is not to provide a detailed account of the verdicts, but to highlight the points that India's apex court made while laying out the foundation of the doctrine and its essential features by reference to the major court judgments in this regard.

One of the first significant judicial steps in this regard was the 1967 *Golaknath* case in which the Supreme Court contributed to the articulation of the doctrine. The primary question that the Supreme Court had raised was whether 'in the exercise of the power of amendment the fundamental structure of the Constitution may be changed or even destroyed or whether the power is restricted to making modification within the framework of the original instrument for its better effectuation'. The answer is equally unambiguous: characterizing the fundamental rights as 'transcendental and immutable or inviolable', the majority of the judges in the bench held the view that

(1) the constitution is intended to be permanent and therefore it cannot be amended in a way which would injure, maim or destroy its indestructible character; (2) the word 'amendment' implies such an addition or change within the lines of the original instrument as will effect an improvement or better carry out the purpose for which it was framed and it cannot be so construed as to enable the Parliament to destroy the permanent character of the Constitution; (3) the amending power cannot be used to abolish the compact of the Union or destroy the democratic character of the Constitution teeing individual and minority rights; and (4) the fundamental rights are a part of the basic structure of the Constitution and, therefore, the said power can be exercised only to preserve rather than destroy the essence of these rights.[13]

In clear terms, the court held that fundamental rights being a part of the basic structure of the Constitution cannot be abrogated. So, Parliament does not have unrestricted authority to amend any of the rights enshrined in Part III of the Constitution. There was a dissenting note too; Justice Wanchoo of the bench felt that the court's insistence on the basic structure could be an impediment to social progress, as the members of the Constituent Assembly had apprehended. He was thus categorical in asserting that no limitation should be implied on the amending power of the Parliament under Article 368 and 'basic structure would lead to the position that any amendment made to any article of the Constitution would be subject to the challenge before the Courts on the ground that it amounts to the amendment of the basic structure.'[14]

Nonetheless, the decision that basic structure cannot be challenged was carried forward as the majority of the bench endorsed the argument. It was now settled that fundamental rights were a part of the essential features of the Constitution that needed to be protected and upheld unconditionally. A revolutionary judgment, for the first time in India's recent political history, it established that Parliament was subservient to the constitution which remained supreme and its authority to amend the constitution was also not absolute. The Parliament took the verdict as an infringement in its constitutional rights for being the voice of the people, and hence it adopted legislations to re-establish its absolute authority in law-making. The result was the enactment of the Twenty-Fourth, Twenty-Fifth and Twenty-Ninth Amendment Acts in 1971. While the Twenty-Fourth Amendment Act was meant to abrogate the *Golaknath* ruling of the court to restore Parliament's unconditional authority in amending the Constitution the Twenty-Fifth and Twenty-Ninth Amendment Acts evolved separate legal tools of safeguarding compulsory acquisition statutes from being struck down for violating fundamental rights.

These amendments were put to test for the first time in the 1973 *Kesavananda Bharati* case in which the Supreme Court, with its full bench of 13 jurists, probed into the constitutional validity of the Kerala Land Reforms Act, 1963, as amended by Kerala Land Reforms (Amendment) Acts, 1969 and 1971. The decision challenging the Twenty-Fourth Amendment Act was clinched by a majority of seven judges as against six; the court ruled that the Article 368 does not enable Parliament to alter the basic structure of the Constitution; there are three different expressions, basic structure, basic elements, and basic features which figured in the judgments. Although the jurists did not conclusively define what constituted basic structure, they left enough inputs to identify those essential characteristics which, according to them, constituted 'the basic structure'. That the apex court avoided defining the basic features categorically was presumably due to the fact that it was not exactly needed and it was also not possible to enumerate them since they were context-driven. The court also held that because 'a particular concept of law cannot be rigidly defined, it does not cease to be a concept of law; principles of natural justice and negligence also cannot be rigidly defined still they are effective concepts of law'.[15] In order to further strengthen the argument, the court advanced the point by saying that,

> the ultimate purpose of the Constitution is the conservation of utility and integrity of the nation and also the dignity of the individual. This can be assured only by promoting fraternity. Any principle of law which, if taken away from the Constitution, would result into a loss of fraternity and unity and integrity of the nation and dignity of the individual would be considered to be an essential feature of the Basic Structure.[16]

The amending power of Parliament was conditional and subject to judicial scrutiny to probe whether it had affected the basic structure. While exercising its constituent power under Article 368, the Parliament cannot, the court held, 'damage, emasculate, destroy, abrogate, change' the basic structure or the fundamental framework of the Constitution. The argument was persuasively justified by Justice S.M. Sikri of the bench that supported the basic structure doctrine by saying that,

> our Constitution is not a mere political document. It is essentially a social document. It is based on a social philosophy and every social philosophy like every religion has two main features, namely basic and circumstantial: the former remains constant but the practices associated with it may change. Likewise, a Constitution like ours contains certain features which are so essential that they cannot be changed or destroyed.[17]

This was a powerful argument in defence of the basic structure doctrine. Being essentially a product of consensus, the 1950 Constitution of India was also an offshoot of a bargain by which the diverse groups constituting the Indian polity came together to form the Union. So, it became a social compact which emerged out of processes in which differences were resolved through dialogues and deliberations without fear or coercion. The founding fathers devoted a great deal of energy to consolidate the social compact by way of reconciliation, accommodation and agreements among the socio-economically diverse groups. And, the basic features evolved out of such intensive dialogues among groups holding contrasting points of view. The idea was captured in its true spirit by Justice Khanna who held that

> amendment of the Constitution necessarily contemplates that the Constitution has not to be abrogated but only changes have to be made in it. The word 'amendment' postulates that the old Constitution survives without loss of its identity despite the change and continues even though it has been subjected to alterations. As a result of the amendment, the old Constitution cannot be destroyed and done away with; it is retained though in the amended form.... Although it is permissible under the power of amendment to effect changes, however important, and to adapt the system to the requirements of the changing conditions, it is not permissible to touch the foundation or to alter the basic institutional pattern. The words 'amendment of the Constitution' with all their wide sweep and amplitude cannot have the effect of destroying the basic structure or framework of the Constitution.[18]

There was unanimity among the seven of thirteen judges of the bench that engaged in the *Kesavananda Bharati* case. The minority view, articulated by a group six jurists, led by Justice A.N. Ray held that all parts of the Constitution were essential and distinction between essential and non-essential did not seem to be constitutional; they also endorsed the Twenty-Fourth Amendment Act and agreed to the view that Parliament was empowered to amend any part of the Constitution.

The majority verdict in *Kesavananda Bharati* case upheld the view that there were features which constituted the core of the constitution and could never be abrogated though there was hardly a compact list of basic features; each of the seven judges gave their own lists of essential features which, of course, are fundamental to the Constitution. The lists are exhaustive, as the following shows:

In Justice Sikri's conceptualization, the list should include:

1. Supremacy of the Constitution;
2. Republican and democratic form of government;
3. Secular character of the Constitution;
4. Separation of powers between the legislature, executive and the judiciary; and
5. Federal character of the Constitution.

According to Justice AN Grover and Justice S.J. Shelat, the following two are important:

1. The mandate to build a welfare state contained in the Directive Principles of State Policy (Part IV of the Constitution);
2. Unity and integrity of the nation.

Justice K.S. Hegde and Justice S.N. Mukherjea incorporated the following:

1. Sovereignty of India;
2. Democratic character of the polity;
3. Unity of the country;
4. Essential features of the individual freedoms secured to the citizens;
5. Mandate to build a welfare state.

Justice Jaganmohan Reddy listed the following:

1. Sovereign democratic republic;
2. Provisions for social, economic and political justice;
3. Liberty of thought, expression, belief, faith, and worship;
4. Equality of status and opportunity.

These are aspects of the basic structure of the Constitution. By identifying the fundamental politico-ideological values and also institutions for constitutional democracy, the court prepared an exhaustive list. In the 1975 *Indira Gandhi v. Raj Narain* case, the court devised a principle to characterize basic structure. Justice K.K. Mathew argued that whether a particular feature forms part of the basic structure needed to be determined on the basis of the specific provisions of the Constitution. According to him,

to be a basic structure it must be a terrestrial concept having its habitat within the four corners of the Constitution. What constitutes basic structure is not like a twinkling star up above the Constitution. For instance, the Preamble enumerates great concepts embodying the ideological aspirations of the people, but these concepts are particularised and their essential features delineated in the various provisions of the Constitution. It is these specific provisions in the body of the Constitution which determine the type of democracy which the founders of that instrument established; the quality and nature of justice, political, social and economic which aimed to realise the content of liberty of thought and expression which they entrenched in that document and the scope of equality of status and of opportunity which they enshrined in it. These specific provisions enacted in the Constitution alone can determine the basic structure of the Constitution. These specific provisions, either separately or in combination, determine the content of the great concepts set out in the Preamble. It is impossible to spin out of any concrete concept of basic structure out of the gossamer concept set out in the Preamble. The specific provisions of the Constitution are the stuff which the basic structure has to be woven.[19]

These are very useful inputs to conceptualize basic structure. There are two important aspects that appear to be critical in capturing the core of the doctrine. On the one hand, instead of pinpointing specific characteristics, the court in this instance preferred to identify basic features in terms of the values that inform them—which means that in the conceptualization of basic structure, the supportive constitutional values and principles remain significant. The court also preferred, on the other, to be indecisive possibly because what constitutes fundamental is also context-dependent – which denotes that the list cannot be conclusive presumably because it is needs to be revised in accordance with the prevalent socio-economic priorities.

Following the *Kesavananda Bharati* judgment, the Congress government, led by Indira Gandhi enacted the Forty-Second Amendment Act in 1976 to dilute the basic structure doctrine. The court intervened again and reaffirmed the idea of the basic structure in the 1980 *Minerva Mills v. the Union of India* case. Striking down the authority of the Parliament to repeal any of the features, identified as part of the basic structure, the court ruled that 'parliament cannot, under Article 368, expand its amending power so as to acquire for itself the right to repeal or abrogate the Constitution or to destroy its basic and essential features'.[20] Reiterating that the Parliament has conditional authority of amendment, the apex court further argues that,

it has no inherent power of amendment of the Constitution and being an authority created by the Constitution, it cannot have such inherent power but the power of amendment is conferred upon it by the Constitution and it is a limited power which is conferred. Parliament cannot in exercise of this power to amend the Constitution as to alter its basic structure or to change its identity. Now, if, by constitutional amendment, Parliament was granted unlimited power of amendment, it would cease to be an authority under the Constitution, but would become supreme over it because it would have power to alter the entire Constitution, including its basic structure and even to put an end to it by totally changing its identity. Therefore, the limited amending power of parliament is itself an essential feature of the Constitution, a part of its basic structure for if the limited power of amendment was enlarged into an unlimited power, the entire character of the Constitution would be changed.[21]

The *Minerva Mills* case reaffirms the limited authority of Parliament in so far as amendment is concerned. The court defended the argument by saying that this was likely to change the fundamental identity of the Constitution. As Justice Y.V. Chandrachud of the Supreme Court bench argued, in a rather poetic language, that 'the theme song of ... *Kesavananda Bharati* is: amend as you may even the solemn document which the founding fathers have committed to your care, for you know best the needs of your generation. But, the Constitution is a precious heritage; therefore, you cannot destroy its identity'.[22] What is emphasized here is the sanctity of the Constitution that can never be compromised which means that Indian system of governance is neither exactly the Westminster form of democracy nor its US counterpart, but a creative blending of the two.

The limited nature of the amendment power is now an established constitutional principle. Furthermore, the Parliament has to respect the basic structure while seeking to enact an amendment to the Constitution. Hence, it is argued that 'since the power to amend the Constitution is not unlimited, if changes brought about by amendments destroy the identity of the Constitution, such amendments would be void'.[23] In order to pursue the argument, Justice Y.K. Sabharwal Singh who wrote the judgment for the *I.R. Coelho (dead) v. State of Tamil Nadu* (2007) thus adumbrated:

the existence of the power of parliament to amend the Constitution at will, with requisite voting strength, so as to make any kind of laws affecting rights, enshrined in Part III including power of judicial review under Article 32 is incompatible with the basic structure doctrine. Therefore such an exercise, if challenged, has to be tested on the touchstone of basic structure as reflected in Article 21 read with Article 14 and Article 19, Article 15 and the principles thereunder.[24]

Here too, the Parliament is told again that it does not have the absolute power of amending the Constitution at will; it has to be respectful to the essential features of the Constitution which the Supreme Court has upheld in a series of its pronouncements. The doctrine of basic structure has now become 'an axiom [which] is premised on the basis that invasion [by parliament] in areas, recognized as the basic structure, is not, at all, permissible [because] it is constitutionally *ultra vires*.'[25] The court prevailed over the Parliament and the validity of the basic structure doctrine was ascertained beyond doubt. Whether it undermines representative democracy is an issue that cannot be settled so easily though there is no doubt that by privileging its role as a reliable custodian of constitutional values and principles the court tilted the balance in its favour. Whatever may have been the consequences of court prevailing over the elected representatives, the fact remains that it was possible for the apex judiciary to overturn a series of executive decisions presumably because of the public trust-deficit in the political authority which cannot be brought back so quickly.

Summarizing the Argument

Out of the tussle between the judiciary and executive emerged the basic structure doctrine. It has also evolved largely due to the judicial concern for sustaining the sanctity of the Constitution which is being violated by the executive as and when opportunity arises. The judiciary is not unanimous, of course, in its assessment of the situation as the majority pronouncements show that, on most occasions, the judiciary was divided, and the decision was endorsed by the majority opinion. The only major exception is 2007 *I.R. Coelho (dead) v. State of Tamil Nadu* where the apex court approved the contention without being split in their opinion. Nonetheless, in view of its growing importance in reviewing the constitutionality of the executive feats, the basic structure doctrine can be said to have become 'the bedrock of constitutional interpretation in

India.[26] The judiciary-executive interaction has thus become far from being amicable, with each trying over-smart the other as soon they get a chance.

Despite the disagreement between the judges on what constitutes the basic structure of the Constitution, the idea that the Constitution has a core has always been upheld in the judicial discourse. As the trajectory of the doctrine shows, there was hardly a fixed list of 'essential' features; the court keeps on adding to the list. Of course, the jurists while deciding the 1973 *Kesavananda Bharati* case provided an exhaustive list of items which, they felt, should be the core of the Constitution and were thus to be protected. In its judgment in the 1980 *Minerva Mills* case, the court privileged the non-justiciable Directive Principles of State Policy since they,

> nourish the roots of our democracy, provide strength and vigour to it and attempt to make it real participatory democracy which does not remain merely a political democracy but also becomes social and economic democracy with Fundamental Rights available to all irrespective of their power, position and wealth. The dynamic provisions of the Directive Principles of State Policy fertilize the static provisions of the Fundamental Rights [which] cannot be considered in isolation from the socio-economic structure in which it is to operate.[27]

So, despite not being enforceable, the court held that the rights enshrined in Part IV of the Constitution are relevant in the changed context of massive democratization of governance. By establishing an obvious link between Part III (Fundamental Rights) and Part IV (Directive Principles of State Policy), the court seems to have been governed by the Forty-Second Amendment Act (1976) which privileged Part IV rights as they were considered to be effective politico-ideological tools for bringing about the required socio-economic changes for the establishment of 'a socialist republic', which the Preamble to the Constitution announces. This was pursued further in the 1994 S.R. Bommai judgment of the apex court. Reiterating that

> the Indian Constitution, being a social document, contains the ideals expected by the nation, the apex court while delivering the verdict, underlined that federalism, social pluralism and pluralist democracy ... form the basic structure of our Constitution, [and] ... if the fabric of pluralism

and pluralist democracy and the unity and integrity of the country are to be preserved, judiciary in the circumstances is the only institution which can act as the saviour of the system and of the nation.[28]

Here too, the basic structure doctrine was expanded to include some of the major socio-economic ideals that are pertinent to effect visible socio-economic transformations. It also implies that the executive did not seem to have paid adequate attention to the goal that the Constitution laid out. What is interesting to note is that the court set aside the presidential decree for dismissal of the Karnataka state government not on procedural grounds but on certain constitutional values which represented the basic structure.

In carving out a specific constitutional position for the basic structure doctrine, the judiciary seems to have upheld two important issues which are critical in parliamentary democracy: one substantive and another institutional.[29] Substantively, the rivalry between judiciary and executive has established that the former retains 'inherent power' to review the parliamentary feats to ascertain whether they are constitutionally justiciable. By implication, it means that the parliamentary supremacy is not absolute and subject to judicial review because the court is not only the final interpreter of the Constitution, but also its saviour. The growing ascendancy of the court has serious institutional implication as well. As the scan of the multiple judgments reveal, the court has both won and asserted its institutional rights by challenging the Parliament 'in constitutional matters through the basic structure doctrine'. There was hardly a significant opposition as it was believed that the court 'rescued the democracy strand of the seamless web from those who would have sacrificed it to genuine or pretended social revolutionary intentions'.[30] Nonetheless, it is difficult to arrive at a definite conclusion since the tussle is far from over which is evident in a series of counterattacks by the executive intending to undermine the judicial supremacy in India's constitutional democracy.

Critiquing the Doctrine

The basic structure doctrine seems to have put the two major organs of governance in a collusion mode. The court has appropriated powers which ordinarily belong to the Parliament since it represents people.

The minority bench in the *Kesavananda Bharati* case, led by Justice A.N. Ray endorsed the view that being people's voice, the Parliament remained supreme in India's constitutional governance which, by implication, means that it was authorized to enact legislations in accordance with what was required to fulfil the politico-ideological mission that the elected representatives had. By striking down Parliament's decision as it is contrary to the basic structure, the Supreme Court appears to have assumed 'a veto power on all constitutional amendments'.[31] Instead of interpreting the amendment clause, the court has, in effect, become the arbiter by suggesting that it will decide whether to permit the legislature to amend the Constitution. The basic structure creates an environment in which 'the constituent power gets transferred from the elected representative of the people to the judges of the Supreme Court', which is a serious threat to constitutional democracy.[32] Highlighting this aspect of the judicial over-reach, H.J. Kania, the first Chief Justice of India thus remarked that 'in a democratic country, the people make the laws through their legislature. It is not the function of the court to supervise or to correct the laws passed by the legislature as an overriding authority'.[33] In the name of protecting the constitution, the judiciary through its 'self-invented doctrine of basic structure' appears to have 'destroyed the most basic feature of Indian polity, namely the primacy of the people and democracy being a government of the people, by the people and for the people'.[34] The argument is based on a fundamental principle of democracy privileging elected representatives since they articulate people's voice and remain accountable to them whereas the judiciary is neither accountable nor institutionally equipped to capture people's voice; it does not therefore seem to be constitutionally-justified because it creates an arrangement contrary to the spirit of parliamentary democracy by allowing concentration of unfettered power in one institution which, incidentally, is not an elected body. This is an endeavour to replace the duly-elected representatives by a small, often-divided set of appointed judges to devise policy preferences.[35] Hence, the basic structure doctrine is charged with being an alibi to tread into an area which, from the point of view of democracy, belongs to Parliament. In a nutshell, the basic structure doctrine is being challenged as 'an illegitimate infringement on majority rule, an attempt to infuse India's constitutional scheme with judicial supremacy'.[36] Being a parliamentary democracy in the

Westminster format, the judicial ascendance is ideologically debilitating since it puts hurdles to the elected representatives when they seek to bring about revolutionary socio-economic changes by way of innovative legislations. So, the basic structure doctrine is a retarding means in India's constitutional democracy which is ideologically restrictive and constitutionally contrarian.

Concluding Observations

Conceptually, the basic structure doctrine is justified given the fact that the Indian constitution clearly 'adopted the American model of constitutionalism with limited government and strong judicial review'. Though some elements of the British parliamentary system were 'adapted to the Indian constitution—the composition of the higher executive and effective collective cabinet responsibility'—it is difficult to accept that it entails 'the doctrine of parliamentary sovereignty'.[37] Despite strong critiques, the basic structure doctrine is being continuously expanded and appears to have created a wave in its favour around the world, especially in South Asia. In a 1989 judgment on *Anwar Husain v. Bangladesh* (or Eighth Amendment case), Justice B.H. Chowdhury while emphasizing the importance of basic structure argued that

> call it by any name—basic structure or whatever, but that is the fabric of the Constitution which cannot be dismantled by an authority created by the Constitution itself, namely, the Parliament. ... Because the amending power is but a power given by the Constitution to Parliament, it is a higher power than any other given by the Constitution to Parliament, but nevertheless [*sic*] it is power within and not outside the Constitution.[38]

The basic structure doctrine has also been appreciated by the Supreme Court of Pakistan. In *Al-Jehad Trust v. the Federation of Pakistan* (1996), the court ruled that in order to resolve a conflict between a constitutional provision and a later amendment, the constitution has to be interpreted as a whole, taking into account 'the spirit and basic features of the Constitution'.[39] This was further pursued in a 1997 judgment when the Supreme Court reiterated that the Pakistan Constitution has salient features—federalism, parliamentary form of government blended with Islamic provisions—'which are beyond the amendment power.'[40] Although the basic structure doctrine did not become integral to Pakistan's constitutional law as in India these are important judgments which created a space for the doctrine more or less on the same arguments which were offered by the Indian Supreme Court.

Notwithstanding the obvious conceptual limitation of the arguments supportive of the doctrine in a parliamentary democracy, there is a powerful defence when it is shown to be an effective means for preventing Parliament from being a self-engineered institution of governance. In the Indian context, the doctrine was conceptualized when the executive resorted to constitutional amendments rather indiscriminately to fulfil its political agenda seemingly at the cost of constitutional propriety. The doctrine that had emerged in the context of the challenges to the validity of constitutional amendments was thus hailed as a panacea which applied brakes; otherwise, 'the engine of amending power would soon', it was apprehended, 'overrun the constitution.'[41] By insisting on the basic structure, the Supreme Court thus acts as an impediment which is required to sustain a healthy balance among the organs of the government. Besides imposing limits on Parliament's amending power, the doctrine also acknowledges that the constitution can be radically changed by the people themselves; it thus emphasizes simultaneously the importance of the elected representatives and 'the democratic pedigree earned by non-representative institutions', including judiciary. The trajectory of the basic structure doctrine confirms that it evolves and gets consolidated when the representative institutions fail to 'maintain democratic essentials' of the country.[42] Hence, the importance of the doctrine cannot be so easily dismissed; in fact, it has gained credibility to the extent of being part and parcel of constitutional democracy in India.

In the final analysis, the basic structure is not merely a judicial decision, but a political intervention in governance which was likely to be derailed due to specific socio-political context reportedly leading to the consolidation of anti-democratic and authoritarian forces, especially in the mid-1970s. By raising concerns, the judiciary seems to have created an environment for 'fostering a democratic dialogue around key constitutional principles between the institutions of government'[43] which not only confirms the importance of the principles of checks and balances in constitutional governance but also consolidates democracy as a collective venture. In principle, the doctrine is thus an important aid for keeping the executive within a limit; in practice however, the judicial intervention through the doctrine of basic structure does not seem to be as fundamental as is construed which Justice Khanna (who was superseded when his turn to become the Chief Justice of India due probably to his dissenting note in the 1976 Habeas Corpus case) articulated by saying that

> there is no modern instance, it is said, in which any judiciary has saved a whole people from the grave currents of intolerance, passion and tyranny which have threatened liberty and free institutions. The attitude of a society and of its organized political forces rather than of its legal machinery, is the controlling force in the character of free institutions. The ramparts of defence against tyranny are ultimately in the hearts of the people. The Constitution, the courts and the laws can act only as aids to strengthen those ramparts; they do not and cannot furnish substitute for those ramparts. If the ramparts are secure, any one who dares to tamper with the liberties of the citizens would do so at his own peril. If, however, the ramparts crack down, no convention, no court would be able to do much in the matter.[44]

This is the crux of the matter; no matter how strong the judiciary is while stream-rolling its diktats, its authority can be effective so long as it is held by the people as an effective instrument for fulfilling some of their cherished socio-economic goals. So, in the ultimate analysis, the basic structure doctrine by itself, does not seem to be an empowering device; that it has acquired the status of being a significant shield against the trespassing by the executive of its constitutionally-recognized boundaries clearly authenticates the critical role of the *demos* in charting-out definite courses for institutions of governance in a democratic polity. This is where the doctrine stands out.

Notes and References

1. Kazi Syed Karimuddin (Central Provinces and Berar), 6 December 1948, *Constituent Assembly Debates*, Book No. 2, p. 843.
2. Krishna Chandra Sharma (United Provinces), 6 December 1948, *Constituent Assembly Debates*, Book No. 2, p. 850.
3. Alladi Krishnaswami Ayyar (Madras), 6 December 1948, *Constituent Assembly Debates*, Book No. 2, p. 854.

4. Alladi Krishnaswami Ayyar (Madras), 6 December 1948, *Constituent Assembly Debates*, Book No. 2, p. 854.

5. Jawaharlal Nehru, 8 November 1948, *Constituent Assembly Debates*, Book No. 2, pp. 322–3.

6. The quoted parts of the sentences are taken from the speech that B.R. Ambedkar made in the Constituent Assembly on 4 November 1948, *Constituent Assembly Debates*, Book No. 2, pp. 43–4.

7. Ernest Rudolf Huber, 'Constitution', in Arthur J. Jacobson and Bernhard Schlink (eds), *Weimer: A Jurisprudence Crisis*, 2002, p. 328—cited in YanivRoznai, *Unconstitutional Constitutional Amendments: A Study of the Nature and Limits of Constitutional Amendment Powers* (unpublished PhD dissertation, London School of Economics, 2014), p. 119.

8. Eivind Smith, 'Old and Protected: On the Supra-constitutional Clause in the Constitution of Norway', *Law Review* 44, 2011, p. 369—cited in Roznai, *Unconstitutional Constitutional Amendments*, p. 119.

9. A.G. Noorani, 'Behind the Basic Structure Doctrine: On India's Debt to a German Jurist, Professor Dietrich Conrad', *Frontline* 18(19), 28 April—11 May 2001, http://www.frontline.in/static/html/fl1809/18090950. htm, (accessed on 18 December 2016).

10. Cited in AG Noorani, 'Behind the Basic Structure Doctrine: On India's Debt to a German Jurist, Professor Dietrich Conrad', *Frontline*, Vol. 18, No. 19, 28 April—11 May 2001, http://www.frontline.in/static/html/fl1809/18090950.htm (accessed on 18 December 2016).

11. *Sajjan Singh v. The State of Rajasthan*, 1965 AIR 845, 1965 SCR (1) 933.

12. *Sajjan Singh v. The State of Rajasthan*.

13. *IC Golaknath v. The State of Punjab*, 1967 AIR 1643, 1967 SCR (2) 762.

14. *IC Golaknath v. The State of Punjab*.

15. *Kesavananda Bharati v. The State of Kerala*, (1973) 4 SCC 225.

16. *Kesavananda Bharati v. The State of Kerala*.

17. *Kesavananda Bharati v. The State of Kerala*.

18. *Kesavananda Bharati v. The State of Kerala*.

19. *Indira Gandhi v. Raj Narain*, Appeal (civil) 887 of 1975, Supplementary, SCC 1.

20. *Minerva Mills Limited and others v. the Union of India*, AIR 1980 SC 1789, 1980 SCR (1), 206-1789, 1981 SCR (1) 206.

21. *Minerva Mills Limited and others v. the Union of India*.

22. *Minerva Mills Limited and others v. the Union of India*.

23. *IR Coelho (dead) v. The State of Tamil Nadu* (2007), 2007 (2), SCC 1.

24. *IR Coelho (dead) v. The State of Tamil Nadu*.

25. *IR Coelho (dead) v. The State of Tamil Nadu*.

26. Granville Austin, *Working a Democratic Constitution: A History of Indian Experience* (New Delhi: Oxford University Press, 1999), p. 258.

27. *Minerva Mills Limited and others v. the Union of India.*

28. *S.R. Bommai and others v. the Union of India,* 1994, 2, SCC 644, Air 1994, SC 1918 (1994), SCC 1.

29. The idea is drawn on Granville Austin, *Working a Democratic Constitution: A History of Indian Experience* (New Delhi: Oxford University Press, 1999), pp. 258–76.

30. Austin, *Working a Democratic Constitution,* p. 258.

31. Subhas C. Kashyap, *Indian Constitution: Conflicts and Controversies* (New Delhi: Vistara Publications, 2010), p. 246.

32. Kashyap, *Indian Constitution,* p. 247.

33. *Hindustan Times,* Delhi, 1950.

34. Kashyap, *Indian Constitution,* pp. 247–8.

35. N.R. Madhava Menon, 'Basic Structure after 30 Years', in Pran Chopra (ed.), *The Supreme Court versus the Constitution: A Challenge to Federalism,* (New Delhi: SAGE, 2006), p. 62.

36. Madhav Khosla, *The Indian Constitution* (New Delhi: Oxford University Press, 2012), p. 155.

37. Sudhir Krishnaswamy, *Democracy and Constitutionalism in India: A Study of the Basic Structure Doctrine* (New Delhi: Oxford University Press, 2009), pp. 218–19.

38. The judgment is cited in Yaniv Roznai, *Unconstitutional Constitutional Amendments: A Study of the Nature and Limits of Constitutional Amendment,* (unpublished PhD dissertation, London School of Economics and Political Science, 2014), p. 59.

39. The judgment is cited in Roznai, *Unconstitutional Constitutional Amendments,* p. 61.

40. The judgment is cited in Roznai, *Unconstitutional Constitutional Amendments,* p. 61.

41. UpendraBaxi, Courage, *Craft and Contention: The Indian Supreme Court in the Eighties,* (Bombay: N.M. Tripathi, 1985), p. 68.

42. Krishnaswami, *Democracy and Constitutionalism in India,* p. 221.

43. Krishnaswami, *Democracy and Constitutionalism in India,* p. 215.

44. Cited in Michael Henderson, 'Setting India's Democratic House in Order', *Asian Survey* XIX, 1979, pp. 955–6.

Conclusion

C onstitutionalizing India is a long analytical statement of how the 1950 Constitution of India was made. As shown above, the Constitution was the culmination of a process in which contrasting ideas converged to evolve an acceptable set of principles for a socio-culturally and economically diverse population. The book thus makes the argument that the Constitution was not just an offshoot of coming together of nationalist leaders appreciative of the values of Enlightenment but also an outcome of their engagement with colonialism through the exercise of popular politics. The account is historical too because the ideas that became pre-eminent in the Constituent Assembly had their roots in the tumultuous days of India's freedom struggle in which various waves of thought were also discernible. By arguing that the Constitution of India was the outcome of a complex ideational battle in different phases of India's struggle for freedom, the book challenges the conventional notion that it is merely a mindless, if not haphazard, borrowing of con-stitutional provisions and practices prevalent elsewhere. The argument supporting the contention that the Indian Constitution is a borrowed doctrine seems vacuous given the fact that it is also a break with the past. One of the most significant break was to constitutionally recognize the principle of representative government in its unalloyed form through universal adult suffrage, an ambition that the nationalists had been nur-turing since the adoption of the 1928 Motilal Nehru Report. Besides the emergent need of tackling contingent circumstances following the partition which created a strong demand for the continuity of the available colonial administrative machinery, the founding fathers also felt the need of a strong administration to translate into reality their ambitious plan of transformation. It has thus been persuasively argued that '[w]hile continuity was sought in the service of the break in this way, the claim of the break itself was called upon to justify certain continuities.'[1] A careful study of the arguments that were marshalled in favour of incorporating mechanisms and institutions from the colonial era confirms the point. For instance, Balkrishna Sharma (a member from Uttar Pradesh) while responding to the criticism that the constitution was 'un-Indian in spirit and [was] more or less a copy of the Government of India Act' defended the design as justified by saying that,

> [h]ere, after all, we are framing a Constitution and the modern tendencies, the modern difficulties, the modern problems that are facing us are there and we have to provide for them all in our Constitution, and if we have learned on the Government of India Act for that matter, then I do not think that we have at all committed any sin.[2]

Notwithstanding disagreements on certain issues, including those related to Gandhi's village swaraj, the Constituent Assembly members converged on the point that India needed a constitution to establish a democratic polity which the nationalists aspired during their struggle against colonialism. This was 'an occasion of the greatest historical significance', argued Raj Bahadur of Rajasthan, who further characterized the effort as 'a wonder'. As he stated, '[t]he wonder is not that we have not been able to produce a better Constitution. The wonder is that we have been able to achieve and arrive at a degree of agreement that is incorporated in the Constitution.'[3] What is evident now is that the constitution evolved out of an intensive deliberations among the members which reflected both agreement and differences. Gandhians were, for instance, unhappy since not only was Gandhi's idea of village swaraj discarded 'the omission of a reference to the Father of the Nation—Respected Bapu [Gandhi]' also disappointed them.[4] Nonetheless, the disagreements never became a source of discontent to the extent of falling apart. Hence, it is conceptually innovative to understand the Constituent Assembly debates as reflective of a unique tension 'between certain aspirations (of creating a democratic constitutional system) and certain necessities (arising from the challenge of creating a viable constitutional order under the given circumstances), which had its resonance in what finally became the Constitution of India.[5]

A cursory look at the processes that influenced constitutionalism in India reveals that there are three critical areas—social justice, liberal constitutionalism, and group representation—in which an ideational battle took place involving those who were responsible for charting out a specific course for India's constitutionalism to follow. The founding fathers addressed these concerns in a historical context which was both derivative and context-driven: derivative because it was drawn on liberalism that had no parallel in India, and context-driven since Indian socio-economic and ideational reality did not seem to favour liberal socio-economic and political practices. A daunting task indeed, and yet, they accomplished their goal by being sensitive to their commitment to constitutional liberalism.

Conceptually, one can argue that the 1950 Constitution of India was a unique response in which the derivative ideas of 'liberal imperialism' were internalized. As soon as the system inspired by the Enlightenment paradigm was put into practice, the nationalists, beginning with the Moderates, instead of challenging, seem to have aligned with the rulers in its sustenance. How was it possible? Besides being enamoured by liberal ideas, the nationalists were also persuaded to accept the system since it allowed them a voice in its running. Hence, it is argued that the continuity of the British rule in India was attributed to the representation of their interests and their co-optation in the system. A smart move nonetheless on the part of the colonialists who created a comprador political class from among the colonized who legitimized the alien rule by being participants. The opinion differed though the majority of the decision-makers favoured the idea of co-optation to develop 'a group of loyalist stakeholders in the Raj [who] may be allowed to voice their views [though] it would be safer', it was further emphasized, 'to have the "natives" selected by nomination and in such small numbers that they would not have the capacity to influence the decision'.[6] For the rulers, it was conceptualized as a strategy while, for the natives, it was an empowering device. As history unfolded, instead of receiving brickbats, the idea of representation became a part of the nationalist discourse and the Indian National Congress from its early days included 'enthusiasts who internalised the idea of interest representation [through legislative devices] though they were unhappy [since] the system devised by the government was not inclusive enough to admit them.[7] India's nationalist history is a testimony to the gradual expansion of the institutions of representation which also gained acceptance even after decolonization presumably because of their conceptual viability and institutional utility in upholding constitutional liberalism in India. In other words, what distinguishes the British colonialism from its European counterparts was its concern to consolidate public opinion its favour by creating avenues of representation for the ruled in the decision-making. As Bhattacharya has shown, by adopting appropriate legislations, the colonial state helped build a strong group of loyal supporters who always remained integral to the government.[8] The process had begun with the promulgation of the 1892 Council Act which partially accommodated the interests of those classes which mattered most in the perception of the rulers. Various legislations followed and increasingly large number of Indians were given opportunities to represent their interests before the rulers. Besides these endeavours, the colonial state seems to have been receptive to the voice, articulated by pressure groups and lobbies. Here too, the colonial state was favourably disposed towards the British interests groups which was obvious given the fact that 'domination was', as the author rightly argues, 'the ultimate basis of colonial state, not the voluntary acceptance of its legitimacy by its subjects'.[9] It is thus fair to argue that the colonial state developed its organic roots in India by employing the twin mechanisms of domination and also the efforts towards legitimizing colonialism because of its ostensible civilizing effects on India. In the ultimate analysis, it was however domination, pure and simple that 'marked the colonial rule in spite of the emotional attachments of the British to liberal principles'.[10] The journey that had begun with the approval of the 1892 Indian Council Act which accommodated the interests of the nobility, landed gentry, and European planting and commercial interests, was uninterrupted in the sense that the idea of accommodating the natives was not shelved; instead, the base of representation was steadily expanded through major ideational and legislative interventions, like the 1919 Franchise Committee (also known as the Southborough Committee) leading to the 1919 Montague-Chelmsford Reforms, and the 1930–2 Round

Table Conferences which culminated in the 1935 Government of India Act respectively. The aim was, of course, to contain 'the political class' who appeared to be threatening to the British rule; it was also a smart design to dispel the apprehension of the British rule being 'racist', as was revealed in a 1930 printed report on constitutional reforms which emphasized that,

> the fact that the dominant power in India is in the hands of a foreign race cannot fail to offer to those who attack existing conditions the opportunity of a racial appeal. Again, a common desire for changes in the form of the Government acts as an inducement to preserve a united front, and to keep in the background such differences as exist.[11]

Although the design was driven by partisan colonial interests it created a class of loyalists that acted favourably for the rulers since the idea of representation was, for them, an empowering device as well. Our purpose here is not to delve into the story of its unfolding which is highly complex in a context when the threat to colonial hegemony dissipated due largely to what the Bhattacharya prefers to call, 'domination effect' which manifested in 'the subordination of the indigenous merchant and moneylending capital [and] ... the reinforcement of the dominance of British private capital in the Indian economy by the government's action';[12] the aim here is to put across the point that an accommodative political design which was articulated by expanding representation in the British decision making, gradually sipped in the nationalist mind as essential to articulate constitutional liberalism in its true spirit and content. The battle that the nationalists had waged was thus never against representation *per se*, but against its restrictive nature. It was therefore not surprising that decision to grant universal adult suffrage was the first one that India's Constituent Assembly had adopted as soon as it convened its deliberations. The point being made here is about the critical role of representation in consolidating constitutional liberalism in India notwithstanding its roots in a very smart imperial design in the containment of nationalist dissent and also in sustaining the rulers' hegemony.

—— •◦• ——

The 1950 Constitution was the outcome of the founding fathers' serious endeavour of evolving an acceptable constitutional design for governance which was perhaps rooted in what is conceptually described as 'the Hobbesian concern' for creating a stable political order out of chaos in 'a united political frame'.[13] While moving the Objective Resolution on 13 December, 1946, Jawaharlal Nehru voiced the same concern by saying that 'we are here not to function as one party or one group, but always to think of India as a whole and always to think of the welfare of the four hundred million that comprise India. ... We have to rise above party and think of the Nation'.[14] After having laid out the foundation of his argument insisting on creating a united social compact, he further exhorted that,

> when I think of this Constituent Assembly, it seems to me, the time has come when we should, so far as we are capable of it, rise above our ordinary selves and party disputes and think of the great problem before us in the widest and most tolerant and most effective manner, whatever we may produce, should be worthy of India as a whole and should be such that the world should recognize that we have functioned, as we should have functioned, in this high adventure.[15]

Nehru's exhortation was not symptomatic of high idealism, but was reflective of a concern which needed to be addressed in unison. The absence of the Muslim League in the Assembly allowed the detractors to substantiate the claim that it was not representative of the India's multitude as was claimed. As the deliberations unfolded, the issue however lost its steam presumably because of the consolidation of the nationalist urge for building a liberal India based on the Enlightenment values. This was not enough because the success of the constitution was contingent on how it was made to work. Hence, Rajendra Prasad, the President of the Constituent Assembly, exhorted that what was critical to the continuity of 'a democratic constitution [was] the willingness to respect the viewpoints of others, capacity for compromise and accommodation, [and for that] ... India needs today nothing more than a set of honest men who will have the interest of the country before them'.[16] Core to Prasad's argument was a concern for evolving a social compact which could not be affected by imposition, but by taking everybody on board regardless of social, economic and political differences.

— •◦• —

The 1950 Constitution was an outcome of coming together of 'a diverse collection of individuals and groups to create a collective identity [on the basis of] their mutual commitment to protect their mutual rights.'[17] The task was not accomplished so easily, as the proceedings of the Constituent Assembly underline. The Assembly became a site of serious contestations where contrasting viewpoints were articulated and fiercely debated with a view to arriving at a negotiated settlement over the suggested provisions of the prospective constitution. A careful analysis of the Constituent Assembly debates suggests that the draft constitution was not an outcome of consensus among the members, as is generally claimed;[18] instead, there are many members who held completely different views which they supported by providing persuasive arguments. The most scathing criticism was made by Hukum Singh of East Punjab; he had no qualms to say that since 'in this Constitution no particular pattern has been followed ... it will not endure because it is neither indigenous nor a complete copy of any other single type. It is neither federal nor unitary. It is an enigmatic production, with every part stranger to the other.'[19] He pursued his argument further by being far more critical when he mentioned that,

[T]he English make of Indian frame was already there as the Government of India Act, 1935. We have substituted an American head in the form of a President, replaced the old limbs by an English Parliamentary system, poured Australian flexibility in bones and flesh, infused Canadian look of a single judiciary and added an Irish appendix of Directive Principles and thus brought out a hybrid which we have been pleased to name the Indian Constitution.[20]

For Singh, the constitution was a direction-less document since it was based on other constitutions which was not going to work in the Indian context in which a strictly liberal constitution in the Western mould was bound to fail. Unhappy with the structure of the constitution which hardly gave 'anything substantial to the individual', Singh further warned that the imposed structure was hardly democratic. With the declining importance of common man in politics and the establishment of the president-driven rule, there was every possibility, he apprehended, that 'an ambitious President would discover a rich find in this Constitution to declare himself as a dictator and yet apparently be acting within this Constitution.'[21] Hukum Singh was not alone in criticizing the

Constitution; he was supported by another member from West Bengal, Arun Chandra Guha. Like Singh, he expressed his discomfort since the Constitution had, in itself, elements of contradictory constitutional designs. According to him,

> This Constitution is something like a hybrid Constitution. It is a Federal Constitution but it has started at the top, not from the bottom, as all Federations should start. It is the Centre that is delegating some of its powers to the federating units—not that the federating units who are enjoying sovereign powers are surrendering some of their sovereign powers to the Centre as was the case in the USA. So naturally the Centre which is devolving some powers must be stingy in this revolution of power. And, in the present context, it is in the fitness of things that the federating units have not their full privileges that in a Federation they ought to have.[22]

Guha was critical of the draft constitution for being heavily tilted in favour of being a unitary state leading to the Centre being hegemonic in governance. It was unacceptable since it was contrary to the very spirt of federalism. The same concern was expressed by P.S. Deshmukh of Central Provinces and Berar. Amused at the blending of different constitutional designs, he thus argued that though 'we have adopted a parliamentary democracy modelled on the British constitution ... we have also decided to encroach on the sovereignty of our parliament in various ways by incorporating Fundamental Rights and many other matter of like nature.'[23] There were therefore serious anomalies in the structure of governance that was preferred.

As is shown above, some of the members expressed their reservation since the Constitution, instead of being a federal constitution, became completely unitary. There was another viewpoint, mainly nurtured by the Gandhians who felt alienated because the draft constitution did not pay adequate attention to the fundamental Gandhian ideals. One of the powerful critics in the Gandhian mould was Jaspat Roy Kapoor of United Provinces. While charging the members for having framed 'a completely alien constitution', he argued that 'our Constitution is a miserable failure [because] ... the spirit of Indian culture has not breathed on it; the Gandhism by which we swear so vehemently at home and abroad, does not inspire it. It is just a piece of legislation like, say, the Motor Vehicles Act.'[24] The argument that Kapoor advanced was pursued further by Nandkishore Das of Orissa who was also appalled since the constitution makers had hardly paid adequate attention to the Gandhian values while preparing the constitution. As he emphatically declared,

> I do not, at all, feel disappointed that this Constitution is not moulded on Gandhian ideal, inasmuch as I least expected a Gandhian Constitution from our constitution-makers. We all swear by the name of the Father of the Nation [Gandhi], but how many of us have been able to assimilate his teaching in our personal activities of the day-to-day life? How many of us have that undying faith in the refashioning of our society on the old village self-sufficiency model? A Gandhian constitution is not to be produced by a mere mechanical process but must grow out of deepest convictions and a determination to shape our society strictly and meticulously in conformity with his ideals. The determination is to be found nowhere in the country. Hence evolving of a Gandhian constitution out of non-Gandhian brains and minds is quite out of the question.[25]

This was a clear attack on B.R. Ambedkar and his colleagues in the Assembly who did not seem to have been persuaded by the Gandhian insistence on making village as the primary unit of governance. It was thus obvious for the Gandhians to have a constitution in which Gandhian ideals remained marginalized because the constitution was framed by what Das characterized as 'non-Gandhian brains and minds'. A careful study of the above points that the Gandhians made while defending their support for a Gandhian constitution reveals that the Assembly was sharply divided and the members of the Drafting Committee, including B.R. Ambedkar, failed to assuage their sentiments and feelings. The Constitution had thus become anything but Gandhian.

Division among the members notwithstanding, the draft constitution was finally approved in the form that the Drafting Committee had suggested. Constitutional democracy was sought to be established and the Constitution was considered to be an important tool in this respect. The success of constitutional democracy was contingent on, as Jadubans Sahay of Bihar explained, the character of a nation, the integrity, the honesty, our love for demo-cratic principles and our zeal to pursue and follow them which can make or mar a constitution. The constitution of a country does not depend upon the cold letters, however beautifully or brilliantly printed in a book. It depends for its growth and development upon the character of a nation. It is the soil—the character of a nation—upon which the seeds of the constitution have got to germinate. If the soil is rocky and barren, then certainly howsoever good the constitution might be and in how-soever grand language it may be worded, it is sure that the constitution cannot lead us to our goal.[26]

This was a fundamental concern, being shared by the members of the Assembly. To be an effective guide for governance, the constitution needs to be upheld by a complementary mindset in support of the values that it represents. A brilliant constitution is futile unless it is made to be functional by those who remain committed to the values, norms and ideals that it seeks to fulfil. Hence, Sahay further argued:

[N]o amount of guarantees in the Constitution or the filling up of the omissions mentioned will carry us to the goal. It depends upon those who work the Constitution. It depends on how we develop the spirit of tolerance and not on Constitution or the letter of the law. It depends on the spirit of love towards those that are down-trodden, ... those who call themselves minorities and 'have-nots'. It does not depend on the Constitution or its articles. It depends upon our own character, our own vitality as a nation.[27]

So the basic point that comes out of Sahay's intervention was the need for developing a complementary mindset in support of a liberal constitu-tion seeking to direct the nation towards those politco-ideological goals that the founding father had set out for themselves. It was Ambedkar who also drew our attention to this aspect when he emphatically argued that 'the Constitution is workable, it is flexible, and it is strong enough to hold the country together both in peace time and in war time [and] ... if things go wrong under the new Constitution, the reason will not be that we had a bad Constitution, but will have to say that Man was vile.'[28] The same point was reiterated. A constitution succeeds if it is endorsed by the people supportive of values on which it rests. What is emphasized by Ambedkar was the importance of a complementary mindset which drew on constitutional morality. A challenging task no doubt though the members were confident to sail through all the difficulties in view of the determination that the nation had shown while fighting for freedom. Now, the time had come to work for those unrealized socio-economic goals. So independence, Ambedkar argued, despite being,

> a matter of joy, has thrown on us great responsibilities [because] … we have lost the excuse of blaming the British for anything going wrong. If hereafter things go wrong, we will have nobody to blame except ourselves. … If we wish to preserve the Constitution in which we have sought to enshrine the principle of Government of the people, for the people and by the people, let us resolve, not be tardy in the recognition of the evils that lie across our path and which induce people to prefer Government for the people to Government by the people, nor to be weak in our initiative to remove them. This is the only way to serve the country.[29]

There are three important points that appear to have been reinforced in what Ambedkar had suggested. First, like his colleagues with similar kind of ideological inclinations, he strongly felt that the success of a constitution was dependent on the socio-economic context in which it evolved. Unless a supportive mindset was created, the constitution would merely become a compilation of rules and regulations with no substance. Being a victim of a highly regimented social system, he was aware that the task of creating a complementary mindset was not an easy one especially when inequality was well-entrenched in India's social and economic life. Nonetheless, the need for a constitution could not be negated since it was certain to contribute to processes for change and reform in the prevalent socio-economic circumstances. Second, by codifying rules and regulations against socio-economic discrimination due to the accident of birth, he also championed the idea of substantial equality which needed to be realized to bring about noticeable changes in the mindset that so far remained committed to birth-driven inequality. This was a great achievement for him especially when feudal socio-economic values did not seem to have lost their steam presumably because the prevalent milieu in which they continued to receive endorsement. Finally, there is no doubt that with its support for liberal democracy, the Constitution initiated processes for change by giving a jolt to the existent socio-economic values shaping inter-personal relationships. Once the constitution was inaugurated in 1950, it was easier for the socially and economically peripheral groups to assert their rightful existence on an equal footing with other socio-economically privileged sections of the demography. This was a revolutionary change not only in their own perceptions, but also in how others viewed them as integral to the same social space which, so far, remained out of their reach due to the accident of birth. It is in this sense that the 1950 Constitution of India is not only an empowering instrument but also a significant determinant of change in independent India.

——— ·•· ———

Constitutionalizing India reinforces the argument that it would be conceptually restrictive if the 1950 Constitution is reduced to being a borrowed doctrine in the light of the long-drawn ideational battle leading to its articulation in the Constituent Assembly. With their commitment to constitutional liberalism, the founding fathers had hardly explored any other ideological alternatives. Even the Gandhians resented when their views were dismissed as being 'inapplicable in a democratic India'. For the dominant section in the Assembly, the constitution was a device to bring about changes that, they felt, were pertinent to India's rise as a liberal polity. This was a design of what is appreciatively identified as 'transformational constitutionalism' which the founding fathers were shown to have adopted 'to mediate a transformation of the prevalent social condition'.[30] Nonetheless, the idea sipped in as a part of India's nationalist imagination out of ideational engagement with constitutional liberalism which became a dominant intellectual discourse in the freedom struggle. The constitution drew on the liberal democratic system of the Western mould from the very beginning though Rajendra Prasad warned that 'we are not bound to have a Constitution which completely and fully falls in line with known categories of the Constitution of the world. We have to take certain facts of history in our own country'.[31] However, in the absence of effective challenges to the extent of disrupting the intellectual wave in favour of constitutional liberalism, the system that the founding fathers preferred seems to have been readily accepted by the Assembly presumably because it was ideologically compatible with what they strove to do. This confirms, at one level, the tremendous influence of Western liberalism to the extent of being 'hegemonic' even when possibilities for alternative systems could have been explored; and, at another, the prevalent ideational model was allowed to continue presumably because of its ideological support to what the founding fathers sought to achieve in the aftermath of decolonization.

Notes and References

1. Sandipta Dasgupta, 'A Language which is Foreign to Us: Continuities and Anxieties in the Making of the Indian Constitution', *Comparative Studies of South Asia, Africa and Middle East* 34(2), 2014, p. 240.

2. Balkrishna Sharma's intervention in the Constituent Assembly, 25 November 1949, *Constituent Assembly Debates*, Book No. 5, Lok Sabha Secretariat, New Delhi, 2003, p. 968.

3. Raj Bahadur's intervention in the Constituent Assembly, 25 November 1949, *Constituent Assembly Debates*, Book No. 5, Lok Sabha Secretariat, New Delhi, 2003, p. 969.

4. Kamaleshwari Prasad Yadav's intervention in the Constituent Assembly, 25 November 1949, *Constituent Assembly Debates*, Book No. 5, Lok Sabha Secretariat, New Delhi, 2003, p. 971.

5. Dasgupta, 'A Language which is Foreign to Us' p. 229.

6. Sabyasachi Bhattacharya, *The Colonial State: Theory and Practice*, (New Delhi: Primus Books, 2016), p. 115.

7. Bhattacharya, *The Colonial State*, p. 116.

8. Bhattacharya, *The Colonial State*, pp. 115–38.

9. Bhattacharya, *The Colonial State*, p. 134.

10. Dipesh Chakrabarty, 'In the Name of Politics: Democracy and the Power of the Multitude in India', in Dipesh Chakrabarty, Rochana Majumdar, and Andrew Sartori (eds), *From the Colonial to the Postcolonial: India and Pakistan in transition*, (New Delhi: Oxford University Press, 2007), p. 39.

11. Governor-General in Council to Secretary of State (Reforms Office), No. 1 of 1930, 20 September 1930, Calcutta, 1930, p. 3, cited in Bhattacharya, *The Colonial State*, p. 123.

12. Bhattacharya, *The Colonial State*, p. 109.

13. Uday S. Mehta, 'Indian Constitutionalism: Crisis, Unity and History', in Sujit Choudhury, Madhav Khosla, and Pratap Bhanu Mehta (eds), *The Oxford Handbook of the Indian Constitution* (New Delhi: Oxford University Press, 2016), pp. 51–4.

14. Jawaharlal Nehru, 13 December 1946, *Constituent Assembly Debates*, Book No. 1, p. 60.

15. Nehru, 13 December 1946, *Constituent Assembly Debates*, Book No. 1, p. 60.

16. Rajendra Prasad, 26 November 1949, *Constituent Assembly Debates*, Book No. 5, p. 993.

17. Rajeev Bhargava, 'Introduction: Outline of a Political Theory of the Indian Constitution', in Rajeev Bhargava (ed.), *Politics and Ethics of the Indian Constitution* (New Delhi: Oxford University Press, 2008), p. 1.

18. One of the prominent scholars supportive of the argument that the 1950 Constitution was an offshoot of 'accommodation and consensus' is Granville Austin who developed this in his *The Indian Constitution: Cornerstone of a Nation* (New Delhi: Oxford University Press, 1966, pp. 311–21.

19. Hukum Singh (East Punjab), 21 November 1949, *Constituent Assembly Debates*, Book No. 5, p. 749.

20. Hukum Singh (East Punjab), 21 November 1949, *Constituent Assembly Debates*, Book No. 5, p. 749.

21. Hukum Singh (East Punjab), 21 November 1949, *Constituent Assembly Debates*, Book No. 5, p. 753.

22. Arun Chandra Guha (West Bengal), 21 November 1949, *Constituent Assembly Debates*, Book No. 5, p. 728.

23. P.S. Deshmukh (Central Provinces and Berar), 22 November 1949, *Constituent Assembly Debates*, Book No. 5, p. 776.

24. Jaspat Roy Kapoor (United Provinces), 21 November 1949, *Constituent Assembly Debates*, Book No. 5, p. 760.

25. Nandkishore Das (Orissa), 23 November 1949, *Constituent Assembly Debates*, Book No. 5, pp. 851–2.

26. Jadubans Sahay (Bihar), 22 November 1949, *Constituent Assembly Debates*, Book No. 5, p. 800.

27. Jadubans Sahay (Bihar), 22 November 1949, *Constituent Assembly Debates*, Book No. 5, p. 800.

28. B.R. Ambedkar, 4 November 1949, *Constituent Assembly Debates*, Book No. 2, p. 44.

29. B.R. Ambedkar, 25 November 1939, *Constituent Assembly Debates*, Book No. 5, pp. 980–1.

30. I borrow this expression from Sandipta Dasgupta who introduced this idea in his *Localizing the Revolution* (unpublished PhD dissertation, Columbia University, 2014), p. 15.

31. Rajendra Prasad, 26 November 1949, *Constituent Assembly Debates*, Book No. 5, p. 987.

Bibliography

Bibliographical Notes and a Select Bibliography

Constitutionalizing India is a biography of constitutional liberalism—an idea that evolved organic roots in the India in the wake of British colonialism. A biographical study, the book thus draws on multiple sources to conceptualize the politico-ideological processes leading to the making of the 1950 Constitution by reference to its intellectual antecedents and also the socio-economic inputs representing concerns and drive for change and empowerment. My purpose here is not to provide an exhaustive list of texts on such a complex theme, but to acquaint the reader with some of the major works which are critical to conceptualize the processes that finally culminated in the making of the Constitution of India with the completion of deliberations in the Constituent Assembly in November 1949. Hence, I have decided to incorporate a select list of texts which I found useful to persuasively elaborate the story. Despite being different in their approaches, these texts offer powerful inputs to build a meaningful story of the evolution of a constitutionalized polity in India. An explanatory note is in order here: I have made extensive use of the *Constituent Assembly Debates* and also volumes edited by B. Shiva Rao entitled *The Framing of India's Constitution*; I have also drawn on the classical texts which are well-known and hence I avoided putting them in this list and the bibliography contains those books and articles which stand out for their analytical depth and conceptual clarity.

Austin, Granville, *The Indian Constitution: Cornerstone of a Nation*, Oxford University Press, New Delhi, 1966.

————. *Working a Democratic Constitution: A History of the Indian Experience*, Oxford University Press, New Delhi, 1999.

Bajpai, Rochana, 'Liberalism in India: A Sketch', in Ben Jackson and Marc Stears (eds), *Liberalism and Ideology: Essay in Honour of Michael Freeden*, Oxford University Press, New York, 2012.

————. *Debating Difference: Group Rights and Liberal Democracy in India*, Oxford University Press, New Delhi, 2011.

Bayly, C.A., *Recovering Liberties: Indian Thought in the Age of Liberalism and Empire*, Cambridge University Press, Cambridge, 2012.

Bhargava, Rajeev (ed.), *Politics and Ethics of the Indian Constitution*, Oxford University Press, New Delhi, 2008.

Bhatia, Gautam, *Offend, Shock or Disturb: Free Speech under the Indian Constitution*, Oxford University Press, New Delhi, 2016.

Bhatia, Udit (ed.), *The Indian Constituent Assembly: Deliberation on Democracy*, Routledge, Oxford and New York, 2018.

Bhattacharya, Sabyasachi, *The Colonial State: Theory and Practice*, Primus Books, New Delhi, 2016.

Chakrabarty, Dipesh, *Provincializing Europe: Postcolonial Thought and Historical Difference*, Oxford University Press, New Delhi, 2001.

————. Rochana Majumdar, and Andrew Sartori (eds), *From the Colonial to the Postcolonial: India and Pakistan in Transition*, Oxford University Press, New Delhi, 2007.

Chakravarthi, Ram-Prasad, 'Pluralism and Liberalism: Reading the Indian Constitution as a Philosophical Document for Constitutional Patriotism', *Critical Review of International Social and Political Philosophy* 16(5), 2013.

Chakravarty, Suhas, *The Raj Syndrome: A Study in Imperial Perceptions*, Penguin, New Delhi, 1991.

Chopra, Pran (ed.), *The Supreme Court versus the Constitution: A Challenge to Federalism*, SAGE, New Delhi, 2006.

Choudhury Sujit, Madhav Khosla, and Pratap Bhanu Mehta (eds), *The Oxford Handbook of the Indian Constitution*, Oxford University Press, New Delhi, 2016.

Cutts, Elmer H., 'The Background of Macaulay's Minute', *The American Historical Review* 58(4), July, 1953.

Das, Samir, 'The Founding Movement: Social Justice in the Constitutional Mirror', in Ashok Agarwal and Bharat Bhusan (eds), *Justice and Law: The Limits of Deliverables of Law*, Vol. II, of *The State of Justice in India: Issues of Social Justice*, SAGE, New Delhi, 2009.

Dasgupta, Sandipto, 'A Language which Is Foreign to Us: Continuities and Anxieties in the Making of the Indian Constitution', *Comparative Studies of South Asia, Africa and Middle East* 34(2), 2014.

————. *Localizing the Revolution* (unpublished PhD dissertation, Columbia University, New York, 2014).

Elangovan, Arvind, 'Constitutionalism, Political exclusion, and Implications for Indian Constitutional History: The Case of Montague Chelmsford reforms (1919)', *South Asian History and Culture*, 2016.

————. 'Provincial Autonomy, Sir Benegal Narsing Rau and the Improbable Imagination of Constitutionalism in India, 1935–38', *Comparative Studies of South Asia, Africa and Middle East* 36(1), 2016.

————. 'The Making of the Indian Constitution: A Case for a Non-nationalist Approach', *History Compass* 12(1), 2014.

————. *A Constitutional Imagination of India: Sir Benegal Narsing Rau Amidst the Retreat of Liberal Idealism (1910–1950)* (unpublished PhD dissertation, University of Chicago, 2012).

————. 'The Road Not Taken: Sir Benegal Narsing Rau and the Indian Constitution in Sekhar Bandyopadhyay (ed.), *Decolonization and the Politics of Transition in South Asia*, Orient Blackswan, New Delhi, 2016.

Fernee, Tadd, 'Gandhi and the Heritage of Non-violence, Secularism and Conflict Resolution', *International Review of Sociology* 24(2), 2014.

Hasan, Zoya, E. Sridharan, and R. Sudarshan (eds), *India's Living Constitution: Ideas, Practices, Controversies*, Permanent Black, New Delhi, 2002.

Holmes, Stephen, 'Making Sense of Liberal Imperialism', in Nadia Urbinati and Alex Zakaras (eds), *J.S. Mill's Political Thought: A Bicentennial Reassessment*, Cambridge University Press, Cambridge, 2007.

Jayal, Niraja Gopal, *Citizenship and Its Discontent: An Indian History*, Permanent Black, New Delhi, 2013.

Kapila, Shruti, 'Self, Spencer and Swaraj: Nationalist Thought and Critiques of Liberalism, 1890–1920', *Modern Intellectual History* 4(1), 2007.

Kashyap, Subhash C., *Indian Constitution: Conflicts and Controversies*, Vistara Publishing Pvt. Limited, New Delhi, 2010.

Khosla, Madhav, *The Indian Constitution*, Oxford University Press, New Delhi, 2012.

Koditschek, Theodore, *Liberalism, Imperialism and the Historical Imagination: Nineteenth-century Vision of a Greater Britain*, Cambridge University Press, Cambridge, 2011.

Kumar, Aishwary, *Radical Quality: Ambedkar, Gandhi and the Risk of Democracy*, Stanford University Press, California, 2015.

Kumaraswamy Sudhir, *Democracy and Constitutionalism in India: A Study of the Basic Structure Doctrine*, Oxford University Press, New Delhi, 2009.

Legg, Stephen, 'Dyarchy: Democracy, Autonomy and the Scaler Sovereignty of Interwar India', *Comparative Studies of South Asia, Africa and Middle East* 36(1), 2016.

Lothian, Arthur Cunningham, *Kingdoms of Yesterday*, John Murray, London, 1951.

Low, D.A., *Britain and Indian Nationalism: The Imprint of Ambiguity, 1929–1942*, Cambridge University Press, Cambridge, 1997.

Majeed, J., 'James Mill's The History of British India and Utilitarianism as a Rhetoric of Reform', *Modern Asian Studies* 24(2), 1990.

Mantena, Karuna, 'Mill and the Imperial Predicament', in Nadia Urbinati and Alex Zakaras (eds), *J.S. Mill's Political Thought: A Bicentennial Reassessment*, Cambridge University Press, Cambridge, 2007.

Mantena, Karuna, *Allibis of Empire: Henry Maine and the Ends of Liberal Imperialism*, Permanent Black, New Delhi, 2010.

————. 'On Gandhi's Critique of State: Sources, Contexts and Conjunctures', *Modern Intellectual History* 9(3), 2012.

————. 'Another Realism: The Politics of Gandhian Nonviolence', *American Political Science Review* 106(2), 2012.

Mehrotra, S.R. and Denyar Patel (eds), *Dadabhai Naoroji: Selected Private Papers*, Oxford University Press, New Delhi, 2016.

Mehta, Uday Singh, *Liberalism and Empire: Indian in British Liberal Thought*, Oxford University Press, New Delhi, 1999.

Mehta, V.R. and Thomas Pantham (eds), *Political Ideas in Modern India: Thematic Explorations*, SAGE, New Delhi, 2006.

Metcalf, Thomas R., *Ideologies of the Raj*, Cambridge University Press, Cambridge, 1998.

Mukherjee, Mithi, *India in the Shadows of Empire: A Legal and Political History, 1774–1950*, Oxford University Press, New Delhi, 2012.

Nanda, B.R., *Gokhale: The Indian Moderates and the British Raj*, Oxford University Press, Delhi, 1977.

Noorani, A.G., *Constitutional Questions in India: The President, Parliament and States*, Oxford University Press, New Delhi, 2000.

O'Hanlon, Rosalind, *Caste, Conflict and Ideology: Mahatma Jotirao Phule and Low Caste Protest in Nineteenth-century Western India*, Cambridge University Press, Cambridge, 1985.

Panthan, Thomas and Kenneth L. Deutsch, *Political Thought in Modern India*, SAGE, New Delhi, 1986.

Parekh, Bhikhu, *Debating India: Essays on Indian Political Discourse*, Oxford University Press, New Delhi, 2015.

Pylee, M.V., *Constitutional Government in India*, Asia Publishing House, London, 1960.

Ramnath, Kalyani, 'We the People: Seamless Webs and Social Revolution in India's Constituent Assembly Debates', *South Asia Research* 32(1), 2012.

Ranganathan, A., 'The Nature of Indian Liberalism: An Essay in Commonwealth Partnership in Relations in Indian democracy', *Civilizations* 14(1/2), 1964.

Rau, B.N., *India's Constitution in the Making*, Orient Longmans, Bombay, 1960.

Reid, Walter, Keeping the Jewel in the Crown: the British betrayal of India, Penguin, New Delhi, 2016.

Roy, Anupama, *Citizenship in India*, Oxford University Press, New Delhi, 2016.

Sen, Sarbani, *The Constitution of India: Popular Sovereignty and Democratic Transformations*, Oxford University Press, New Delhi, 2007.

Seth, Sanjay, 'Rewriting Histories of Nationalism: The Politics of "Moderate Nationalism" in India, 1870–1905', *American Historical Review* 104(1), February, 1999.

Shankar, Shylashri, *Scaling Justice: India's Supreme Court, Anti-terror Laws and Social Rights*, Oxford University Press, New Delhi, 2009.

Skaria, Ajay, *Unconditional Equality: Gandhi's Religion of Resistance*, University of Minnesota Press, Minneapolis, 2016.

Stokes, Eric, *The English Utilitarians and India*, Oxford University Press, Oxford, 1959.

Vajpeyi, Ananya, *Righteous Republic: The Political Foundations of Modern India*, Harvard University Press, Cambridge, 2012.

Index

About the Author

Bidyut Chakrabarty has been professor of political science at the University of Delhi, India, since 1998. He has been widely cited for his original contribution to Gandhi's social and political thought. His book *Confluence of Thought: Mohandas Karamchand Gandhi and Martin Luther King, Jr.* (Oxford University Press, 2013) discusses the ideas of M.K. Gandhi and Martin Luther King Jr. His other works, for example, *Communism in India* (Oxford University Press, 2014); *Non-violence: Challenges and Prospects* (Oxford University Press, 2014); *Coalition Politics in India* (Oxford University Press, 2014), among others, have also been widely appreciated. Further, several of his works have also been translated in more than one language.

In addition to University of Delhi, Chakrabarty works with the Union Public Service Commission (UPSC), University Grants Commission (UGC), and the Indian Council of Social Science Research (ICSSR). He is a member of the Board of Studies, Nabakrushna Chaudhury Institute, Utkal University, Bhubaneswar, India. He is involved in various academic assignments (as a visiting professor) in renowned universities across the globe. He was a part of the Organisation for Economic Co-operation and Development (OECD) project on Education for the Future, 2030, where he was responsible for the India chapter.

Chakrabarty is currently appointed as the DAAD Visiting Professor in Germany, housed in the University of Hamburg.